GW00982494

The Complete
Field Guide to
Ireland's Birds

Eric Dempsey & Michael O'Clery

Gill & Macmillan

Gill & Macmillan Ltd
Hume Avenue, Park West, Dublin 12
with associated companies throughout the world
www.gillmacmillan.ie

© Text: Eric Dempsey, 2010
© Paintings and Maps: Michael O'Clery, 2010
978 07171 4668 0

Index compiled by Cover to Cover
Design and print origination by Michael O'Clery
Printed in Italy by Printer Trento

The paper used in this book comes from the wood pulp of managed forests.
For every tree felled, at least one tree is planted, thereby renewing natural resources.

A CIP catalogue record for this book is available from the British Library.

5 4 3 2 1

For our parents, Ann, Conor & Della

Find a bird

The tabs to the right of each page will help you find the main bird families.

Bird families and individual species are arranged in a systematic order, which places the more 'primitive' groups first and follows with progressively more 'evolved' species.

Species are also listed in systematic order in the Contents on pages vii to xi, and all species are listed in alphabetical order in the index on page 265.

Wildfowl

Seabirds

Birds of prey

Waders

Gulls

Auks, etc

Larks

Warblers

Crows

Sparrows

Rare

Contents

Preface

Since the publication of the second edition of *The Complete Guide to Ireland's Birds* in 2002, Ireland has seen many changes in bird populations and distributions. We have seen the reintroduction and successful breeding of both Golden Eagles and Red Kites while White-tailed Eagles are now establishing themselves in the south-west. In addition to this, natural colonisations have also taken place with Great Spotted Woodpeckers now breeding in areas along the east and north, while Little Ringed Plovers have also bred for the first time.

Other species continue to do well with Little Egrets present in regions of the north-west. Recent winter influxes of Cattle Egrets may also result in the colonisation of that species into Ireland in the coming years. While Corncrakes have maintained their low numbers, the distribution of the birds has moved from the concentrations around the Shannon Callows in the midlands to the more remote islands and regions of the north and west. Roseate Terns are also doing very well with breeding populations increasing year on year since 2002. In addition, many new species have been recorded in Ireland for the first time while changes in the taxonomic classification of species have resulted in some birds being afforded full species status.

In this new field guide we have reflected the changes that have occurred in relation to the distribution and breeding status of Ireland's birds. The rare species accounts include all species added to the Irish list. As a result, this book details all species of birds recorded in Ireland up to 1 June 2010.

Eric Dempsey & Michael O'Clery
June 2010

Acknowledgments

There are many people (too numerous to mention here) who have offered us encouragement, advice and practical assistance. Without them, this book would not have been possible.

We are particularly grateful to Anthony McGeehan for his comments on early drafts of the book, and to Joe Hobbs for his advice on taxonomic and classification issues.

Special thanks also to John Fox, Irene Kavanagh and Paul and Andrea Kelly for their support and friendship.

Our thanks also to Philip Clancy, Richard Collins, Dick Coombes, Davey Farrar, Fergus Fitzgerald, Terry Flanagan, Éanna Flynn, Gerald Franck, Kieran Grace, Niall Hatch, Aidan Kelly, Suzanne Ledwith, Derek Mooney, Éanna Ní Lamhna and Michael O'Keeffe.

We would also like to thank the staff of Birdwatch Ireland, the members of the IRBC and the students of the People's College in Dublin for their assistance.

Finally, we would like to thank our families for their invaluable support and encouragement over the years.

Eric Dempsey & Michael O'Clery

How to use this book

If you know the name of a species, you can find it listed in either the Contents on pages vii to xi, or alphabetically in the index at the back of the book, where English, Irish and Latin names are listed. It is helpful to know the approximate systematic order in which birds are listed in the main part of the book, but to help find particular groupings of birds, e.g. waders, or birds of prey, refer to page v. Here, the main groupings are linked to a coloured tab to enable rapid location in the main body of the book. Irish species names are also listed on page 257.

Time of year bar
The illustration of each species is accompanied by a 'Time of year' coloured bar. The colour key appears at the foot of each page, allowing an immediate assessment of the likelihood of encountering a given species at a particular time of year. A second 'Time of year' bar is also used to illustrate the occurrence of some distinctive sub-species, where appropriate, e.g. White Wagtail (pages 158, 159).

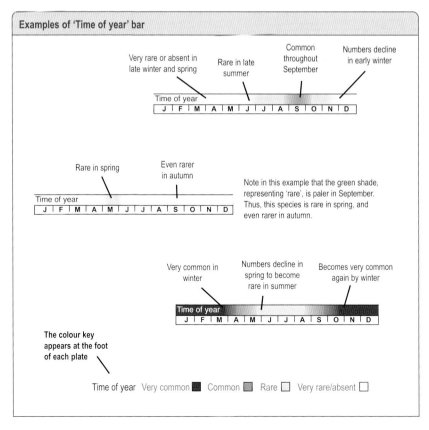

1

Maps

The colour key for all maps appears at the foot of each page. Used in conjunction with the 'Time of year' bar, it should allow you make a reasonable judgment about when and where in Ireland the species is likely to occur. Some very rare species have no map, usually when there have been too few occurrences to map accurately, or where the species has been recorded in widely scattered localities.

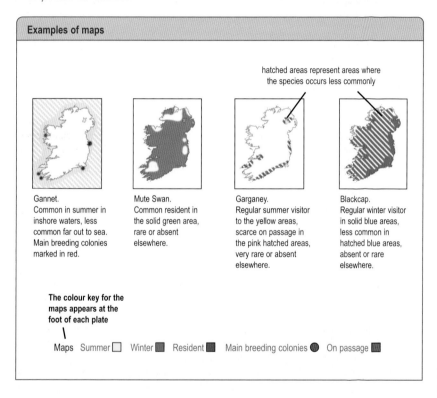

Examples of maps

hatched areas represent areas where the species occurs less commonly

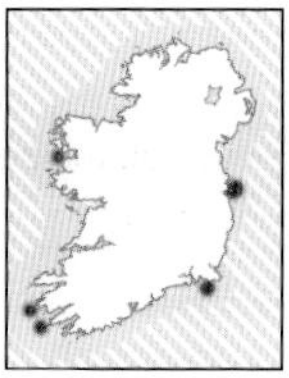

Gannet.
Common in summer in inshore waters, less common far out to sea. Main breeding colonies marked in red.

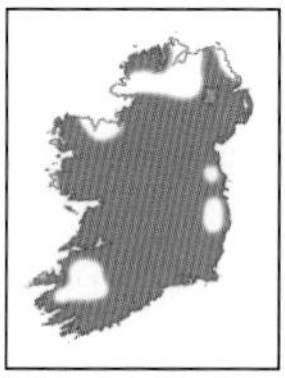

Mute Swan.
Common resident in the solid green area, rare or absent elsewhere.

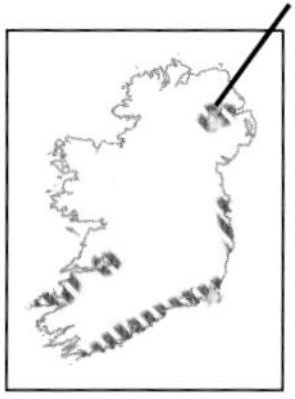

Garganey.
Regular summer visitor to the yellow areas, scarce on passage in the pink hatched areas, very rare or absent elsewhere.

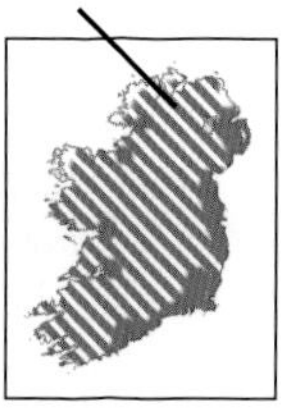

Blackcap.
Regular winter visitor in solid blue areas, less common in hatched blue areas, absent or rare elsewhere.

The colour key for the maps appears at the foot of each plate

Maps Summer Winter Resident Main breeding colonies On passage

Introduction

Taxonomy and bird names

With new developments in the classification of birds, the taxonomic order of species is constantly changing. In this book we have placed species in the latest order, as adopted and recommended by the Irish Rare Bird Committee (IRBC). However, in order to aid identification, we have placed several species out of their taxonomic order to allow them appear alongside similar-looking species. Birds are assigned scientific names. These are usually in Latin and comprise two sections. The first is the genus name and the second is the species name. Within some species, there are also races (or sub-species). Where this occurs, a race name appears after the species name. For example, Pied Wagtails are a race of White Wagtail *(Motacilla alba)* and, as a result, have the scientific name *Motacilla alba yarrellii* (see pages 158, 159).

Approaching bird identification

Encountering a species of bird for the first time, or finding a bird in a plumage that you may not recognise, can be a daunting experience. While some species can be extremely difficult to identify and require very detailed and careful observation, it is worth remembering that there are very few birds you will encounter in Ireland that cannot be easily identified, given good views and time. Bird identification can often be simply a process of elimination.

General information

There are many things that can assist this process. These include taking note of the time of year or the habitat the bird is in. In Ireland we have summer migrants and winter visitors as well as birds on passage in spring and/or autumn. Of course there are many species found in Ireland throughout the year, so checking the 'Time of year' bars against each species will offer very useful indications of when species can be seen. Habitat preference can also be helpful when identifying birds. For example, Purple Sandpipers prefer rocky coastlines and are rarely found with other waders on open mudflats. Again, the preferred habitat types for each species in the main section of this book is covered in detail.

The bird's behaviour and size are also vital elimination factors in the identification process. Among ducks on a freshwater lake there are some that will be diving while others are surface feeding species. Noting such easily observed behaviours can lead to the identification of the bird. The way a bird flies can also be a useful method to aid identification. For example, at sea, shearwaters glide effortlessly while petrels flutter over the waves. It is also worth remembering that some birds are even named according to their behaviour: wagtails wag their tails; Turnstones turn stones over; Treecreepers creep up trees, etc. Judging the size of a bird can be difficult. It is always best to compare a bird with a familiar, and if possible, a similar looking bird. Use certain species within families to accurately judge size. With waders, for example, use birds like Dunlin and Redshank, while in the garden, birds such as Robin and Blackbirds make ideal species for comparing size.

Understanding plumage and feathers

There are three different types of feathers found on birds. The first are the soft, down feathers which are closest to the skin and effectively keep the bird warm. The second group of feathers are known as contour feathers. These cover all the external areas of the bird. Contour feathers overlap each other to provide water and wind-proofing as well as streamlining the bird for flight. Have you ever noticed that birds always roost facing into the wind? This keeps the contour feathers against the body. If they faced tail to the wind, the feathers would be ruffled and the insulation breached! A bird's temperature can also be regulated by fluffing up these feathers to trap air in cold conditions which explains why birds always look rounded, fat and 'fluffy' in the snow. Alternatively, in warm weather their temperature is cooled by pressing the feathers tightly against the body giving the bird a lovely sleek appearance. So, a bird's shape can change according to weather conditions. Many species can also look tall and sleek when alert or more short-necked and rounded when relaxed.

The last group of feathers are remiges (the flight feathers). These, along with the retrices (the tail feathers), are the longest and most hardwearing. Flight feathers comprise two main groups, the secondaries and the primaries, of which there are usually ten arranged from the tip of the wing inwards.

Bird topography
It is worth learning the topography of a bird. This gives an understanding of where the bird's feathers lie on the body, the correct descriptions for the head markings, the way wingbars are formed, etc. It will also show the different 'bare parts' of a bird (areas not normally covered by feathers) such as the bill, legs and eyes. The diagrams below detail the topography of a bird in full.

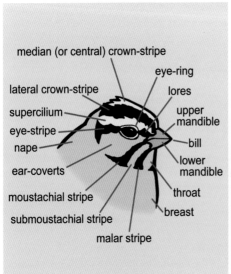

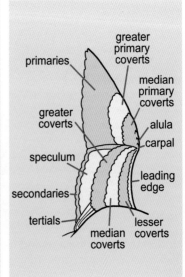

Understanding moult

Feathers do not grow continuously so, once a feather is grown, it is effectively dead. Over the course of time, feathers become worn and damaged. This can make birds appear paler than usual, while many features normally used for identification become difficult to observe as the feathers wear. More importantly, feather wear reduces a feather's ability to provide water-proofing or adequate strength for flight. For that reason feathers are moulted (replaced) annually. Growing new feathers is a slow and energy consuming process so a moult is under-taken over several weeks with old feathers gradually being replaced by new ones. This gradual replacement of feathers is an important evolutionary development as most species need to retain the powers of flight during moult (some species of geese and duck being an exception). Most species moult their feathers immediately following the breeding season (the post-nuptial moult) when, for many birds, they grow a completely new set of body and wing feathers.

   Many species also go through a partial moult in early spring. During these partial moults they usually replace head, body and some wing feathers, but never the important flight feathers. This spring moult gives birds their 'summer plumage' and explains why birds in spring are usually in immaculate condition. Not all birds acquire their summer plumage through moult. Birds like Linnets, Stonechats and Reed Buntings actually reach this stage when the tips of their head and body feathers wear away to reveal the brighter colours that lie underneath. These are the exception rather than the rule.

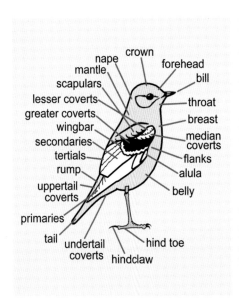

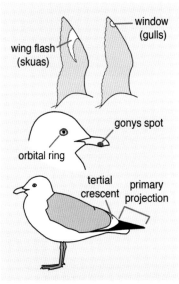

Ageing

When a young bird fledges (leaves the nest) it will have a complete set of wing and tail feathers but usually 'juvenile' head and body feathers which, in most cases, are moulted very quickly in time for its first winter. In small birds, this 'first-winter' plumage is essentially the same as that of an adult but will usually show pale tips to some of the wing feathers. By the following spring, another partial moult produces an adult plumage. The bigger the bird, the longer it usually takes for it to become a full adult. In medium-sized species it may take two years before reaching adulthood, while in larger birds like gulls, it may take four or five years. As they grow older, each time they moult a new plumage emerges, and an understanding of each plumage phase allows us to accurately age each bird. Hence we often refer to individual birds as a 'second winter' or a 'third summer', etc. Once they reach their full adult plumage it becomes almost impossible to age them.

Understanding the ageing process

Learning the ageing process of some large species (such as gulls) may require a lot of detailed observation. It is worth noting that as birds mature and go through a feather moult they change their appearance slightly. In larger birds, as each year passes, each moult brings them closer to adult plumage. In some birds, their bare part (bill and leg) colour also changes each year. Birds are aged according to the stages of moult they are at. The different stages are as follows:

Juvenile – this is just after the bird has left the nest. It has a full set of feathers for flying but many of the upperpart and head feathers are designed for camouflage.

First-winter – this is the bird's first ever winter plumage. This plumage is reached when a juvenile moults some of its body and head feathers (a partial moult) in late summer. In small birds this is often referred to as immature plumage because, by the following spring, they will essentially appear the same as adults.

First-summer – the bird is one year old. This plumage is reached when the bird moults some of its body and head feathers in spring (after the bird's first winter). For small birds, this is an adult plumage as they reach breeding age when one year old.

Second winter – this is the bird's second winter. It is now a year and a half old. This plumage is reached by a complete moult of wing, body and head feathers just after the summer (the bird's first summer).

Second summer – the bird is now two years old. This plumage is reached by a partial moult of head and body feathers in spring (after the bird's second winter).

Third winter – the bird is now two and a half years old. This plumage is reached by a complete moult after the summer (the bird's second summer).

Third summer/Adult summer – reached by a partial moult of some head and body feathers in spring. Most adult birds reach full adult breeding plumage by this stage.

Adult winter – a full winter-plumaged adult bird reached by a complete moult after the summer.

Of course, during the entire course of this process, birds are often in the middle of moulting so sometimes birds are referred to as being in two plumages (e.g. a bird moulting from its first summer plumage to its second winter plumage would be a first-summer/second winter bird).

Songs and calls

Learning and understanding the vocalisations of birds is a very useful way to aid identification. Birds can often be identified by song and calls. In summer, for example, Willow Warblers and Chiffchaffs appear very similar but have very distinctive songs, allowing the species to be easily separated. Birds sing for three main reasons. Firstly, it is a non-confrontational method of proclaiming ownership of a territory. It is the males that lay claim to, and defend, territories so it is usually only the males that sing. Secondly, it is a way of attracting a female. Thirdly, it is a way for a male bird to inform all of his neighbours that he is still alive. For these reasons, bird song in Ireland is usually only heard during the breeding season.

However, bird vocalisations are not confined to song. Chicks and young birds have begging calls to encourage their parents to feed them. Alarm calls are one of the most frequently heard bird sounds. They are often given in flight or by birds in deep cover. Flight calls can be very distinctive and, in some species, can be a real key to their identification. Alarm calls are usually far-carrying, sharp calls and many species give very similar alarm calls. Birds that flock together also keep in touch by using calls. Contact calls are essential for night flying migrants like Redwings. Most flocking species such as waders, geese and ducks are very vocal when feeding or flying. Even in woodlands, the short, low calls of Long-tailed Tits help to keep the flock in the same area while they are feeding. Simple questions such as whether the song is delivered from deep in cover, from the top of a tree or in the air may assist in the identification of the bird.

Trying to learn bird song and calls can be difficult, but it is worth remembering that birds are often heard before they are seen. Try to note key phrases of the song. Record whether the call has an upward or downward inflection, if the notes are sharp or soft and the number of notes in the call.

Swans

Mute Swan *Cygnus olor* Eala bhalbh   144-160cm

An all-white plumage and long, curved neck make this species easy to identify. The long, pointed tail is another useful feature, especially when birds are up-ending. **Male** (the cob) and **female** (the pen) are identical in plumage, with both having orange bills with black edges and a black base which continues up to meet the dark eye. Best told apart by the size of the knob on the top of the bill, which is larger and more obvious on the cob. Legs black. **Immatures** are brownish-grey with pinkish bills, and lack the bill knob of adults.

Voice & Diet Gives a variety of calls including hissing sounds and muffled 'nasal' grunts. Silent in flight but the wings make a whistling, throbbing sound. Feeds on water plants pulled from lake and river bottoms while up-ending. Also feeds on grasslands and cereal crops.

Habitat and Status A common resident bird found on lakes, rivers and canals throughout Ireland. Gathers in large, sociable herds in winter at traditional sites. Can also graze on crop fields and arable lands. Nests are enormous, round constructions found by rivers, canals and lakes, often hidden in reeds.

Bewick's Swan *Cygnus columbianus* Eala Bewick   116-129cm

The smallest swan to occur in Ireland, Bewick's is more likely to be confused with Whooper than Mute. Both sexes are identical with an all-white plumage, often with pale brown staining on the head, a short, straight, thick neck and a short black and yellow bill. The combination of size and body proportions give Bewick's Swan an almost goose-like appearance. The black on the bill is more extensive than on Whooper, with a rounded, rather than wedge-shaped, yellow area confined to the base of the bill. **Juveniles** show a pale greyish plumage and a pale creamy-pink bill, with black confined to the edges and extreme tip of the bill. The North American race known as **Whistling Swan** shows a tiny yellow spot on an all-dark bill.

Voice & Diet A quieter species than Whooper, giving a goose-like honking call. When in herds, can often give more melodic, 'babbling' calls. Feeds on grass, roots and water plants. Usually found alongside Whooper and Mute Swans.

Habitat and Status A scarce winter visitor from northern Russia and Siberia. Frequents lakes and marshes, crop fields and arable lands. Whistling Swan is a very rare winter visitor.

Whooper Swan *Cygnus cygnus* Eala ghlórach   145-158cm

The larger of the two migratory swans, Whooper is slightly smaller than Mute. Easily separated from Mute Swan by the short tail and the bill colour. It is more often confused with the smaller Bewick's but identified from that species by the long, slender, straight neck, sloped forehead, size, and the extent and shape of yellow on the larger bill. On Whooper, the yellow is large and triangular in shape with the black confined to the lower edge and tip. Like Bewick's, both sexes are identical, with an all-white plumage which sometimes shows pale brown head staining. Legs blackish. **Immatures** show a pale creamy-pink bill, with black confined to the tip, and a pale greyish plumage.

Voice & Diet In flight gives loud honking-type calls. During territorial or aggressive displays gives loud, excitable, trumpeting calls. Feeds on grasses, roots and water plants, often alongside other swans and geese.

Habitat and Status A common winter visitor from Iceland and northern Europe, and a rare breeding species. Found on lakes and marshes. Can also form large herds to graze on crop fields and arable lands. Small numbers breed in Ireland each year in northern counties.

Bewick's Swan

Whooper Swan

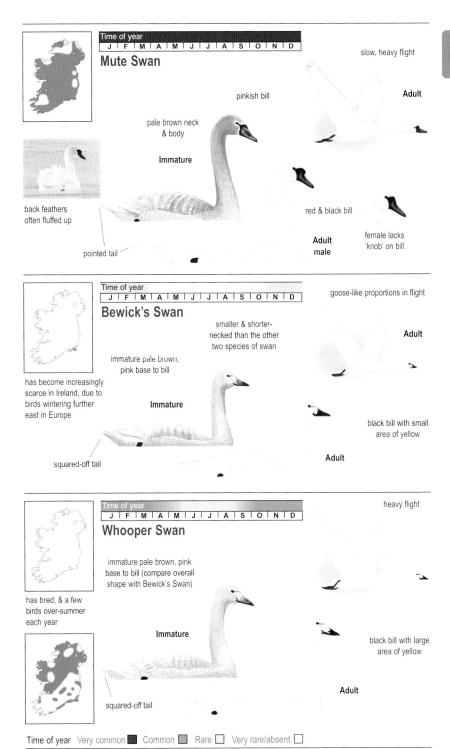

Time of year

J | F | M | A | M | J | J | A | S | O | N | D

Mute Swan

slow, heavy flight

pinkish bill

Adult

pale brown neck
& body

Immature

back feathers
often fluffed up

red & black bill

pointed tail

**Adult
male**

female lacks
'knob' on bill

Time of year

J | F | M | A | M | J | J | A | S | O | N | D

Bewick's Swan

goose-like proportions in flight

smaller & shorter-
necked than the other
two species of swan

Adult

immature pale brown,
pink base to bill

Immature

has become increasingly
scarce in Ireland, due to
birds wintering further
east in Europe

black bill with small
area of yellow

squared-off tail

Adult

Time of year

J | F | M | A | M | J | J | A | S | O | N | D

Whooper Swan

heavy flight

immature pale brown, pink
base to bill (compare overall
shape with Bewick's Swan)

has bred, & a few
birds over-summer
each year

Immature

black bill with large
area of yellow

squared-off tail

Adult

Time of year   Very common ■   Common ■   Rare □   Very rare/absent □

Maps   Summer □   Winter ■   Resident ■

9

Geese

Brent Goose *Branta bernicla* Cadhan   56-61cm

A small, short-necked goose with a black head, neck and breast, a small white neck collar, dark blackish-brown upperparts and a short dark bill. **Pale-bellied Brent** is a common winter visitor to Ireland and shows a whitish lower breast and belly, and dark barring along whitish flanks. Undertail white. **Immatures** similar, but show a thinner neck collar and broad white edges to the wing coverts. **Dark-bellied Brent**, an eastern race, shows a blackish breast, belly and flanks which do not contrast with the upper breast. **Black Brant** shows a large white neck collar, a dark belly contrasting with a white crescent on the upper flanks, and very dark upperparts. In flight shows darkish upper and underwings, a black tail and white uppertail coverts. Legs dark.

    Voice & Diet Gives a nasal *rronk* call. Feeds on grass, coastal vegetation and other plants.

    Habitat and Status Pale-bellied Brent is a common winter visitor from Arctic Greenland and Canada. Found on coastal estuaries and mudflats, and on open areas of grassland including football pitches. Dark-bellied Brent is a scarce winter visitor from Arctic Siberia. Black Brant is a rare winter visitor from North America.

Barnacle Goose *Branta leucopsis* Gé ghiúrainn   59-69cm

A small, distinctive goose with a black crown, neck and breast and a contrasting creamy-white face which shows a black line from the dark eye to the dark bill. Upperparts pale grey with broad, black, white-tipped barring. Underparts whitish with pale grey barring on the flanks. Undertail white. **Immatures** show a duller plumage and diffuse barring on flanks. In flight shows a pale grey underwing with darker flight feathers, a greyish upperwing with black barring and a black rump and tail contrasting with white uppertail coverts. Legs blackish.

    Voice & Diet Gives very distinctive, short, repeated, barking calls in flight. When feeding gives a chattering *hugug, hugug* call. Feeds on grass, rushes and other plant material.

    Habitat and Status A winter visitor from north-east Greenland. Found on quiet, undisturbed grazing areas, especially favouring uninhabited islands. Also found on coastal grasslands.

Canada Goose *Branta canadensis* Gé Cheanadach   80-108cm

A long-necked goose with a black head and neck, a diagnostic white throat and cheek patch, and a long dark bill. The upperparts are brownish with pale fringes to the feathers. Underparts show a pale creamy breast and a brownish belly and flanks with narrow pale barring. Undertail white. **Immatures** show a slightly duller plumage. In flight shows a black rump and tail, a narrow white crescent formed by white uppertail coverts and dark underwings. Legs dark.

    Voice & Diet Gives a loud, trumpeting *ah-honk* call. Feeds on grass, grain and other plants.

    Habitat and Status Feral populations are now established in many parts of the country. Wild birds are rare winter vagrants from Arctic Canada and are usually found on open pastures with Greenland White-fronted or Barnacle Geese.

Cackling Goose *Branta hutchinsii*   60-70cm

Similar to Canada Goose but smaller with a shorter, thicker neck and a shorter dark bill. Head and neck black with a white throat and cheek patch. Upperparts pale brownish with pale fringes to the feathers. Underparts show a dark creamy breast and a brownish belly and flanks with narrow creamy barring. Undertail white. **Immatures** show a duller plumage. In flight shows a black rump and tail, white uppertail coverts and dark underwings. Legs blackish.

    Voice & Diet Gives a high-pitched, loud *ah-honk* call. Feeds on grass, grain and other plants.

    Habitat and Status A very rare winter vagrant from Arctic Canada. Usually found on open pastures and most often seen with Barnacle Geese.

| J | F | M | A | M | J | J | A | S | O | N | D |

Brent Goose

Pale-bellied Brent

young birds have barred upperparts

black neck & head

Pale-bellied Brent

dark upperwing

adult

Immature

larger white collar

adult

dark belly

adult

darker back, black underparts

Black Brant

Immature

Dark-bellied Brent

Pale-bellied Brent

Dark-bellied Brent & Black Brant

Time of year

| J | F | M | A | M | J | J | A | S | O | N | D |

Barnacle Goose

like most geese, flies in V formation

black neck, white (or pale yellow) face

Adult

Time of year

| J | F | M | A | M | J | J | A | S | O | N | D |

Canada Goose

black neck, white chinstrap

Cackling Goose is smaller, darker & shorter necked

Canada Goose

feral birds

feral birds are large, long-necked & pale-bellied

Canada Goose

Cackling Goose

wild birds

Time of year

| J | F | M | A | M | J | J | A | S | O | N | D |

Cackling Goose

Time of year   Common ■   Rare □   Very rare/absent □

Maps   Winter ■   Resident ■

11

Geese

White-fronted Goose *Anser albifrons* Gé bhánéadanach   66-76cm
A thick-necked, greyish-brown goose, with **adults of the Greenland race** (Greenland White-fronted Goose) showing an orange bill and legs, and a striking white patch around the base of the bill. Head and neck brown, with thin black streaking on the sides of the neck. Upperparts greyish-brown with narrow, pale fringes. Underparts greyish-brown with black patches on the belly and flanks, and a thin white line along upper flanks. Undertail white. **Immatures** lack belly patches and white base to the bill. The **Siberian race** (Russian White-fronted Goose) has a pinkish bill. In flight shows pale coverts on a plain upperwing. Underwing dark. Rump and tail dark, with a white tail band and white uppertail coverts.

   Voice & Diet Gives a loud, melodious, high-pitched *kow-lyok* call in flight. Feeds on grass, grain, fodder, beet and other plant material.

   Habitat and Status Ireland holds approximately half of the world's wintering population of the Greenland race. Found on open grasslands, wetlands and loughs. At coastal locations can roost on sandbanks. The Siberian race is a very rare winter visitor.

Pink-footed Goose *Anser brachyrhynchus* Gé ghobghearr   60-74cm
A small, short-necked, greyish-brown goose with a small, round-headed appearance. Adults show a dark chocolate-brown head and neck contrasting with a pale, fawn breast. Darker rear flanks show a narrow white upperflank line. Undertail white. Upperparts pale, frosted, greyish-brown with pale greyish fringes to the feathers. Short, stubby bill black with a pink subterminal band and can show a white base. Legs pink. **Immatures** similar, but show a duller and browner plumage, lacking greyish tones to upperparts. In flight shows a contrasting pale grey forewing, a darkish underwing and a white-bordered dark tail. Uppertail coverts white.

   Voice & Diet Gives a loud, repeated *wink-wink* or *wink-wink-wink* call, which is shriller and more high-pitched than other species of grey geese. Also gives an *ang-unk* call. Feeds on grass, grain, potatoes, fodder and other plants and roots.

   Habitat and Status An uncommon but regular winter visitor from Iceland and Greenland. Found on open grassland, stubble fields, lakes and wetlands, usually with other goose species.

Bean Goose *Anser fabalis* Síolghé   71-88cm
A large, greyish-brown goose, with adults showing a dark brown head and neck with pale neck streaking, and a pale fawn-coloured breast contrasting with the darker rear flanks which show whitish edges to feathers. White upper-flank line present. Undertail white. Upperparts brownish with pale edges. Lacks the frosted appearance of Pink-footed. European birds of the race *fabalis* (**Taiga Bean Goose**) are larger, show a long, slender, black bill with varying amounts of orange, a longer neck and can have a narrow white base to bill. Birds from Siberia of the race *rossicus* (**Tundra Bean Goose**) appear smaller, with shorter, thicker necks and a deep base to the short bill which shows a neat orange subterminal band. The cutting edge on the bill of Taiga Bean Goose is straight while that of Tundra Bean Goose shows an open 'grinning' effect. Both races show dull orange legs. In flight, shows a relatively plain upperwing. Underwing dark grey. Rump, back and tail dark, with white uppertail coverts and narrow white tail band. **Immatures** show a duller, browner plumage.

   Voice & Diet Gives deep, repeated *hank-hank* and *ang-unk* calls which are lower pitched and shriller in tone than the similar calls given by Pink-footed Goose. Feeds on grass, root crops, fodder and other plant material.

   Habitat and Status Taiga Bean Goose is a rare winter vagrant from northern Europe. Tundra Bean Goose is a very rare winter vagrant from Siberia. Found on open grasslands and wet pastures.

Time of year

| J | F | M | A | M | J | J | A | S | O | N | D |

White-fronted Goose

white patch

orange bill & legs

Immature

Adult

Adult

black patches on belly & flanks (lacking on immature)

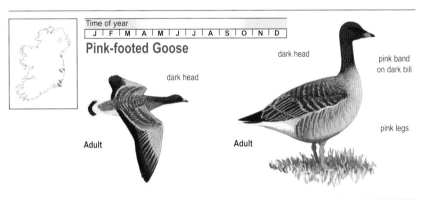

Time of year

| J | F | M | A | M | J | J | A | S | O | N | D |

Pink-footed Goose

dark head

pink band on dark bill

dark head

pink legs

Adult

Adult

Time of year

| J | F | M | A | M | J | J | A | S | O | N | D |

Bean Goose

orange variable, some have white at base of bill

long, slender bill

compared with 'Tundra' Bean Goose, 'Taiga' has longer neck & more orange on a longer, more slender bill

'Taiga' Bean Goose

dark head

both races very rare

dark head

'Tundra' Bean Goose

orange legs

Adult 'Taiga' Bean Goose

Time of year   Common ■ Rare □ Very rare/absent □

Maps   Winter ■   13

Greylag Goose *Anser anser* Gé ghlas   76-90cm

A large, thick-necked, heavy goose with a broad orange bill and pinkish legs. On **adults**, the head and neck are greyish-brown with dark neck streaking. Breast and belly slightly paler with variable amounts of black markings on belly. Flanks show dark centres to the feathers with pale, greyish-brown edges. Undertail white. Upperparts pale greyish-brown with paler grey fringes to the feathers. **Immatures** similar but lack black belly spots. In flight shows a strikingly pale grey forewing and pale grey underwing coverts. The rump is greyish. The uppertail coverts are white and form a narrow white crescent which does not contrast strongly with the rump. Tail dark with white border.

Voice & Diet Gives a loud, cackling, *aahng-unng-ung* call. Feeds on grass, grain, roots and other plant matter.

Habitat and Status A locally common winter visitor from breeding grounds in Iceland. In several parts of Ireland small pockets of feral birds are present, these having escaped from wildfowl collections. Found on open grasslands, arable fields, marshes and lakes.

Snow Goose *Anser caerulescens* Gé shneachta   64-78cm

A large goose with a broad, pale-tipped, pink bill which shows a dark cutting edge, and pinkish legs. Occurs in two forms, the white and blue phases. The unmistakable **white phase** shows an all-white plumage with black primaries and bluish-grey primary coverts. The **blue phase** shows a white head and upper neck, and dark bluish-grey lower neck, breast, mantle and underparts, and a white undertail. The elongated scapulars show white edges. The wing coverts are pale grey. Primaries dark. In flight the white phase shows contrasting black primaries against the all-white plumage, while the blue phase shows pale grey wing coverts and a grey rump and tail.

Voice & Diet Gives a harsh, nasal *kaank* call as well as deep, gabbling *ung-ung* calls. Feeds on grass, fodder, grain and other plants.

Habitat and Status A rare winter visitor from Arctic Canada and north-west Greenland. Often found associating with Greenland White-fronted Geese. Found on open pastureland, sloblands and arable fields.

Shelduck *Tadorna tadorna* Seil-lacha   57-64cm

A large duck with a bright red bill and pinkish legs. **Males** show a large bill knob, a blackish-green head and neck, and a white lower neck and upper breast. A broad, chestnut band extends from mantle onto breast. Underparts white with a black belly stripe from breast to vent. Undertail coverts chestnut. Upperparts white with a black scapular stripe, chestnut-coloured tertials, dark green secondaries and black primaries. Bill knob reduced in winter. **Females** show no bill knob, white mottling around base of bill and duller plumage. **Immatures** blackish-grey on head and upperparts, and white below. In flight shows a striking black and white plumage, a white rump and a white, dark-tipped tail.

Voice & Diet Relatively noisy in the breeding season, with males giving melodious whistling calls. Females give a repeated *ag-ag-ag-ag* call. Feeds on small molluscs, crustaceans and insects. Feeds by sifting in mud or by up-ending in deeper water.

Habitat and Status A common resident breeding species found in all coastal counties. Nests in old rabbit burrows and other holes. In July most adults depart to moult their feathers, leaving the immatures in large creches, usually attended by a small number of adult birds. Moulting takes place on sandbanks off north-west Germany, with birds returning in early winter. Feeds on estuaries and mudflats. Nests in sand-dune systems and around some inland lakes.

wild birds, in winter

feral population

Time of year											Feral birds
Time of year											Wild birds
J	F	M	A	M	J	J	A	S	O	N	D

Greylag Goose

orange bill

thick-necked, stocky

pale grey forewing

Adult

pinkish legs

| Time of year | | | | | | | | | | | |
| J | F | M | A | M | J | J | A | S | O | N | D |

Snow Goose

Adult white phase

Adult white phase

white body, black wingtips

white head & neck, black body

white head & neck, dark body

Adult blue phase

Adult blue phase

| Time of year | | | | | | | | | | | |
| J | F | M | A | M | J | J | A | S | O | N | D |

Shelduck

striking black & white plumage

female lacks 'knob' on bill

Juvenile
(July/August)

Female

Male

chestnut breast band

| Time of year | Common ■ | Rare ☐ | Very rare/absent ☐ |

Maps Summer ☐   Winter ■   Resident ■

Ducks

Mandarin Duck *Aix galericulata* Lacha mhandrach   41-49cm

A medium-sized but very striking and colourful Asian species with a large-headed, crested appearance. **Males** show a bright red bill with a white nail. Face shows a white stripe from above the eye to the rear of the nape. Forehead appears green, contrasting with the orange cheeks and lores. Breast dark with two white stripes. Upperparts dark with striking orange sails on back. Undertail white. **Females** similar in shape but show a paler bill with a white nail and a white throat. A white eye-ring and stripe from behind the eye contrasts with a greyish head. Upperparts dark brown with greyish underparts showing pale, buff, rounded spots. Female **Wood Duck** very similar but shows a dark nail to the bill, a broader white eye-ring and thinner, duller spotting on the underparts.

Voice & Diet A relatively silent species. Gives a sharp, whistling call when disturbed. Males can give a *prruib* call. Feeds on a wide variety of aquatic plants and seeds.

Habitat and Status Found on small lakes and ponds, usually with overhanging vegetation. Will freely perch in trees and nests in holes in trees. A small, self-sustaining feral population is now established in Co. Down. Rarely recorded away from this area.

Wigeon *Anas penelope* Rualacha   43-49cm

A short-necked duck with a black-tipped, blue-grey bill. **Males** show a chestnut head, a creamy-yellow forehead and crown, a greyish-pink breast, grey, vermiculated flanks, a white ventral patch and black undertail. Belly white. Grey and white vermiculated upperparts show black- and white-edged tertials and white coverts. In flight shows a white covert patch and a black-bordered dark green speculum. **Females** grey-brown on head with a dull, warm brown breast and flanks, a white belly and a spotted whitish undertail. Brownish upperparts show pale fringes and white-edged tertials. In flight shows a greyish forewing. Blackish-green speculum shows a white upper edge and a pale trailing edge. Underwing shows greyish axillaries.

Voice & Diet Males give a very distinctive, whistling *wheeoo* call, while females give a growling *krrr*. Feeds on a wide variety of aquatic plants and seeds. Will also graze on grasslands. Feeds on eel-grass at coastal locations in winter.

Habitat and Status A very common winter visitor from Iceland, Scandinavia and Siberia. Very small numbers may spend the summer in Ireland, with breeding being recorded on only a few occasions, mainly in northern counties. Found on coastal estuaries, lagoons, freshwater lakes, marshes and grassland close to water.

American Wigeon *Anas americana* Rualacha Mheiriceánach   45-55cm

Males show a steep, white forehead and crown, a flecked, pale head and neck, and a dark green eye patch. Breast and flanks pinkish-brown. Belly and ventral patch white. Undertail black. Upperparts finely vermiculated pinkish-brown. Dark tertials show white edges. In flight shows white covert patch and a dark green and black speculum. **Females** like female Wigeon, but show a greyish head with fine flecking, a darkish eye patch, an orangy breast and flanks, and a white belly and edges to brown rump. Upperparts brownish with broad, buff edges. In flight shows white axillaries, a whitish upperwing panel, and a black and green speculum with a white trailing edge. Bill bluish-grey with black tip and thin black border to base.

Voice & Diet Males give a soft, repeated, whistling *whee* call, with females giving growling *krrr* calls. Feeds on a wide variety of aquatic plants and seeds. Like Wigeon, can sometimes graze on land.

Habitat and Status A rare autumn and winter visitor from North America. Usually found associating with Wigeon. Frequents lakes, marshes, coastal lagoons and estuaries, although tends to prefer freshwater areas.

Wildfowl

Mandarin Duck

Time of year
J F M A M J J A S O N D

small population established
on the Shimna River &
Tollymore Forest Park in
Co. Down

unique plumage

Male

striking white eye-ring
& white tip to bill

Female

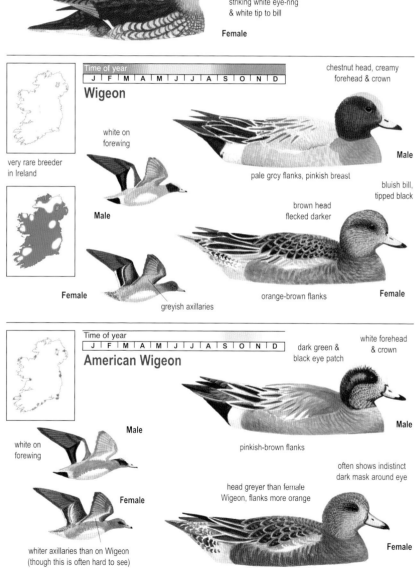

Time of year
J F M A M J J A S O N D

Wigeon

chestnut head, creamy
forehead & crown

very rare breeder
in Ireland

white on
forewing

pale grey flanks, pinkish breast

Male

bluish bill,
tipped black

brown head
flecked darker

Male

Female

greyish axillaries

orange-brown flanks

Female

Time of year
J F M A M J J A S O N D

American Wigeon

dark green &
black eye patch

white forehead
& crown

Male

white on
forewing

pinkish-brown flanks

Male

often shows indistinct
dark mask around eye

Female

head greyer than female
Wigeon, flanks more orange

whiter axillaries than on Wigeon
(though this is often hard to see)

Female

Time of year   Common ☐   Rare ☐   Very rare/absent ☐

Maps   Summer ☐   Winter ■   Resident ■

17

Ducks

Gadwall *Anas strepera* Gadual   48-53cm

A slender duck with a steep forehead and yellowish-orange legs. **Males** greyish on head, with crown and nape streaking. Breast and flanks grey with vermiculations heaviest on breast. Stern black. Upperparts vermiculated grey with elongated buff-edged scapulars and paler grey tertials. Bill dark. **Females** show dark scalloping on brownish-grey upper and underparts, and a whitish belly. Head pale buffish-grey with dark crown and eye-stripe, and a whitish throat. Bill dark with clear-cut yellowish or orange edges. In flight males show a black and white speculum, a chestnut median covert panel and white trailing edge to secondaries. Females show a whitish speculum on inner secondaries and a thin white trailing edge.

Voice & Diet Relatively silent, although males give whistling and dry, croaking type calls. Females give a high-pitched, repeated *quack* in flight or when disturbed. Feeds by up-ending or dabbling, taking aquatic plants and seeds. Occasionally feeds on stubble and crops.

Habitat and Status A scarce breeding species, with very small populations in the west, north and south-east. Breeds on freshwater lakes with good vegetation, suitable for cover when nesting. Uncommon in winter, despite the arrival of birds from Iceland, Britain and Europe. Winters on open freshwater lakes and marshes.

Mallard *Anas platyrhynchos* Mallard   55-62cm

A very familiar, large duck with a broad bill and orange legs. **Males** show a dark, glossy, green head, a white neck collar and purple-brown breast. Central tail feathers black and curled, contrasting with white outertail. Flanks greyish with fine vermiculations. Black undertail shows white edges. Back blackish. Upperparts greyish with fine vermiculations. Wing coverts brownish. Rump black. Bill olive-yellow with black nail. **Females** buff-brown with coarse, dark mottling. Face shows a pale buff super-cilium and throat, and a dark eye-stripe. Bill grey with pale yellow at base and tip. In flight shows a black-bordered blue speculum with even, white trailing and upper edges.

Voice & Diet The familiar, laughing *quack, quack, quack* call is given by females only. Males give soft, weak *kairp* calls, as well as grunts and whistles. Feeds by dabbling or up-ending, taking aquatic plants, seeds and invertebrates. Will also graze on crops and stubble.

Habitat and Status An extremely common and widespread breeding species. In winter populations increase with the arrival of birds from northern Europe. Found on lakes, ponds, marshes and estuaries. This species is widely reared and released for shooting.

American Black Duck *Anas rubripes* Lacha chosrua   53-61cm

A dark, Mallard-sized duck with bright orange-red legs. **Males** sooty-black on underparts. Pale greyish edges to tertials contrast with sooty-black upperparts. Head and throat pale buff with fine streaking. Crown and eye-stripe dark. Pale head contrasts with darker body. Bill olive-yellow with black nail. **Female** similar but body browner and head more coarsely streaked. Bill duller, occasionally with dark centre. Legs brownish-red. In flight shows a black-bordered, deep blue speculum and a very thin white trailing edge. Lacks the white upper edge of speculum present on Mallard. Underwing silvery-white, contrasting strongly with dark body.

Voice & Diet Calls similar to Mallard, with females giving *quack* calls and males giving weak *kairp* calls. Feeds by dabbling or up-ending, taking aquatic plants, seeds and invertebrates.

Habitat and Status An extremely rare winter visitor from North America. Found associating with Mallard on lakes, marshes and estuaries. Also found on crop and stubble fields.

Gadwall

Time of year

| J | F | M | A | M | J | J | A | S | O | N | D |

rather featureless pale grey
upperparts, flanks & head

rare but regular
breeder in Ireland

Male

white on inner
secondaries

black undertail

dark grey
bill

Male

yellowish or
orange bill

more slender-
necked than
female Mallard

Female

Female

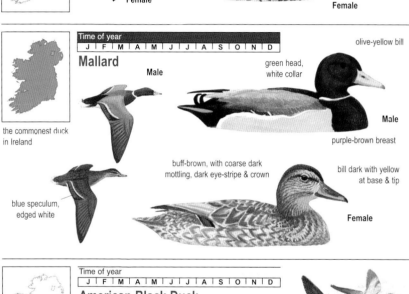

Mallard

Time of year

| J | F | M | A | M | J | J | A | S | O | N | D |

the commonest duck
in Ireland

Male

green head,
white collar

olive-yellow bill

Male

purple-brown breast

buff-brown, with coarse dark
mottling, dark eye-stripe & crown

blue speculum,
edged white

bill dark with yellow
at base & tip

Female

American Black Duck

Time of year

| J | F | M | A | M | J | J | A | S | O | N | D |

dark body, paler head

white
underwing

very rare, though
several individuals
have returned in
successive winters

Male

yellow
bill

vagrants to Ireland
often consort with Mallard,
& are, by comparison,
always noticeably darker

overall very
dark, paler
head

Male

bill olive-
green

purple
speculum
not edged
white

**Female/
immature**

**Female/
immature**

Time of year   Very common ■   Common ▨   Rare ▢   Very rare/absent ▢

Maps   Summer ▢   Winter ▨   Resident ■

19

Ducks

Pintail *Anas acuta* Biorearrach

A long-necked, elegant duck. **Males** show a chocolate-brown head and throat, with a thin white stripe meeting white neck and breast. Belly white. Creamy ventral patch contrasts with black undertail. Fine grey vermiculations on upperparts and flanks. Tertials and elongated scapulars black with white and grey edges. White-edged black tail shows long central feathers. Bill dark grey with blue-grey edges. In flight shows a chestnut covert panel, and a dark green and black speculum with a white trailing edge. **Females** show a plain, buff-brown head, a coarsely marked, pale grey-brown body and a longish, pointed tail. Shows a dark speculum with a white trailing edge. Bill dark greyish.

Voice & Diet A relatively quiet species, males can give a Teal-like *krrip* call and low, whistling calls. Females give a repeated, weak, Mallard-like *quack*. Feeds by dabbling, up-ending or grazing on land. Takes a wide variety of aquatic plants, seeds and other plant material. Will also take aquatic invertebrates.

Habitat and Status A rare breeding species, with records from the midlands and north. A scarce winter visitor from Iceland and continental Europe, found on freshwater lakes, coastal lagoons and estuaries. Breeds on wet meadows and lakes, nesting in short vegetation.

(Common) Teal *Anas crecca* Praslacha
34-39cm

A small duck. **Males** show a chestnut head with a green face mask which extends from the eye towards the nape. The face mask shows a broad, yellow-buff border which extends towards the base of the bill. Breast buff with dark spotting. Flanks grey, finely vermiculated. Yellow, black-bordered undertail patches obvious. Upperparts grey with fine vermiculations and black and white scapular stripes. Bill dark. **Females** greyish-brown with heavy mottling, and show a dark eye-stripe on a plain face, a diagnostic white undertail covert stripe and a pale base to bill. In flight shows a black and green speculum with a broad pale buff and white upper border, and a thin, white trailing edge. Flight fast and agile.

Voice & Diet Males give a very distinctive, bell-like *prrip* call, while females give a sharp, Mallard-like *quack*. Feeds by up-ending in shallow water or by dabbling on the surface. Takes aquatic plants, seeds and aquatic invertebrates.

Habitat and Status A very common species in winter, with birds from Scandinavia, Britain and Iceland arriving in late autumn. An uncommon breeding species, found nesting on small lakes, pools and rivers. Winters on lakes, marshes and estuaries.

Green-winged Teal *Anas carolinensis* Praslacha ghlaseiteach
34-39cm

Similar in size and structure to Teal. **Males** differ by showing a bold white vertical bar on the side of the breast and by lacking a horizontal white stripe on the upperparts. Head dark rufous with a dark green face mask showing a thin, dull yellowish border which, unlike Teal, does not extend towards the base of the bill. Breast orange-buff with dark spotting with dark brownish-grey upperparts and grey flanks showing fine vermiculations. Yellow, black-bordered undertail patches very obvious. **Female** Green-winged Teal very difficult to separate from female Teal, but tends to show a darker line on the cheek and a whiter wingbar in flight.

Voice & Diet Males give a very distinctive, bell-like *krrip* call, while females give a weak, Mallard-like *quack*. Behaviour as Teal, feeding by up-ending in shallow water or by dabbling on the surface. Takes aquatic plants, seeds and aquatic invertebrates.

Habitat and Status A rare but annual autumn and winter vagrant from North America. Found associating with Teal on marshes, lakes and estuaries. Can breed with Teal, producing offspring showing features that are a combination of both species.

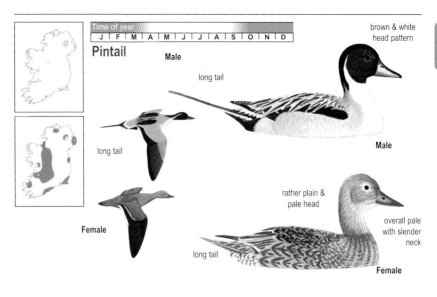

Time of year
J F M A M J J A S O N D

Pintail

Male

long tail

brown & white head pattern

Male

long tail

Female

long tail

rather plain & pale head

overall pale with slender neck

Female

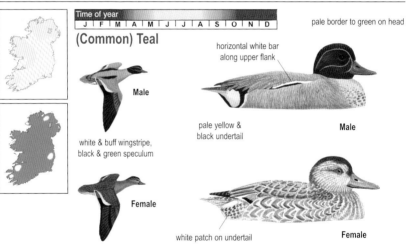

Time of year
J F M A M J J A S O N D

(Common) Teal

Male

white & buff wingstripe, black & green speculum

Female

pale border to green on head

horizontal white bar along upper flank

pale yellow & black undertail

Male

white patch on undertail

Female

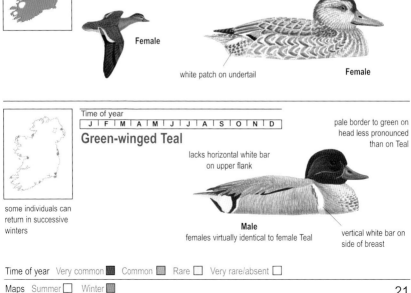

Time of year
J F M A M J J A S O N D

Green-winged Teal

lacks horizontal white bar on upper flank

pale border to green on head less pronounced than on Teal

some individuals can return in successive winters

Male
females virtually identical to female Teal

vertical white bar on side of breast

Time of year   Very common ■   Common ■   Rare □   Very rare/absent □

Maps   Summer □   Winter ■

21

Ducks

Shoveler *Anas clypeata* Spadalach   47-54cm

A large spatulate bill gives Shoveler a striking profile. **Males** show a black bill, a glossy, dark green head and white breast. A chestnut belly contrasts with a white ventral spot and a black undertail. Upperparts white with a dark central stripe. Long black scapulars show white edges. Forewing pale blue. Shows white tips to greater coverts, a green speculum in flight, blackish primaries, a black rump and white sides to a black tail. **Females** pale brown with dark spotting, best recognised by the large bill which shows an orange cutting edge. In flight females show a grey-blue forewing and dull green speculum. Legs and feet orange. Eye yellowish on male, duller on female.

    Voice & Diet A relatively quiet species, males can give a hollow *tunk-tunk* call, while females give quacking-type calls. Feeds by sifting the surface of the water with the large bill or by up-ending. Takes molluscs, insects, crustaceans, seeds and water plants.

    Habitat and Status A common wintering species from Iceland, Scandinavia and northern Russia. Found on freshwater lakes and marshes, as well as estuaries and mudflats. Shoveler are a rare breeding species, nesting in grass or rushes close to water. The main breeding populations are concentrated in the midlands and north-east.

Garganey *Anas querquedula* Praslacha shamhraidh   37-42cm

A small duck which holds the rear end of the body high out of the water. **Males** show a rich brown head with a striking white stripe from above eye onto nape. A brown breast shows dark mottling. Flanks pale grey with dark vermiculations. Brown undertail shows dark spotting. Upperparts dark. Elongated scapulars show white edges. **Females** and **immatures** greyish-brown with broad dark mottling. Head shows a whitish supercilium contrasting with a dark crown and eye-stripe, a whitish loral patch and throat, and a dark cheek stripe. In flight males show a pale grey-blue forewing, and a green and black speculum which has even white upper and trailing edges. Females show duller forewing, a white trailing edge and a thin, white upper edge to the secondaries.

    Voice & Diet Males give a distinctive, croaking, rattling call, while females give a short *quack*. Feeds on aquatic plants, seeds and invertebrates. Dabbles and immerses head in water, but rarely up-ends like Teal.

    Habitat and Status An uncommon spring, summer and autumn visitor. Very rare in winter. A very rare breeding species with most reports referring to northern and south-eastern regions. Found along fringes of reeds and sedges on freshwater lakes, pools and marshes. Nests in dense vegetation close to water.

Blue-winged Teal *Anas discors* Praslacha ghormeiteach   37-41cm

A small duck with a broad, dark bill. **Males** show a dark blue-grey head, a blackish crown and a broad white crescent between eye and bill. Breast and flanks warm buff with dark spotting. Rear flanks barred. White ventral patches contrast with black undertail. Upperparts dark with striped elongated scapulars. **Females** greyish-buff with broad, dark mottling and showing a striking whitish loral patch, a whitish supercilium and a broken, pale eye-ring. In flight males show a bright blue forewing with a broad, white upper edge and a dark trailing edge to a black and green speculum. Females show a duller forewing, a dark trailing edge, and an obscure whitish upper edge to a darker speculum.

    Voice & Diet Males can give soft, whistling calls in flight while females give a high-pitched *quack*. Feeds by dabbling, occasionally up-ending. Takes a variety of aquatic plants, seeds and invertebrates.

    Habitat and Status A very rare autumn and winter vagrant from North America. Found on freshwater lakes, coastal lagoons and estuaries. Can associate with flocks of Shovelers.

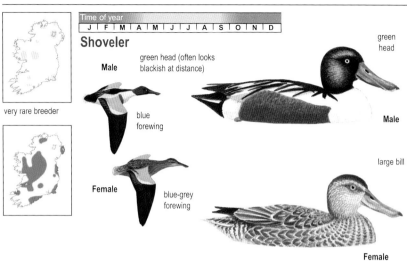

Shoveler

Time of year

| J | F | M | A | M | J | J | A | S | O | N | D |

very rare breeder

Male — green head (often looks blackish at distance)

blue forewing

Female — blue-grey forewing

green head

Male

large bill

Female

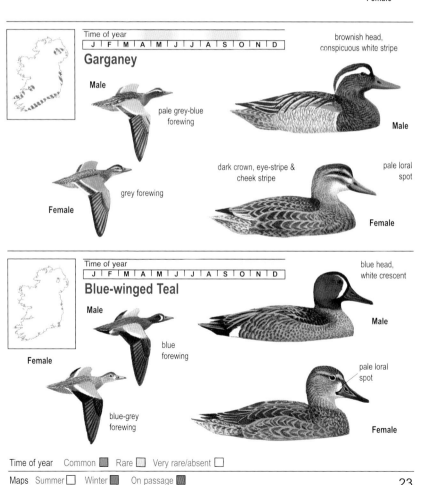

Garganey

Time of year

| J | F | M | A | M | J | J | A | S | O | N | D |

Male — pale grey-blue forewing

Female — grey forewing

brownish head, conspicuous white stripe

Male

dark crown, eye-stripe & cheek stripe

pale loral spot

Female

Blue-winged Teal

Time of year

| J | F | M | A | M | J | J | A | S | O | N | D |

Male

Female — blue forewing

blue-grey forewing

blue head, white crescent

Male

pale loral spot

Female

Time of year Common ■ Rare ▨ Very rare/absent □

Maps Summer □ Winter ■ On passage ▧

23

Ducks

Red-crested Pochard *Netta rufina* Póiseard cíordhearg 53-57cm

A large diving duck with a long neck and a rounded crown. **Males** unmistakable with a bright, slightly shaggy, golden crown, and a chestnut face. Neck and breast black, with whitish flanks becoming brownish on upper border. Belly and undertail black. Upperparts greyish-brown with a black back, rump and tail. Eye orange-red with black pupil. Bill bright red with a pale tip. **Females** show a dark brownish crown and nape contrasting with a pale grey lower face and throat. Breast and flanks greyish-brown with pale barring. Ventral area pale. Upperparts and rump greyish. Eye dark. Bill dark with pinkish edges and a pink subterminal band. In flight shows a white wing stripe and pale underwings.

Voice & Diet Rarely heard in Ireland. Red-crested Pochard tends to feed by dabbling on the surface of the water or by up-ending and is also known to feed on stubble and crop fields close to water. Takes seeds, water plants and other plant material.

Habitat and Status A very rare winter visitor from southern Europe. Widely kept in wildfowl collections, so some sightings might refer to escaped birds. Found on freshwater lakes, brackish lagoons and reservoirs. Usually seen associating with mixed diving duck flocks.

Pochard *Aythya ferina* Póiseard 44-48cm

A diving duck with a high, domed crown and a long bill. **Males** show a rich chestnut head, a black breast, tail and undertail, and whitish-grey flanks. Upperparts pale grey. Eye reddish. Bill black with a grey central patch. **Females** show a brownish crown, with paler lores and throat. Eye dark, with thin pale orbital ring which can extend back as line over ear-coverts. Breast brownish with pale barring. In summer upperparts brownish with grey scalloping. Flanks warm brown with buff scalloping. Upperparts and flanks show pale grey scalloping in winter. Tail and undertail brown. Bill dark, usually with a pale subterminal band, which can be absent on some birds. In flight, Pochard shows a broad greyish wing stripe.

Voice & Diet During the breeding season males can give a wheezing-type call. Females give a growling call in flight. An active diving species, feeding on aquatic invertebrates and water plants.

Habitat and Status A common winter visitor from Europe, with a very small breeding population concentrated in the midlands and north. In winter the largest concentration occurs on Lough Neagh, with smaller numbers found throughout the country. Occurs on freshwater lakes, ponds and reservoirs.

Ferruginous Duck *Aythya nyroca* Póiseard súilbhán 38-43cm

A diving duck with a sloped forehead, a peaked crown and a long, slender bill. **Males** show a dark, rich chestnut head, neck and breast, with paler chestnut flanks. Belly whitish. Undertail conspicuously white. Upperparts, rump and tail dark brown. Males show a striking white eye with a black pupil. Bill blue-grey with a paler subterminal band and a black tip. **Females** similar, but show a dark eye, a duller brown head, breast and underparts, and blackish upperparts. Undertail white. Females show a dark grey bill, a paler subterminal band and a black tip. In flight shows a white, conspicuous wing stripe. Underwing pale.

Voice & Diet Rarely heard when found in Ireland, although females can utter a harsh *gaaa* when flushed. An active diving species, feeding on invertebrates, water plants and seeds.

Habitat and Status A very rare winter visitor from eastern and southern Europe. Found on freshwater lakes and ponds, tending to favour those with a rich growth of vegetation. Usually found associating with flocks of Pochard.

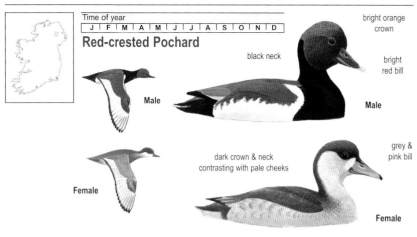

Time of year

| J | F | M | A | M | J | J | A | S | O | N | D |

Red-crested Pochard

bright orange crown

black neck

bright red bill

Male

Male

dark crown & neck contrasting with pale cheeks

grey & pink bill

Female

Female

Time of year

| J | F | M | A | M | J | J | A | S | O | N | D |

Pochard

chestnut head, black neck

Male

orange head

Male

dark grey bill, pale subterminal band, black tip

Female

Female

Time of year

| J | F | M | A | M | J | J | A | S | O | N | D |

Ferruginous Duck

white eye

Male

Male

white undertail

Female

Female

Time of year   Common ■   Rare □   Very rare/absent □

Maps   Summer □   Winter ■   25

Tufted Duck *Aythya fuligula* Lacha bhadánach   41-46cm

A small, tufted, diving duck with yellow eyes. **Males** show a black head, breast, ventral area, tail and upperparts. Head shows a purple-blue sheen and a long, loose crest. Belly and flanks white. **Females** are brownish on the head, upperparts, breast and tail. Flanks pale brown. Belly pale. The crest is short on females and sometimes difficult to see. Females can also show an area of white around the base of the bill which could lead to confusion with female Scaup. Tufted, however, lack the full-bodied, round-headed shape of Scaup and show a neater bill. Females can also show a whitish undertail. In flight shows a long, broad, white wing stripe and a whitish underwing. Bill pale grey with a diffuse subterminal band and a black tip.

Voice & Diet During the breeding season, males can give low whistling calls, with females giving growling-type calls. Feeds by diving for marine invertebrates. Also feeds on aquatic plants.

Habitat and Status A common winter visitor and breeding species, found on freshwater lakes, reservoirs and small ponds. Breeds on lakes in the midlands and the north, with smaller populations in the south-east, south and west. Nests in thick cover close to water. In winter numbers increase with the arrival of birds from Scotland, Iceland and Europe.

Ring-necked Duck *Aythya collaris* Lacha mhuinceach   37-45cm

A small diving duck with a distinctive peaked rear crown and a longish tail which can be held cocked. **Males** show a black head, breast, upperparts, tail and undertail, and a faint brown neck collar. Flanks greyish, contrasting with a white crescent on the fore-flanks. Eye yellow. Bill grey with a thin white base, a broad white subterminal band, and a black tip. **Females** show a dark greyish crown and pale lores and throat. Eye dark with a distinctive pale orbital ring which, on occasions, extends back in a line over the ear coverts. Breast and upperparts brownish with warm rufous flanks. Bill greyish with a white subterminal band and a black tip. In flight shows a greyish wing stripe.

Voice & Diet Usually silent when found in Ireland, although females can give a growling-type call in flight. Feeds by diving for marine invertebrates. Will also feed on aquatic plants.

Habitat and Status A rare but regular autumn and winter visitor from North America. Found on freshwater lakes, ponds and reservoirs, usually with flocks of Tufted Ducks.

Goldeneye *Bucephala clangula* Órshúileach   41-48cm

A small diving duck with a peaked head, pale yellow eyes, orange-yellow legs and a blunt bill. **Males** show a dark, green-glossed head and a white spot on face at the base of the dark grey bill. Neck, breast, flanks and belly white. Upperparts black with a white, black-striped wing patch formed by white secondaries and coverts, and black scapulars. Tail greyish. Undertail coverts black. In flight shows a striking black and white wing pattern. Duller **females** show a reddish-brown head, a whitish neck collar, dark upperparts with grey mottling, and a greyish breast and flanks. Belly white. The dark grey bill shows an orange-yellow subterminal band. Also shows white wing patches in flight.

Voice & Diet During courtship displays males can give whistling-type calls. These displays can be seen from late winter into spring. Otherwise, a silent species. Dives for insects, molluscs and crustaceans.

Habitat and Status A very rare breeding species but a common wintering species from northern Europe and Russia. Found on coasts, bays, reservoirs and lakes.

Wildfowl

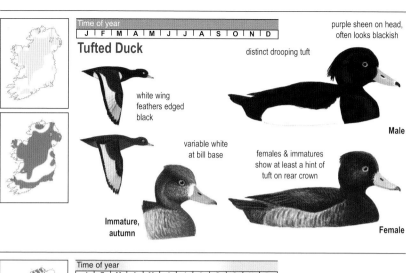

Tufted Duck

Time of year
J F M A M J J A S O N D

distinct drooping tuft

purple sheen on head, often looks blackish

Male

white wing feathers edged black

variable white at bill base

females & immatures show at least a hint of tuft on rear crown

Female

Immature, autumn

Ring-necked Duck

Time of year
J F M A M J J A S O N D

peaked crown, in all plumages

Male

grey wing feathers edged black

grey bill, black & white tip

the most frequent North American duck in Ireland

distinctive head pattern & shape, white eye-ring

blue bill, black & white tip

Immature male

Female

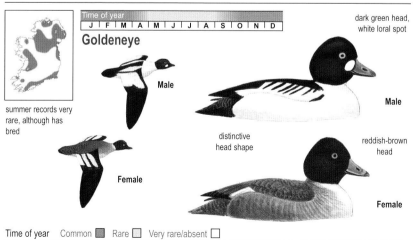

Goldeneye

Time of year
J F M A M J J A S O N D

dark green head, white loral spot

Male

Male

summer records very rare, although has bred

distinctive head shape

reddish-brown head

Female

Female

Time of year   Common ■   Rare □   Very rare/absent □

Maps   Summer □   Winter ■   27

Ducks

(Greater) Scaup *Aythya marila* Lacha iascán   46-52cm

A large, full-bodied, round-headed diving duck with pale yellow eyes. **Males** show a black head and breast, with a green sheen to head. Belly and flanks white. Tail and undertail blackish. Mantle pale greyish with dark, narrow barring on the lower mantle. Rump black. Wing coverts blackish-grey. **Females** show a brownish head and breast, and an extensive white patch at base of bill, more extensive than that of female Tufted. In spring can show a whitish ear covert patch. Upperparts greyish-brown. Flanks pale grey-brown, appearing broadly barred. Belly whitish. Tail and undertail brownish. In flight shows a long, broad, white wing stripe across secondaries and onto inner primaries. Broad, bluish-grey bill shows a large black nail.

Voice & Diet Rarely hear in Ireland but females can give a gruff *karr* call. Dives for molluscs and crustaceans, as well as feeding on marine plants.

Habitat and Status A common winter visitor from breeding grounds in Iceland and Scandinavia. Found on open coastal water and bays and also on coastal lakes.

Lesser Scaup *Aythya affinis* Mionlacha iascán   41-45cm

Very similar to Scaup, but appearing smaller, with a peaked rear crown, and showing a blue-grey bill with a narrow black tip confined to the nail. **Males** show a purple gloss to a black head, unlike the green of Scaup, and a black breast. The scapulars appear more vermiculated than Scaup while the flanks show greyish tones. Tail, rump and undertail black. In flight shows a dark upperwing with a white wingbar on secondaries fading to grey on the primaries. Scaup show a white wingbar across the secondaries onto inner primaries. **Females** resemble female Scaup and are best told by the peaked rear crown, the smaller size, the narrow black nail on the blue-grey bill, a smaller white patch at the base of the bill, more greyish tones to the flanks as well as the white wing stripe fading to grey on the primaries.

Voice & Diet Rarely heard in Ireland but females can give harsh calls when flushed. Feeds by diving for marine invertebrates, but will also feed on aquatic plants.

Habitat and Status A very rare but regular winter visitor from North America. Found on freshwater lakes and reservoirs, usually associating with Tufted Ducks.

Ruddy Duck *Oxyura jamaicensis* Lacha rua   36-42cm

A small diving duck with a large, broad bill and a stiff tail, which can, on occasions, be held upright. **Summer males** show a striking black crown and nape, with a pure white face and a bright blue bill. Breast, flanks and upperparts rich chestnut with white belly and undertail. Wings and tail brownish. **Winter males** show a mottled grey-brown breast and flanks, and brownish upperparts. The crown and nape are dark brown in winter with a clean whitish face and a duller bill. **Females** similar to winter males but show a dark line from base of bill onto cheeks and a dull grey-blue bill. In flight shows a plain brown upperwing and a whitish underwing panel.

Voice & Diet Can give low, belching calls as well as bill slaps and rattles. Females can also give low, hissing calls. Feeds by diving for insect larvae. Also takes aquatic plant seeds.

Habitat and Status An uncommon species found on reservoirs and lakes. A North American species, Ruddy Ducks were introduced into Britain in the 1960s and have since become established in Ireland. Attempts are being made to eradicate Ruddy Ducks from Europe due to the species hybridizing with White-headed Ducks *Oxyura leucocephala* in Spain. A small breeding population exists in Northern Ireland and the south-east.

Time of year

| J | F | M | A | M | J | J | A | S | O | N | D |

(Greater) Scaup

black head, green sheen — **Male**

light vermiculation on mantle

broad white stripe across secondaries & onto primaries

Male

head shape rounded, with peak towards front of forehead

Female

Female

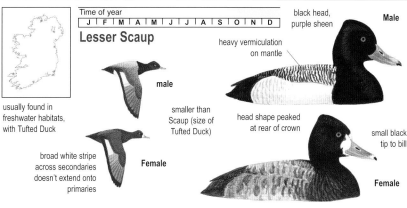

Time of year

| J | F | M | A | M | J | J | A | S | O | N | D |

Lesser Scaup

black head, purple sheen — **Male**

heavy vermiculation on mantle

usually found in freshwater habitats, with Tufted Duck

male

smaller than Scaup (size of Tufted Duck)

head shape peaked at rear of crown

small black tip to bill

broad white stripe across secondaries doesn't extend onto primaries

Female

Female

Time of year

| J | F | M | A | M | J | J | A | S | O | N | D |

Ruddy Duck

Male, summer

blue bill

tail often held cocked

Male

Male, winter

plain, grey bill

small, dark wings

Female

Female

dark line on cheek

Time of year   Common ▦   Rare ☐   Very rare/absent ☐

Maps   Summer ☐   Winter ▦

29

Ducks

Eider *Somateria mollissima* Éadar   55-65cm

A stocky duck with a diagnostic wedge-shaped head. **Males** black on forehead and crown, with white stripes through pale green nape and neck patches. Face and neck white. Breast tinged pink. Belly, flanks and undertail black with white ventral patch. Upperparts black and white. Bill olive-green. In flight black primaries and secondaries contrast with white forewing and back. **Immature males** show a dark head, mottled brown underparts, a white breast and pale upperparts. **Females** greyish-brown with heavy barring and mottling. Best told by the large, stocky size, the wedge-shaped head profile and the wedge-shaped feathering on the base of the bill. In flight plain wing shows a thin white covert bar and trailing edge to secondaries. Males of the northern race *borealis,* from the Arctic, show more orange tones to the bill and can show small scapular 'sails'.

Voice & Diet Very vocal in late winter and early spring when males give a cooing *oo-oh-wah* call. Females give a growling *krrr* call. Feeds by diving for mussels and other molluscs. Will also take invertebrates.

Habitat and Status A common sea duck along the northern and north-eastern coastlines. Scarce elsewhere, with birds wintering and breeding in small numbers in other regions. Found along rocky coasts and offshore islands. Nests in down-lined hollows on short grass, bracken or heather close to water.

King Eider *Somateria spectabilis* Éadar taibhseach   55-62cm

Adult males show a greyish-blue crown, nape and hindneck, a greenish-white face and a large black-bordered, orange-yellow shield over a bright orange-red bill. Lower neck and mantle white. Breast shows a pinkish wash. Black belly, flanks and undertail show a white ventral patch. Black upperparts show a white covert stripe with raised inner scapulars forming two prominent sails. In flight shows white covert patch on a black wing. **Females** rufous-brown with coarse barring, a rounded rear crown, and a pale eye-ring. Short, dark bill with upcurve at gape gives a smiling expression. Bill feathering not wedge-shaped as in Eider. In flight shows a thin pale covert bar and trailing edge to secondaries. **Immature males** show a dark head, a brownish back and underparts, a white breast and a small, buff-yellow shield over a pale bill.

Voice & Diet In flight can give a croaking call. Feeds by diving for a variety of marine molluscs and invertebrates.

Habitat and Status A very rare vagrant from the high Arctic regions of North America and northern Europe. Found in winter associating with Eiders. Found along rocky coasts and offshore islands.

Long-tailed Duck *Clangula hyemalis* Lacha earrfhada   41-46cm

A small sea duck, most likely to be seen in winter plumage when **males** show a white head, a pale pink-brown eye patch and a dark lower ear covert patch. Breast, mantle and centre of upperparts blackish. Wings blackish with white scapulars. Tail shows elongated black central feathers. Belly, flanks and undertail white. In flight shows dark wings. **Females** whitish on face and neck, with a dark crown and ear covert patch. Breast and upperparts brownish-grey. Underparts white. **Summer females** similar, but show a dark head with a pale eye patch. **Summer males** show a pale grey eye patch on a dark head, neck and breast. Bill dark grey with broad, pinkish, central band on males. Immatures like females but darker on face and breast.

Voice & Diet Rarely heard in Ireland. Males can occasionally give a yodelling *aw-awlee* call in spring. Females give low quacking calls. Dives for molluscs, crustaceans and invertebrates.

Habitat and Status A scarce winter visitor from northern Europe and Greenland. The largest wintering populations are along northern and western coasts. Found on open coastal waters and bays.

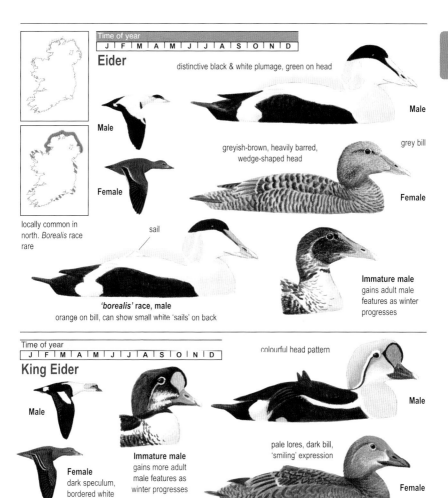

Eider

distinctive black & white plumage, green on head

Male

Male

greyish-brown, heavily barred, wedge-shaped head

grey bill

Female

Female

locally common in north. *Borealis* race rare

sail

Immature male
gains adult male features as winter progresses

'borealis' race, male
orange on bill, can show small white 'sails' on back

Time of year
J F M A M J J A S O N D

King Eider

colourful head pattern

Male

Male

Female
dark speculum, bordered white

Immature male
gains more adult male features as winter progresses

pale lores, dark bill, 'smiling' expression

Female

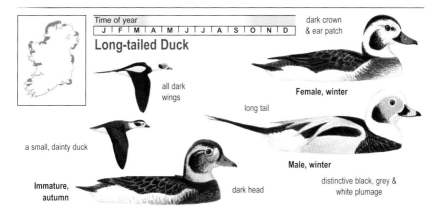

Time of year
J F M A M J J A S O N D

dark crown & ear patch

Long-tailed Duck

all dark wings

Female, winter

long tail

a small, dainty duck

Immature, autumn

dark head

Male, winter

distinctive black, grey & white plumage

Time of year   Common ◼   Rare ◻   Very rare/absent ◻

Maps Summer ◻ Winter ◼

Ducks

Common Scoter *Melanitta nigra* Scótar   46-52cm

A distinctive sea duck with a square head, a long neck and a longish tail. **Males** are totally black. Black bill shows a small knob and a yellow central patch. **Females** dark brown, with contrasting pale brown cheeks and throat. Can sometimes show pale barring on breast and flanks. Bill dark grey. **Immature males** also show a dark brown plumage with pale face patches on some birds. The longish tail can be held cocked, especially at rest. Usually dives with wings closed. In flight appears uniformly blackish or dark brownish, with a slight contrast between the darker wing coverts and the flight feathers. When wing flapping, droops the neck and head in a distinctive S-shape.

Voice & Diet Males on the breeding grounds give high, piping, whistling calls. Females give harsh, grating calls. In winter birds in flocks call frequently, a fluting *pyew,* more often heard during calm weather. Feeds by diving for crustaceans, cockles, mussels, larvae and worms. Occasionally takes seeds.

Habitat and Status A rare breeding species found in small numbers on large inland lakes in the west. Common in winter with the arrival of birds from Iceland and northern Europe. Found on open coastal water, often in very large flocks.

Velvet Scoter *Melanitta fusca* Sceadach   53-60cm

A large, thick-necked, bulky sea duck with a wedge-shaped head. **Males** all black, with a small white crescent below the whitish eye and pure white secondaries. The large bill is orange-yellow with a black basal knob. **Females** appear dark brown, with white secondaries and pale, oval face patches on the loral area and towards the rear of the cheek. Females also show a dark eye and a greyish bill. **Immature males** lack the white eye crescent and show a duller bill. Legs orange-red. In flight the white wing patches are striking. However, on the water, the white secondaries are not always obvious and may appear as a small white patch towards the rear of the wing. Tends to open wings when diving.

Voice & Diet Usually silent when found in Ireland, although males can give a piping call in flight. Females can give a harsher *garr* call in flight. Feeds by diving for mussels, worms, crabs, shrimps and cockles.

Habitat and Status An uncommon but regular winter visitor from northern Europe. Found on open coastal waters, usually associating with flocks of Common Scoters.

Surf Scoter *Melanitta perspicillata* Scótar toinne   45-56cm

A bulky sea duck with a thick neck and a broad-based, heavy bill. **Adult males** are all black, with white forehead and nape patches, white eyes and a large, multi-coloured bill which is red and yellow towards the tip, white on the base and showing a black basal patch. **Females** are brownish with two whitish face patches on the loral area and on the cheek. Adult females may also show a small whitish nape patch. The eyes are dark and the large bill greyish. **Immature males** similar to females, but can show orange-yellow on the bill. **Sub-adult males** show an adult-like bill and a white nape patch, but can lack the white forehead patch. In flight the wings appear uniform. Tends to dive with open wings.

Voice & Diet Rarely heard in Ireland. Feeds by diving for mussels, worms, crabs, shrimps and cockles.

Habitat and Status A rare but regular winter visitor from North America. Found on open coastal water and bays, usually associating with Common Scoter flocks. Some birds are known to return to the same wintering area for several years in succession.

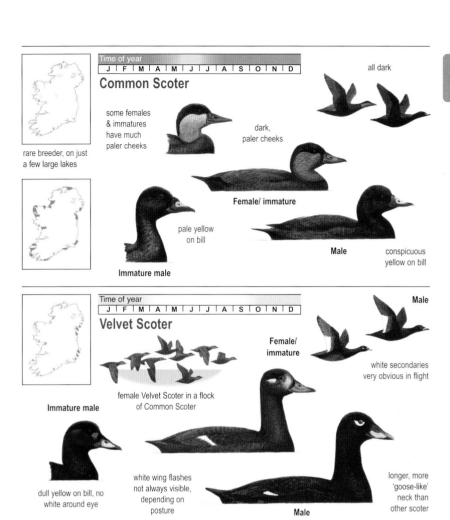

Common Scoter

Time of year
J F M A M J J A S O N D

rare breeder, on just a few large lakes

some females & immatures have much paler cheeks

dark, paler cheeks

all dark

Female/ immature

pale yellow on bill

Immature male

Male conspicuous yellow on bill

Velvet Scoter

Time of year
J F M A M J J A S O N D

Male

Female/ immature

white secondaries very obvious in flight

female Velvet Scoter in a flock of Common Scoter

Immature male

dull yellow on bill, no white around eye

white wing flashes not always visible, depending on posture

Male

longer, more 'goose-like' neck than other scoter

Surf Scoter

Time of year
J F M A M J J A S O N D

some individuals return to the same areas in successive winters

square-shaped head

Immature

Female

some females show pale nape

Immature male acquires adult plumage as winter progresses

Male

unique head & bill pattern

Time of year Common ▨ Rare ☐ Very rare/absent ☐

Maps Summer ☐ Winter ▨

33

Ducks

Smew *Mergus albellus* Síolta gheal   36-42cm

An attractive, compact diving duck with a steep forehead and a short crest. **Males** are unmistakable, with a striking black and white plumage. Head white with a large black patch around eye, a black line along rear crown, and a short crest. Breast white, with two narrow black lines on breast sides. Flanks greyish with fine vermiculations. Upperparts black and white. In flight shows black wings with a broad, white wing patch and a grey rump and tail. **Females** show a reddish-brown crown and nape, with a slightly darker brown patch around the eye and a bold white cheek patch. Upperparts dark greyish with paler grey underparts. In flight shows a whitish wing patch and a grey rump and tail.

Voice & Diet Rarely heard in Ireland. An active feeder, diving for small fish and invertebrates.

Habitat and Status A scarce but annual winter visitor from breeding grounds in northern Europe. Found on lakes, reservoirs and, occasionally, estuaries.

Red-breasted Merganser *Mergus serrator* Síolta rua   52-61cm

A slender, thin-necked duck with a long, slightly up-curved, thin bill. **Males** show a blackish-green head with long, wispy head crests, a white lower neck and a spotted, reddish-buff breast. Vermiculated greyish flanks contrast with black and white breast sides. Mantle black. In flight shows a white inner wing, broken by two black bars. Outer wing and leading edge black. Rump and tail greyish. Eye and bill bright red. **Females** rufous-brown on head with wispy crests, a whitish loral stripe and a whitish throat. Head colour merges into pale breast. Flanks greyish-brown. Upperparts mottled brownish-grey. In flight shows a broken, white wing patch on the inner rear wing. Eye brownish. Bill dull red.

Voice & Diet Usually a quiet species but males can give low, purring calls during elaborate courtship displays. Females give harsher, grating calls. Feeds by diving for fish and invertebrates.

Habitat and Status A common resident species breeding on inland lakes and large river systems in most regions except the south and east. A small breeding population is also present in the south-east. In autumn large flocks of moulting birds can occasionally be seen at coastal locations. A common coastal duck in winter, found in harbours, bays and estuaries.

Goosander *Mergus merganser* Síolta mhór   57-69cm

A slender duck, very similar to Red-breasted Merganser. **Males** show a dark blackish-green head with a full, bulging rear head crest. White breast and flanks can show a pink wash. Upperparts black and white. Eye dark. Bill red. In flight shows an unbroken, white inner wing, a black leading edge and outer wing, and a greyish rump and tail. **Females** show a dark rufous-brown head, a bulging rear head crest and a clear-cut white throat patch. Rich head colour is sharply demarcated from the pale neck and breast. Flanks and upperparts greyish. Red bill is broader-based and shorter than on Red-breasted Merganser. In flight females show a white patch on the rear inner wing.

Voice & Diet Usually a quiet species, but on the breeding grounds males can give strange, twanging-type calls. Females give harsher *karr* calls. Dives for fish and invertebrates.

Habitat and Status A rare breeding species with small populations concentrated on remote lakes and rivers in the north-west and upland areas of eastern counties. Uncommon but annual in winter with birds arriving from northern Europe. Found on inland lakes, reservoirs and occasionally on estuaries.

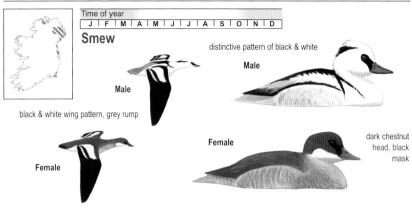

Time of year

| J | F | M | A | M | J | J | A | S | O | N | D |

Smew

distinctive pattern of black & white

Male

Male

black & white wing pattern, grey rump

Female

dark chestnut head, black mask

Female

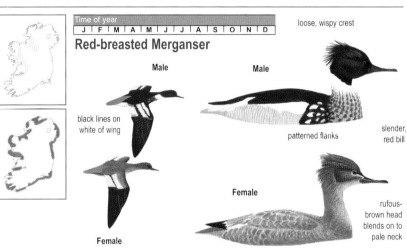

Time of year

| J | F | M | A | M | J | J | A | S | O | N | D |

Red-breasted Merganser

loose, wispy crest

Male

Male

black lines on white of wing

patterned flanks

slender, red bill

Female

rufous-brown head blends on to pale neck

Female

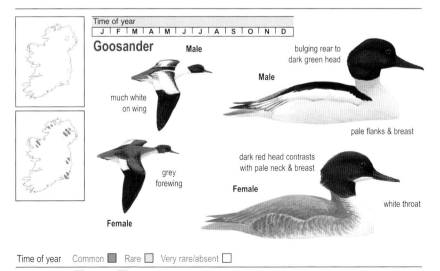

Time of year

| J | F | M | A | M | J | J | A | S | O | N | D |

Goosander

Male

bulging rear to dark green head

Male

much white on wing

pale flanks & breast

dark red head contrasts with pale neck & breast

grey forewing

Female

white throat

Female

Time of year Common ■ Rare □ Very rare/absent □

Maps Summer □ Winter ■

35

Divers

Great Northern Diver *Gavia immer* Lóma mór   69-81cm

A large, thick-necked, black and white diver. Shows a long, flat crown, a steep forehead, a distinctive bump where the crown meets the forehead and a long, heavy, pale grey bill. **Summer adults** show a completely black head, with black and white striped patches on the sides of the neck and throat. Black upperparts show a white chequered pattern. **In winter** the head and nape are black, contrasting strongly with a white throat, neck and breast. A black half collar extends from the nape onto the neck. Upperparts black. **Immatures** similar, but show pale fringes to the upperpart feathers. Deep red eye appears blackish at a distance. Flies with neck extended.

Voice and Diet Although usually quiet, birds returning in autumn can give a far-carrying, wailing, gull-like call. Dives for fish and marine invertebrates. Can stay submerged for long periods, covering good distances under water.

Habitat and Status A common winter visitor to Ireland from breeding grounds in Greenland and Iceland. Found on open seas, bays and harbours in all coastal counties. Can also occur on inland lakes and reservoirs. In early spring some can show a full summer plumage.

White-billed Diver *Gavia adamsii* Lóma gobgheal   75-90cm

The largest diver species and easily mistaken for Great Northern. **Summer adults** show a black head with striped neck and throat patches, and black upperparts showing a white chequered pattern. Shows a steep forehead, a flat crown and a bump on the upper forehead, as on Great Northern. The pale, uptilted, yellowish-white bill is very striking, giving a large, Red-throated Diver-like head profile. Differs from Great Northern **in winter** by showing a diffuse brownish nape which does not contrast strongly with the paler neck. Half collar also present. Upperparts blackish-brown. **Immatures** show pale feather edges to browner upperparts. Eyes deep red.

Voice and Diet Although rarely heard in Ireland, White-billed Diver can give a wailing, gull-like call. Dives for fish and marine invertebrates.

Habitat and Status An extremely rare winter visitor to Ireland from high Arctic regions from western Russia to Canada. Occurs on open coastal waters, bays and harbours.

Black-throated Diver *Gavia arctica* Lóma Artach   55-68cm

An elegant species with a slender, straight bill. **Summer adults** show a matt greyish head and nape with a black chin and throat. Black and white stripes extend from the sides of the neck onto the white breast. Belly white. Black upperparts show a white chequered pattern. **In winter** the black crown extends down to eye. The blackish-grey nape extends well onto the sides of the neck and is strongly demarcated from the white throat. Underparts white. Shows a gently-angled forehead and a slightly rounded crown. Upperparts blackish. **Immatures** show pale fringes to upperpart feathers. Often shows a prominent white patch on the rear flanks. Eyes deep red.

Voice and Diet Although normally quiet in Ireland, autumn birds can give a croaking-type call or a plaintive, wailing *airu-uub*. Feeds by diving for fish and a variety of marine invertebrates.

Habitat and Status A rare but regular winter visitor to Irish coastlines. Can occur in good numbers in western, north-western and northern coastal regions. In spring frequently reported off south-eastern counties. Usually found on open coastal waters, bays and harbours. Can occur on inland freshwater lakes.

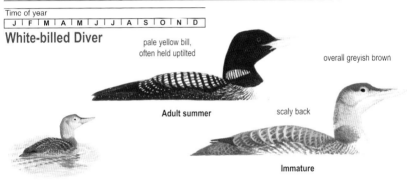

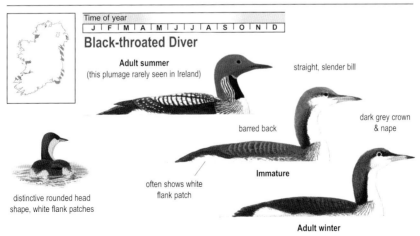

Great Northern Diver

Time of year
J F M A M J J A S O N D

some non-breeders
can be seen in
mid-summer

heavy, dagger-like bill

Adult summer
this plumage usually seen in April & May

long neck,
heavy build

Immature

Adult winter

Time of year
J F M A M J J A S O N D

White-billed Diver

pale yellow bill,
often held uptilted

overall greyish brown

Adult summer

scaly back

Immature

Time of year
J F M A M J J A S O N D

Black-throated Diver

Adult summer
(this plumage rarely seen in Ireland)

straight, slender bill

barred back

dark grey crown
& nape

distinctive rounded head
shape, white flank patches

often shows white
flank patch

Immature

Adult winter

Time of year   Common ▣ Rare ▢ Very rare/absent ▢

Maps   Winter ▣

Divers & Grebes

Red-throated Diver *Gavia stellata* Lóma rua 53-60cm

A small diver with a narrow, uptilted, pale greyish bill giving a distinctive head-in-the-air profile. **Summer adults** show a pale greyish head and a narrow, red throat patch. Black and white stripes extend from the neck onto the sides of the breast. Upperparts brownish with small, faint, pale spots. **In winter** appears very pale, with a grey, rounded crown and nape lacking a strong contrast with the whitish throat and breast. Upperparts show pale feather edges. Can show a white flank patch but is not usually as contrasting as on Black-throated. **Immatures** appear dirtier, and show a small, dull red throat patch. Dark red eye conspicuous in a plain face.

Voice and Diet Gives a quacking *kruuk* call and a loud, wailing *ruu-aruu*. These calls are usually heard on the breeding grounds. Dives for fish and marine invertebrates. Can move considerable distances under water.

Habitat and Status A rare Irish breeding bird found nesting on small islets on loughs or lakes. The main Irish breeding populations are based in north-western regions. A common winter visitor to all coastal counties. Found on open coastal waters, bays and harbours.

Great Crested Grebe *Podiceps cristatus* Foitheach mór 46-52cm

Large, elegant, slender-necked grebe with a long, pointed, pink bill. **In summer** shows a black crown which extends back to form double crest. Long, rufous and black feathers from the rear of crown to the throat form a frill which is used during elaborate courtship displays. Dark line extends from base of bill to eye. Diagnostic white supercilium extends from the bill over the eye and blends with the white cheeks. Throat and breast whitish. Nape and upperparts plain brown. Shaggy, pale greyish flanks can show a rufous wash. **In winter** the head frill and long double crest are lost. Eye red. In flight shows white patches on forewing and secondaries.

Voice and Diet On the breeding grounds gives a variety of harsh, croaking *kar-rraar* calls and whirring notes. An active diver, feeding on fish, insects and aquatic invertebrates.

Habitat and Status A common Irish breeding bird found on inland lakes throughout the year. Builds a large floating nest among reeds and sedges. In winter common in harbours and on open coastal waters in most regions. Tends to be scarce in some south-western areas. Breeding populations are highest in more northern regions of the country.

Red-necked Grebe *Podiceps griseigena* Foitheach píbrua 41-47cm

A smaller, stockier and thicker-necked grebe than Great Crested. In all plumages shows a black crown which extends down below eye. Cheeks dusky white. Nape and upperparts blackish-brown. Flanks pale brown but can show a striking white flash. **In summer** lower throat, neck and upper breast chestnut-red, becoming greyish-white and diffuse **in winter** and lacking a strong contrast with the nape. Black bill shows a bright yellow basal patch, this being more conspicuous and extensive on **immatures**. In flight shows white on secondaries and a white forewing patch. Eyes dark on adults, pale yellow on immatures. When diving, often leaps clear of water.

Voice and Diet A usually silent species in Ireland. Dives for small fish and other small aquatic invertebrates.

Habitat and Status A rare but regular winter visitor from the Baltic regions. Normally found on open coastal waters and bays and occasionally in harbours. Can also occur on reservoirs and inland lakes.

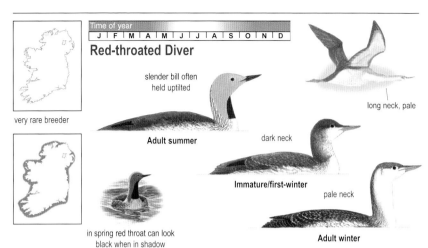

Time of year

| J | F | M | A | M | J | J | A | S | O | N | D |

Red-throated Diver

slender bill often held uptilted

long neck, pale

very rare breeder

Adult summer

dark neck

Immature/first-winter

pale neck

in spring red throat can look black when in shadow

Adult winter

Time of year

| J | F | M | A | M | J | J | A | S | O | N | D |

Great Crested Grebe

white patches on forewing & secondaries

rufous & black

Juvenile (June & July)

slender neck pink bill

Adult summer

Winter

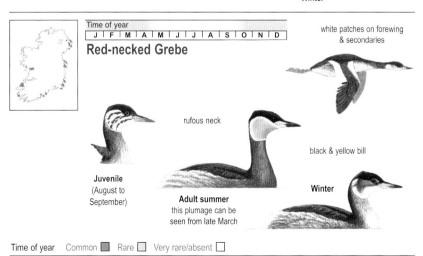

Time of year

| J | F | M | A | M | J | J | A | S | O | N | D |

Red-necked Grebe

white patches on forewing & secondaries

rufous neck

black & yellow bill

Juvenile
(August to September)

Winter

Adult summer
this plumage can be seen from late March

Time of year   Common ■   Rare ☐   Very rare/absent ☐

Maps   Summer ☐   Winter ■

Grebes

Slavonian Grebe *Podiceps auritus* Foitheach cluasach   32-37cm
Small, flat-crowned grebe with a stubby, pale-tipped, black bill. **Summer adults** show a black crown separated from black cheeks and chin by golden horns extending from base of bill, through eye, and forming a crest on the rear of crown. Nape and upperparts blackish. Neck, upper breast and flanks chestnut-red. **In winter** is strikingly black and white. Crown black, extending down to the red eye and sharply demarcated from the white cheeks. Also shows a thin stripe from eye to bill, and a pale loral spot. Nape and upperparts black, contrasting with the white breast and neck. Flanks greyish. Shows white secondaries and small, white wedge on forewing in flight.
    Voice & Diet Silent in Ireland. Dives for small fish, insects and other small aquatic invertebrates.
    Habitat and Status An uncommon winter visitor from breeding grounds in Iceland and Scandinavia. Found in coastal bays and harbours and occasionally on inland lakes and reservoirs.

Black-necked Grebe *Podiceps nigricollis* Foitheach píbdhubh   29-33cm
A small grebe which can give a fluffed-up appearance. Shows a steep forehead and rounded crown. Thin, black pointed bill is uptilted. **Summer adults** show a black crown which forms a stubby crest. Nape, cheeks, throat and neck black. Bright golden feathers form a fan behind the deep red eye. Flanks bright chestnut-red. **In winter**, unlike Slavonian Grebe, the black of the crown extends below the eye onto ear coverts. Cheeks, chin and throat white. Nape black, fading into the dusky-grey sides of neck. Breast white. Flanks greyish. Upperparts blackish. In flight shows white inner primaries and secondaries, but no white on forewing.
    Voice & Diet On the breeding grounds, gives a flute-like *poe-eet* call. Silent in winter. Dives for small aquatic invertebrates. Does not take fish as frequently as other grebes.
    Habitat and Status Formerly a rare breeding species but now an uncommon winter visitor from continental Europe. Found on coastal bays or freshwater areas close to the coast. Most reports refer to southern counties.

Little Grebe *Tachybaptus ruficollis* Spágaire tonn   24-29cm
Tiny, short-necked, stubby-billed grebe with a fluffed-up, short-bodied appearance. **Summer adults** show a black crown, nape and upper breast. Black on crown extends down to the eye. Cheeks, chin, throat and sides of neck deep chestnut-red. Also shows a pale yellow spot at the base of the bill. Upperparts blackish. Breast and flanks dark brownish-black. **In winter** shows a dark brown crown, nape and upperparts, and greyish flanks. Cheeks, throat and neck pale buff-brown with a paler breast. **Immatures** similar to winter adults, but show a dark mark below the eye. In flight shows a plain wing.
    Voice & Diet On the breeding grounds can give a high-pitched, rattling call. Also gives a sharp *pit-pit* or *wit-wit* call when alarmed. Dives for small insects and molluscs.
    Habitat and Status A common breeding bird found on ponds, lakes, reservoirs and marshes. Builds a floating nest among reeds and sedges. In winter found on ponds, lakes, reservoirs and, occasionally, on estuary channels and in harbours.

Pied-billed Grebe *Podilymbus podiceps* Foitheach gob-alabhreac   31-38cm
A stocky grebe, slightly larger than Little Grebe and showing a thick, short, stubby bill. **Summer adults** show a whitish bill with a thick black band, a dark crown and nape, a greyish head and neck, and a black throat patch. Shows dark brown upperparts and dingy-buff flanks. Belly and undertail white. **In winter** shows a yellowish-grey bill, a pale throat and a warm brownish-buff head and neck.
    Voice & Diet In spring gives cooing calls but usually silent in winter. Dives for small aquatic insects and invertebrates.
    Habitat and Status A very rare vagrant from North America. Most records refer to southern and western regions. Found on lakes and ponds, often with Little Grebes.

Time of year
J F M A M J J A S O N D

Slavonian Grebe

rounded crown

Adult   Winter

Time of year
J F M A M J J A S O N D

Black-necked Grebe

yellow ear tufts

peaked crown

Adult   all black neck   Winter

Time of year
J F M A M J J A S O N D

Little Grebe

chestnut neck

yellow spot at
base of bill

dark crown

Winter

Adult

Time of year
J F M A M J J A S O N D

Pied-billed Grebe

black band on bill

black throat

thin, white
trailing edge
to wing

Adult   Winter

Time of year   Common ■   Rare □   Very rare/absent □

Maps   Winter ■   Resident ■   41

Seabirds

Gannet *Morus bassanus* Gainéad　　　　　　　　　　　　　　85-95cm

A large seabird with long, narrow wings, a pointed tail and a spear-like bill. **Adults** are white with striking black wing tips, a creamy-yellow head and black lores. Pointed bill bluish-grey with dark lines. Forward-facing eyes show a pale iris. Legs and feet greyish. **Juveniles** blackish-brown with pale speckling on upperparts and head, a paler lower breast and belly, and pale uppertail coverts. Bill and legs dark. As birds mature, the plumage becomes gradually whiter, so that **third year birds** are very similar to adults but show some dark feathering on the inner wings, and can show a dark centre to the tail. Flight is graceful, with strong wing beats interspersed with long, easy glides.

　　Voice & Diet Noisy on the breeding colonies with birds giving loud, barking *arrah* calls. Usually silent at sea. Feeds on a wide variety of fish which are caught by diving into the water, sometimes from substantial heights.

　　Habitat and Status A common bird of open sea found off the Irish coastline throughout the year, although scarcer in winter. Nests on steep, rocky cliffs. Breeds at colonies in Clare, Cork, Dublin and Wexford, with the largest colony found on Little Skellig, Kerry.

Black-browed Albatross *Thalassarche melanophris* Albatrass dú-mhalach　76-90cm

An enormous seabird with extremely long, narrow wings and a chunky head and body. **Adults** show a large, yellow bill with blackish basal lines, a white head with a blackish eye patch giving a frowning expression, and white underparts. Back and upperwings blackish, contrasting with the white rump and uppertail coverts. Short tail dark greyish. Underwing shows a white central stripe with a broad black border. **Immatures** similar, but show a greyish bill with a dark tip, a greyish wash on the nape and hindneck, and a greyish band on the foreneck. Underwings show a very narrow, ill-defined, whitish central stripe. Glides with ease on stiff wings.

　　Voice & Diet A silent species, rarely heard away from the breeding grounds. Feeds on a variety of marine life including fish, jellyfish and squid. Will readily take offal from trawlers.

　　Habitat and Status An extremely rare vagrant from breeding grounds in the southern hemisphere. Usually seen at sea in autumn, with records from sites in the south-west, west and south-east. Most reports of albatrosses off Ireland probably refer to this species.

Fulmar *Fulmarus glacialis* Fulmaire　　　　　　　　　　　　　45-51cm

A rather gull-like species with a thickset neck and long, narrow, stiff wings. **Adults** and **immatures** similar, showing a thick, tube-nosed, yellowish bill with a green or bluish-green base. Head and neck white with conspicuous black patches in front of eyes. Back and upperwings bluish-grey with pale inner primary patches. Underwings white with dusky edges. Tail and rump pale greyish. Flight strong with long glides and rapid, stiff wing beats. When alarmed can spurt an oily substance which is foul-smelling and repulsive. The northern phase, known as **Blue Fulmar**, shows a smoky-grey head, neck and underparts.

　　Voice & Diet On the nest, gives a cackling, grunting, repeated *urg-urg-urg* call. Can also give a warning, growling call before spurting oil. Feeds on a wide range of marine fish, molluscs and crustaceans. Will also take fish offal from trawlers and can feed on carrion found at sea.

　　Habitat and Status A common and widespread breeding species found nesting in most coastal counties in summer. In winter found at sea, often well away from the coast. Fulmars are strictly pelagic, rarely venturing inland. Nests in small colonies on coastal cliffs. Small numbers of Blue Fulmars are recorded on passage annually.

like petrels & shearwaters, has a 'tube-nose'

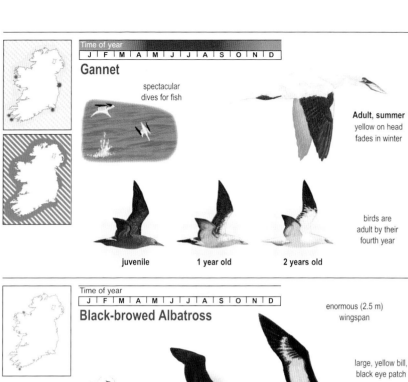

Time of year

| J | F | M | A | M | J | J | A | S | O | N | D |

Gannet

spectacular dives for fish

Adult, summer
yellow on head fades in winter

birds are adult by their fourth year

juvenile   **1 year old**   **2 years old**

Time of year

| J | F | M | A | M | J | J | A | S | O | N | D |

Black-browed Albatross

enormous (2.5 m) wingspan

large, yellow bill, black eye patch

much larger than Fulmar

Adult

Adult

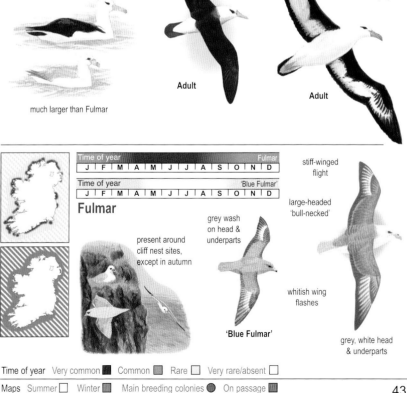

Time of year   Fulmar

| J | F | M | A | M | J | J | A | S | O | N | D |

Time of year   'Blue Fulmar'

| J | F | M | A | M | J | J | A | S | O | N | D |

Fulmar

stiff-winged flight

large-headed 'bull-necked'

grey wash on head & underparts

present around cliff nest sites, except in autumn

whitish wing flashes

'Blue Fulmar'

grey, white head & underparts

Time of year   Very common ■   Common ■   Rare ☐   Very rare/absent ☐

Maps   Summer ☐   Winter ■   Main breeding colonies ●   On passage ▨

43

Seabirds

Great Shearwater *Puffinus gravis* Cánóg mhór 42-50cm

A large shearwater which glides effortlessly on bowed wings, or flies with stiff, fast wing beats. **Adults** and **immatures** similar, showing a black bill, a dark brownish cap which contrasts strongly with a white throat, and a whitish collar which almost extends around the nape. Underparts white with diagnostic dark brownish patches on the sides of the breast, and a dark belly patch. Mantle and rump greyish-brown. Wings show greyish-brown coverts and contrasting blackish wing tips and secondaries. Whitish underwings show black edges, and black markings on the coverts and axillaries. White tips to the uppertail coverts form a narrow horseshoe patch above the dark tail.

Voice & Diet When feeding, can give a gull-like call. Feeds on a wide range of small fish, squid and offal from trawlers.

Habitat and Status An annual autumn visitor to Irish waters from the South Atlantic. Most are recorded from seawatching sites in the south-west or on open seas during pelagic trips. Has been recorded off all coastal regions.

Cory's Shearwater *Calonectris diomedea* Cánóg Cory 43-49cm

A large shearwater which glides on bowed wings and flies in a lazy, gull-like manner. **Adults** and **immatures** show a pale yellow bill and a rather featureless plumage. Head greyish-brown, becoming diffuse as it merges into a whitish throat. Lacks the diagnostic dark cap and pale collar of Great Shearwater. Underparts pure white with no breast or belly patches. Upperparts and wings greyish-brown with no contrast between the wing coverts, wing tips and secondaries. Underwing clean white with dark border. Pale tips to uppertail coverts can show as a thin, pale horseshoe patch above darker tail. Fulmars, seen in silhouette or in poor conditions, can be mistaken for Cory's Shearwater.

Voice & Diet Usually silent in Irish waters. Feeds on a wide variety of small fish and crustaceans. Will readily take offal from trawlers.

Habitat and Status A bird of open seas, Cory's Shearwaters are a rare but annual autumn visitor to Irish waters from breeding grounds in the Mediterranean regions and in the central Atlantic. Most records refer to birds passing seawatching sites in the south-west. Birds are occasionally found in summer at Manx Shearwater colonies.

Sooty Shearwater *Puffinus griseus* Cánóg dhorcha 38-44cm

A distinctive, stocky bird, showing an all-dark body plumage and long, narrow wings. Head, upperparts, upperwings and tail sooty-brown. Underparts can appear slightly paler or greyish-brown. In flight the conspicuous silvery centre to the underwing contrasts strongly with the dark plumage. Bill dark. Flies with long, angled-back wings, gliding in arcs over the water. On the water, appears wholly dark and could be mistaken for a dark-phase Arctic Skua at a distance. Could also be mistaken for Mediterranean Shearwater but the all-dark underparts, the angled-back wings, larger size and flight are diagnostic.

Voice & Diet Silent in Irish waters. Feeds on a wide range of small fish, squid and crustaceans.

Habitat and Status A bird of open oceans and seas, Sooty Shearwaters are regular late summer and autumn visitors from breeding grounds in the southern hemisphere. Usually seen off seawatching points in most coastal counties, with the largest movements recorded in the south and south-west. Often seen with flocks of Manx Shearwaters.

Time of year

| J | F | M | A | M | J | J | A | S | O | N | D |

Great Shearwater

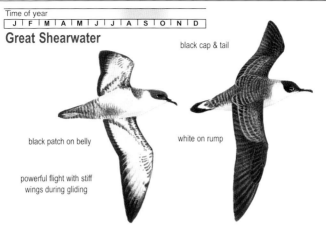

black cap & tail

black patch on belly

white on rump

powerful flight with stiff wings during gliding

Time of year

| J | F | M | A | M | J | J | A | S | O | N | D |

Cory's Shearwater

yellow bill with blackish tip

underwing white with neat blackish border

greyish-brown upperparts

can show a narrow, white band on rump

relaxed flapping flight & gliding

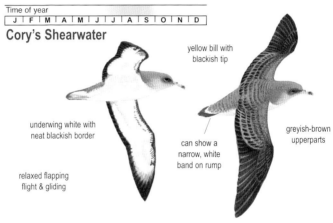

Time of year

| J | F | M | A | M | J | J | A | S | O | N | D |

Sooty Shearwater

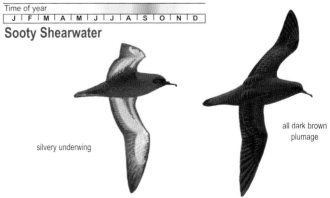

all dark brown plumage

silvery underwing

Time of year   Common ■   Rare □   Very rare/absent □

Seabirds

Mediterranean Shearwater *Puffinus mauretanicus* Cánóg Bhailéarach   32-38cm
A brown and white shearwater, slightly bulkier and larger than Manx Shearwater, with a shortish tail and long, narrow, pointed wings. Upperparts brown, with a slightly darker brown cap fading into a paler throat. Underparts pale whitish-brown, but can show very dark underparts with a pale belly. Underwing whitish with a thick, dark border. The underwing can appear quite greyish or silvery. Bill dark. Legs pinkish. In bad light can appear all-dark, and could be confused with Sooty Shearwater. However, Mediterranean is smaller with shorter, less angled wings. Glides and shears like Manx Shearwater, but flight tends to appear more fluttery with rapid, stiff wing beats.
   Voice & Diet Rarely heard in Irish waters. Feeds on a wide range of small fish and molluscs.
   Habitat and Status A bird of the open seas and oceans. A scarce but annual late summer and early autumn visitor from breeding grounds in the western regions of the Mediterranean. Usually seen moving with flocks of Manx Shearwaters at sea.

Manx Shearwater *Puffinus puffinus* Cánóg dhubh   30-35cm
A slender, black and white shearwater with long, narrow, pointed wings. Upperparts black. Crown black, extending below eye. Underparts white. Underwing white with a black border and extensive dark wing tips. Bill dark. Legs pinkish. Very distinctive in flight, with quick, stiff wing beats followed by long glides, shearing and banking low over the waves. In very calm weather can fly with rapid wing beats and very little gliding.
   Voice & Diet Silent at sea. At the breeding grounds gives a range of wild, crooning and crowing calls. These raucous calls are given both in flight and on the ground when returning to nesting burrows. Feeds on a wide range of small fish and molluscs.
   Habitat and Status A very common, numerous, breeding seabird found off all coastal counties on passage and in summer. Winters far out into the Atlantic Ocean. Found breeding at many sites on quiet islands and headlands, with the largest concentrations in the south-west. Found on open sea and oceans.

Macaronesian Shearwater *Puffinus baroli* Cánóg bheag   25-31cm
A stocky shearwater, very similar to Manx Shearwater but noticeably smaller with shorter, blunter wings. Upperparts and upperwing black with pale panels on innerwing. Unlike Manx, the black crown does not extend below eye, giving a whiter face with a white circle around eye. Underparts white. Whitish underwing shows a blackish border, but the wing tips are not as extensively dark as on Manx. Short bill dark. Legs bluish. Flies with fast, auk-like, fluttering wing beats. Glides and banks less than Manx Shearwater.
   Voice & Diet A silent species in Irish waters. Feeds on a wide variety of small fish and molluscs.
   Habitat and Status An extremely rare late summer and early autumn vagrant from breeding grounds in the Azores and Canary Islands. A bird of open sea and ocean, often seen with Manx Shearwaters.

Fea's Petrel *Pterodroma feae*   33-36cm
An agile petrel, similar in size to Manx Shearwater. Shows a dark, blackish crown and cheeks, a whitish forehead, a dark grey nape and back, dark upperwings with a distinctive W pattern, and a long, pale tail. White underparts contrast strongly with blackish underwings. Shows a diffuse greyish patch on the sides of the breast near the base of the wings. Flies with long, arcing glides over the sea.
   Voice & Diet Silent in Irish waters. Feeds on a variety of small fish and marine invertebrates.
   Habitat and Status A rare but annual autumn vagrant from breeding grounds in the Cape Verde and Madeira Islands. A bird of open sea and ocean.

Time of year

| J | F | M | A | M | J | J | A | S | O | N | D |

Mediterranean Shearwater

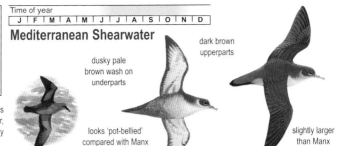

dark brown
upperparts

dusky pale
brown wash on
underparts

can look as dark as
Sooty Shearwater,
but smaller, pale belly

looks 'pot-bellied'
compared with Manx
Shearwater

slightly larger
than Manx

Time of year

| J | F | M | A | M | J | J | A | S | O | N | D |

Manx Shearwater

all black upperparts
white underparts

upperparts can look
dark brown in bright
sunlight

long glides,
sometimes
wheeling high

Time of year

| J | F | M | A | M | J | J | A | S | O | N | D |

Macaronesian Shearwater

whiter underwing
than Manx

whiter face
than Manx

noticeably smaller
than Manx Shearwater

flight straight & low, glides
interspersed with brief periods of flapping

Time of year

| J | F | M | A | M | J | J | A | S | O | N | D |

Fea's Petrel

black 'mask'
around eye

pale grey
uppertail

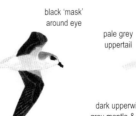

flies effortlessly in
long, high arcs

dark upperwing,
grey mantle & neck

dark underwing

Time of year Very common ▮ Common ▮ Rare ▢ Very rare/absent ▢

Maps Summer ▢ Main breeding colonies ● On passage ▨

Seabirds

Storm Petrel *Hydrobates pelagicus* Guairdeall   13-16cm

A small, dark petrel with a square tail, a white rump and short, rounded wings. **Adults** and **immatures** show a sooty-black head, underparts, mantle and upperwing, contrasting strongly with a square, white rump which extends onto the lower flanks. Tail dark. Upperwing plain, lacking any pale covert panel as seen on other petrel species. However, the underwing does show a striking white line on the coverts. Legs dark and short, not extending beyond tail. Bill small and dark. Flight is fluttery and bat-like, with fast wing beats interspersed with glides. When feeding, can paddle the feet in the water as it moves back and forth on raised wings.

Voice & Diet Silent at sea. At night, around the breeding colonies, gives a variety of repeated, squeaking and growling *tur-wik* and *pee* calls. At the nest, gives a purring call which ends in a distinctive hiccup-type note. Feeds on a wide variety of small fish and plankton. Will readily take offal from trawlers.

Habitat and Status A common bird of open sea and ocean, breeding on small, undisturbed islands with most colonies concentrated in north-western, western and south-western counties. Nests in crevices in walls, under rocks and in burrows. Following breeding, disperses to open seas, with large numbers often recorded off seawatching sites in the south-west. Occasionally found inland after storms.

Leach's Petrel *Oceanodroma leucorhoa* Guairdeall gabhlach   19-23cm

A dark petrel, larger and paler than Storm Petrel, and showing long, pointed wings, a forked tail and a white rump. **Adults** and **immatures** show a dark blackish-brown head, mantle and underparts. Upperwing dark with a distinctive greyish band across the coverts. Underwing wholly dark. Narrow rump can show a dark central line. Tail dark and forked. Bill and legs dark. In flight shows long, pointed wings which are swept back at the carpals. Flight appears easy, with slow wing beats and glides. Moves back and forth across the water when feeding, pattering the feet in the water while holding the wings flat or slightly bowed.

Voice & Diet Silent at sea. At breeding sites at night gives a variety of chatters and screeches. At the nest gives purring-type calls and a distinctive, wheezing *wick* call. Feeds on a variety of small fish and plankton.

Habitat and Status An uncommon petrel, with a small Irish breeding population based on remote islands off western counties. Nests under rocks or boulders, or in burrows. Regularly reported off western and northern coasts in autumn. Disperses to open seas and oceans in winter.

Wilson's Petrel *Oceanites oceanicus* Guairdeall Wilson   15-19cm

A dark petrel, larger than Storm Petrel, with rounded wings, a white rump and long legs extending beyond the tail. **Adults** and **immatures** show a blackish head, mantle and body. Rounded blackish wings show a greyish upperwing panel like Leach's Petrel. Unlike Leach's, can show a pale line on the underwing. Broad, white rump extends further onto flanks than on Storm Petrel. Tail square and dark. In moult can show long outer primaries, giving the wings a pointed appearance. Bill dark. Long legs dark with yellow webbed feet. Flight direct, with fast wing beats and short glides. When feeding, dangles the long legs or patters the feet in the water. Moves slowly with wings raised high above the body.

Voice & Diet Silent in Irish waters. Feeds on a wide range of small fish and plankton. Will readily take offal from trawlers.

Habitat and Status A very rare but annual late summer or early autumn vagrant to the North Atlantic from the southern hemisphere. A bird of open seas and oceans.

Time of year

| J | F | M | A | M | J | J | A | S | O | N | D |

Storm Petrel

dark upperwing

white rump

small size

diagnostic white underwing bar

bat-like flight, rapid wingbeats interspersed with brief glides

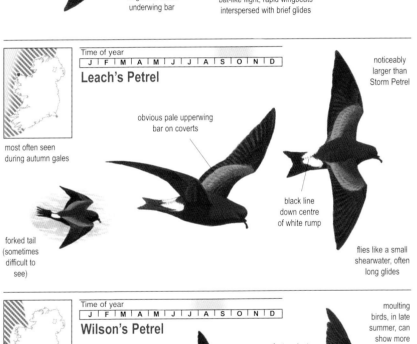

Time of year

| J | F | M | A | M | J | J | A | S | O | N | D |

Leach's Petrel

noticeably larger than Storm Petrel

obvious pale upperwing bar on coverts

most often seen during autumn gales

black line down centre of white rump

forked tail (sometimes difficult to see)

flies like a small shearwater, often long glides

Time of year

| J | F | M | A | M | J | J | A | S | O | N | D |

Wilson's Petrel

moulting birds, in late summer, can show more pointed wings

feet project beyond tail

extensive white rump

yellow webs only visible at very close range

pale upperwing bar on coverts

direct flight, short glides

Time of year Very common ■ Common ■ Rare ☐ Very rare/absent ☐

Maps Summer ☐   Main breeding colonies ●   On passage ▨   49

Cormorants & Glossy Ibis

Cormorant *Phalacrocorax carbo* Broigheall   83-97cm

A stockier, thicker-necked bird than Shag, with a heavier bill, a large area of bare skin on the lores, face and chin, and a slanted forehead. **Summer adults** show yellow around eye, a white throat and cheek patch, white head and neck feathers, a blue gloss on head and underparts, and white thigh patches. Upperparts show a bronzy gloss. **Winter adults** lack thigh patches, are less glossy, and show dark mottling on the white face patch. Eyes green. **Immatures** show a yellow or orange face, a blackish-brown plumage, mottled or whitish underparts, and brownish eyes. Legs dark. In flight appears heavy and goose-like. Swims low in the water. Often seen perched on rocks or buoys, drying open wings. '**Continental Cormorants**' of the race *sinensis*, from eastern and southern Europe, show a square-shaped throat patch and, in spring, more extensive white feathering on the head and neck.

    Voice & Diet On the breeding cliffs can give low, guttural *rr-rah* calls. Feeds by diving, jumping clear of the water. Takes a wide variety of fish.

    Habitat and Status A common breeding species found nesting in colonies on cliffs and islands along most coastal counties. Also breeds on large inland lakes, nesting on islands and in trees. In winter found on estuaries, offshore waters, inland lakes, rivers and canals. Continental Cormorants are a very rare winter visitor from Europe.

Shag *Phalacrocorax aristotelis* Seaga   72-80cm

A smaller, thinner-necked bird than Cormorant with a steep forehead and a slim bill. **Summer adults** show a dark bill with a yellow gape line, an upcurved forehead crest, and a dark, glossy-green head, neck and underparts. Upperparts dark with a purple gloss. **In winter** shows a pale throat, a duller plumage and no crest. Eyes green. Legs dark. Brownish **immatures** show pale wing coverts, yellowish eyes and a pale brown throat and breast. Belly can also be pale. Underparts rarely as white as immature Cormorant. Legs yellow-brown. In flight appears light, with pointed wings. Tends to fly low over the water. Swims higher on the water than Cormorant. Often seen perched, drying open wings.

    Voice & Diet On the breeding cliffs can be heard to give a range of croaks, grunts and hisses. Feeds on a wide variety of small fish and some crustaceans. Jumps clear of the water when diving.

    Habitat and Status A common breeding species found nesting in colonies on rocky cliffs and islands off most coastal counties. Shags are more maritime than Cormorants and are rarely found inland. In winter occurs on open coastal waters and harbours. Found less frequently in estuaries.

Glossy Ibis *Plegadis falcinellus* Íbis niamhrach   54-65cm

A large, all-dark, long-necked bird with a long, curved, Curlew-shaped bill. **Summer adults** appear blackish, but show a deep bronze plumage with a purple gloss on the upperparts, a green gloss on the wings and chestnut on the shoulders. Long, curved bill and legs dark. In winter the plumage is less glossy and appears blackish, with white streaking on the head and neck. **Immatures** appear dull brown, with very little gloss and varying amounts of mottling or streaking on the head and neck. In flight shows a slim body, long, rounded wings, an extended neck and trailing legs. Flies with fast wing beats and occasional glides. Walks and feeds in a slow, methodical manner.

    Voice & Diet When disturbed, gives a long, harsh, croaking call. Feeds in a slow manner, picking or probing with the long bill. Takes a wide range of food items including insects, worms, larvae and molluscs.

    Habitat and Status A rare vagrant from south-eastern Europe. Found on marshes, open farmland and mudflats. Will also readily perch in trees.

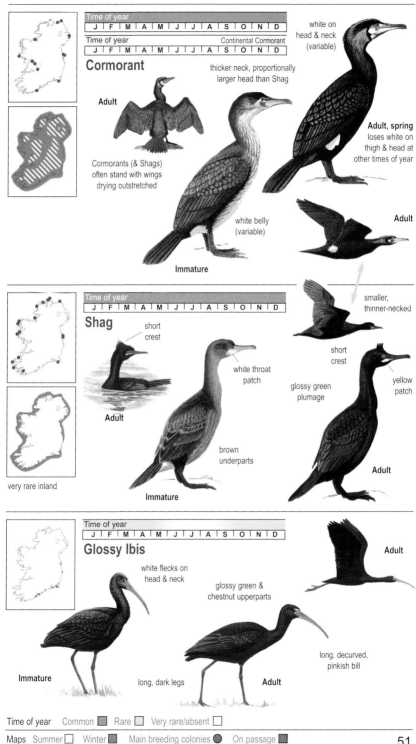

Seabirds

Time of year

| J | F | M | A | M | J | J | A | S | O | N | D |

Time of year — Continental Cormorant

| J | F | M | A | M | J | J | A | S | O | N | D |

Cormorant

thicker neck, proportionally
larger head than Shag

white on
head & neck
(variable)

Adult

Cormorants (& Shags)
often stand with wings
drying outstretched

Adult, spring
loses white on
thigh & head at
other times of year

Adult

white belly
(variable)

Immature

smaller,
thinner-necked

Time of year

| J | F | M | A | M | J | J | A | S | O | N | D |

Shag

short
crest

white throat
patch

short
crest

glossy green
plumage

yellow
patch

Adult

Adult

brown
underparts

very rare inland

Immature

Time of year

| J | F | M | A | M | J | J | A | S | O | N | D |

Glossy Ibis

Adult

white flecks on
head & neck

glossy green &
chestnut upperparts

long, decurved,
pinkish bill

Immature

long, dark legs

Adult

Time of year — Common ▓ Rare ▒ Very rare/absent ☐

Maps — Summer ☐ Winter ▓ Main breeding colonies ● On passage ▓

51

Herons

Bittern *Botaurus stellaris* Bonnán   71-80cm

A stocky, short-necked, heron-like species with a pointed, dagger-like, yellowish bill, orange-yellow eyes and greenish legs. Shows a blackish crown, nape and moustachial stripe contrasting with the warm buff neck which shows brownish barring. Chin and throat whitish with brownish stripes. Pale buffish underparts show dark streaking. Upperparts warm buff and brown, with blackish-brown mottling, barring and stripes. Brownish wings show heavy, dark mottling. In flight the large, rounded wings give an owl-like impression. Legs trail behind the short, brownish, barred tail. Stretches neck upwards when alarmed, blending into and swaying with the surrounding vegetation.

Voice & Diet Gives a loud, harsh, raucous *aarrk* when disturbed or in flight. The distinctive booming song of the male is rarely heard in Ireland. Feeds by walking in a slow, methodical, hunched manner, watching for suitable prey items. Feeds on fish, frogs, newts, small mammals and birds.

Habitat and Status Formerly a widespread breeding species but now a rare migrant from Britain and Europe, with most records referring to winter months. Found in areas of extensive reed-beds. Also found feeding among rank vegetation on the fringes of lakes and slow rivers. Can also climb reed stems. Very active at dusk.

Night Heron *Nycticorax nycticorax* Corr oíche   58-64cm

A compact, short-necked heron with a thick, pointed, dark bill and deep reddish eyes. **Adults** are very distinctive, with a black loral stripe contrasting with a whitish forehead, and a black crown and nape showing long, white plumes. Throat and underparts greyish-white. Mantle black, contrasting with grey wings and tail. Legs yellowish but can show red tones in spring. In flight the black crown, nape and mantle contrast with the grey wings and tail. Flies with rapid wing beats on short, rounded wings. **Immatures** show brownish upperparts with heavy, buffish-white spots and streaks, and pale, greyish-white underparts with heavy, dark streaking. Active at dusk.

Voice & Diet When leaving a roost at dusk, or when disturbed, gives a hoarse, croaking, Raven-like call. Feeds on a wide range of insects, frogs, newts, worms, molluscs and fish.

Habitat and Status A rare spring and autumn vagrant from southern Europe. Inactive during the day, roosting in trees near marshes, rivers, swamps or lakes. Best seen at dusk when leaving the daytime roost. Feeds in shallow waters close to vegetation, hunting in a methodical manner.

Little Bittern *Ixobrychus minutus* Bonnán beag   32-38cm

A tiny, skulky species with a long, dark-tipped, yellowish bill and yellow-green legs. **Males** show a black crown, a pale greyish-buff neck and pale buff underparts with orange-buff stripes. Mantle, rump and tail black, contrasting with a large, pale buff patch on the black wings. Underwings show pale coverts contrasting with black flight feathers. **Females** show a dark crown, warm orange-buff tones on the nape and sides of the neck, and stronger brown stripes on the pale buff underparts. Pale-streaked, brownish upperparts contrast with an orangy carpal and a pale buff wing patch. **Immatures** brown with dark streaking. When alarmed, adopts a Bittern-like, stretched-neck posture. Flight fast with shallow wing beats.

Voice & Diet When disturbed gives a short, abrupt, low *querk* call. Although rarely heard in Ireland, the song consists of muffled, repeated, barking notes which may recall a dog barking in the distance. Feeds on fish, insects and frogs.

Habitat and Status A very rare spring passage vagrant from continental Europe. Found in dense reed-beds or in vegetation and trees along rivers, lakes or marshes. Can climb up reed stems or tree branches. Also recorded in open areas on coastal islands and headlands, these reports usually referring to exhausted birds or fresh arrivals.

Time of year

| J | F | M | A | M | J | J | A | S | O | N | D |

Bittern

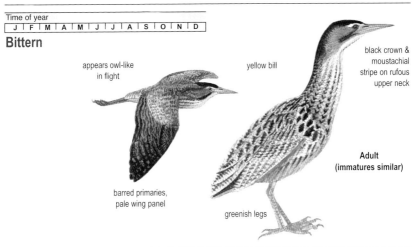

appears owl-like
in flight

yellow bill

black crown &
moustachial
stripe on rufous
upper neck

Adult
(immatures similar)

barred primaries,
pale wing panel

greenish legs

Time of year

| J | F | M | A | M | J | J | A | S | O | N | D |

Night Heron

Immature

grey body,
black mantle

rounded wings,
bill often pointing
downward

heavy pale
spotting on
brown
upperparts

black bill, crown, nape
& mantle, white plumes

heavily
streaked
underparts

Adult

most active
around dusk

Time of year

| J | F | M | A | M | J | J | A | S | O | N | D |

Little Bittern

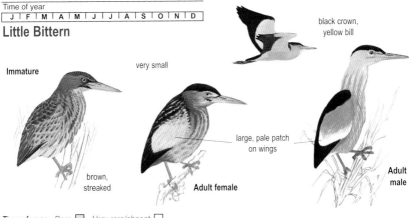

Immature

very small

black crown,
yellow bill

large, pale patch
on wings

brown,
streaked

Adult female

**Adult
male**

Time of year   Rare ▢   Very rare/absent ▢

Maps   On passage ▨

53

Herons

Cattle Egret *Bubulcus ibis* Éigrit eallaigh   45-52cm

A stocky, short-necked egret, smaller than Little Egret. In **summer** shows white plumage with long, pinkish-buff crown, breast and mantle feathers. Bill and legs pinkish-orange. In **winter** shows a white plumage with pale buff tones on the breast, crown and mantle, a yellow bill and dark greyish-green legs. In flight shows rounded wings. Usually found following livestock.

Voice & Diet When disturbed, gives a harsh *recc* call. Feeds on a wide variety of insects which are usually caught when disturbed by livestock. Will also take worms and larvae.

Habitat and Status Formerly a rare vagrant from southern Europe but a species considered to be expanding its range. In some winters have been recorded in small flocks in southern and south-western regions, with some birds reported summering in suitable breeding locations. Found on grasslands, farmlands and dry habitats, usually associating with livestock. Nests in trees and small bushes.

Little Egret *Egretta garzetta* Éigrit bheag   55-64 cm

An elegant, thin-necked, all-white heron, with a long, dagger-like bill and an all-white plumage. **Summer adults** show two long, white plumes on the head and long aigrettes (back and mantle plumes). Shows greyish-blue lores throughout the year which turn reddish in the breeding season. In **winter** the head plumes are lost and the aigrettes are reduced. The long, pointed, dagger-like bill is blackish. The legs are black, with contrasting yellow feet. **Immatures** can show yellowish lores and pale yellow feet with the yellow extending onto the back of the legs. In flight withdraws the neck and shows white, rounded wings and long, trailing legs.

Voice & Diet When disturbed gives a croaking *arrk* call. At the nest site gives a gurgling-type call. Feeds actively in shallow water, catching fish, insects or frogs. Can also follow livestock in search of insects disturbed by the animals.

Habitat and Status Formerly a rare vagrant from Europe, Little Egrets are now a resident breeding species on coastal regions along the east, south and south-west. Also seen inland, with birds present in small numbers along western and northern coastal areas. Nests in colonies in trees and bushes. Usually found in marshes, lakes and estuaries where they feed in the channels at low tide. Also found on dry open farmland, often associating with livestock. This can lead to birds being mistaken for Cattle Egrets. Hard winters with prolonged snow and ice makes feeding difficult and such conditions may reduce the resident population.

Great White Egret *Ardea alba* Éigrit mhór   85-100cm

A very large, slim, elegant egret similar in size to Grey Heron. Shows a long, slender neck, an all-white plumage with long, wispy scapular aigrettes and loose breast feathering. Lacks the head plumes of Little Egret. In **summer** shows greenish lores, a yellow base to a dark bill and black lower legs and yellowish upper legs. In **winter** loses the scapular aigrettes, has darker legs and shows a dark tip to a yellow bill. Flies with slow, deep wingbeats with very long legs extending well beyond the tail.

Voice & Diet When disturbed gives a loud, harsh *crr-rr-ack* call. Feeds on a wide range of fish and aquatic insects.

Habitat and Status Formerly a very rare vagrant from Europe and possibly North America but now recorded annually. Considered to be expanding its range in Europe. Most reports refer to spring and early summer, with some over-wintering on occasions. Found on lakes, rivers, marshes and estuaries.

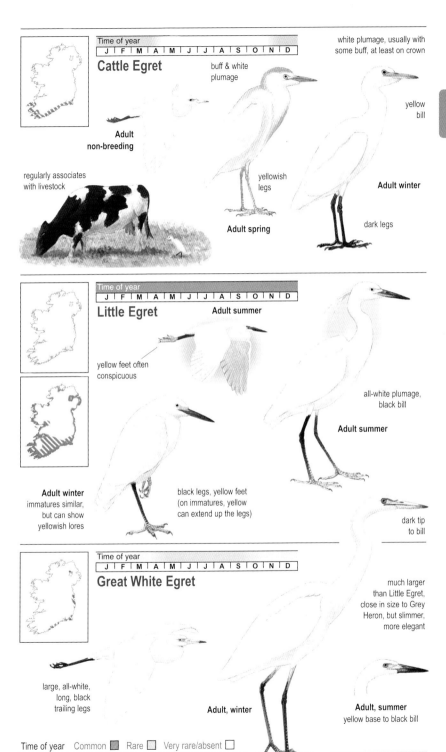

Time of year

J F M A M J J A S O N D

Cattle Egret

buff & white plumage

white plumage, usually with some buff, at least on crown

yellow bill

Adult non-breeding

regularly associates with livestock

yellowish legs

Adult winter

Adult spring

dark legs

Time of year

J F M A M J J A S O N D

Little Egret

Adult summer

yellow feet often conspicuous

all-white plumage, black bill

Adult summer

Adult winter
immatures similar, but can show yellowish lores

black legs, yellow feet (on immatures, yellow can extend up the legs)

dark tip to bill

Time of year

J F M A M J J A S O N D

Great White Egret

much larger than Little Egret, close in size to Grey Heron, but slimmer, more elegant

large, all-white, long, black trailing legs

Adult, winter

Adult, summer
yellow base to black bill

Time of year Common ▨ Rare ☐ Very rare/absent ☐

Maps Summer ☐ Winter ▨ On passage ▨

55

Herons & (Common) Crane

Grey Heron *Ardea cinerea* Corr réisc   90-100cm

Large, long-necked bird with a long, stout, pointed bill. **Adults** show a white head and neck with a black crown stripe which forms a loose crest. Black stripes obvious on foreneck extending onto loose, shaggy breast. Upperparts blue-grey with a black shoulder patch and pale, elongated scapulars forming plumes. Black on sides of breast continues down as flank stripe, meeting on the ventral area. Flanks and belly white. Bill orange-yellow. Flies on bowed wings, showing contrasting grey wing coverts and blackish primaries and secondaries. Flies with neck retracted, dull-greenish legs extending beyond the tail. **Immatures** show a dark crown, greyish sides to neck and a duller bill.

Voice & Diet Gives a harsh, grumpy *krarnk* call, especially when disturbed. At the nest site gives croaking calls. Feeds by standing patiently, watching for prey items which are caught with a fast, sudden stab of the dagger-like bill. Takes fish, insects, frogs and small mammals.

Habitat and Status A common resident species found throughout the country. Breeds in colonies known as heronries, building nests on tops of trees and bushes. In winter populations may increase with the arrival of birds from Scandinavia and Britain. Found on lakes, rivers, canals, marshes and estuaries. Will occasionally visit garden ponds.

Purple Heron *Ardea purpurea* Corr chorcra   77-89cm

A thin-necked bird with a long, yellowish bill. **Adults** show a chestnut head and neck, a pale throat and foreneck, and black crown and face stripes forming a crest. Shows a black stripe down sides of neck, with thinner black stripes on foreneck. Upperparts dark purple-grey with chestnut shoulder patch. Elongated scapulars yellow-brown. Underparts purple-chestnut with dark purple-brown flank stripe. In flight purple-grey wing coverts do not contrast with darker flight feathers, although buff carpal patches are obvious. Underwing reddish-brown. In flight yellowish legs trail beyond the tail and the retracted neck forms a prominent bulge. **Immatures** show pale buff face, sides of neck and upperparts, a dark crown with thin stripes on face extending onto foreneck and pale underparts.

Voice & Diet When disturbed gives a *krarnk* call similar to that of Grey Heron, although delivered in a higher-pitched tone. Feeds on a wide range of fish, insects and small amphibians.

Habitat and Status A very rare visitor from southern Europe, with most records referring to spring and early summer. Found in reed-beds or marshes, rarely on open estuaries or rivers. Can stand motionless for long periods within cover, making them very difficult to see.

(Common) Crane *Grus grus* Grús   115-130cm

A very tall, long-necked bird with a shortish bill and long, drooping tertials. **Adults** unmistakable, with a black head showing a small red crown patch and a broad white stripe from behind eye down neck. Lower neck, breast and underparts grey. Upperparts grey with a brownish wash on mantle. Most striking feature is the long, drooping black and grey tertials which fall over the tail. In flight shows a large wing span with darker primaries and secondaries, and a dark-tipped grey tail. Extended neck and trailing legs give an almost goose-like profile in flight. Bill pale and pointed. Legs dark. **Immatures** show a sandy-brown head and neck with an overall greyish-brown plumage.

Voice & Diet Can give a loud *krroh* call as well as trumpeting, bugle-like calls in flight. Feeds on insects, small mammals and a wide variety of plant material and seeds.

Habitat and Status Bred in Ireland in the Middle Ages but now only occurs as a very rare visitor from northern and central Europe. Most records refer to winter sightings. Found on marshes and open, arable lands.

Grey Heron

Time of year
J F M A M J J A S O N D

grey on crown

Immature

white crown & forehead

white crown & forehead, long black plumes (in early spring)

Adult

Adult

slow, heavy flight, dark grey & black wing feathers

grey wash on neck

Time of year
J F M A M J J A S O N D

Purple Heron

usually in cover, in or near large reed-beds

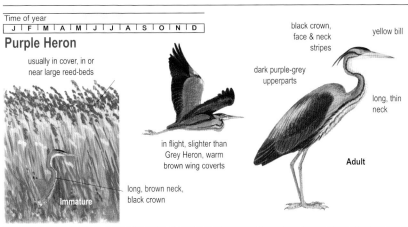

black crown, face & neck stripes

yellow bill

dark purple-grey upperparts

long, thin neck

Adult

in flight, slighter than Grey Heron, warm brown wing coverts

long, brown neck, black crown

Immature

Time of year
J F M A M J J A S O N D

(Common) Crane

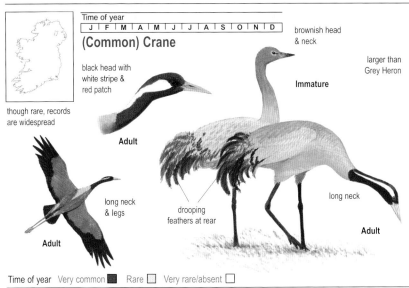

brownish head & neck

larger than Grey Heron

black head with white stripe & red patch

Immature

though rare, records are widespread

Adult

long neck & legs

drooping feathers at rear

long neck

Adult

Adult

Squacco Heron *Ardeola ralloides* Corr scréachach   41-49cm

A small, thickset heron with a short neck and elongated crown feathers forming a long, striped, cream and black mane. Appears yellow-buff on head, breast and upperparts with a strong peach wash on the mantle. In flight shows strikingly white wings, rump and tail. **Summer adults** show a dark tip to a thick, pointed, blue-grey bill and have pinkish legs. **Immatures** and **winter adults** show browner upperparts, heavy streaking on sides of neck and breast, a dark tip to a yellow-green bill, and greenish legs.

Voice & Diet When disturbed gives a harsh *ka-aah* call. Feeds on a wide range of small fish, insects and small amphibians.

Habitat and Status Found in small pools, wetlands and marshes. A very rare spring vagrant from southern Europe with most records from southern coastal regions in spring and early summer.

Spoonbill *Platalea leucorodia* Leitheadach   81-90cm

An unmistakable, white, heron-like bird with a long neck and legs and a distinctive long, spatulate bill. **Adults** show an all-white plumage with a yellow throat, a black, yellow-tipped bill and black legs. Shows yellowish neck plumes and a yellow wash around the base of the neck in summer. In flight shows an outstretched neck and trailing legs. Flies with fast wing beats, interspersed with short glides. **Immatures** are similar to adults, but show a pinkish throat and bill, pinkish legs and black tips to the wings, obvious in flight. Feeds with diagnostic, side-to-side sweeps of the bill.

Voice & Diet Although usually silent in Ireland, can occasionally give grunting-type calls. An active feeder, taking fish, molluscs and insects from shallow water by side-to-side sweeps of the sensitive bill.

Habitat and Status A rare visitor from Europe, Spoonbills can occur at any time of the year, with some birds over-wintering. Feeds in shallow water and can be found on marshes or lakes. Often found on estuaries feeding in shallow channels at low tide.

White Stork *Ciconia ciconia* Storc bán   101-115cm

A large, long-necked, black and white bird with a long, red bill and long, red legs. Plumage all white except for black greater coverts, tertials, secondaries and primaries, which form a large, glossy, black wing patch. Also shows a thin, black loral stripe. Eye blackish. The bright red bill is thick, long and pointed. Legs bright red. **Immatures** show a dull wing patch, a blackish tip to a reddish bill and dull red legs. Flies with long, outstretched neck and trailing legs. Wings appear long and narrow in flight and show a striking black and white underwing pattern. Flies with slow wing beats, soaring frequently. On the ground, walks slowly with outstretched neck.

Voice & Diet A silent bird, only heard during the breeding season. Feeds on a wide variety of prey, including insects, small mammals, frogs, nestlings, fish and worms. Feeds by walking slowly, watching carefully before stabbing at prey with the long bill.

Habitat and Status A very rare vagrant to Ireland from Europe, normally recorded in spring. Usually found on open grasslands, flooded meadows and marshes. Can be quite tame and approachable on occasions.

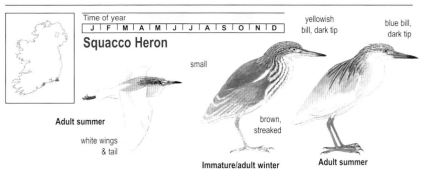

Time of year
J F M A M J J A S O N D

Squacco Heron

small

Adult summer

white wings
& tail

yellowish
bill, dark tip

blue bill,
dark tip

brown,
streaked

Immature/adult winter

Adult summer

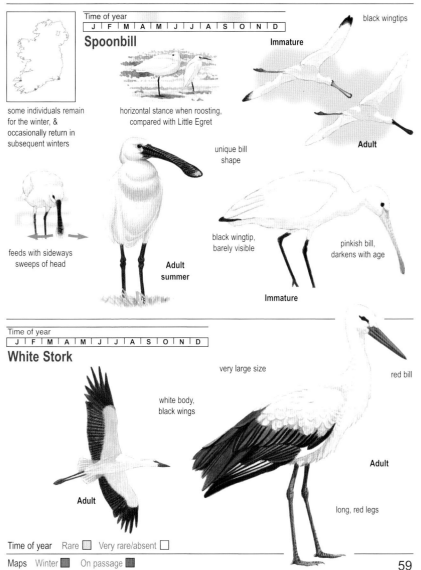

Time of year
J F M A M J J A S O N D

Spoonbill

some individuals remain
for the winter, &
occasionally return in
subsequent winters

horizontal stance when roosting,
compared with Little Egret

black wingtips

Immature

Adult

feeds with sideways
sweeps of head

unique bill
shape

**Adult
summer**

black wingtip,
barely visible

pinkish bill,
darkens with age

Immature

Time of year
J F M A M J J A S O N D

White Stork

very large size

red bill

white body,
black wings

Adult

Adult

Adult

long, red legs

Time of year   Rare ☐   Very rare/absent ☐

Maps   Winter ▨   On passage ▨

59

Birds of Prey

Hen Harrier
Circus cyaneus Cromán na gcearc   43-52cm

A slim, narrow-winged raptor. **Adult males** show whitish underparts, a white rump, a pale grey head, breast, tail and upperwing with black tips and a dark trailing edge. Underwing paler. **Females** brown above with a pale upperwing covert panel, a large, white rump and barring on a brown tail. Owl-like face streaked brown, showing a dark crescent on rear cheeks. Underparts pale with brown streaking on neck, breast and flanks. Underwing shows mottled brown coverts, barred flight feathers and a dark trailing edge. **Immatures** buffier on underparts. Legs and cere yellowish. Flies with fast wing beats and short glides. Soars on raised wings. Rounded wings usually show five fingered primaries.

Voice and Diet Males at the breeding sites give chattering *tchuc-uc-uc* calls. Females give high-pitched *ke-ke-ke* and whistling-type calls. Feeds on a wide variety of small birds and rodents. Hunts by gliding low over an area before suddenly swooping down on prey.

Habitat and Status A scarce breeding species. In summer found on mountains and moorlands, nesting on the ground. Also nests in young conifer plantations. In winter birds can roost communally and are found in most parts of Ireland including coastal areas.

Montagu's Harrier
Circus pygargus Cromán liath   39-45cm

A light raptor, similar to Hen Harrier. **Males** grey with a white rump, a whitish belly and flank streaking. Upperwing shows black tips and a black secondary bar. Underwing shows black bars and black mottling on coverts. **Females** brown with a pale upperwing panel, a thin white rump and a barred, brown tail. Three or four fingered primaries make wings appear pointed. Face pattern diagnostic with whitish sides to head, a dark rear cheek crescent and a dark eye-stripe. Underparts pale with brown streaking. **Immatures** show unstreaked, rufous underparts and a dark secondary bar. Legs and cere yellowish. Flight more buoyant than Hen Harrier, appearing falcon-like on occasions. Soars on raised wings.

Voice and Diet Rarely heard on passage. Can give a soft, high-pitched *yick-yick* call at the nest. Feeds on a wide range of prey items, including frogs, small birds, eggs, rodents, worms and large insects.

Habitat and Status A rare spring and autumn passage migrant from Europe. Breeding has occurred on several occasions in eastern and south-western counties. Frequents crop fields, dune systems, reeds, moorlands and areas with young conifer plantations. On passage found on coastal areas including headlands and islands.

Marsh Harrier
Circus aeruginosus Cromán móna   49-56cm

A broad-winged, heavy raptor. **Adult males** show a dark brown mantle and wing coverts, a pale head, black wing-tips, and pale grey flight feathers. Underwing shows brown coverts, pale flight feathers and a dark trailing edge. Underparts streaked brown. Tail grey. **Adult females** are larger and show a dark brown plumage, a dark eye-stripe, and a creamy-yellow crown and throat. Underparts brown with a paler breast. Wings dark brown with creamy-yellow forewing patches on the upperwing. Tail brown. **Immatures** similar but lack forewing patches. **Immature males** show greyish inner primaries. Cere and legs yellowish. Flight heavy with deep wing beats. Glides with wings raised in a shallow V.

Voice and Diet Usually silent on passage, with males giving shrill *key-eoo* calls only at the nesting site. Feeds on a wide range of marshland birds, mammals and frogs. Will also take eggs, nestlings and carrion.

Habitat and Status Formerly a widespread breeding species, Marsh Harrier is now a scarce but regular spring and autumn passage migrant from Europe, with birds recorded summering in suitable breeding habitat. Most reports refer to eastern, south-eastern and south-western counties. Found over large reed-beds and marshes.

Hen Harrier

Time of year
J F M A M J J A S O N D

scarce breeder, usually in young conifer plantations

more widespread & slightly more numerous in winter

pale grey

Male

wings & tail barred brown

Female

white rump

Female

darker 'hood'

Male

pale grey, black wingtips

white rump

broader wings than Montagu's Harrier

Male

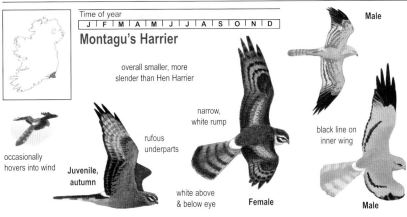

Montagu's Harrier

Time of year
J F M A M J J A S O N D

occasionally hovers into wind

overall smaller, more slender than Hen Harrier

Juvenile, autumn

rufous underparts

narrow, white rump

white above & below eye

Female

Male

black line on inner wing

Male

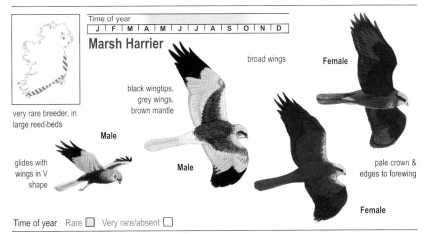

Marsh Harrier

Time of year
J F M A M J J A S O N D

very rare breeder, in large reed-beds

glides with wings in V shape

black wingtips, grey wings, brown mantle

Male

Male

broad wings

Female

pale crown & edges to forewing

Female

Time of year   Rare ☐   Very rare/absent ☐

Maps   Summer ☐   Winter ■   On passage ▨

Birds of Prey

White-tailed Eagle *Haliaeetus albicilla* Iolar mara   77-93cm

An extremely large eagle with long, broad wings and a short, wedge-shaped tail. **Adults** show a pale yellow-brown head and upper breast, brown underparts, greyish-brown upperparts and a white tail. In flight, shows a large head, dark underwings and grey-brown upperwings with yellowish coverts. Large bill pale yellow. Legs yellow. **Immatures** dark brown, with a paler breast and undertail. In flight dark underwings show pale axillary patches and a faint covert bar. Dark brown upperwing shows a faint covert panel. Lacks white wing panels and patches of immature Golden. Short, dark tail shows white centres to feathers from below. Bill dark with a paler cere. Soars on flat wings.

Voice and Diet White-tailed Eagle can give a harsh, repeated *kri-ick* call. Feeds on a wide range of prey items, including fish which are snatched from, or just below, the surface of the water. Hunts low over the ground in a strong, cruising flight, taking mammals and birds. Also attracted to carrion.

Habitat and Status A very rare vagrant from Scotland and northern Europe. A reintroduction scheme is currently taking place in Co. Kerry and birds from this programme have been recorded in many regions. Found along rocky coasts and mountainous regions. Perches on cliffs, on trees and, occasionally, on the ground.

Golden Eagle *Aquila chrysaetos* Iolar fíréan   76-91cm

A very large, powerful raptor. **Adults** show a golden-buff crown and nape, and brown upper and underparts. In flight shows a large head and a long, brownish, faintly barred tail. Long wings dark brown below, with faint barring and paler primary bases. Underparts dark brown with paler undertail coverts. Brown upperwing shows a pale buff covert panel and greyish-brown flight feathers. Large hooked bill shows a yellow cere. Legs yellow. **Immatures** dark brown with a buff-yellow head. Dark underwing shows a striking white panel across flight feathers. White patches obvious on dark brown upperwing. Tail shows a broad white base. Soars with wings held in a shallow V.

Voice and Diet Usually a silent species, Golden Eagle can occasionally give a whistling *wee-u* call. Hunts by flying reasonably low over the ground and swooping on prey. Feeds on a wide range of mammals and birds. Will also take carrion, which makes this species susceptible to poisoning.

Habitat and Status This species has been reintroduced into Co. Donegal and is now a rare breeding species in the region. Birds from Scotland occasionally fly over to north-eastern regions. Can occur at any time of the year. Frequents wild coastal islands and headlands and inland mountainous regions.

Black Kite *Milvus migrans* Cúr dubh   55-61cm

A large, dark raptor with a shallow fork on a long tail, and long wings angled back at the carpal. Soars on flat or bowed wings. Flies with deep, elastic wing beats. **Adults** show a greyish-brown head and dark brown plumage. Breast and belly warmer brown. In flight shows dark brown underwings with an inconspicuous pale patch on base of primaries. Upperwing dark brown with a pale covert bar. Long, slightly forked tail can appear square-ended and is often twisted in flight. Bill dark. Cere and legs yellow. **Immatures** show a brighter plumage. Appears less contrasting than Red Kite. Distant Marsh Harriers appear similar, but soar with wings held in a shallow V.

Voice and Diet Black Kites give harsh, gull-like calls but are usually silent on passage and therefore rarely heard in Ireland. Feeds on a wide range of amphibians, birds, rodents and insects. Also attracted to carrion.

Habitat and Status An extremely rare vagrant from continental Europe. Most records refer to eastern, south-eastern and south-western counties, with most birds recorded in spring. Found in open areas with scattered trees or woods, and usually close to rivers and lakes. On passage can be seen anywhere along coastal counties. Can occur close to human habitation.

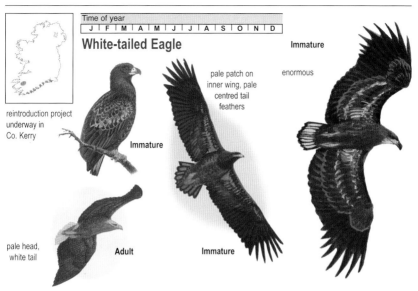

White-tailed Eagle

Immature

reintroduction project underway in Co. Kerry

pale patch on inner wing, pale centred tail feathers

enormous

Immature

Immature

pale head, white tail

Adult

Immature

Golden Eagle

Immature

white on wings, pale base to tail

reintroduction project underway in Co. Donegal

top: soaring Golden Eagle
bottom: soaring White-tailed Eagle

Adult

pale upperwing panel & crown

very large, broad wings

Adult

Black Kite

long tail with shallow fork

Adult

Birds of Prey

Osprey *Pandion haliaetus* Coirneach   51-60cm
A large raptor with a contrasting plumage. When perched, shows dark brown upperparts, a crested white crown and a striking black eye-stripe which extends down side of neck. Underparts white with a brownish breast band. Hooked bill pale with a dark tip. Legs greyish. In flight a pale underwing shows a blackish carpal patch, a black covert bar and dark wing tips. Shortish tail is pale below, dark above, and shows narrow barring. **Immatures** show pale tips to underwing coverts. Flies with strong, shallow wing beats on long, narrow wings. Soars on bowed wings. In the air can look gull-like. Hunts by hovering before plunging feet-first into the water. Shakes water from the plumage when rising.

Voice and Diet Although seldom heard in Ireland, can give loud, repeated, whistling-type calls. Feeds exclusively on large fish. Always carries fish head-first in talons in flight.

Habitat and Status An uncommon but regular spring and autumn passage migrant from Europe, occurring annually. In recent years birds have been reported in suitable breeding areas in spring and late summer. Found on large lakes and rivers, often with suitable perches such as dead trees. Also reported on passage at coastal sites. Has been seen out at sea.

Buzzard *Buteo buteo* Clamhán   50-57cm
A large, stocky, short-necked raptor with broad wings and a shortish tail. Plumage can vary greatly, but most show a dark brown head, breast and upperparts with brown mottling on underparts. Lower breast can be paler, appearing as a pale crescent. Shortish tail pale brown below, darker above, with narrow barring. Upperwing plain dark brown. Underwing shows dark brown coverts, dark carpal patches, blackish wing tips, pale base to primaries and a dark trailing edge. **Immatures** lack dark trailing edge to wings. Bill dark with a yellowish cere. Legs yellowish. Soars with wings held in a shallow V. When gliding the wings can be held flat or just slightly raised.

Voice and Diet Gives a distinctive, high-pitched, drawn-out, mewing *pee-oo* call. Feeds on a wide range of prey, including rats, rabbits, frogs, insects, worms and young birds. Will also be attracted to carrion.

Habitat and Status Formerly an uncommon breeding species but now common in northern, north-western, eastern and some midland counties. Also present in small numbers in other regions. Found in a wide range of habitats including undisturbed coasts and islands, farmlands, mountains and wooded demesnes. Nests in trees or on cliffs.

Rough-legged Buzzard *Buteo lagopus* Clamhán lópach   51-61cm
A sturdy raptor, larger than Buzzard, with long wings. **Adults** show a well-defined, black terminal band on a white tail with two or three narrower bands. Head and breast brown, with a paler lower breast and black belly patches. Underwing shows brown coverts, black tips to barred flight feathers, and black carpal patches. Upperwing brown with pale primary base patches. Bill dark with yellowish cere. Legs yellowish. **Immatures** similar, but show a diffuse terminal tail band, a paler, streaked head and underparts, and pale underwing coverts. Upperwings also show pale covert panels and primary patches. Flies with deep wing beats. Soars on raised wings. Hovers more than other buzzard species.

Voice and Diet The long, mewing call is seldom given away from the breeding grounds. Feeds on a wide variety of rodents, including rabbits, rats and mice. Will also occasionally take birds.

Habitat and Status A rare autumn and winter vagrant from Scandinavia, with most records referring to coastal counties. Frequents barren, open country and farmland. Also found on coastal dunes, marshes, headlands and islands. Most are seen on passage but some may over-winter.

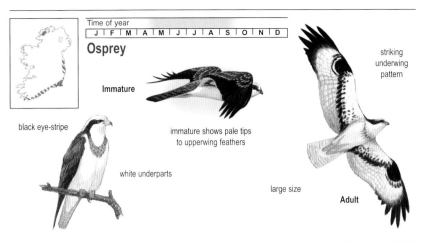

Osprey

Time of year
J F M A M J J A S O N D

Immature

black eye-stripe

white underparts

immature shows pale tips to upperwing feathers

large size

striking underwing pattern

Adult

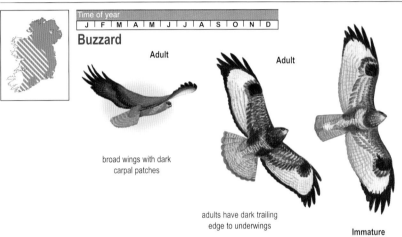

Buzzard

Time of year
J F M A M J J A S O N D

Adult

Adult

broad wings with dark carpal patches

adults have dark trailing edge to underwings

Immature

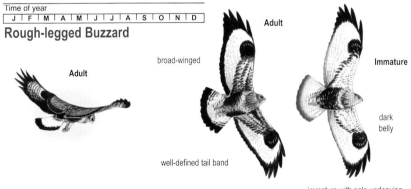

Time of year
J F M A M J J A S O N D

Rough-legged Buzzard

Adult

broad-winged

Immature

Adult

dark belly

well-defined tail band

immature with pale underwing coverts & diffuse tail band

Birds of prey

Red Kite *Milvus milvus* Cúr rua   60-66cm

A striking species with a deeply-forked, bright orange tail. Long, narrow wings are angled back at the carpal, and are held flat or slightly bowed when soaring. Flies with deep, elastic wing beats. **Adults** show a streaked whitish head and a warm rufous-brown plumage with dark underpart streaking. In flight shows rufous-brown underwings with conspicuous pale primary bases forming square underwing patches. Upperwing brown with a pale rufous covert panel. Long, deeply-forked, orangy tail is twisted in flight. Bill dark. Cere and legs yellow. **Immatures** as adults, but show paler underparts and a broader, paler upperwing covert panel.

Voice & Diet Gives a shrill, mewing *weeh-oo* call which is often repeated. Call is similar to Buzzard, but is higher-pitched and delivered more rapidly. Feeds on small mammals, birds, amphibians and worms. Also attracted to carrion.

Habitat and Status Formerly a rare but regular passage migrant from breeding grounds in Wales and continental Europe but now resident in eastern and north-eastern counties following reintroduction schemes. Birds from these programmes have been recorded in other regions. Found in open country with farmland, hills and woodland. On passage seen over islands and headlands.

Sparrowhawk *Accipiter nisus* Spioróg   28-37cm

A small raptor with yellow-orange eyes. In flight shows rounded wings and a long, square-ended tail. **Adult males** blue-grey on crown and upperparts, and show a white supercilium and rufous cheeks. White underparts show orange-red barring extending onto underwing coverts. Underwing flight feathers barred. Undertail shows dark bars. **Females** larger, with a grey-brown crown and upperparts, a white supercilium, and greyish barring on white underparts, on underwing coverts and on flight feathers. Tail shows dark bars. Bill dark. Legs and cere yellow. **Immatures** similar to females, but show pale edges to upperpart feathers and brown barring on buffish underparts.

Voice & Diet Gives a loud, shrill, repeated *kek-kek-kek*, when close to the nest. Hunts by gliding low over the ground, along hedgerows or through trees. Occasionally perches quietly, watching for prey. Feeds on a variety of small birds and mammals. Will also take large insects.

Habitat and Status A common resident breeding species found in all counties. Frequents coniferous and mixed woodland, open farmland with trees and hedgerows, parks and suburban gardens. Nests high in trees. Numbers may increase in winter with the arrival of birds from Britain and Europe.

Goshawk *Accipiter gentilis* Spioróg mhór   48-59cm

A powerful raptor, much larger than Sparrowhawk, with longer wings, a deeper chest and a rounded tail. In flight shows a bulge to the secondaries. **Adult males** show a dark cap due to a white supercilium and nape, greyish upperparts, and dark barring on white underparts and underwing coverts. Underwing flight feathers barred. Tail shows dark bars. Larger **females** show a dark brown cap, a white supercilium and nape, brown upperparts, and barring on white underparts and underwing coverts. Undertail coverts white. Underwing flight feathers barred. Tail shows dark bars. Eyes orange-yellow. Legs and cere yellow. **Immatures** show dark streaking on pale buff underparts.

Voice & Diet Gives agitated *gek-gek-gek* calls if disturbed near the nest. Engages in slow, soaring, display flights when plaintive, whistling *ee-aa* notes can be given. Feeds by flying and gliding quickly through trees, swooping on suitable prey. Takes mammals and birds up to Pheasant size.

Habitat and Status A rare passage vagrant and an extremely rare breeding species. Frequents coniferous and mixed woodlands in both low-lying and mountainous areas. Secretive in breeding areas, but best seen in early spring when birds perform aerial displays. Occurs on passage on coastal islands and headlands.

Birds of prey

Time of year

| J | F | M | A | M | J | J | A | S | O | N | D |

Red Kite

greyish head

striking, pale
wing patches

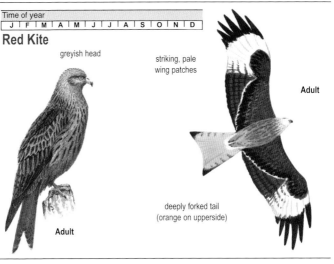

Adult

two reintroduction
projects currently
under way, in counties
Down & Wicklow

orange tail,
deeply forked

deeply forked tail
(orange on upperside)

Adult

Time of year

| J | F | M | A | M | J | J | A | S | O | N | D |

Sparrowhawk

Male

grey
upperparts

Juvenile female
pale tips to
upperwing coverts

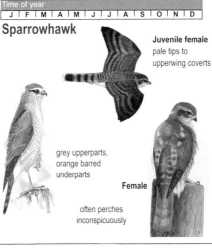

the commonest raptor
in Ireland, though often
inconspicuous

fine, grey barring on
underparts looks
grey at a distance

Male

grey upperparts,
orange barred
underparts

Female

squared-off
tail corners

male noticeably
smaller than female

often perches
inconspicuously

Female

Time of year

| J | F | M | A | M | J | J | A | S | O | N | D |

Goshawk

dark cap, white
supercilium

smallest males
still larger than
largest (female)
Sparrowhawks

bulging
secondaries

large, heavy
build

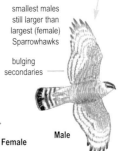

very rare breeding
resident, usually
associated with large
areas of coniferous
forest

Female

Female

Male

broad,
rounded tail

Time of year   Common ▨   Rare ☐   Very rare/absent ☐

Maps   Resident ▨

Birds of Prey

Kestrel *Falco tinnunculus* Pocaire gaoithe   33-37cm

A long-tailed falcon with pointed wings, often seen hovering in mid-air. **Adult males** show a blue-grey crown and nape, a dark moustachial stripe, black spotting on chestnut upperparts, and a black band and white tip to a grey tail. Creamy underparts show dark spotting. In flight shows dark wing tips and dark spots on underwing coverts. **Adult females** and **immatures** show a streaked brown head, a dark moustachial stripe and heavy, dark barring on rufous upperparts. Brown tail shows dark bars and a white tip. Creamy-buff underparts and underwing coverts show heavy streaking. Shows dark tips to upperwing and barred underwing flight feathers. Legs and cere yellow.

Voice & Diet Gives harsh, loud, repeated *kee-kee-kee* calls when agitated or close to the nest. Hunts by hovering motionless in mid-air, searching for suitable quarry below, before diving onto prey. Will also sit on an open perch, watching for insects. Feeds on a wide range of small rodents, birds, insects and worms.

Habitat and Status A common, widespread breeding species found in a wide range of habitats, including mountainous cliffs, moorlands and bogs, open farmland, woodlands, parks, towns and cities. Frequently seen hovering over road verges. A small autumn and spring movement is noted annually on southern headlands and islands.

Merlin *Falco columbarius* Meirliún   27-33cm

A small, agile falcon with short, pointed wings. **Males** show a dark grey crown, a faint moustachial stripe, a whitish supercilium, streaked cheeks and a buff to rust-brown nape. Grey upperparts show thin streaking. Grey tail shows broad bars. Buff to rust-brown underparts show dark streaking. In flight shows a streaked and barred underwing. **Females** and **immatures** show a brown crown, streaked cheeks, a diffuse moustachial stripe and a pale nape. Upperparts grey-brown. Creamy tail shows dark bars. Creamy underparts heavily streaked. In flight shows a heavily streaked and barred underwing. Legs yellow. Cere yellow on adults, bluish on immatures.

Voice & Diet Gives a shrill, repeated, Kestrel-like *kiik-kiik-kiik* call when agitated or disturbed at the nest. Prey consists mainly of birds, with small mammals and insects taken occasionally. Hunts by flying fast and low over the ground, sometimes snatching feeding or perched birds.

Habitat and Status A scarce, resident breeding species found in all regions. In summer found on upland moorland and bogs and in conifer plantations. Nests on the ground or in old crow nests. In winter found along coastal saltmarshes and estuaries, and on low-lying inland bogs. Numbers increase in winter with the arrival of birds from Iceland and Scotland.

Red-footed Falcon *Falco vespertinus* Fabhcún cosdearg   28-32cm

Adult males show a dark grey head, upperparts and tail, silvery flight feathers, grey underparts, and red thighs, undertail and feet. Cere and eye-ring orange-red. **First-summer males** show a pale throat, orange upper breast and neck, brown flight feathers, and a barred tail. Underwing heavily barred and streaked. Thighs and bare parts yellow-orange. **Adult females** show an orange-buff crown and underparts, a white throat, and a black moustachial and eye-stripe. Upperparts and tail greyish with heavy barring. In flight shows orange-buff underwing coverts and heavily barred flight feathers. Bare parts reddish-orange. **First-summer females** show a dark crown.

Voice & Diet Generally silent on passage. Hovers with deep wing beats and also watches for insects on the ground from a perch, swooping down in a shrike-like manner. Also hawks insects on the wing. Prey consists of a variety of insects, lizards, frogs and small mammals.

Habitat and Status An extremely rare spring and autumn vagrant from central Europe. Can be very tame and approachable.

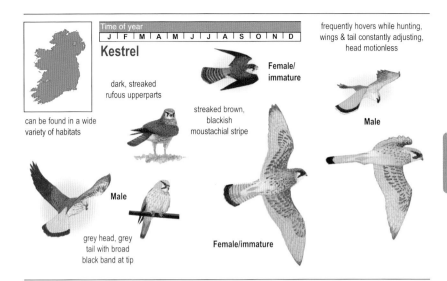

Kestrel

Time of year
J F M A M J J A S O N D

frequently hovers while hunting, wings & tail constantly adjusting, head motionless

dark, streaked rufous upperparts

Female/immature

streaked brown, blackish moustachial stripe

Male

can be found in a wide variety of habitats

Male

grey head, grey tail with broad black band at tip

Female/immature

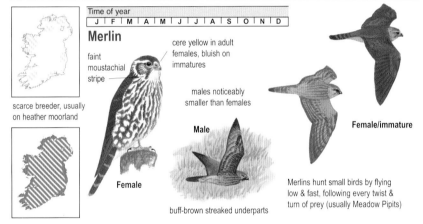

Merlin

Time of year
J F M A M J J A S O N D

cere yellow in adult females, bluish on immatures

faint moustachial stripe

males noticeably smaller than females

scarce breeder, usually on heather moorland

Male

Female/immature

Female

Merlins hunt small birds by flying low & fast, following every twist & turn of prey (usually Meadow Pipits)

buff-brown streaked underparts

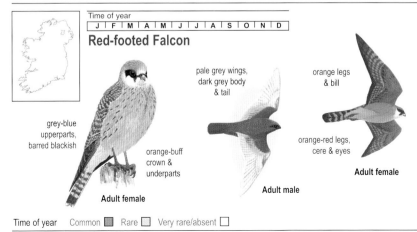

Red-footed Falcon

Time of year
J F M A M J J A S O N D

pale grey wings, dark grey body & tail

orange legs & bill

grey-blue upperparts, barred blackish

orange-red legs, cere & eyes

orange-buff crown & underparts

Adult female

Adult female

Adult male

Time of year   Common ▣   Rare ▢   Very rare/absent ☐

Maps   Summer ☐   Winter ▣   Resident ▣

69

Hobby *Falco subbuteo* Fabhcún coille   30-36cm

A slim falcon with long, Swift-like wings. **Adults** show a blackish head, a prominent black moustachial stripe and a white face. Heavily streaked, creamy underparts show bright rufous-red thighs and undertail coverts. Upperparts slate-grey. Greyish uppertail unbarred. Shows heavily streaked and barred underwings. Pale undertail shows dark bars. Legs and cere yellow. **Immatures** show pale buff fringes to dark brown upperparts and wings. Brown uppertail unbarred, but shows a pale tip. Shows a moustachial stripe, heavily streaked, pale underparts and buffish thighs and undertail coverts. Underwings heavily streaked and barred. Pale undertail barred. Cere bluish.

Voice & Diet Gives a clear, slow, plaintive *kew-kew-kew* call. A very agile and skilful aerial hunter, often seen hawking insects. Will twist and turn in the air, snatching large insects in the talons and transferring them to the bill in flight. Also pursues birds and is capable of catching Swifts and swallows in the air. Occasionally hunts by watching from a perch and swooping to the ground in a shrike-like manner.

Habitat and Status A rare but annual spring and autumn passage migrant from Europe. Most records refer to eastern, south-eastern and south-western counties, with most being recorded on headlands and islands. Also found inland over marshes, lakes and open farmland with scattered trees.

Peregrine Falcon *Falco peregrinus* Fabhcún gorm   38-49cm

A powerful, stocky, heavy-chested falcon with broad, pointed wings. **Adults** show a thick, blackish moustachial stripe, a dark crown, and a white face and throat. Upperparts bluish-grey. Darker tail shows dark bars. Underparts white with fine, delicate barring. In flight underwing shows heavy barring on flight feathers and coverts. Undertail pale with dark bars. Cere and legs yellow. **Females** larger. **Immatures** show pale-fringed, brownish upperparts, a dark moustachial stripe, and heavy streaking on creamy underparts. Dark uppertail shows pale bars. Undertail as adult. Underwing heavily barred. Cere bluish. Legs yellow. Soars on stiff, slightly bowed wings.

Voice & Diet At the nest gives loud, repeated, chattering, *keyak-keyak-keyak* calls. Hunts by climbing to a great height and circling before diving at enormous speeds with wings held tight into the body. Feeds on birds and mammals up to the size of rabbits.

Habitat and Status A widespread, resident breeding species found in all counties. Frequents coastal and mountainous regions, nesting on cliff edges. Occasionally nests on high-rise buildings in cities. In winter most leave upland breeding areas, moving to coastal estuaries and mudflats.

Gyr Falcon *Falco rusticolus* Fabhcún mór   55-60cm

A powerful falcon, larger and heavier than Peregrine, with broader, longer wings. **White phase birds** show a white plumage, light upperpart barring, dark wing tips and faint underpart spotting. **Dark phase birds** resemble Peregrine but show a diffuse moustachial stripe, greyish-brown upperparts, pale, streaked nape and forehead, and heavy, dark underpart spotting and barring. Heavily barred and spotted underwing coverts contrast with pale, faintly barred flight feathers. **Grey phase birds** are intermediate between light and dark phases. Cere and legs yellow. **Immatures** as adults but show clear moustachial stripes and underpart streaking. Cere and legs bluish.

Voice & Diet Silent in Ireland. Hunts low over the ground, gliding on slightly bowed wings and flying with shallow wing beats. Takes a wide range of bird species as well as mammals like rabbits and hares.

Habitat and Status A very rare vagrant from Greenland, Iceland and Scandinavia, recorded in coastal counties in all provinces. Most sightings involve white-phase-type birds. Usually found in winter, but also reported in early spring. Frequents open country, rocky sea cliffs and islands, mudflats, estuaries and saltmarshes.

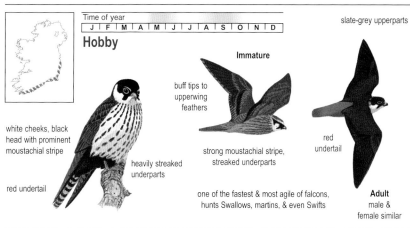

Hobby

Time of year
J F M A M J J A S O N D

slate-grey upperparts

Immature

buff tips to upperwing feathers

white cheeks, black head with prominent moustachial stripe

red undertail

heavily streaked underparts

strong moustachial stripe, streaked underparts

red undertail

one of the fastest & most agile of falcons, hunts Swallows, martins, & even Swifts

Adult
male & female similar

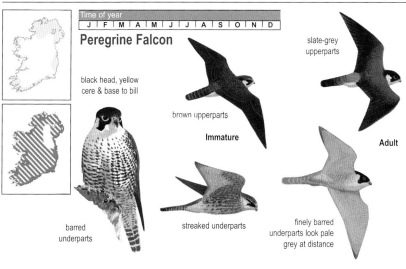

Time of year
J F M A M J J A S O N D

Peregrine Falcon

slate-grey upperparts

black head, yellow cere & base to bill

brown upperparts

Immature

Adult

barred underparts

streaked underparts

finely barred underparts look pale grey at distance

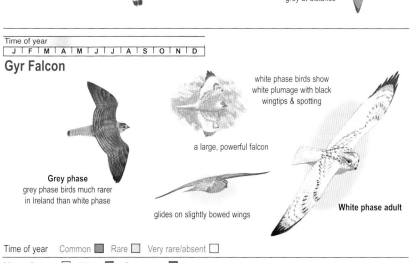

Time of year
J F M A M J J A S O N D

Gyr Falcon

white phase birds show white plumage with black wingtips & spotting

a large, powerful falcon

Grey phase
grey phase birds much rarer in Ireland than white phase

glides on slightly bowed wings

White phase adult

Time of year Common ■ Rare ☐ Very rare/absent ☐

Maps Summer ☐ Winter ■ On passage ▨

71

Gamebirds

Red Grouse *Lagopus lagopus* Cearc fhraoigh   33-40 cm

A dark, plump bird showing a stout, short bill and short, rounded wings. Usually only seen when flushed. **Summer males** show a deep red-brown plumage with heavy, dark barring, white-feathered legs and a bright red comb above the eye. **Winter males** appear darker. **Females** smaller, and show a yellower plumage with coarse barring and spotting, and lack red comb. **Immatures** similar to females, but lack red combs and show a duller plumage. Flushes noisily from the ground, flying with rapid, whirring wing beats and long glides on bowed wings.

Voice & Diet When disturbed gives a fast, cackling *kowk-ko-ko-ko* call. During the breeding season Red Grouse engage in displays which involve the distinctive, crowing *go-bak, go-bak, go-bak-bak-bak-bak* call. Feeds on heather shoots, flowers, seeds, berries, buds and some insects.

Habitat and Status A scarce but widespread resident breeding species. Found on upland blanket bog, low-lying bogs, open moorland and heather slopes. Numbers appear to be gradually declining due to habitat loss. Nests in cover of heather, rushes and tussocks on the ground.

Grey Partridge *Perdix perdix* Patraisc   29-32cm

A shy, rotund species which shows short, rounded wings and a short, bright rufous tail. **Males** show an orange-red face, a grey neck and upper breast, a brown crown and nape, and pale streaking and dark spotting on brown upperparts. Pale lower breast shows a conspicuous, inverted dark chestnut 'horseshoe', while buff-washed flanks show chestnut barring. **Females** similar, but show a paler face, browner upperparts and a buff-grey breast. The inverted chestnut horseshoe is usually reduced to blotches on the lower breast and, on some birds, may be totally absent. Short, stout bill and legs greyish. Flies with rapid, whirring wing beats and glides on bowed wings.

Voice & Diet When alarmed Grey Partridge can give a slow, cackling *krikric-ric-ric-ric* call while the song consists of loud, hoarse *kirr-ic, kirr-ic* notes. Feeds on a wide variety of seeds, grain, roots, fruit, small insects and, occasionally, slugs and worms.

Habitat and Status A rare, resident breeding species present in the wild only in the midlands. Found on bogs, moorlands and pastures with hedgerow borders or overgrown verges. Also found in wheat and corn-growing areas. A reintroduction programme has resulted in an increase in the population in the midland region. Nests in dense cover on the ground.

Pheasant *Phasianus colchicus* Piasún   53-89cm

A large, striking species showing a very long, barred tail. **Males** show a metallic blackish-green head, bright red facial skin and small tufts on rear of crown. Some can show a white collar and eyebrow. Plumage copper-red with black crescents on underparts, and black and white fringes on upperparts. Short, rounded wings greyish-brown. In flight shows a grey rump and a long, barred buff tail. Small bill ivory-white. **Females** show a shorter tail, a buff-brown plumage with dark barring and spotting on the breast, flanks and upperparts. **Immatures** resemble short-tailed, dull females. Flushes noisily, flying with rapid, whirring wing beats and gliding on bowed wings.

Voice & Diet Males give distinctive, far-carrying, resonant, choking *korrk-kook* calls and a repeated *kutok, kutok* note. When disturbed females can give whistling-type notes. Feeds on a wide range of plant material, including roots, seeds, fruit, berries, leaves and stems. Will also take insects, worms, slugs and occasionally small rodents and amphibians.

Habitat and Status An extremely common, widespread, resident breeding species found in all counties. Frequents agricultural lands, rough pastures, woodlands and upland scrub. Nests on the ground in dense cover. First introduced into Ireland from Asia in the 16th century.

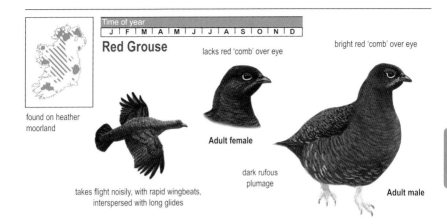

Red Grouse

Time of year

| J | F | M | A | M | J | J | A | S | O | N | D |

found on heather moorland

lacks red 'comb' over eye

bright red 'comb' over eye

Adult female

dark rufous plumage

takes flight noisily, with rapid wingbeats, interspersed with long glides

Adult male

Grey Partridge

Time of year

| J | F | M | A | M | J | J | A | S | O | N | D |

only one population left in Ireland, at Boora Bog, Co. Offaly

orange face

rufous tail, rapid, whirring wingbeats

Adult

dark chestnut horseshoe on lower breast

Adult

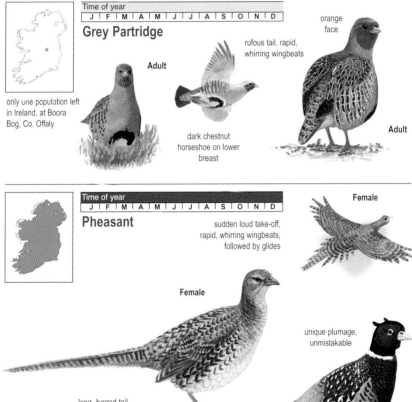

Pheasant

Time of year

| J | F | M | A | M | J | J | A | S | O | N | D |

sudden loud take-off, rapid, whirring wingbeats, followed by glides

Female

Female

unique plumage, unmistakable

long, barred tail

Male

Time of year   Very common ■   Common ■   Rare □

Maps   Resident ■

73

Gamebirds, Rails & Crakes

Quail *Coturnix coturnix* Gearg   17-19cm

A tiny, elusive gamebird, more often heard than seen. **Adult males** show a whitish central crown-stripe, a dark crown and a whitish supercilium. Whitish throat shows a black central stripe and lower border. Underparts sandy rufous with warmer smudges on breast and black-edged, pale streaking on the flanks. Upperparts dark with buff barring and black-edged, whitish streaks which are very conspicuous in flight. Tail brownish, short and appears pointed. **Females** show unmarked pale throats, brown and cream head markings, and dark spotting on breast. Bill short. When flushed, Quail fly short distances on bowed wings before dropping back into cover.

Voice & Diet Adult males give a very distinctive *kwit, kwit-wit* song which is loud, repeated and far-carrying. Quail are also ventriloquial, making their precise locations difficult to judge and can call by night. Females give a low, wheezing *quep-quep* call. Feeds on a wide range of seeds and insects.

Habitat and Status A scarce summer visitor, with small breeding populations based mostly in midland counties. Some breeding may also take place in western, northern and south-eastern regions. Seen regularly on passage on coastal headlands and islands, more frequently reported in spring than autumn. Nests in crop fields and rough pastures.

Corncrake *Crex crex* Traonach   25-27cm

Corncrakes are shy and elusive, their distinctive call often being the only indication of their presence. **Adult males** show a brown, streaked crown with blue-grey cheeks and supercilium, and a chestnut eye-stripe. Breast buffish-grey with chestnut smudges on breast sides. Flanks show chestnut, white and thin black barring, fading on undertail. Upperparts show yellow-buff and greyish edges to dark-centred feathers. Wings bright chestnut, striking in flight. Short tail yellow-buff. **Females** show less grey in plumage. Short bill and legs yellow-brown. Prefers to run through thick cover, dropping quickly back into cover if flushed. Flight weak and floppy, with legs dangling.

Voice & Diet Males give a very distinctive, loud, rasping *kerrx-kerrx* call which is repeated. Tends to call more frequently at night, but will call during the day. Feeds on seeds, plants and invertebrates.

Habitat and Status Formerly an extremely common summer visitor but now a very rare breeding species, with birds present in small numbers in the midlands and in some areas of the south-west, west and north-west. Found in rough pastures, meadows, flooded meadows and crop fields.

Spotted Crake *Porzana porzana* Gearr breac   21-24cm

A shy bird with a short, yellow bill showing a red base and an olive tip. Legs pale olive-green. **Adult males** show a dark, streaked crown, white spotting on rear of blue-grey supercilium and throat, and black lores. Breast brownish-grey with heavy, white spotting. Flanks strongly barred brown and white with thin black edges, fading on belly. Undertail buffish. White spotting extends onto upperparts which show dark-centred feathers with greyish-brown and white edges. Tail short, and can be held cocked. **Adult females** tend to show more extensive spotting on face. **Immatures** show white spotting on a brownish-buff head and breast, a whitish throat and a dark bill with a paler base.

Voice & Diet Gives a clear, loud, whistling *whett* call which is delivered in an explosive manner. The call is usually repeated, with birds tending to call more frequently at dusk and at night. Feeds on a wide range of plants, seeds and invertebrates.

Habitat and Status A very uncommon visitor from Europe, Spotted Crakes may occasionally breed in Ireland. Most reports refer to autumn, with small numbers recorded in song in spring and summer. Has also occurred in winter months. Frequents areas of shallow water with dense vegetation around lakes, marshes, pools and rivers.

Time of year

| J | F | M | A | M | J | J | A | S | O | N | D |

Quail

heard far more often than seen

found in grassland & cereal crops

in flight, small, plump body, longish wings

Female

lacks black throat

Male

direct flight with quick, flickering wingbeats, drops quickly back into cover

Time of year

| J | F | M | A | M | J | J | A | S | O | N | D |

Corncrake

streaked brown upperparts, grey on face

pink bill

Adult

wings bright chestnut

Adult

distinctive loud song delivered from meadow

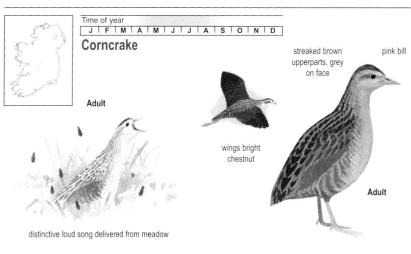

Time of year

| J | F | M | A | M | J | J | A | S | O | N | D |

Spotted Crake

yellow bill, red base

has bred in Ireland

Adult summer

white spotting on grey throat & breast

secretive, rarely showing at edges of wetland vegetation

pale olive-green legs

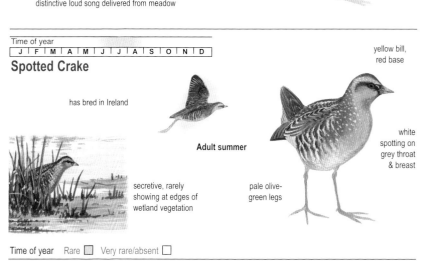

Time of year   Rare ▢   Very rare/absent ▢

Rails & Crakes

Water Rail *Rallus aquaticus* Rálóg uisce — 27-30cm

A secretive bird with a long red bill. **Adults** show dark streaking on olive-brown crown, nape and upperparts. Wing feathers olive-brown with dark centres. Face, throat and breast blue-grey with a dark line through eye. Chin white. Flanks barred black and white. Undertail white. Eye reddish with a black pupil. Legs pinkish-brown. **Juvenile** birds show a paler bill, a whitish throat, brown mottling on buff face and underparts, and brown and buff flank barring. **Sub-adults** similar to adults, but show a large whitish chin patch, a brownish face, and dark barring on grey-brown throat and breast. Walks in a slow, deliberate manner with tail cocked. Flies on rounded wings with trailing legs.

Voice & Diet Gives loud, explosive, pig-like squealing calls. Also gives a variety of grunting calls. Song is a rhythmic, hammering, repeated *kupp* call. Feeds on invertebrates, plants, berries and seeds.

Habitat and Status A widespread, common resident species, with numbers increasing in winter due to the arrival of birds from Iceland and Europe. Found in dense reed-beds, sedges and marshes, and rivers with dense vegetation. Nests in sedges, reeds and dense grass close to water.

Moorhen *Gallinula chloropus* Cearc uisce — 30-35cm

A very distinctive bird with a brightly-coloured frontal shield and bill, and a blackish plumage. **Adults** blackish-brown on head and upperparts with short, brownish wings. Underparts greyish-black with a broad, broken, white flank stripe. Undertail white with a black central stripe. Eye reddish-brown with a black pupil. Shows a bright red frontal shield and a short, yellow-tipped red bill. Legs and feet olive-green with small red 'garters' on tibia. **Immatures** show brownish upper and underparts, a whitish throat and belly, a buffish flank stripe, a white undertail and a greenish-brown bill. Swims buoyantly with a jerking head and cocked tail. Flies with rounded wings and trailing legs.

Voice & Diet Gives a throaty *kurruk* alarm call and a repeated, high-pitched *krik* call. Feeds on seeds, aquatic plants, grass, worms and insects. Seldom dives for food, preferring to pick from water surface. Can also graze on pastures, walking in a deliberate, hen-like manner.

Habitat and Status A widespread, common resident species. Found along slow streams and rivers, canals, marshes, lakes, flooded fields and ditches. Also found feeding on pastures and along hedgerows. Nests in reeds, grass, bushes or trees close to water.

Coot *Fulica atra* Cearc cheannann — 36-41cm

A distinctive, slaty-black bird with a heavy, rotund body and short, rounded wings. **Adults** show a glossy black head with a contrasting broad, white frontal shield and a white bill. Upperparts and wings greyish-black with white tips to secondaries, showing as a thin, white trailing edge to the wings in flight. Underparts greyish-black. Eye reddish with a black pupil. Legs greenish-grey with red garters on the tibia and long, lobed toes. **Immatures** show paler upperparts, a whitish face with a dark ear covert patch and a whitish neck, breast and belly. The small frontal shield and bill are greyish. Runs across the water when taking off. Flies on rounded wings with trailing legs.

Voice & Diet Gives a high-pitched, sharp *pitt* call. Can also give a loud, piping, repeated *kock* call. Feeds by diving or by grazing on land close to water. Takes a variety of insects and other invertebrates and also aquatic plants, grasses and seeds.

Habitat and Status A common, resident species. In winter populations may increase with the arrival of birds from continental Europe. Can gather in large flocks. Found on areas with open water such as lakes and reservoirs, occasionally wintering in salt-water areas. Nests in reeds, grasses and other aquatic vegetation.

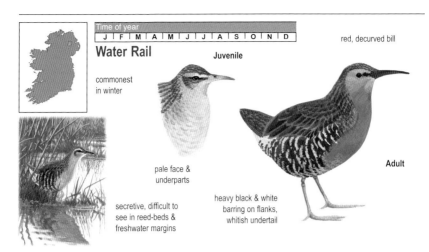

Time of year
J F M A M J J A S O N D

Water Rail

commonest in winter

Juvenile

red, decurved bill

pale face & underparts

Adult

secretive, difficult to see in reed-beds & freshwater margins

heavy black & white barring on flanks, whitish undertail

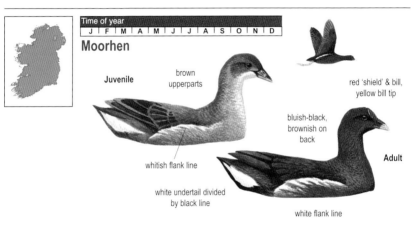

Time of year
J F M A M J J A S O N D

Moorhen

Juvenile

brown upperparts

red 'shield' & bill, yellow bill tip

bluish-black, brownish on back

Adult

whitish flank line

white undertail divided by black line

white flank line

Time of year
J F M A M J J A S O N D

Coot

dark crown & ear coverts

sooty grey upperparts

thin, white trailing edge to secondaries

white 'shield' on forehead, white bill

Juvenile

Adult

slaty-black plumage

Waders

Oystercatcher *Haematopus ostralegus* Roilleach   40-45cm

A noisy, stocky, black and white wader, best recognised by the long, orange bill, which is tipped yellowish. **Summer adults** show a black head and breast, with black upperparts showing a white wingbar, obvious in flight. Underparts white. White tail shows a black subterminal band. White rump extends as a conspicuous white wedge onto back. **Winter adults** show a white band from the throat to the sides of the neck. Adults have red eyes and an orange-red eye-ring. Stout legs are flesh-pink on adults. **Immatures** show browner upperparts, a duller bill, a white neck band, yellowish eye-rings and greyish legs.

    Voice & Diet Oystercatchers give a loud, sharp *peik*, sometimes finished with *kapeik* in flight. In song, or when disputing feeding territories, these notes develop into long, loud, trilling calls. Probes for worms on tidal mudflats or fields. Also feeds on molluscs which are either prised or hammered open.

    Habitat and Status A very common species, primarily found on coastal estuaries and mudflats. Can form large flocks in winter. Nests in scrapes made in shingle, sand or grass, usually along coastal stretches. Rarely nests inland. In winter can sometimes be found on playing fields or farmland probing for worms. A resident species, numbers increase with wintering birds from northern Europe and Iceland.

Black-winged Stilt *Himantopus himantopus* Scodalach dubheiteach   35-41cm

An elegant, long-legged, black and white wader. **Males** show a white head with a black nape extending up onto the rear crown. The extent of the black on the crown varies greatly and some birds can show a completely white head. Mantle and wings black, with long, pointed primaries giving an elegant, attenuated appearance. Underparts and tail white. **Females** similar but show brownish tones to the upperparts. Shows a long, thin, black bill and extraordinarily long, pinkish-red legs. Usually feeds in deep water, moving with long, slow strides. In flight shows black wings, a white wedge on the back, a white tail and long, trailing legs.

    Voice & Diet The call is a short, sharp *kiyik*, repeated two or three times. This call is usually delivered in flight, when disturbed or during disputes. Feeds on insects which are picked off the surface of the water.

    Habitat and Status A very rare visitor to Ireland from southern Europe, normally seen in spring or early summer, with a few autumn records. Normally found in marshland or wetland areas with deep pools and occasionally along channels on coastal estuaries.

Avocet *Recurvirostra avosetta* Abhóiséad   41-46cm

A striking, black and white wader with a long, up-curved bill. The black forehead, crown and nape contrast with the white throat and neck. A strong black scapular stripe and thick black stripe on the wing coverts form the diagnostic black oval pattern which contrasts sharply with the otherwise white upperparts. The primaries are also black. The underparts and tail are white. The long, up-curved bill is black and the legs are bluish-grey. In flight black wing tips and black covert and scapular stripes create a striking pattern. **Males** told from **females** by neater, blacker head markings. Feeds with distinctive side-to-side head sweeps. In deep water head may be totally submerged.

    Voice & Diet Gives a loud, excited, fluty *klo-whitt* call when disturbed or alarmed. Also gives a shorter *klip* call. The sweeping feeding motion allows the sensitive bill to sift water for worms, insects and crustaceans.

    Habitat and Status An uncommon winter and spring visitor from Europe. Normally found on estuaries and mudflats as well as on shallow lagoons. Small influxes can occur in some winters.

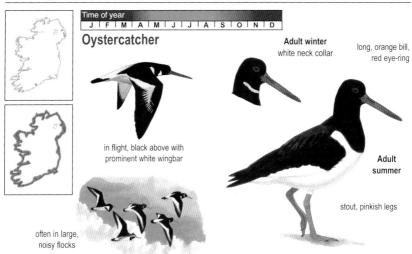

Time of year

J F M A M J J A S O N D

Oystercatcher

Adult winter
white neck collar

long, orange bill,
red eye-ring

in flight, black above with
prominent white wingbar

**Adult
summer**

stout, pinkish legs

often in large,
noisy flocks

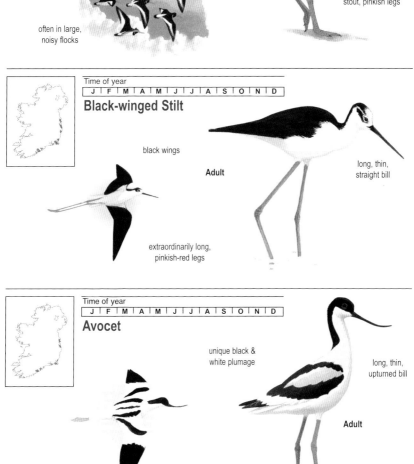

Time of year

J F M A M J J A S O N D

Black-winged Stilt

black wings

Adult

long, thin,
straight bill

extraordinarily long,
pinkish-red legs

Time of year

J F M A M J J A S O N D

Avocet

unique black &
white plumage

long, thin,
upturned bill

Adult

long, grey-blue legs

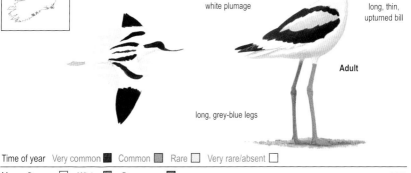

Time of year Very common ■ Common ■ Rare □ Very rare/absent □

Maps Summer □ Winter ▨ On passage ▨

Waders

Ringed Plover *Charadrius hiaticula* Feadóg chladaigh   18-21cm
Small, banded plover with a striking face pattern and bright orange legs. **Breeding adults** show a white forehead patch, a black forecrown patch, and black from base of bill onto ear coverts. White supercilium above and behind dark eye. Thin, indistinct eye-ring. White throat and collar contrasts with black breast band. Thick, short bill is orange with a black tip. Crown and upperparts greyish-brown. Underparts white. Females usually show a duller head pattern. **Winter adults** show a duller plumage and bill. **Immatures** show duller legs, a blackish bill, greyish-brown head and upperparts, and a white supercilium and forehead patch. Thin, brownish breast band usually incomplete. In flight shows a white wingbar and white sides to the rump. Tail dark.
   Voice & Diet Gives a distinctive, fluty *too-ip* call which rises in pitch. On the breeding grounds can give a trilling display song. Feeds in the typical stop-start fashion of plovers. Takes a variety of insects, molluscs and other invertebrates which are picked from the surface.
   Habitat and Status A very common coastal species found on estuaries, mudflats and beaches throughout the year. Nests in a scrape in the ground on shingle and sandy coastal beaches. In autumn and winter numbers increase with the arrival of birds from Iceland and Europe.

Little Ringed Plover *Charadrius dubius* Feadóigín chladaigh   14-16cm
A small, slim plover, with a bright yellow eye-ring and pale, flesh-pink legs. Bill short and blackish. **Summer adults** show a black forecrown patch, a white forehead patch and black from base of bill onto ear coverts. The white supercilium extends onto crown behind black forecrown patch. White collar contrasts with black breast band. Crown and upperparts greyish-brown. Underparts white. **Winter adults** duller. **Immatures** pale greyish-brown on head and upperparts, showing a thin, yellow eye-ring but lacking a clean white supercilium and forehead patch. Thin, pale, greyish-brown breast band, usually incomplete. In flight shows a uniform upperwing and white sides to tail and rump.
   Voice & Diet Gives a clear, whistling, far-carrying *pee-uu* call, which, unlike Ringed Plover, descends in pitch. Feeds on a variety of insects and molluscs which are picked from the surface of the ground.
   Habitat and Status A rare but regular visitor from Europe, with most records from spring, summer and autumn. Has bred in Ireland and has also been recorded in winter. Found on mudflats and coastal lakes but, when breeding, found at inland locations such as gravel pits and shingle banks close to fresh water.

Kentish Plover *Charadrius alexandrinus* Feadóigín chosdubh   14-17cm
Small, short-necked plover with a slender, black bill and blackish-grey legs. **Summer adult males** show a thin black line from base of bill onto ear coverts and a black forecrown patch. A white forehead patch extends back to form a broad white supercilium. Crown and upperparts sandy-brown with a rufous patch on nape. White collar contrasts with thin, black breast patches. Underparts white. **Females** and **winter males** show sandy-brown breast patches and brown face markings, lacking any rufous tones. **Immatures** similar to females, but show pale edges to upperpart feathers. In flight shows a white wingbar and extensive white on sides of tail.
   Voice & Diet Gives a sharp but soft *twit* call in flight. When alarmed can give a hard *prrip* call. Feeds on a wide variety of invertebrates in the stop-start manner of plovers, although movements appear fast and may recall Sanderling.
   Habitat and Status A very rare vagrant from Europe with records from spring, late summer and autumn. Found on coastal estuaries, mudflats, wetlands and sandy areas usually associating with mixed flocks of plovers and waders.

Time of year

| J | F | M | A | M | J | J | A | S | O | N | D |

narrow, dull yellow eye-ring

orange bill, black tip

Ringed Plover

Adult

prominent wingbar

Adult male
(female head pattern slightly duller)

orange legs

white supercilium

Adult winter

nests on most Irish coasts (less commonly inland), on undisturbed shingle beaches

Immature

duller head pattern & bill

Time of year

| J | F | M | A | M | J | J | A | S | O | N | D |

Little Ringed Plover

small black bill

striking yellow eye-ring

small, slim

mainly a spring migrant, though has bred & exceptionally, overwintered

Immature

narrow neck collar

faint, narrow, whitish wingbar

pinkish legs

Adult male

Adult

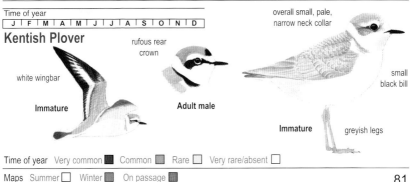

Time of year

| J | F | M | A | M | J | J | A | S | O | N | D |

overall small, pale, narrow neck collar

Kentish Plover

rufous rear crown

white wingbar

small black bill

Immature

Adult male

Immature

greyish legs

Time of year Very common ■ Common ■ Rare □ Very rare/absent □

Maps Summer □ Winter ■ On passage ▨

81

Waders

Dotterel *Charadrius morinellus* Amadán móinteach   20-24cm

A tame plover with a large black eye and a broad supercilium which meets in a V on the nape. **Immatures** and **autumn adults** show a streaked crown and a pale buff supercilium. Breast and belly buff-brown, separated by a narrow, creamy breast band. Upper breast streaked. Upperpart feathers show pale fringes, warmer buff on immatures. In flight wings appears uniform. Underwing pale. **Summer adults** show a black crown and a white supercilium and throat. A blue-grey neck and upper breast is separated from the chestnut-brown of the lower breast and upper belly by a white breast band. Belly black, undertail white. Upperpart feathers show buff fringes. **Females** show brighter plumage than males in summer. Short bill, dark. Legs yellowish.

   Voice & Diet Usually silent but can give a soft, repeated *peet* call or a trilling alarm call. Feeds on a wide variety of insects, including flies, spiders and beetles.

   Habitat and Status A rare but regular visitor from Europe. Can occur in mountainous regions on spring migration. Most records refer to autumn, when birds are found on coastal islands and headlands, or on short grassy areas along coast. Usually very tame but excellent camouflage can make Dotterels difficult to find at times.

Lapwing *Vanellus vanellus* Pilibín   29-33cm

A distinctive plover with a broad, dark breast band. **Summer males** show a long crest with black on the crown and face. Chin and throat black, meeting breast band. Neck white. Nape dark. Upperparts deep green with copper sheens. **Females** show white flecking on chin and throat, a shorter crest and duller upperparts. Underparts white. Undertail orange-buff. **Winter adults** show white chin and throat, black patches on a buff face, and buff tips to some wing feathers. **Immatures** similar but show a shorter crest and buff fringes to upperpart feathers. Flight bouyant with dark, rounded upperwings, and striking black and white underwings. Tail white with a black subterminal band. Legs pinkish-red. Bill dark.

   Voice & Diet Gives a distinctive, loud, bubbling *pee-wit* call. On the breeding grounds gives a repeated *perr-u-weet-weet* call often delivered during flight displays. Feeds on a variety of invertebrates, insects and seeds.

   Habitat and Status A common bird, found on grasslands and wetlands. In recent years breeding numbers have decreased due to habitat loss. The nest consists of a simple scrape in the ground. In winter populations increase with the arrival of birds from northern Britain and Europe. In winter found on coastal mudflats and estuaries as well as on inland grasslands and ploughed fields.

Killdeer *Charadrius vociferus* Feadóg ghlórach   23-27cm

A long-tailed plover with two blackish breast bands. **Males** show a black forecrown, a white forehead patch which continues under eye, black from the base of the bill onto ear coverts, an orange-red eye-ring and a whitish supercilium behind the eye. Crown and nape brown. White collar contrasts with nape and breast bands. Underparts white. Upperparts brown with long wings. **Females** duller. **Immatures** lack the black on the face and show pale fringes to the upperpart feathers. In flight shows a white wingbar and a bright rust-orange rump. Long tail rust-orange with white edges, a darker centre and a black subterminal band. Bill long and blackish. Legs greyish-pink.

   Voice & Diet Gives a very distinctive, loud, far-carrying *kill-dee* call from which the bird derives its name. Feeds on a variety of insects, molluscs and crustaceans.

   Habitat and Status An extremely rare autumn vagrant from North America. Found on open grasslands or ploughed fields as well as on coastal marshes and fields. Some birds have over-wintered.

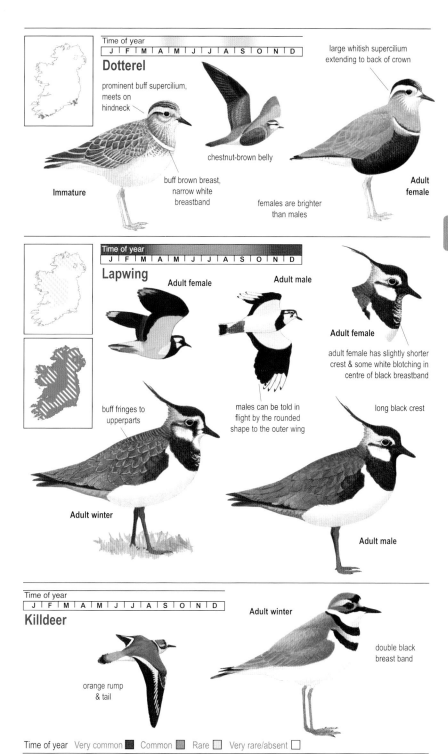

Dotterel

Time of year
J F M A M J J A S O N D

prominent buff supercilium, meets on hindneck

large whitish supercilium extending to back of crown

chestnut-brown belly

buff brown breast, narrow white breastband

females are brighter than males

Immature

Adult female

Lapwing

Time of year
J F M A M J J A S O N D

Adult female

Adult male

Adult female

adult female has slightly shorter crest & some white blotching in centre of black breastband

buff fringes to upperparts

males can be told in flight by the rounded shape to the outer wing

long black crest

Adult winter

Adult male

Killdeer

Time of year
J F M A M J J A S O N D

Adult winter

double black breast band

orange rump & tail

Time of year Very common ■ Common ■ Rare □ Very rare/absent □

Maps Summer □ Winter ■ On passage ▦

83

Waders

Grey Plover *Pluvialis squatarola* Feadóg ghlas 28-32cm
A large plover with a stout, dark bill, dark legs, and black axillaries contrasting with white underwings. **Summer adults** show a black face, breast, belly and flanks. Broad, white supercilium continues onto sides of neck and breast. Undertail white. Crown and nape pale grey. Upperparts grey with black spotting. **Winter adults** shows a large dark eye in a pale grey face, dark streaking on breast and pale grey upperparts. **Immatures** similar to winter adults, but show buffish tones to the upperparts. In flight shows a white wingbar and rump, and a barred tail.

Voice & Diet Gives a diagnostic, loud, whistling *tee-oo-ee* call. Feeds on marine molluscs, crustaceans and worms.

Habitat and Status A common winter and passage visitor from breeding grounds in western Siberia. Small numbers summer at coastal locations. Found on coastal estuaries, mudflats and beaches.

Golden Plover *Pluvialis apricaria* Feadóg bhuí 27-30cm
A large plover with a short dark bill, dark legs, gold-spangled upperparts and white underwings and axillaries. **Summer adults** show a black face, throat, breast and belly. White supercilium extends as white stripe down sides of neck, breast and onto flanks. Undertail whitish. Crown, nape and upperparts dark with gold spangling. Wing tips equal to tail length. **Immatures** and **winter adults** show pale golden upperparts, a large black eye in a yellow-buff face and dark streaking on the breast. Belly and undertail whitish. In flight shows a narrow white wingbar.

Voice & Diet Gives a rather plaintive, whistling *too-lee* call. On the breeding grounds gives a mournful *per-wee-oo* song, often delivered in flight. Feeds on insects, beetles, earthworms and other invertebrates, as well as seeds and berries.

Habitat and Status Breeds in small numbers on mountains and bogs in the west and north-west. In autumn numbers increase with the arrival of migrant birds from Europe and Iceland. Common in winter, found on inland arable lands as well as coastal mudflats and estuaries.

American Golden Plover *Pluvialis dominica* Feadóg bhuí Mheiriceánach 24-28cm
A medium-sized plover with a fine, dark bill, long dark legs, an upright, attenuated appearance, and a diagnostic dusky-grey underwing. **Summer adults** show a black face, breast, belly, flanks and undertail. Broad, white supercilium continues down sides of neck but stops abruptly on the sides of the breast. Crown and upperparts dark with pale gold spangling. Long primaries extend beyond tail but tertial length is shorter than tail length. **Immatures** and **winter adults** appear greyish on the upperparts, with a broad, white supercilium conspicuous against a dark crown. Face and breast pale grey with faint streaking. In flight shows a thin, pale wing stripe.

Voice & Diet Gives a distinctive, sharp *clu-ee* call. Feeds on insects, larvae, worms and molluscs.

Habitat and Status A rare but regular late summer and autumn vagrant from North America. Found in a variety of coastal habitats.

Pacific Golden Plover *Pluvialis fulva* Feadóg bhuí Áiseach 21-25cm
Very similar to American Golden Plover but shows a slightly longer, heavier bill, a shorter primary projection and tertials equal or slightly shorter in length than the tail. Shows a dusky, grey underwing. **Summer adults** show a black face and underparts, and a white supercilium extending down sides of neck and continuing as a white flank stripe. Flank stripe and undertail can show dark barring and smudges. Shows yellow-buff spotting on mantle and whitish spotting on wing coverts. **Immatures** more yellow-buff than immature American Golden Plover with a less contrasting head pattern.

Voice & Diet Gives a sharp *chu-iit* call. Feeds on insects, larvae, worms and molluscs.

Habitat and Status A very rare, late summer and autumn vagrant from Siberia. Found on a variety of coastal habitats.

Grey Plover

Time of year
J F M A M J J A S O N D

small numbers summer in Ireland, on some of the major wetlands

Adult winter
white wingbar & rump

stout black bill

black axillaries contrast with paler underwing

Adult summer

black legs

Immature
adults in autumn similar, but lack buffish tones

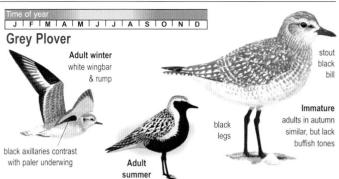

Time of year
J F M A M J J A S O N D

Golden Plover

scarce breeder on heather moorlands

gold-spangled upperparts

Adult winter

white underwing

Adult winter

Adult male summer

in summer plumage, males show the most black on underparts

Time of year
J F M A M J J A S O N D

American Golden Plover

Adult summer

black flanks

American Golden Plovers have greyer tones, more prominent white supercilium, & a slightly longer primary projection

Immature

Time of year
J F M A M J J A S O N D

Pacific Golden Plover

both American & Pacific Golden Plovers show greyish underwing

Immature

some white on flanks

Adult summer

Time of year   Common ▣   Rare ▣   Very rare/absent ☐

Maps   Summer ☐   Winter ▣   On passage ▣

85

Waders

Ruff *Philomachus pugnax* Rufachán 22-32cm

A highly variable, small-headed, medium-sized wader with a shortish, slightly decurved bill. **Males** (Ruffs) are larger than **females** (Reeves). **Immatures** are orange-buff on the head and breast, with neat pale fringes to the dark upperpart feathers giving a strongly scalloped appearance. Belly and undertail white. Bill dark. **Summer adult males** show head and neck plumes which vary greatly in colour and a pale bill, while **females** show strong but variable markings on the head, breast and flanks, and dark bills. In flight shows two white, oval rump patches, a white wing stripe and a white underwing. **Winter males** lack the head and neck plumes and show a pink base to a dark bill. Leg colour varies, from greenish on immatures to orange or pink on adults.

Voice & Diet Generally a quiet species but gives a gruff *ku-uk* call on occasions. Feeds in a Redshank-like manner, walking with deliberate strides, occasionally wading into deep water. Eats worms, insects, molluscs, crustaceans, as well as seeds.

Habitat and Status An uncommon but regular autumn visitor from Europe, with small numbers over-wintering. Found on muddy verges of coastal, freshwater or brackish pools and lakes, and occasionally on mudflats and estuaries.

Buff-breasted Sandpiper *Tryngites subruficollis* Gobadán broinn-donnbhuí 18-21cm

A tame, attractive wader with a short, pointed, dark bill, a large, conspicuous, black eye and mustard-yellow legs. **Immatures** show pale buff underparts, with a paler rear belly and undertail, a plain buff-coloured face, fine streaking on the crown and nape, and dark spotting on the sides of the breast. Buff-centred upperpart feathers have sharp whitish buff edges and dark submarginal crescents, giving a neat scalloped appearance. **Adults** similar but show darker centres to upperpart feathers and plainer wing coverts. In flight shows a plain upperwing and rump. Underwing white, with dark tips to the primary coverts forming a distinctive dark crescent. An extremely tame species preferring to crouch down or walk when approached instead of flying.

Voice & Diet Normally a quiet species, can give a low *pr-r-reet* call and, on occasions, a sharp *tic* call. Feeds in a dainty, active fashion, picking flies, insects and larvae from the ground.

Habitat and Status A rare but regular autumn vagrant from North America. Usually found on short grass or sandy areas close to coastal marshes or lakes. Rarely found feeding in water.

Pectoral Sandpiper *Calidris melanotos* Gobadán uchtach 19-23cm

A very tame wader with heavy streaking on the breast which stops abruptly on the lower breast and appears sharply demarcated from the pure white belly and undertail. The slightly decurved bill is dark with a pale base. Legs yellowish. The warm rufous crown, nape and ear coverts show dark streaking. Supercilium whitish contrasting with a dark loral smudge before the eye. **Immatures** show dark-centred upperpart feathers with warm chestnut, buff and white fringes creating white braces on the mantle and scapulars. **Adults** show duller upperparts. In flight shows white sides to rump and a faint white wing stripe. Underwing white, contrasting with the streaked breast. An extremely tame bird, easy to overlook as it feeds in wetland grass or sedges.

Voice & Diet Gives a distinctive, harsh, sharp, often repeated, loud *krrit* or *trrit* call in flight. Feeds in a deliberate, steady, head-down manner, either picking from the surface or probing. Feeds on insects, larvae, worms and crustaceans.

Habitat and Status An uncommon but regular autumn visitor from North America. Occasionally seen in summer. Found along edges of reed-fringed pools and wetlands, usually at coastal locations. Occasionally found on open mudflats.

Time of year

| J | F | M | A | M | J | J | A | S | O | N | D |

Ruff

rather plain-faced, pale lores

thin, white wingbar

neatly pale-fringed upperpart feathers

two white ovals on rump

short, decurved, black bill

Summer males

Immature male

summer males have ornate, elongated neck feathers in a variety of colours

males (Ruffs) are larger than females (Reeves)

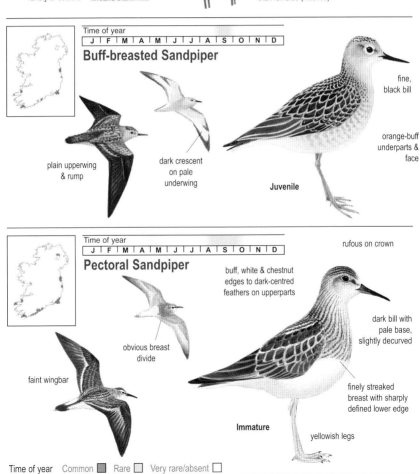

Time of year

| J | F | M | A | M | J | J | A | S | O | N | D |

Buff-breasted Sandpiper

fine, black bill

plain upperwing & rump

dark crescent on pale underwing

orange-buff underparts & face

Juvenile

Time of year

| J | F | M | A | M | J | J | A | S | O | N | D |

Pectoral Sandpiper

rufous on crown

buff, white & chestnut edges to dark-centred feathers on upperparts

dark bill with pale base, slightly decurved

faint wingbar

obvious breast divide

finely streaked breast with sharply defined lower edge

Immature

yellowish legs

Time of year   Common ▨   Rare ▢   Very rare/absent ▢

Maps   Winter ▨   On passage ▨   87

Little Stint *Calidris minuta* Gobadáinín beag   12-14cm

A tiny wader with a fine, short, black bill and black legs. **Immatures** show bright chestnut-buff edges to the upperpart feathers with white fringes to the mantle, creating distinctive, white mantle braces. A whitish supercilium extends onto the warm brown crown, creating a diagnostic split supercilium. Ear coverts and breast sides warm buff and streaked. Underparts clean white. **Summer adults** show streaking on a warm buff head and breast, a white throat, and chestnut-buff, dark-centred upperpart feathers with whitish fringes to the mantle. **Winter adults** show brown-grey upperparts and white underparts. In flight shows a narrow, white wing stripe, white sides to rump, and a dark-centred greyish tail.

Voice & Diet Gives a short, sharp, high-pitched and often repeated *stit* call. Feeds in a busy, animated fashion taking insects, worms and molluscs.

Habitat and Status A regular late summer and autumn visitor from breeding grounds in north-eastern Europe and Siberia. Occasionally recorded in winter and spring. Usually found in mixed wader flocks on coastal estuaries, mudflats or lakes.

Semipalmated Sandpiper *Calidris pusilla* Gobadáinín mionbhosach   13-15cm

A small, dull wader showing a broad, black, 'blob-ended' bill, black legs and partially-webbed toes. The dull **immature** plumage shows grey-brown upperparts with pale buff or whitish feather fringes while wing coverts show a dark 'anchor' pattern. Lacks the warm tones and the striking white mantle braces of immature Little Stint. Dark streaking on the crown combined with a clear white supercilium gives a capped effect. Dark eye-stripe. Nape and breast streaked, with a pale buff wash on breast sides. Underparts white. Bright immatures can show warm tones to the crown and upper scapulars but still appear dark capped and duller than Little Stint. **Summer adults** show greyish-buff upperparts and a streaked breast. Crown warm brown. **Winter adults** are pale grey above and white below. Narrow white wing stripe obvious in flight. White sides to rump. Some birds can show long, slightly decurved bills.

Voice & Diet Gives a short, low-pitched, hoarse *churp* call, quite different from Little Stint. Feeds in a slower manner than Little Stint, taking a wide variety of insects, molluscs and worms.

Habitat and Status A very rare autumn vagrant from North America. Usually found with mixed wader flocks on coastal mudflats, estuaries and coastal lakes.

Temminck's Stint *Calidris temminckii* Gobadáinín Temminck   12-14cm

A small, dull wader with a short, fine, blackish bill and yellow-green legs. **Immatures** show a brownish crown, ear coverts and nape, a faint supercilium, a white chin and throat, and brownish upperparts with a scaly pattern due to a unique subterminal line and buff fringe to each feather. Sides of breast buff-brown, usually joining to form a breast band. Belly and undertail whitish. Tail equal to, or just longer than, wing length. **Summer adults** show black centres to mantle and scapulars with buff and grey tips, a faint supercilium and heavy streaking on the breast and head. **Winter adults** appear pale grey above with white underparts and a grey breast band. In flight shows a short, narrow white wingbar and diagnostic white sides to the tail and rump.

Voice & Diet Gives a distinctive, short, trilling, often repeated *tirrr* call. Feeds in a slower manner than Little Stint, occasionally with a crouched profile, searching carefully for food items. Takes a wide variety of small molluscs, insects, larvae and worms.

Habitat and Status A very rare, north European autumn vagrant. Usually seen singly, Temminck's Stints rarely associate with other waders. Frequently feeds among vegetation at wetland edges, seldom feeding on open, exposed mudflats.

Time of year
J F M A M J J A S O N D

Little Stint

white 'tramlines' on mantle

split supercilium

chestnut, black & white on upperparts

Immature

tail grey with black centre

plain grey upperparts

very small compared with Dunlin (left)

short black bill

warm buff head & breast

black legs

Adult winter

Adult summer

Waders

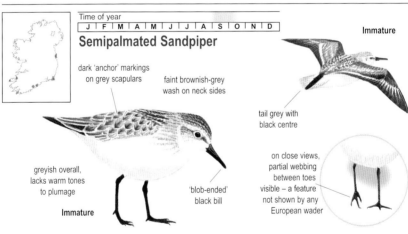

Time of year
J F M A M J J A S O N D

Semipalmated Sandpiper

Immature

dark 'anchor' markings on grey scapulars

faint brownish-grey wash on neck sides

tail grey with black centre

greyish overall, lacks warm tones to plumage

'blob-ended' black bill

on close views, partial webbing between toes visible – a feature not shown by any European wader

Immature

Time of year
J F M A M J J A S O N D

narrow, pale wingbar

Immature

Temminck's Stint

tail white with black centre

black centres to mantle feathers

scaly pattern on scapulars

tail longer than wings

short, dark bill

Adult summer

breast band

pale legs

Immature

Time of year   Rare ☐   Very rare/absent ☐

Waders

White-rumped Sandpiper *Calidris fuscicollis* Gobadán bánphrompach   15-18cm

A long-winged wader with a short, straight, slightly drooped bill. In flight shows a narrow, white wingbar and a white rump similar to Curlew Sandpiper. **Immatures** show a streaked, chestnut crown, a white supercilium and streaked, rufous-washed ear coverts. The streaked nape and breast are greyish-buff, with some diffuse spotting on flanks. Underparts white. Upperparts dark with white and chestnut fringes to dark-centred mantle and upper scapulars, and thin white mantle and scapular lines. Long primaries extend beyond tail. **Summer adults** show rufous tones to mantle and upper scapulars, heavy streaking on breast and flanks, and a pale base to lower mandible. **Moulting adults** appear dull, with pale grey upperparts often showing some dark-centred summer feathers, and dark breast streaking extending onto the flanks. Legs dark.

    Voice & Diet Gives a distinctive, high-pitched *tseet* call. Feeds in a fast manner, picking from the surface or probing for small molluscs, worms and insects. Can feed in an almost phalarope-manner, feeding in deep water and picking insects from the surface.

    Habitat and Status A rare but regular autumn vagrant from North America. Found with mixed wader flocks on coastal estuaries, mudflats, freshwater lakes and lagoons.

Baird's Sandpiper *Calidris bairdii* Gobadán Baird   14-16cm

A slim, elongated wader with a short, fine, slightly drooped black bill and blackish legs. **Immatures** show a streaked, buff-brown crown and ear coverts, and a whitish supercilium which can be broken to show as a pale spot above the lores. Buff-washed, streaked breast shows as a clearly defined breast band. Underparts white. Flanks unstreaked. Upperparts appear neatly scalloped with dark feathers fringed buffish-white. Long primaries extend beyond tail. In flight shows a very narrow white wingbar and a dark rump with narrow white edges. Tail appears dark. **Adults** show buff upperparts with broad black centres to scapulars, a heavily streaked breast and clean white flanks and underparts.

    Voice & Diet Gives a short, trilling *preeep* call. Feeds in a methodical manner, preferring to pick from the surface rather than probing into soft mud. Takes a wide variety of insects, larvae, worms and small molluscs.

    Habitat and Status A rare autumn vagrant from North America. Found on coastal estuaries, mudflats and lagoons. Although can be found with large mixed wader flocks, tends to be less gregarious than other species and is sometimes found singly or within a small flock.

Sanderling *Calidris alba* Luathrán   19-22cm

A small, hyperactive wader with a short, straight, black bill and black legs which lack a hind toe. In winter shows pale grey upperparts with a distinctive black patch on the bend of the wing and pure white underparts. **Summer adults** show bright chestnut-brown head, face and breast with dark streaking on the crown and breast. Also shows broad black and buff centres to the upperpart feathers. **Immatures** similar to adult winter, but show black spangled upperparts, black streaking on crown and faint streaking on the sides of the neck which can also show a buff wash. In flight shows a prominent white wingbar, white sides to rump, and a dark-centred grey tail.

    Voice & Diet Gives a hard, quiet, often repeated *kick* call. Feeds in a hyperactive fashion, almost recalling a clockwork toy. Takes a wide variety of invertebrates, including insects, worms, molluscs and small fish.

    Habitat and Status A common winter visitor to the coastline, arriving in early autumn from breeding grounds in the Arctic. Some non-breeding birds can be found in summer. Usually found chasing the waves up and down the beach, or feeding along the tideline on debris and seaweed washed ashore. On migration can also occur on mudflats or on coastal marshes.

Waders

Time of year

J F M A M J J A S O N D

White-rumped Sandpiper

rufous fringes

dark-centred feathers on mantle

black bill with paler base to lower mandible, slightly decurved

Immature

long primary projection

white rump

black legs

streaking extends lightly onto flanks

Adult, autumn

Immature

Time of year

J F M A M J J A S O N D

Baird's Sandpiper

scaly upperparts

pale spot on lores

fine, black bill, slightly decurved

long primary projection

unstreaked flanks

thin, pale wingbar

Immature

black legs

Immature

Time of year

J F M A M J J A S O N D

Sanderling

spangled upperparts

stout, black bill

pale, black on bend of wing

Immature

Adult winter

black legs

Adult winter

dark-centred grey tail

a common bird of sandy shorelines, often in large flocks

lacks a hind toe

Adult summer
this plumage seen in May & in August/September

Time of year   Common ▣   Rare ☐   Very rare/absent ☐

Maps   Winter ▣   On passage ▨

91

Waders

Dunlin *Calidris alpina* Breacóg 16-19cm

A small wader with black legs and a blackish bill, decurved at the tip. Dunlin vary greatly in size, plumage and bill length. **Winter adults** show greyish-brown upperparts, white underparts and faint streaking on the breast. **Summer adults** show a striking black belly patch and rufous edges to mantle and scapular feathers. The brightness of the upperparts can vary. Crown and nape warm buff, with heavy streaking on the breast. **Moulting adults** show a mixture of both plumages. **Immatures** show black centres to mantle and scapular feathers with warm buff fringes and white edges forming narrow white braces. Wing coverts fringed buff. Breast shows a diffuse buff wash and dark streaking extending onto belly and flanks as dark spotting. In flight shows a white wingbar, white sides to rump and a dark-centred greyish tail.

Voice & Diet Gives a distinctive, sharp *treep* call in flight. On the breeding grounds the song consists of a purring trill. A fast, active feeder, probing and picking off the surface. Feeds on molluscs, worms, insects and crustaceans.

Habitat and Status Common in autumn and winter, with a small breeding population in the midlands, west and north-west. Winters on estuaries, mudflats and coastal lakes. Nests in grass and tussocks on marshes, bogs and wetlands.

Curlew Sandpiper *Calidris ferruginea* Gobadán crotaigh 18-20cm

A slender wader with a long, slightly decurved bill and black legs. **Immatures** show neatly scalloped upperparts with pale fringes to the feathers and a well-defined supercilium. Underparts clean, creamy white, with a delicate peach wash on breast sides. **Adult summers** show chestnut-red underparts, neck and head with scapulars and mantle feathers showing black centres with pale and rufous fringes. Wing coverts appear greyish. **Moulting adults** can show blotchy red underparts and some dark-centred upperpart feathers. **Winter birds** are greyish-brown above and white below, with a strong supercilium. In flight shows a white rump, a dark tail and a white wingbar.

Voice & Diet Gives a rippling, gentle *chirrup* call. Feeds by probing or picking from the surface. Takes a variety of worms, molluscs, crustaceans and insects.

Habitat and Status A regular autumn visitor from breeding grounds in Siberia. Occasionally seen in large numbers, with wintering birds sometimes reported. Found on coastal lakes, estuaries and mudflats. Curlew Sandpipers can associate with Dunlin flocks but have a tendency to feed in deeper water, making them more noticeable when in large, mixed flocks.

Broad-billed Sandpiper *Limicola falcinellus* Gobadán gobleathan 16-18cm

A small wader, with a long, black bill which shows a kink at the tip, and short, dark legs. **Immatures** show neatly patterned upperparts with rufous and creamy fringes to dark-centred feathers and obvious scapular and mantle stripes. Broad, creamy-white supercilium is split before the eye and extends onto crown to form lateral crown stripe. **Summer adults** show a heavily streaked breast and spotted flanks, a dark crown, dark upperparts with pale and buff edges to the feathers, and a contrasting split supercilium. **Winter adults** grey above and white below. In flight shows a narrow white wingbar, white sides to rump and a dark-centred greyish tail.

Voice & Diet Gives a distinctive, hard, trilling *chr-rr-eek* call in flight. Feeds by picking from the surface or probing in soft mud. Takes small molluscs, insects, worms and crustaceans.

Habitat and Status A very rare autumn vagrant from breeding grounds in northern Europe. Found on coastal lake edges, estuaries, mudflats and saltmarshes.

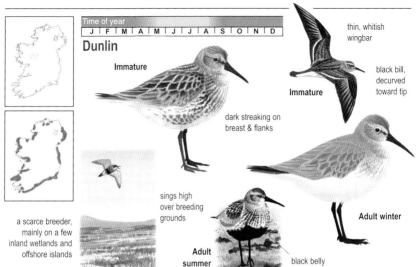

Dunlin

Time of year
J F M A M J J A S O N D

Immature

thin, whitish
wingbar

Immature

black bill,
decurved
toward tip

dark streaking on
breast & flanks

a scarce breeder,
mainly on a few
inland wetlands and
offshore islands

sings high
over breeding
grounds

**Adult
summer**

black belly

Adult winter

Curlew Sandpiper

Time of year
J F M A M J J A S O N D

white rump

well-defined pale
supercilium

black-centred
feathers on
mantle

neatly scalloped
upperparts

longish,
decurved bill

**Adult
winter**

buff wash
on breast

blotchy red
underparts

Adult
this plumage seen in
late July/August

longish,
black legs

Immature

Broad-billed Sandpiper

Time of year
J F M A M J J A S O N D

split supercilium

dark upperparts,
thin, whitish
wingbar

Immature

short, dark legs

long, black bill,
down-curved
at tip

Time of year   Common ▇   Rare ▢   Very rare/absent ▢

Maps   Summer ▢   Winter ▇   On passage ▨

93

Waders

Knot *Calidris canutus* Cnota   14-27cm

A medium-sized wader with a short, straight, black bill and greenish legs. **Winter adults** are plain grey on the upperparts with pale fringed feathers. The underparts are whitish, with streaking on a grey-washed breast, and barring on the flanks. **Immatures** similar, but show a buff wash on the breast, yellow-green legs and buffish-grey upperpart feathers appearing scalloped due to pale buff fringes and dark subterminal crescents. **Summer adults** show chestnut-red face and underparts, with thin dark streaking on the sides of the breast and a barred whitish undertail. Upperparts show black-centred feathers with rufous and buff fringes. In flight shows a narrow white wingbar, a pale rump and uppertail, and a greyish tail.

    Voice & Diet Gives a soft *knut* call but tends to call less than other wader species. Feeds in flocks, probing or picking from the surface. Eats a variety of molluscs, crustaceans, worms and insects, but can occasionally take vegetable matter.

    Habitat and Status A common autumn and winter visitor from breeding grounds on the high Arctic regions of Greenland, Canada and Iceland. Found on coastal estuaries, mudflats and saltmarshes.

Purple Sandpiper *Calidris maritima* Gobadán cosbhuí   17-21cm

A tame, rather drab wader with a long, slightly decurved, yellow-based dark bill and orange-yellow legs. **Winter adults** show a dark grey head and upperparts, with a faint purple gloss on scapulars and mantle, and greyish fringes to the coverts. Throat and breast dark grey with streaking on breast extending onto flanks. Belly and undertail white. **Immatures** show rufous tones on the crown, a faint supercilium and dark upperpart feathers with whitish and buff fringes. **Summer adults** show a brown crown, a white supercilium, a heavily streaked, brown-washed breast, and dark spots on flanks. Dark-centred upperpart feathers show chestnut and white fringes. In summer legs duller greenish-yellow. In flight shows a striking white wingbar, white sides to the rump and a dark-centred greyish tail.

    Voice & Diet Gives a short, twittering *wheet* call when disturbed. Feeds on a variety of insects, molluscs and crustaceans which are found on rocky shorelines.

    Habitat and Status An uncommon winter visitor from breeding grounds in Greenland, Iceland and northern Europe. Found along rocky shorelines, occasionally searching for prey items among seaweed. They can be extremely tame and this, as well as their coloration, can make them easy to overlook. Often found feeding with flocks of Turnstones.

Turnstone *Arenaria interpres* Piardálaí trá   21-24cm

A small, stocky wader with a stubby, dark bill and orange-yellow legs. **Summer males** show a white head with black crown streaking and a black line from forehead, through eye, down to broad, black breast band. White neck collar contrasts with breast band. Mantle and scapulars blackish, contrasting with chestnut upperparts. Underparts white. **Females** similar, but show rufous tones to head. **Winter adults** show a duller plumage with a brownish-grey head and upperparts, a dark breast band and white underparts. **Immatures** similar to winter adults, but show buff edges to dark brownish upperpart feathers. In flight shows blackish tail with a contrasting white uppertail, rump and back. Wings dark with a white wingbar and inner coverts. Underwing white.

    Voice & Diet When disturbed gives a rolling *tuk-i-tuk* call, with shorter *tuk* calls given when in feeding parties. Feeds by turning over stones or tossing seaweed aside in search of food items. Will take insects, worms, crustaceans and also carrion.

    Habitat and Status A very common passage migrant and winter visitor from breeding grounds in Greenland, Iceland and northern Europe. Found feeding in parties along rocky coasts and shorelines with stones and seaweed. Also frequents harbours and piers.

J F M A M J J A S O N D

Knot

narrow white wingbar

Adult winter

greyish tail

small numbers of non-breeding birds are usually present throughout summer on larger wetlands

Adult summer

chestnut-red underparts

greenish legs

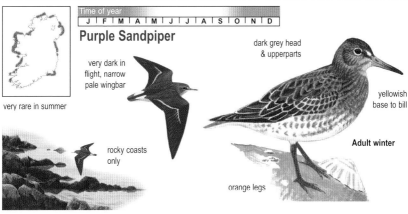

J F M A M J J A S O N D

Purple Sandpiper

dark grey head & upperparts

very dark in flight, narrow pale wingbar

very rare in summer

rocky coasts only

yellowish base to bill

Adult winter

orange legs

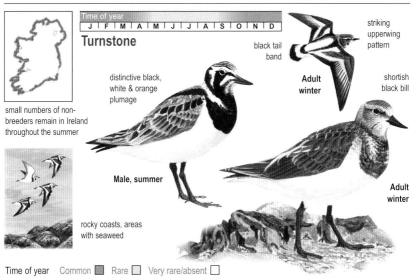

J F M A M J J A S O N D

Turnstone

black tail band

striking upperwing pattern

distinctive black, white & orange plumage

Adult winter

shortish black bill

small numbers of non-breeders remain in Ireland throughout the summer

Male, summer

Adult winter

rocky coasts, areas with seaweed

Time of year   Common ■   Rare □   Very rare/absent □

Waders

Waders

Whimbrel *Numenius phaeopus* Crotach eanaigh   40-45cm

A short-necked wader, smaller and with a shorter, more kinked bill than Curlew. **Adults** show a distinctive head pattern of a creamy crown-stripe, a dark lateral crown-stripe, a whitish supercilium and a prominent, dark eye-stripe. Cheeks, throat and neck whitish with heavy streaking. Pale breast shows heavy streaking extending onto flanks. Belly and undertail whitish. Upperparts brownish, with pale fringes and notches on feathers. **Immatures** like adults but show a shorter bill, a buff wash on the streaked breast and more clearly defined edges to the scapulars. In flight shows a coarsely marked upperwing, pale underwings, a barred tail and a white rump extending as a wedge up the back. Bill dark, occasionally with a paler base to lower mandible. Legs bluish-grey. Birds of the North American race, known as **Hudsonian Whimbrel**, differ by showing a brown rump and back, and darker, more strongly barred underwings.

Voice & Diet Gives a distinctive, whistling, rolling *ti-ti-ti-ti-ti* call which is flat-toned and delivered in a faster manner than Curlew. Feeds by probing for insects, molluscs, crabs and worms.

Habitat and Status A common spring and autumn passage migrant, moving to and from the breeding grounds of Iceland and northern Europe. Small numbers present in summer, with birds occasionally wintering. Found on estuaries, mudflats, coastal wetlands and coastal pastures. Hudsonian Whimbrel is an extremely rare autumn vagrant from North America.

Curlew *Numenius arquata* Crotach   51-60cm

A large wader with a long, decurved bill. **Adults** show a pale buff, rather plain head with an indistinct supercilium and eye-stripe. Heavy streaking on crown, nape and sides of neck extends onto breast and along flanks. Throat pale. Belly and undertail whitish. Mantle and scapulars show buff edges. Coverts show dark centres with pale edges. Secondaries and greater coverts dark with pale notches. **Immatures** similar, but show a shorter bill and buff tones to breast. In flight shows a coarsely marked plain wing with paler secondaries and greater coverts, a barred tail and a white rump extending as a wedge up the back. Underwing whitish with barring. Long bill shows a pinkish base to lower mandible. Legs bluish-grey.

Voice & Diet Gives a very distinctive, rolling, far-carrying *cour-lee* call. When alarmed gives a repeated *kyuyu* call. Feeds by probing with the extremely long bill for molluscs, crabs, worms and insects.

Habitat and Status A scarce but widespread breeding species, nesting in small numbers on moorlands, bogs, damp meadows and farmlands. Breeding occurs in most regions. Winters on estuaries, mudflats and coastal grasslands as well as on inland pastures. In winter numbers increase with the arrival of birds from Scotland, northern England and Scandinavia.

Stone Curlew *Burhinus oedicnemus* Crotach cloch   38-45cm

A striking, stocky species with staring, bright yellow eyes and a shortish, thick, yellow-based black bill. **Adults** shows a broad white supercilium and a striking white stripe below the eye. Also shows a heavily streaked brownish crown, nape and breast, and a white throat. Belly and flanks white. Undertail cinnamon-washed. Upperparts brown with dark streaking. Shows a distinctive, horizontal white covert bar with black upper and lower borders. Covert bars less striking on **females**. Tail considerably longer than wings. **Immatures** similar to adults but lack prominent supercilium and coverts bars. In flight dark outer wings show white patches and contrast with two black-edged wingbars. Sturdy, long legs yellowish. Most active at dusk and night.

Voice & Diet In flight gives a Curlew-like, *kruuee-lii* call. Feeds on a variety of inverebtrates but can take young birds, rodents and frogs.

Habitat and Status A very rare spring and summer vagrant from Europe. Found on grasslands and ploughed fields.

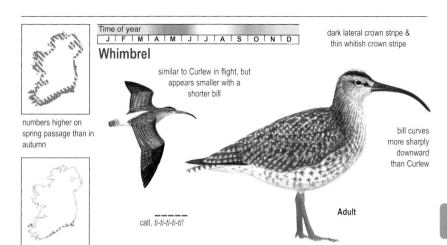

Time of year

J F M A M J J A S O N D

Whimbrel

numbers higher on spring passage than in autumn

similar to Curlew in flight, but appears smaller with a shorter bill

dark lateral crown stripe & thin whitish crown stripe

bill curves more sharply downward than Curlew

Adult

call, *ti-ti-ti-ti-ti!*

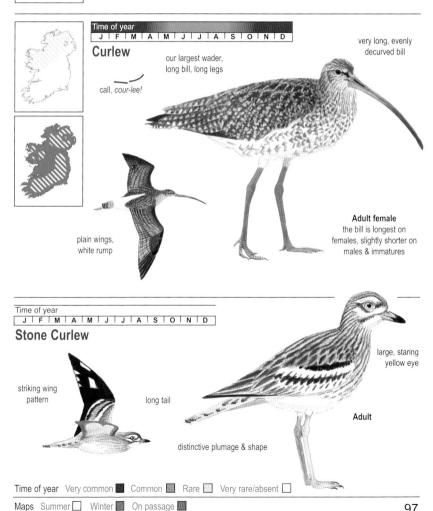

Time of year

J F M A M J J A S O N D

Curlew

call, *cour-lee!*

our largest wader, long bill, long legs

very long, evenly decurved bill

plain wings, white rump

Adult female
the bill is longest on females, slightly shorter on males & immatures

Time of year

J F M A M J J A S O N D

Stone Curlew

striking wing pattern

long tail

large, staring yellow eye

distinctive plumage & shape

Adult

Time of year   Very common ■   Common ■   Rare □   Very rare/absent □

Maps   Summer □   Winter ■   On passage ▩

97

Waders

Bar-tailed Godwit *Limosa lapponica* Guilbneach stríocearrach   33-41cm

A large wader with a long, slightly up-curved, pink-based, dark bill and dark legs. Like Black-tailed Godwit, but in flight shows plain wings, a barred tail and a white rump extending as a wedge up the back. In **winter** shows streaked, brownish-grey upperparts. Underparts white with streaking on the breast. Head brownish-grey, with a whitish supercilium, prominent behind the eye. In **summer** shows a brick-red head and underparts, a streaked crown and dark upperpart feathers with notched, chestnut edges. **Immatures** like winter adults, but show a buff wash on the breast.

    Voice & Diet In flight gives a low, barking *kirruk* call and also a short, repeated *ik* call. Feeds on lugworms, flatworms, molluscs and insects.

    Habitat and Status A common winter visitor from northern Europe. Occasionally recorded in summer. Found on sandy estuaries, beaches and mudflats in all coastal counties.

Black-tailed Godwit *Limosa limosa* Guilbneach earrdhubh   36-44cm

A large wader with a long, straight, pink-based, dark bill and long, dark legs. Like Bar-tailed Godwit, but in flight shows a white wing stripe, a black tail and a white rump. In **winter** shows unstreaked, grey upperparts. Underparts white with a grey wash on breast. Head grey with a short supercilium, prominent before eye. In **summer** shows a chestnut head, a streaked crown and a pale supercilium fading behind the eye. Throat pale orange, with dark barring on white belly. Upperparts plain grey, with some black and chestnut feathers. **Immatures** like winter adults but show a warm buff wash on the throat and breast, and warm buff edges to dark upperpart feathers.

    Voice & Diet In flight gives repeated *wikka-wikka* and short *tuk* calls. On the breeding grounds gives a loud *krru-wit-tsew* song during display flights which almost sounds like *whatta-we-do.* Feeds on worms, molluscs, insects and larvae.

    Habitat and Status A common winter visitor from Iceland and a very rare breeding species. Found on mudflats and estuaries in all coastal counties.

Long-billed Dowitcher *Limnodromus scolopaceus* Guilbnín gobfhada   28-31cm

A stocky wader with a very long, dark bill and dull yellowish-green legs. In **summer** shows a dark crown, a broad, pale supercilium and a dark eye-stripe. Dark upperpart feathers show rufous and white edges. Underparts chestnut-red, with barring on the sides of the breast onto flanks. In **winter** shows a grey crown, a whitish supercilium and a dark eye-stripe. Dark grey upperparts show pale edges to feathers. Underparts white with a grey-washed breast and barring on flanks. **Immatures** show brownish upperparts with thin, pale edges to plain tertials, white underparts and a buff wash on the breast. In flight shows plain wings, and a dark, barred rump and tail contrasting with a white wedge on the back.

    Voice & Diet Gives a distinctive, sharp *keek* call. Feeds on a variety of aquatic invertebrates.

    Habitat and Status A rare but regular autumn vagrant from North America. Can over-winter. Found on freshwater and coastal wetlands. Occasionally feeds along the shoreline.

Short-billed Dowitcher *Limnodromus griseus* Guilbnín gobghearr   25-29cm

Like Long-billed Dowitcher, but shows a slightly shorter bill, although there is some overlap between the species. **Immatures** show warmer buff underparts than immature Long-billed, and show warm edges to tertials, greater coverts and scapulars. Tertial centres barred. **Summer adults** show pale chestnut underparts, a whitish belly and dark spotting on sides of breast. In flight shows plain wings and a white wedge on back. Barred tail appears darker than tail of Long-billed.

    Voice & Diet Gives a distinctive, soft, rolling *che-tu-weet* call. Feeds on aquatic invertebrates.

    Habitat and Status An extremely rare vagrant from North America. Found on coastal wetlands and mudflats.

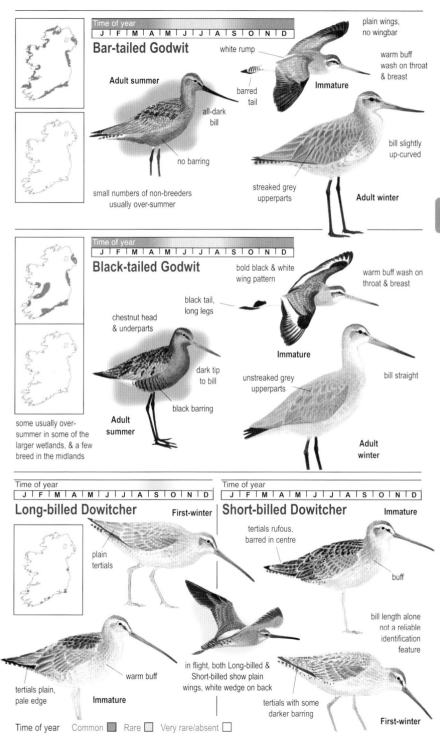

Waders

Time of year
J F M A M J J A S O N D

Bar-tailed Godwit

plain wings, no wingbar

white rump

warm buff wash on throat & breast

Adult summer

Immature

barred tail

all-dark bill

bill slightly up-curved

no barring

streaked grey upperparts

Adult winter

small numbers of non-breeders usually over-summer

Time of year
J F M A M J J A S O N D

Black-tailed Godwit

bold black & white wing pattern

warm buff wash on throat & breast

black tail, long legs

chestnut head & underparts

Immature

dark tip to bill

unstreaked grey upperparts

bill straight

black barring

Adult summer

Adult winter

some usually over-summer in some of the larger wetlands, & a few breed in the midlands

Time of year
J F M A M J J A S O N D

Time of year
J F M A M J J A S O N D

Long-billed Dowitcher

First-winter

Short-billed Dowitcher

Immature

tertials rufous, barred in centre

plain tertials

buff

bill length alone not a reliable identification feature

warm buff

tertials plain, pale edge

Immature

in flight, both Long-billed & Short-billed show plain wings, white wedge on back

tertials with some darker barring

First-winter

Time of year   Common ◼   Rare ☐   Very rare/absent ☐

Maps   Summer ☐   Winter ◼   On passage ◼

99

Waders

Redshank *Tringa totanus* Cosdeargán   26-31cm

A medium-sized, greyish-brown wader with bright orange-red legs and a reddish base to a straight, medium-length, dark bill. **Winter adults** show plain greyish-brown head and upperparts, and a white eye-ring obvious against a dark eye-stripe. Underparts pale greyish-white, with dull breast and flank spotting. **Summer adults** show heavy streaking on the head, breast and underparts. Upperparts brown, buff and cinnamon, with a variety of dark brown barring. **Immatures** show heavily streaked underparts, warm buff edges and spots to upperpart feathers, paler legs and a duller base to the bill. In flight shows all-white secondaries and inner primaries, a barred tail and a white rump extending as a white wedge onto back

Voice & Diet Gives a loud, repeated *teeuu-u* call. During display flights gives rapid, loud *ty-uu* song notes. Feeds by probing or picking from the surface, taking worms, insects, molluscs and crustaceans.

Habitat and Status A very common, resident species. Breeds in very small numbers in midland and northern regions, nesting on open, wet grasslands. In autumn and winter numbers increase with the arrival of birds from Iceland and Europe. Found on coastal estuaries and mudflats.

Spotted Redshank *Tringa erythropus* Cosdeargán breac   29-33cm

An elegant wader with long, red legs and a long, dark bill, showing a red base to the lower mandible and a slight droop towards the tip. **Winter adults** show pale grey upperparts, white underparts and a strong white supercilium contrasting with dark eye-stripe. **Summer adults** show an all-black plumage with white spots on the upperparts and white barring on flanks. **Immatures** show dusky grey-brown upperparts with white spots and edges to the feathers. Told from immature Redshank by the white supercilium obvious before the eye, the longer bill, and the underparts which appear more barred than streaked. In flight shows a plain wing with a white oval on the back, contrasting with darkish rump and tail. Legs extend well beyond the tail in flight.

Voice & Diet Gives a distinctive, sharp, loud *tch-uit* call in flight. Feeds in a very active manner, taking a wide variety of aquatic invertebrates including molluscs, crustaceans, worms and insects.

Habitat and Status An uncommon winter migrant from breeding grounds in northern Europe. Also seen in autumn and spring on passage. Found on coastal estuaries in winter, occasionally feeding in deep water. On passage also recorded on brackish coastal lakes and lagoons.

Greenshank *Tringa nebularia* Laidhrín glas   29-33cm

A large, grey and white wader with a long, slightly up-curved bill and long, pale green legs. **Winter adults** show a pale head and grey upperparts. Faint streaking obvious on nape and sides of breast. Underparts white. **Summer adults** show a heavily streaked head and breast, some flank streaking and black centres to some upperpart feathers. **Immatures** appear greyish-brown on the upperparts, with buff fringes on the scapulars and streaking on the head and breast sides. In flight shows a dark, plain upperwing, contrasting with a white rump extending as a white wedge on the back. Tail pale with faint barring and appears white at a distance. Dark bill shows a pale green base.

Voice & Diet Gives a very loud, distinctive and repeated *tue-teu-teu* call. On the breeding grounds gives a soft, repeated *teo-oo* call. Feeds in a very active manner, walking with deliberate strides, sometimes chasing prey in shallow water with lunges and sweeps. Also probes in soft mud. Takes molluscs, crustaceans, insects, worms and small fish.

Habitat and Status A common late summer, autumn and winter visitor from breeding grounds in Scotland and Europe. Very rare breeding species, nesting on open moorland. Usually found on estuaries, mudflats and saltmarshes.

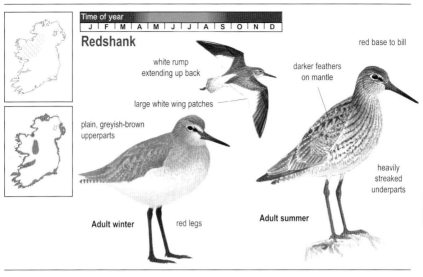

Time of year

| J | F | M | A | M | J | J | A | S | O | N | D |

Redshank

red base to bill

white rump extending up back

darker feathers on mantle

large white wing patches

plain, greyish-brown upperparts

heavily streaked underparts

Adult winter   red legs

Adult summer

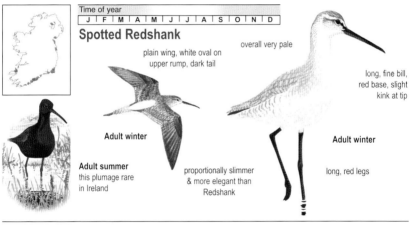

Time of year

| J | F | M | A | M | J | J | A | S | O | N | D |

Spotted Redshank

plain wing, white oval on upper rump, dark tail

overall very pale

long, fine bill, red base, slight kink at tip

Adult winter

Adult summer
this plumage rare in Ireland

proportionally slimmer & more elegant than Redshank

Adult winter

long, red legs

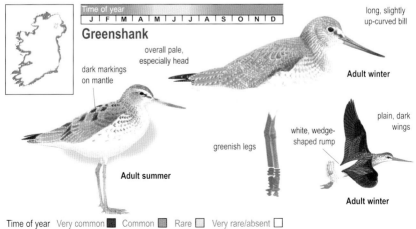

Time of year

| J | F | M | A | M | J | J | A | S | O | N | D |

Greenshank

long, slightly up-curved bill

overall pale, especially head

dark markings on mantle

Adult winter

plain, dark wings

white, wedge-shaped rump

greenish legs

Adult summer

Adult winter

Time of year   Very common ■   Common ▨   Rare ▢   Very rare/absent ▢

Maps   Summer ▢   Winter ■

101

Waders

Wood Sandpiper *Tringa glareola* Gobadán coille   19-22cm

Small, slim, elegant wader, similar to Green Sandpiper, but with a long, dark-tipped bill and greenish-yellow legs. Most sightings refer to **immatures** which show a clear white supercilium extending beyond eye, a dark brown crown with creamy streaking, a dark eye-stripe, and coarse, pale buff spotting on brown upperparts. Underparts white with delicate breast streaking and spotting. **Summer adults** similar, but show white spotting on darker brown upperparts, and heavy streaking on foreneck and breast extending as barring onto flanks. In flight similar to Green Sandpiper, showing a plain upperwing and a white rump, but differing by showing pale underwings and longer legs.

   Voice & Diet Gives a very distinctive, rapid, high-pitched, shrill *chiff-iff-iff* call, especially when flushed. Feeds in a delicate, busy manner, taking a variety of insects, larvae, worms, molluscs, small crustaceans and occasionally small fish.

   Habitat and Status A scarce but regular autumn passage migrant from north-eastern Europe. Rarer in spring and summer. Very rare in winter. Found on muddy edges of coastal lakes, pools and marshes. Occasionally found along open shoreline.

Lesser Yellowlegs *Tringa flavipes* Mionladhrán buí   23-26cm

A long-winged wader, larger than Wood Sandpiper, with a long, thin, dark bill, and long, bright yellow legs. Smaller and more elegant than Redshank. **Immatures** show a white supercilium fading above eye, white streaking on a brownish-grey crown, a white eye-ring, and brownish-grey upperparts with extensive pale spotting. White underparts show dark streaking on breast and neck. **Summer adults** show heavy streaking on head and breast. Brownish upperparts show some blackish scapular and mantle feathers, and pale fringes and spots to wing feathers. **Winter adults** show white underparts and dark speckling on pale grey upperparts. In flight shows a plain upperwing, a small, square white rump and long legs.

   Voice & Diet Gives a quiet, subdued *tu* call, usually only given once or twice in flight. Feeds in a busy, active manner, taking a variety of aquatic insects, larvae, worms, small fish and crustaceans.

   Habitat and Status A rare but annual autumn vagrant from North America. Rare in spring and summer. Some birds, arriving in late autumn, remain faithful to one area and over-winter. Found on coastal marshes, lakes, ponds, estuaries and mudflats. Often associates with Redshanks.

Greater Yellowlegs *Tringa melanoleuca* Ladhrán buí   29-33cm

A medium-sized wader, larger than Lesser Yellowlegs and similar to Greenshank. Shows a long, dark tipped, upturned bill and long, bright yellow legs. **Immatures** show a white supercilium, a streaked, dark grey crown, and extensive pale spotting on dark grey upperparts. Underparts white. Neck and breast streaked. **Summer adults** show a heavily streaked head and breast, and, unlike summer Greenshank, shows barred flanks. Dark grey upperparts show white spots and black mantle feathers and scapulars. **Winter adults** show white underparts, pale spots to grey upperparts, faint barring on flanks, and streaking on foreneck. In flight shows a plain upperwing. Differs from Greenshank by showing a square, white rump. Tail shows faint, dark streaking.

   Voice & Diet Gives a very loud, ringing, repeated *thew-thew-thew* call, not unlike the call of Greenshank. A busy, active feeder, taking a variety of aquatic invertebrates.

   Habitat and Status An extremely rare autumn and winter vagrant from North America. Has been recorded in spring. Has also over-wintered. Found on coastal estuaries, mudflats and brackish lagoons but also on inland wetlands.

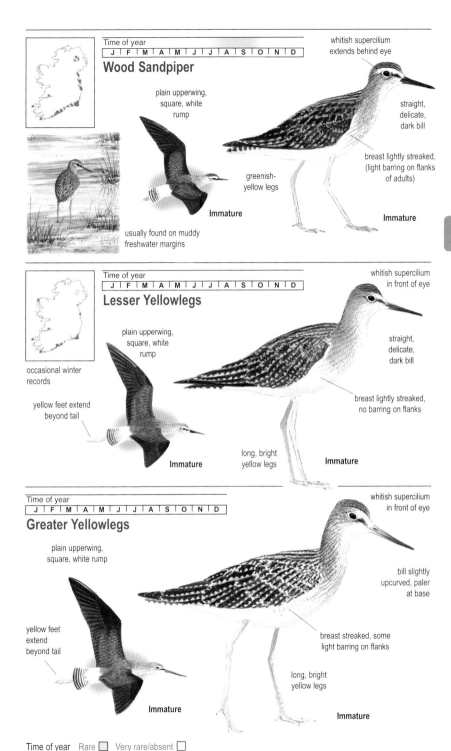

Time of year

J F M A M J J A S O N D

Wood Sandpiper

whitish supercilium extends behind eye

plain upperwing, square, white rump

straight, delicate, dark bill

greenish-yellow legs

breast lightly streaked, (light barring on flanks of adults)

Immature

Immature

usually found on muddy freshwater margins

Time of year

J F M A M J J A S O N D

Lesser Yellowlegs

whitish supercilium in front of eye

plain upperwing, square, white rump

straight, delicate, dark bill

occasional winter records

yellow feet extend beyond tail

breast lightly streaked, no barring on flanks

long, bright yellow legs

Immature

Immature

Time of year

J F M A M J J A S O N D

Greater Yellowlegs

whitish supercilium in front of eye

plain upperwing, square, white rump

bill slightly upcurved, paler at base

yellow feet extend beyond tail

breast streaked, some light barring on flanks

long, bright yellow legs

Immature

Immature

Time of year   Rare ☐   Very rare/absent ☐

Maps   On passage ▧

Waders

Green Sandpiper *Tringa ochropus* Gobadán glas   22-25cm

A stocky, dark wader with greenish legs. Straight bill shows a greenish base and a dark tip. **Summer adults** show dark greenish-brown upperparts with coarse pale spots, a dark crown, a white supercilium prominent before eye, and a white eye-ring. Neck and breast show heavy streaking. Underparts white. **Immatures** show buff spots and notches on dark upperparts and on tertial edges. **Winter adults** show darker upperparts and breast. In flight shows a square, white rump, a white tail with black barring, a plain upperwing and a dark underwing. Shy and easily flushed.

Voice & Diet Gives a loud, high-pitched, repeated *weet-twee-weett* call. Also gives loud *too-leet* notes. Feeds on a variety of aquatic invertebrates.

Habitat and Status A common late summer and autumn passage migrant from northern Europe. Also recorded in winter and spring. Found on coastal pools, rivers and brackish lagoons.

Solitary Sandpiper *Tringa solitaria* Gobadán aonarach   18-21cm

Like Green Sandpiper, but appears smaller and more attenuated. Shows pale spots on olive-brown upperparts, a prominent white orbital ring, and a short, pale supercilium. Crown, neck and sides of breast coarsely streaked. Underparts white. Dark bill shows a pale base and appears slightly decurved towards the tip. Legs greenish. In flight differs from Green Sandpiper by showing a dark rump, uppertail coverts and tail centre. Outer-tail conspicuously white with black barring. Underwings dark.

Voice & Diet Gives a soft, high-pitched, *tweet-weet* call. Feeds on various aquatic invertebrates.

Habitat and Status An extremely rare autumn vagrant from North America. Found on coastal pools, rivers and brackish lagoons.

Spotted Sandpiper *Actitis macularius* Gobadán breac   18-20cm

A small wader with a constantly bobbing tail which does not extend far beyond the wings. Legs yellowish. **Summer adults** show brown spots on white underparts and streaking on sides of breast. Upperparts greyish-brown with thin barring and streaking, a white eye-ring and supercilium, and dark lores. Pinkish-orange bill shows a dark tip. **Immatures** like Common Sandpiper, but show plain brownish upperparts and heavy buff, brown and black barring on the coverts. Unlike Common Sandpiper, shows plain edges to tertials. In flight shows a white wingbar, more extensive on outer wing than inner wing. Dark barred tail shows narrow white edges. Flies on stiff, bowed wings.

Voice & Diet Gives a quiet, piping, repeated *pett* call which can be extended to give a Green Sandpiper-like *peet-weet-weet* call. Feeds on a variety of aquatic invertebrates.

Habitat and Status An extremely rare autumn and winter vagrant from North America. Has been recorded in summer. Found on coastal estuaries and rivers.

Common Sandpiper *Actitis hypoleucos* Gobadán coiteann   18-21cm

A small wader with a constantly bobbing, long tail extending well beyond the wings. Legs dull green-yellow. Pale greyish bill shows a dark tip. **Summer adults** show brownish upperparts with thin streaking and barring, a brownish crown, dark lores, an indistinct, pale supercilium, and a white eye-ring. Underparts white, with brown streaking on sides of breast. **Immatures** show pale brown and dark edges to upperpart feathers, with pale tips and brown subterminal bars on coverts. Unlike Spotted Sandpiper, tertial edges show buff notches. In flight shows a white wingbar and trailing edge to secondaries. Tail shows faint barring and white edges. Flies on stiff, bowed wings.

Voice & Diet Gives a clear *swee-wee-wee* call. During flight displays gives rapid *kitli-weeti* song notes. Feeds on insects, larvae, worms, molluscs, tadpoles and crustaceans.

Habitat and Status A common spring and autumn passage migrant, and widespread summer breeding species. Winters occasionally. In summer found along rocky streams, lakes and rivers. On passage found on coastal wetlands.

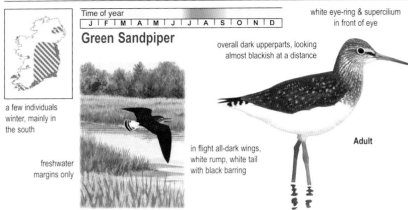

Green Sandpiper

white eye-ring & supercilium in front of eye

overall dark upperparts, looking almost blackish at a distance

a few individuals winter, mainly in the south

freshwater margins only

in flight all-dark wings, white rump, white tail with black barring

Adult

Waders

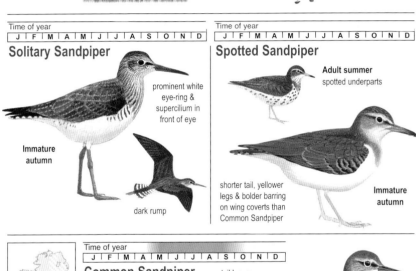

Solitary Sandpiper

prominent white eye-ring & supercilium in front of eye

Immature autumn

dark rump

Spotted Sandpiper

Adult summer
spotted underparts

shorter tail, yellower legs & bolder barring on wing coverts than Common Sandpiper

Immature autumn

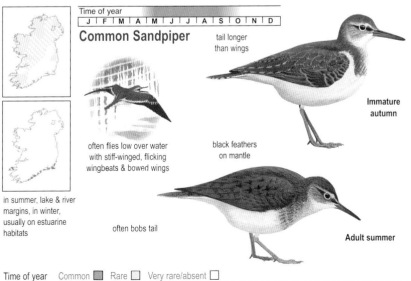

Common Sandpiper

tail longer than wings

Immature autumn

often flies low over water with stiff-winged, flicking wingbeats & bowed wings

black feathers on mantle

in summer, lake & river margins, in winter, usually on estuarine habitats

often bobs tail

Adult summer

Time of year   Common ▓   Rare ▢   Very rare/absent ☐

Maps   Summer ☐   Winter ▓   On passage ▨

Waders

Jack Snipe *Lymnocryptes minimus* Naoscach bhídeach   18-20cm

Small, long-billed wader with rounded wings and prominent golden stripes on the back. When flushed, rarely calls and flies in a straight line before quickly dropping into cover. Told from Snipe by smaller size, shorter bill, more rounded wings with a prominent, white trailing edge, prominent golden stripes on the back and darker tail. Head shows a dark crown and a dark, isolated line within a creamy double supercilium. A dark eye-stripe continues to form a dark border to ear coverts. Underparts pale, with heavy streaking on breast and flanks. Dark upperparts contrast with golden upperpart stripes. Bill pale with dark tip. Legs greenish.

Voice & Diet Usually silent when flushed, but can give a weak *gach* call. Feeds in a crake-like manner, picking off the surface. Probes less often than Snipe and, when feeding, has a habit of bobbing the body up and down. Takes insects, worms and seeds.

Habitat and Status Uncommon winter visitor from northern Europe. Found in grassy wetlands, freshwater marshes, bogs and saltmarshes. Rarely found in open water or exposed mudflats.

Snipe *Gallinago gallinago* Naoscach   25-29cm

A long-billed wader with creamy stripes on the back and crown. When flushed, usually calls loudly and flies rapidly, zig-zagging to a height before dropping back into cover a good distance away. Told from Jack Snipe by the larger size, longer bill, less prominent back stripes, less rounded wings and dark barring on a rufous tail. Head shows a creamy central crown-stripe and supercilium, and a dark lateral crown-stripe. Dark eye-stripe does not form border to ear coverts. Underparts pale, with heavy streaking on the breast. Flanks barred. Upperparts dark with creamy back stripes. Straight, dark tipped, pale brownish bill. Legs greenish.

Voice & Diet When flushed gives a loud, harsh *sccaap* call. On the breeding grounds gives a short, repeated *chic-a* call. During display flight dives with spread outer-tail feathers creating a rapid, muffled, 'bleating' sound. Feeds by probing with fast, 'sewing machine' head movements. Feeds on insects, worms and seeds.

Habitat and Status A common resident breeding species. Numbers increase in winter with the arrival of birds from the Baltic and Britain. Nests on the ground in wetlands, bogs, river and lake shorelines. In winter can also occur on coastal marshes. Can feed in deep, open water or on exposed mudflat areas.

Woodcock *Scolopax rusticola* Creabhar   32-36cm

A large, chunky bird with a long, heavy, straight bill and shortish legs. Unlike most waders, found in damp woodland areas and are usually seen at dusk and dawn. The large, black eye is set high and back in the head. The steep forehead is greyish, with broad dark and pale bars on the crown and nape. Pale supercilium contrasts with dark loral stripe. Upperparts a complicated pattern of black, buff and cream barring with a broad, creamy mantle stripe. Underparts pale with greyish-brown barring. Sides of breast show rufous tones. In flight shows broad, plain, rounded wings. Tail dark brown with pale tips. Bill shows a pale base and a dark tip. Legs pale.

Voice & Diet Usually silent when flushed, but can give a 'squeaky' call in flight. During the breeding season males give a display flight (known as roding) low over treetops, giving a low, guttural song consisting of *quorr-quorr-quorr-tsietz*. Feeds in damp woodland areas and fields, taking earthworms, insects and larvae.

Habitat and Status An uncommon but widespread breeding species, found in woodlands with open clearings. Nests in scrapes under cover of trees and bushes. Populations increase in winter with birds arriving from northern Britain and Europe.

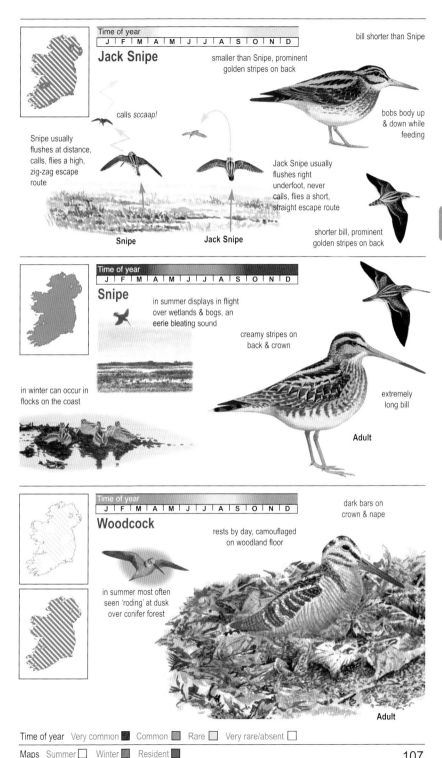

Time of year

| J | F | M | A | M | J | J | A | S | O | N | D |

Jack Snipe

bill shorter than Snipe

smaller than Snipe, prominent golden stripes on back

bobs body up & down while feeding

calls *sccaap!*

Snipe usually flushes at distance, calls, flies a high, zig-zag escape route

Jack Snipe usually flushes right underfoot, never calls, flies a short, straight escape route

shorter bill, prominent golden stripes on back

Snipe   Jack Snipe

Waders

Time of year

| J | F | M | A | M | J | J | A | S | O | N | D |

Snipe

in summer displays in flight over wetlands & bogs, an eerie bleating sound

creamy stripes on back & crown

extremely long bill

in winter can occur in flocks on the coast

Adult

Time of year

| J | F | M | A | M | J | J | A | S | O | N | D |

Woodcock

dark bars on crown & nape

rests by day, camouflaged on woodland floor

in summer most often seen 'roding' at dusk over conifer forest

Adult

Time of year   Very common ■   Common ■   Rare □   Very rare/absent □

Maps   Summer □   Winter ■   Resident ■

107

Waders

Red-necked Phalarope *Phalaropus lobatus* Falaróp gobchaol   17-19cm

An elegant wader with a fine, black bill and greyish legs. **Summer females** show a blue-grey crown and neck, darker ear coverts, a white spot above eye, a white throat, and a red foreneck extending up sides of neck to rear of ear coverts. Upperparts dark with warm buff mantle stripes and edges to wing feathers. Breast and flanks grey. Belly and undertail whitish. Tail greyish. **Summer males** drabber. In flight shows white wing stripes and sides to uppertail coverts and rump. **Immatures** show dark upperparts with prominent buff stripes, a dark buff breast, a whitish face with a dark crown, and a dark ear patch curving down behind eye. **Winter adults** pale grey above and white below, with a thin, black ear patch.

Voice & Diet Gives short, low-pitched *prek* or *whit* calls. Feeds by wading or swimming buoyantly, occasionally spinning in circles or up-ending. Takes a wide range of insects and larvae.

Habitat and Status A rare summer and autumn passage migrant from Iceland and northern Europe. A former breeding species with birds still occasionally recorded at suitable nesting sites in summer. Found in freshwater marshes with open pools and dense vegetation. Nests in vegetation. Incubation and chick rearing performed by males only. On passage found on coastal freshwater marshes. Winters at sea.

Grey Phalarope *Phalaropus fulicarius* Falaróp gobmhór   19-22cm

Small wader with a thick black bill showing a yellow base, and bluish-grey legs. **Immatures** show a dark crown, a whitish face and a square, blackish ear patch which does not curve behind eye. Whitish underparts can show a peach-tinged breast. Dark upperparts show buff edges to feathers and an inconspicuous buff mantle stripe. Some grey winter feathers can show on mantle and scapulars. **Winter adults** are pale grey above and white below with a black ear patch. In flight shows white wingbars and white sides to uppertail coverts and can recall Sanderling. **Summer adults** show completely red underparts with a white face, a dark crown, lores and chin, dark buff-fringed upperparts and a yellow bill with a dark tip.

Voice & Diet Gives a short, sharp *wit* call in flight. Feeds by swimming buoyantly, occasionally spinning, and wading. Takes a wide variety of insects, larvae, worms and, at sea, marine invertebrates.

Habitat and Status A regular autumn passage bird from Arctic regions. Can occur in winter. Rarely seen in spring. In autumn frequently seen during seawatches. Also found on coastal lakes, freshwater pools and marshes. Extremely tame.

Wilson's Phalarope *Phalaropus tricolor* Falaróp Wilson   22-25cm

An elegant wader with a long, thin bill. **Immatures** show a white head, a grey crown and a thin, dark eye-stripe which extends onto sides of neck. Underparts white, with a greyish wash on breast. Upperparts dark with pale edges but can show grey winter feathers on mantle and scapulars. Legs yellow. Bill black. **Winter adults** pale grey above and white below. In flight shows plain wings and a white rump. **Summer females** show a grey crown and nape, a white patch above eye, and a black eye-stripe extending down side of neck. Underparts white, with orange-buff on sides of neck onto breast. Upperparts grey, with chestnut stripes on scapulars and sides of mantle. Legs black. **Summer males** duller.

Voice & Diet Can give a nasal, grunting *chup* call. Swims less than other phalarope species. Takes a wide variety of insects, larvae, worms, crustaceans and seeds.

Habitat and Status A rare autumn vagrant from North America. Has been recorded in summer. Found on freshwater shallow lakes, pools, lagoons and also tidal mudflats and estuaries. Rarely seen at sea.

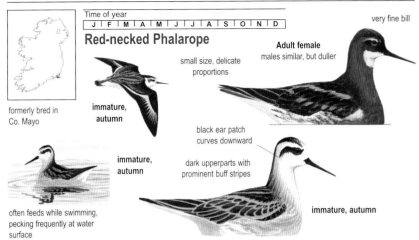

Time of year

J F M A M J J A S O N D

Red-necked Phalarope

very fine bill

Adult female
males similar, but duller

small size, delicate
proportions

**immature,
autumn**

formerly bred in
Co. Mayo

black ear patch
curves downward

**immature,
autumn**

dark upperparts with
prominent buff stripes

immature, autumn

often feeds while swimming,
pecking frequently at water
surface

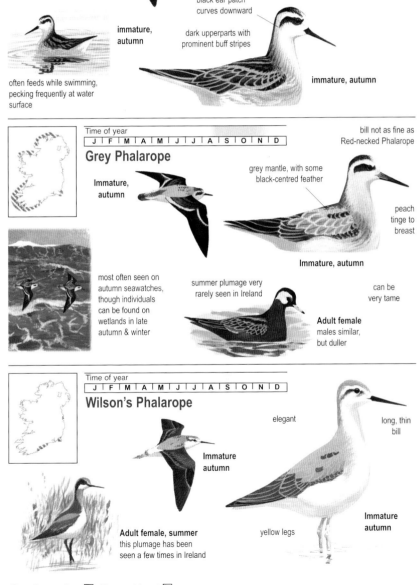

Time of year

J F M A M J J A S O N D

Grey Phalarope

bill not as fine as
Red-necked Phalarope

**Immature,
autumn**

grey mantle, with some
black-centred feather

peach
tinge to
breast

Immature, autumn

most often seen on
autumn seawatches,
though individuals
can be found on
wetlands in late
autumn & winter

summer plumage very
rarely seen in Ireland

can be
very tame

Adult female
males similar,
but duller

Time of year

J F M A M J J A S O N D

Wilson's Phalarope

elegant

long, thin
bill

**Immature
autumn**

**Immature
autumn**

Adult female, summer
this plumage has been
seen a few times in Ireland

yellow legs

Time of year   Rare ☐   Very rare/absent ☐

Waders

Skuas

Great Skua or Bonxie *Stercorarius skua* Meirleach mór   56-62cm
Adults show a dark brown crown, a yellowish-streaked brown neck, streaked brown upperparts and a dark brown tail. Greyish-brown underparts show brown streaking and barring. In flight appears deep-chested, with dark brown wings showing darker flight feathers and striking white primary flashes. **Immatures** appear darker and lack streaking. Shows a large, dark bill. Legs dark.

Voice & Diet Can give deep, guttural *tuk-tuk* calls. Feeds by chasing and attacking other seabirds until they either drop or disgorge food. Will also take fish, birds, eggs and offal.

Habitat and Status A very rare breeding species and a common passage migrant from Iceland and the Scottish Isles. Seen on passage off all coastal regions. Can occur in winter.

Pomarine Skua *Stercorarius pomarinus* Meirleach pomairíneach   43-54cm
Pale-phase adults show a yellowish face, a dark cap, whitish underparts and a dark breast band. Upperwing brown with whitish outer primary shafts. Underwing shows white crescents and dark underwing coverts. **Dark-phase adults** show dark underparts and head. Tail shows long, blunt, twisted, central tail feathers. In flight appears deep-chested with broad-based wings. Bill shows a pale base. Legs dark. **Immatures** show brown, buff-edged upperparts, a grey-brown head and barred brownish underparts. In flight shows white primary bases, double white underwing patches, barring on rump, and short, blunt, central tail feathers. Bill shows a greyish base. Legs greyish. **Second years** like adults but show barred underwings.

Voice & Diet Can give a harsh *whit-yuu* call. Feeds by chasing other seabirds until they drop or disgorge food. Also takes fish, small mammals, birds, eggs and offal.

Habitat and Status A regular but uncommon spring and autumn passage migrant from Arctic Russia. Seen on passage off all coastal counties. Can occur in winter.

Arctic Skua *Stercorarius parasiticus* Meirleach Artach   38-49cm
Pale-phase adults show a dark cap, a yellowish face, whitish underparts and a diffuse breast band. Dark, plain brown upperwings show whitish shafts to outer primaries appearing as crescents on the underwing. Rump brown. Dark tail shows long, pointed, central feathers. Can show white around base of bill. **Dark-phase adults** show all-dark underparts and head. Bill and legs dark. **Immatures** show warm brown, buff-edged upperparts and rump. Crown and underparts buff with dark barring and streaking. In flight shows white primary bases, barred underwing and undertail coverts, and short, pointed, central tail feathers. Bill shows a dark grey base. Legs greyish. **Second years** like adults but show barred underwings.

Voice & Diet Can give high-pitched *tuuk-tuuk* calls. Feeds by chasing seabirds until they drop or disgorge food. Will also feed on fish, small mammals, birds, eggs and offal.

Habitat and Status A common spring and autumn passage migrant from the Scottish Isles, northern Europe and Iceland. Seen on passage off all coastal counties. Can occur in winter.

Long-tailed Skua *Stercorarius longicaudus* Meirleach earrfhada   38-55cm
Adults show very long central tail feathers, a yellowish nape, a black cap and a whitish breast contrasting with a dusky grey belly, flanks and undertail. In flight greyish wings show a dark secondary bar and little white on primaries. Underwings dark. **Immatures** show grey-brown upperparts and wings, a black secondary bar and little white on primaries. Barred underwings show pale crescents. Nape and sides of head pale. Greyish underparts barred, heaviest on undertail. Rump barred. Dark tail shows blunt tip. Some immatures appear very dark overall. Bill shows a greyish base. Legs greyish. Seldom chases other seabirds.

Voice & Diet Usually silent in Irish waters. Feeds on fish and offal.

Habitat and Status A rare but regular passage migrant from Arctic Europe. Seen off coastal counties.

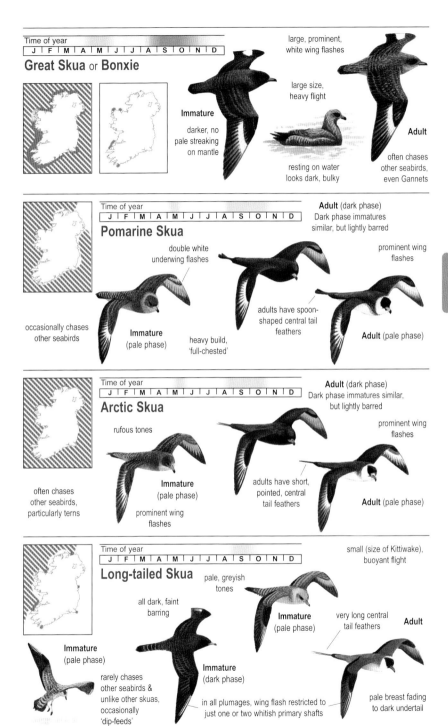

Skuas

Great Skua or Bonxie

Time of year
J F M A M J J A S O N D

large, prominent, white wing flashes

large size, heavy flight

Immature
darker, no pale streaking on mantle

resting on water looks dark, bulky

Adult

often chases other seabirds, even Gannets

Pomarine Skua

Time of year
J F M A M J J A S O N D

Adult (dark phase)
Dark phase immatures similar, but lightly barred

double white underwing flashes

prominent wing flashes

adults have spoon-shaped central tail feathers

occasionally chases other seabirds

Immature (pale phase)

heavy build, 'full-chested'

Adult (pale phase)

Arctic Skua

Time of year
J F M A M J J A S O N D

Adult (dark phase)
Dark phase immatures similar, but lightly barred

rufous tones

prominent wing flashes

adults have short, pointed, central tail feathers

often chases other seabirds, particularly terns

Immature (pale phase)

prominent wing flashes

Adult (pale phase)

Long-tailed Skua

Time of year
J F M A M J J A S O N D

small (size of Kittiwake), buoyant flight

pale, greyish tones

all dark, faint barring

Immature (pale phase)

very long central tail feathers

Adult

Immature (pale phase)

rarely chases other seabirds & unlike other skuas, occasionally 'dip-feeds'

Immature (dark phase)

in all plumages, wing flash restricted to just one or two whitish primary shafts

pale breast fading to dark undertail

Time of year   Common ▨   Rare ▨   Very rare/absent ☐

Maps   Summer ☐   Winter ▨   On passage ▨

111

Gulls

Sabine's Gull *Xemas sabini* Sléibhín Sabine   32-35cm

Summer adults show a blackish-grey hood, white underparts, rump and tail, and a yellow-tipped black bill. In flight shows a black leading edge, dark grey coverts and mantle, and white inner primaries and secondaries forming a striking white triangle. Outer primaries show white tips. **Winter adults** show a dark smudge on the head. Legs dark. **Juveniles** show a grey-brown mantle extending onto head and sides of breast, grey-brown coverts contrasting with a black leading edge and white 'triangle'. Forked tail shows a black terminal band. Bill dark. Immature Kittiwakes can resemble Sabine's Gulls but are larger, show a mostly white head, a black W on the wings and a black collar on the neck.

Voice & Diet Can give a soft, mewing-type call. Feeds on a wide range of crustaceans, molluscs, worms, small fish and insects.

Habitat and Status A rare but regular autumn passage vagrant from the high Arctic regions of Canada, Greenland and Spitzbergen. Has been recorded in winter, spring and summer. Sabine's Gulls are almost wholly pelagic, rarely being found inland. Can follow trawlers at sea.

Kittiwake *Rissa tridactyla* Saidhbhéar   38-42cm

A slender gull with long, pointed wings. **Summer adults** show a white head, underparts, rump and tail. Upperparts dark grey. In flight shows clear-cut, black wing tips and dark grey coverts fading to a white trailing edge to secondaries and primaries. **Winter adults** show a greyish hindneck and rear crown, and a dark ear spot. Bill greenish-yellow. Legs dark. Eye dark with a red orbital ring. **First-year birds** show a greyish rear crown, a dark ear spot and a black half-collar on the hindneck. In flight the greyish-white secondaries and inner primaries contrast with the black leading edges and covert bars which form a distinctive W on the wings. Forked tail shows a black terminal band. Bill dark.

Voice & Diet Gives distinctive, loud, repeated *kitti-waak* calls. Feeds on a wide range of fish, crustaceans, molluscs, worms and insects.

Habitat and Status A common, widespread breeding species present in most coastal counties. During the breeding season, found on sheer cliffs, nesting on narrow ledges. Will occasionally build nests on sides of buildings or piers. Passage movements to and from more northern European breeding areas occur in spring and autumn. In winter disperses to open oceans and seas, although small numbers are usually present in ports and harbours. Rarely found inland.

Ross's Gull *Rhodostethia rosea* Faoileán Ross   29-32cm

A small gull with a wedge-shaped tail. **Winter adults** show a grey-washed crown, dark eye crescents and ear spots, a full or partial dark neck ring, and can show a pink flush on whitish underparts. In flight slender, pale grey wings show a white trailing edge and a narrow, black leading edge. Underwings pale grey. Tail white. Legs reddish. Bill and eye dark. **Summer adults** show a black neck ring and deep pink underparts. **First-winter** birds show a greyish wash on the head, sides of breast and flanks, dark ear spots and eye crescents, and a black W across the wings formed by black leading edges and covert bars which contrast with a white innerwing and grey coverts. Tail shows a dark subterminal band. Flight buoyant.

Voice & Diet Gives high-pitched *ar-wo* and *cla* calls. Feeds on small fish and invertebrates.

Habitat and Status An extremely rare winter vagrant from Arctic regions of Siberia, Canada and Greenland. Has been recorded in spring. Usually found in coastal fishing ports and harbours, often associating with other gull species.

Time of year

| J | F | M | A | M | J | J | A | S | O | N | D |

Sabine's Gull

mostly adults are seen in July & August, mostly juveniles from September on

scaly brown mantle & forewing

grey mantle & inner forewing

usually seen in small flocks, on autumn seawatches, often with migrating Arctic Terns & Kittiwakes

Juvenile

black tail band, forked tail

black bill, yellow tip

Adult summer

although mostly seen at sea, occasional individuals are found on beaches or coastal wetlands

Adult

adults in July or early August usually have all or most of their black hood

Juvenile

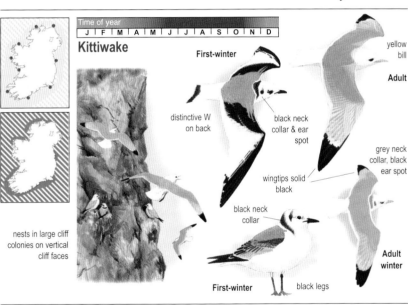

Time of year

| J | F | M | A | M | J | J | A | S | O | N | D |

Kittiwake

First-winter

yellow bill

Adult

distinctive W on back

black neck collar & ear spot

grey neck collar, black ear spot

wingtips solid black

black neck collar

nests in large cliff colonies on vertical cliff faces

Adult winter

First-winter

black legs

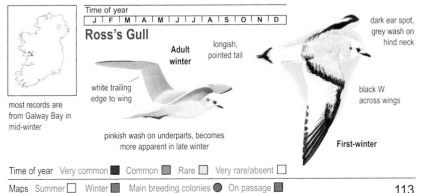

Time of year

| J | F | M | A | M | J | J | A | S | O | N | D |

Ross's Gull

Adult winter

longish, pointed tail

dark ear spot, grey wash on hind neck

white trailing edge to wing

black W across wings

most records are from Galway Bay in mid-winter

pinkish wash on underparts, becomes more apparent in late winter

First-winter

Time of year   Very common ▓   Common ▒   Rare ░   Very rare/absent ☐

Maps   Summer ☐   Winter ▓   Main breeding colonies ●   On passage ▓

Gulls

Gulls

Black-headed Gull *Chroicocephalus ridibundus* Sléibhín   35-39cm
Summer adults show a chocolate-brown hood, white eye crescents, a dark red bill and legs, and white underparts. Upperparts pale grey with black-tipped primaries. In flight wings show a white leading edge and contrasting dusky under-primaries. Tail white. **Winter adults** show a white head with a dark ear spot and brighter legs and bill. **First-winter** birds similar to adult winter, but wings show a pale brown carpal bar, a black secondary bar and a dark tail band. Like adults, wings show a white leading edge and dusky under-primaries. **First-summers** can show a dark hood. **Juveniles** warm-buff on head, hindneck, sides of breast and upperparts.

Voice & Diet Gives harsh *kuarr* and short *kwup* calls. Feeds on small fish, worms, insects, seeds and berries. Will also hawk for flying ants and insects in the air.

Habitat and Status A very common, widespread, resident breeding species found in all counties. Nests in colonies on dunes, coastal islands, moorland pools and freshwater lake islands. In winter found on inland pastures, reservoirs, and coastal estuaries and mudflats.

Little Gull *Hydrocoloeus minutus* Sléibhín beag   27-30cm
Winter adults show a white head, a blackish ear spot, a greyish crown and a blackish bill. Underparts white. Upperparts pale grey. In flight shows pale grey wings, with white-tipped primaries and secondaries forming a white trailing edge, and contrasting blackish underwings. Legs red. **Summer adults** show a black hood and a pink flush on underparts. In flight **first-winter birds** show a blackish covert bar and leading edge, forming a striking W upperwing pattern. Underwing whitish. Head as winter adult. **Second winters** as adults, but show black on wing tips and paler underwings. **Juveniles** show barring on upperparts, more extensive areas of dark on crown and face, and a dark mantle extending onto the breast.

Voice & Diet Gives low-pitched *kek* and harsher *ke-aa* calls. Feeds on a variety of small fish, molluscs, worms and insects. Will also hawk for flying insects on the wing.

Habitat and Status A scarce but regular winter and passage visitor from breeding colonies in Europe. Found on coastal lakes, marshes and harbours. Occasionally found on inland lakes.

Bonaparte's Gull *Chroicocephalus philadelphia* Sléibhín Bonaparte   28-31cm
Summer adults show a black hood, white eye crescents, a black bill, pale red legs, and white underparts. Upperparts pale grey with black-tipped primaries. In flight shows white leading edges and black edge to white under-primaries. Tail white. **Winter adults** show a white head, a neat, dark ear spot, and a grey wash on sides of breast and hindneck. **First-winter birds** as adult winter, but wings show a dark covert bar, a black secondary bar, white under-primaries and a dark tail band. Legs pinkish.

Voice & Diet Gives harsh, chattering calls. Feeds on a wide range of invertebrates.

Habitat and Status A rare vagrant from North America. Found on mudflats, harbours and coastal lakes.

Laughing Gull *Larus atricilla* Sléibhín an gháire   36-40cm
Summer adults show a black hood, white eye crescents, dark grey upperparts and black primaries with small, white tips. Underparts white. Bill dark red. Legs reddish. **Winter adults** show a cleaner head with dark shading behind eye, a red-tipped, dark bill and dark legs. **First-year birds** show a dark patch behind eye onto crown, grey on nape extends onto breast and flanks, a dark grey mantle, brownish coverts and long dark primaries. Bill and legs dark. In flight shows a dusky underwing and a tail band. **Second years** as adult winter, but shows grey wash to nape and underparts.

Voice & Diet Gives loud, harsh, laughing calls. Feeds on small fish, worms and invertebrates.

Habitat and Status A very rare vagrant from North America. Found on estuaries and harbours.

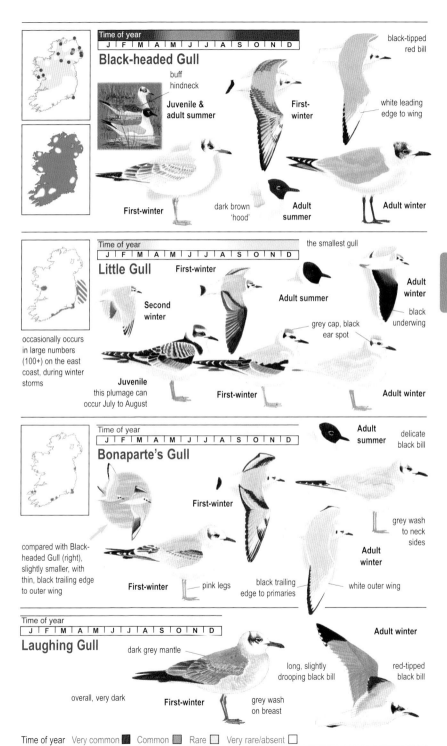

Time of year

| J | F | M | A | M | J | J | A | S | O | N | D |

Black-headed Gull

black-tipped red bill

buff hindneck

Juvenile & adult summer

First-winter

white leading edge to wing

First-winter

dark brown 'hood'

Adult summer

Adult winter

Time of year

| J | F | M | A | M | J | J | A | S | O | N | D |

Little Gull

First-winter

the smallest gull

Adult winter

black underwing

Second winter

Adult summer

grey cap, black ear spot

occasionally occurs in large numbers (100+) on the east coast, during winter storms

Juvenile
this plumage can occur July to August

First-winter

Adult winter

Time of year

| J | F | M | A | M | J | J | A | S | O | N | D |

Bonaparte's Gull

Adult summer

delicate black bill

First-winter

grey wash to neck sides

Adult winter

compared with Black-headed Gull (right), slightly smaller, with thin, black trailing edge to outer wing

First-winter

pink legs

black trailing edge to primaries

white outer wing

Time of year

| J | F | M | A | M | J | J | A | S | O | N | D |

Laughing Gull

dark grey mantle

Adult winter

long, slightly drooping black bill

red-tipped black bill

overall, very dark

First-winter

grey wash on breast

Time of year Very common ■ Common ■ Rare □ Very rare/absent □

Maps Summer □ Winter ■ Main breeding colonies ●

115

Gulls

Common Gull *Larus canus* Faoileán bán   38-42cm

Adults show a slender, pointed yellow-green bill and legs, a dark eye, a white head, tail and underparts, and dark grey upperparts with a broad, white tertial crescent. White-tipped, black primaries show large white mirrors. **Winter adults** show a narrow dark band on the bill and a streaked head. **First-year** birds show a pinkish-grey base to a slender, dark-tipped bill, dark spots on head, a dark grey mantle, pale-edged brown tertials and coverts, and dark brown primaries. In flight shows a clear, dark tail band. **Second years** as adults, but show dark primary coverts and a dark band on a dull yellowish bill.

Voice & Diet Gives shrill, whistling *keee-ya* calls. Feeds on a wide range of insects, molluscs, worms and fish. Will also take offal, dead fish, small birds and mammals, and eggs.

Habitat and Status A widespread, resident species. Breeds in colonies on small lake or coastal islands. Nests on the ground. In winter numbers increase with the arrival of birds from Europe and Iceland. Found on estuaries, coastal fields and inland lakes and fields.

Ring-billed Gull *Larus delawarensis* Faoileán bandghobach   41-46cm

Adults show a black ring on a broad, parallel yellow bill. Iris yellow with a dark pupil. Legs yellow. Upperparts pale grey with small mirrors on the primaries and a thin tertial crescent. Head and underparts white. Head streaked in winter. **First-year** birds show a dark tip to a heavy, orange-pink bill. Head and breast heavily spotted. In flight shows a pale grey mantle, dark primaries and secondaries, pale grey greater coverts, and a blotchy tail band. **Second years** as adults, but show dark primary coverts and can show traces of the tail band.

Voice & Diet Gives high-pitched *keee-yo* calls. Feeds on molluscs, fish, worms and scraps.

Habitat and Status A rare but regular winter vagrant from North America. Found with gull flocks on estuaries, mudflats, marshes and inland fields.

Mediterranean Gull *Larus melanocephalus* Sléibhín Meánmhuirí   37-41cm

Larger than Black-headed Gull. **Summer adults** show a black hood, a drooped, heavy, deep red bill with a black subterminal band and a yellow tip. Legs red. Upperparts pale grey. Primaries white. Underparts and tail white. **Winter adults** show a black patch behind eye. **First-winter** birds show a pale base to a dark bill, a pale grey mantle and dark brown primaries. In flight shows a striking upperwing pattern, resembling Common Gull, and a dark tail band. **Second years** as adults, but show variable amounts of black on the primaries and duller bills.

Voice & Diet Gives deep, harsh *kee-oh* calls. Feeds on a variety of small fish, worms and scraps.

Habitat and Status A regular winter visitor from Europe and a rare breeding species. Found on coastal estuaries and rocky outcrops, harbours and inland fields.

Franklin's Gull *Larus pipixcan* Sléibhín Franklin   32-37cm

Summer adults show a black hood with striking, white eye crescents, white underparts and dark, slate-grey upperparts with large white tips to the primaries. In flight shows a white trailing edge to wings. Short, red bill shows a dark tip. Legs bright red. **Winter adults** show a reduced hood, confined to the rear of the crown and behind the eye, a dark bill and dull-coloured legs. **First-winter** birds show greyish-brown wing coverts, black wing tips and a neat, black tail band. **Second years** like adults but show darker wing tips.

Voice & Diet Gives a soft *krrik* call. Feeds on a variety of small fish, worms and scraps.

Habitat and Status A very rare vagrant from North America. Found on coastal estuaries and harbours.

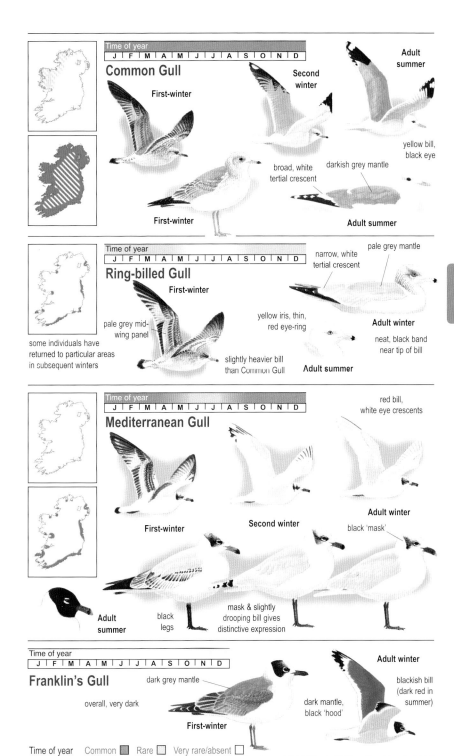

Time of year

| J | F | M | A | M | J | J | A | S | O | N | D |

Common Gull

First-winter

Second winter

Adult summer

yellow bill, black eye

broad, white tertial crescent

darkish grey mantle

First-winter

Adult summer

Time of year

| J | F | M | A | M | J | J | A | S | O | N | D |

Ring-billed Gull

First-winter

pale grey mantle

narrow, white tertial crescent

pale grey mid-wing panel

yellow iris, thin, red eye-ring

Adult winter

some individuals have returned to particular areas in subsequent winters

slightly heavier bill than Common Gull

neat, black band near tip of bill

Adult summer

Gulls

Time of year

| J | F | M | A | M | J | J | A | S | O | N | D |

Mediterranean Gull

red bill, white eye crescents

Adult winter

First-winter

Second winter

black 'mask'

Adult summer

black legs

mask & slightly drooping bill gives distinctive expression

Time of year

| J | F | M | A | M | J | J | A | S | O | N | D |

Franklin's Gull

dark grey mantle

Adult winter

blackish bill (dark red in summer)

overall, very dark

dark mantle, black 'hood'

First-winter

Time of year   Common ■   Rare □   Very rare/absent □

Maps   Summer □   Winter ■

117

Gulls

Great Black-backed Gull *Larus marinus* Droimneach mór — 62-73cm

A very large gull with a heavy bill and pinkish legs. **Adults** show a white head, underparts and tail. Head shows little streaking in winter. Upperparts black with white scapular and tertial crescents, large white tips to black primaries and, in flight, a white trailing edge to wing. Bill yellow with a red gonys spot. Eye yellow. **First-year birds** show a black bill, a dark eye, a whitish head and underparts, barred, brownish-grey upperparts and dark primaries. In flight shows a narrow tail band. **Second years** show whiter underparts and head, a pale-based bill and some black mantle feathers. **Third years** like adult, with some immature feathering and dark markings on bill. **Sub-adults** can show immature feathering on wings and tail, and dark markings towards bill tip.

Voice & Diet Gives loud, deep, barking *aouk* and long, trumpeting *ee-aouk-ouk-ouk* calls. Also gives deep *uk-uk-uk* calls. Feeds on a variety of fish, worms, crustaceans and carrion. Also takes small mammals and seabird chicks.

Habitat and Status A common resident breeding species found in all coastal counties. Breeds in small colonies or singly on coastal cliffs or islands, and on lake islands at inland sites. In winter found on estuaries, mudflats and around harbours.

Lesser Black-backed Gull *Larus fuscus* Droimneach beag — 50-56cm

A large gull, similar in size to Herring Gull. **Adults** show a white head and underparts, and yellow legs. Head streaked and legs duller in winter. Dark grey upperparts contrast with white-tipped black primaries. Underwing dusky on inner primaries and secondaries. Bill yellow with red spot. Eye yellow. **First-year birds** show a black bill, a dark eye, barred brownish upperparts, dark primaries and a streaked whitish head, often showing a dark wash through the eye. Whitish underparts show dark mottling. In flight shows a broad tail band, a whitish rump and a dark upperwing pattern. Legs pinkish. **Second years** show a pale-based bill and some grey mantle feathers. **Third years** as adult, with some immature feathering and dark subterminal markings on bill.

Voice & Diet Gives loud, deep *kyow* and long, shrill, trumpeting *kyee-kyee-kyee-aou-aou-aott* calls. Also gives loud *kee-ya* and deep *gak-gak-gak* calls. Feeds on a variety of fish, worms, crustaceans, offal and carrion as well as small mammals and seabird chicks.

Habitat and Status A common breeding species found on coastal headlands and islands, and on inland lake islands. In winter found on estuaries, mudflats and inland pastures. More numerous in summer, with birds arriving from southern Europe and North Africa.

Yellow-legged Gull *Larus michahellis* Faoileán buíchosach — 52-58cm

Adults show yellow legs, with the grey upperparts being a shade between Herring and Lesser Black-backed. Head and underparts white with little streaking in winter. Bill yellow with red gonys spot. Eye yellow. In flight shows small white tips and mirrors on extensive black wing tips, and dusky-grey inner primaries and secondaries on the underwing. **First-year birds** show barred, brownish upperparts, dark primaries, a whitish head and underparts, and a black bill. In flight shows a neat tail band contrasting with a white uppertail and rump, and dark primaries and secondaries. **Second years** show a grey mantle and scapulars, and a well-defined tail band. **Third years** as adult, with some immature feathering and dark markings on bill. Appears deeper-chested than Lesser Black-backed Gull.

Voice & Diet Gives loud *kyo* and long, trumpeting *kyee-kyee-kyo-kyo-kyo* calls. Also gives deep *gak-gak-gak* calls. Feeds on a variety of fish, worms, crustaceans, offal and carrion.

Habitat and Status An uncommon passage migrant from southern Europe. Found in gull flocks on estuaries, mudflats and around harbours.

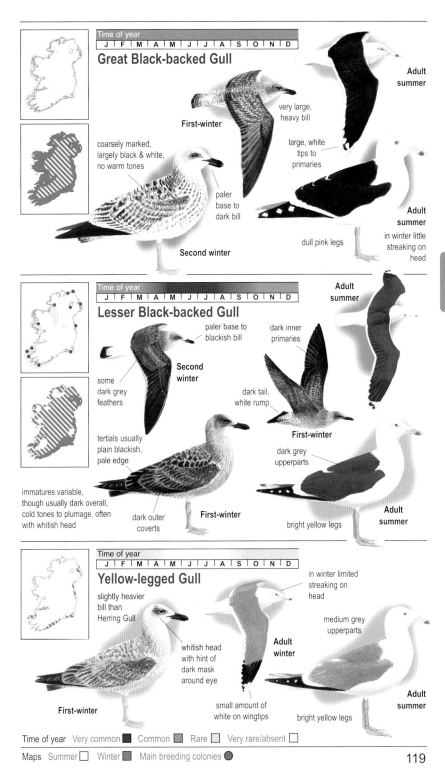

Great Black-backed Gull

Time of year
J F M A M J J A S O N D

Adult summer

First-winter

very large, heavy bill

coarsely marked, largely black & white, no warm tones

large, white tips to primaries

paler base to dark bill

Adult summer

Second winter

dull pink legs

in winter little streaking on head

Lesser Black-backed Gull

Time of year
J F M A M J J A S O N D

Adult summer

paler base to blackish bill

dark inner primaries

Second winter

some dark grey feathers

dark tail, white rump

First-winter

tertials usually plain blackish, pale edge

dark grey upperparts

immatures variable, though usually dark overall, cold tones to plumage, often with whitish head

dark outer coverts

First-winter

bright yellow legs

Adult summer

Yellow-legged Gull

Time of year
J F M A M J J A S O N D

in winter limited streaking on head

slightly heavier bill than Herring Gull

medium grey upperparts

whitish head with hint of dark mask around eye

Adult winter

First-winter

small amount of white on wingtips

bright yellow legs

Adult summer

Time of year Very common ■ Common ■ Rare □ Very rare/absent □

Maps Summer □ Winter ▨ Main breeding colonies ●

119

Gulls

Herring Gull *Larus argentatus* Faoileán scadán   54-62cm

A large gull, similar in size to Lesser Black-backed, but showing pink legs. **Adults** show a white head and underparts. Head streaked in winter. Pale grey upperparts contrast with white-tipped black primaries. Bill yellow with red spot. Eye yellow. **First-year birds** show a slightly paler base to black bill, a dark eye, barred brownish upperparts, dark primaries, and a pale brownish head and underparts. In flight shows a tail band and a dark outer wing contrasting with paler inner primaries. **Second years** show some grey mantle feathers and a blotchy tail band. **Third years** as adult, with some immature feathering and dark subterminal markings on bill. Winter adults of the northern race, *argentatus*, show slightly darker upperparts, more white on the wingtips, and heavy streaking on the head.

    Voice & Diet Gives loud *kyow* and long, shrill, trumpeting *kyee-kyee-aou-aou-aou* calls. Also gives loud *kee-ya* and deep *gak-gak-gak* calls. Feeds on a wide variety of fish, molluscs, worms, offal and carrion as well as taking small mammals and seabird chicks.

    Habitat and Status A very common, widespread, resident breeding species. Breeds in colonies on coastal cliffs or islands, and on lake islands at inland sites. Also nests on rooftops in towns and cities. In winter found on coastal estuaries, around harbours and on inland pastures and lakes.

American Herring Gull *Larus smithsonianus* Faoileán scadán Mheiriceánach 52-59cm

A large gull very like Herring Gull. **First-year birds** most easily recognisable of all plumages showing dark, uniform underparts, a paler head, dark brown upperparts which show some greyish feathers, and an all-dark tail. Rump and undertail heavily barred. Large bill shows pink base and dark tip. Eye dark. Legs pink. In flight shows dark outer primaries, dark secondaries and a dark base to the greater coverts. **Second years** show some grey mantle feathers and a dark tail. **Third years** grey above but show some immature feathering. **Adult winters** very like adult Herring Gull but show heavy streaking on the head and breast, and slightly paler grey upperparts. Bill yellow with red gonys spot. Eye yellow.

    Voice & Diet Gives loud *kyow* and long, high-pitched *kyee-kyee-aou-aou-aou* calls. Also gives loud *kee-ya* and deep *gak-gak-gak* calls. Feeds on fish, molluscs, worms and carrion.

    Habitat and Status A very rare vagrant from North America. Found on coastal estuaries and harbours.

Caspian Gull *Larus cachinnans* Faoileán Chaispeach   55-61cm

Similar to Herring Gulls but appears more slender with longer wings, longer legs and appearing full-chested. **Adults** show a white head with a long, sloping forehead and white underparts. Upperparts dark grey with obvious white spots on black wing tips. In flight white inner primary webs appear as white 'tongues' intruding onto the black of the wing tip. In winter shows no streaking on head. Long, slender bill pale yellow with a small, red gonys spot. Eye dark and appears small. Legs pinkish-yellow. **First-year birds** appear white-headed with dark streaking on the base of the hind-neck. Greyish upperparts show barring on the wing coverts. In flight shows a dark tail band. Bill dark. Legs pale. **Second years** show some grey mantle feathers and a blotchy tail band. **Third years** as adult, with some immature upperpart feathering and dark subterminal markings on bill.

    Voice & Diet Gives loud *kyo* and long, fast, high-pitched trumpeting *kyee-kyee-kyu-kyo-kyo* calls. Also gives *gak-gak-gak* calls. Feeds on fish, worms, crustaceans and carrion.

    Habitat and Status A very rare vagrant from eastern Europe, the Black Sea and the Caspian Sea. Found in gull flocks on estuaries and mudflats.

Time of year

| J | F | M | A | M | J | J | A | S | O | N | D |

Herring Gull

dark outer primaries

Third winter

grey upperparts, some brown feathers

mottled dark brown

dark tail band

blotchy tail band

First-winter

yellow bill with red gonys spot, yellow eye

coarsely marked brown upperparts

Adult

black bill, paler base

white-tipped black primaries

First-winter

highly variable, some much darker

pink legs

Adult

Gulls

Time of year

| J | F | M | A | M | J | J | A | S | O | N | D |

American Herring Gull

a highly variable species, generally darker & with a heavier build than Herring Gull

First-winter

all-dark tail

black tail **First-winter**

dark brown underparts, often contrasting with paler head

rump & undertail heavily barred

third years & adults almost indistinguishable from Herring Gull

dark underparts & underwing coverts

Time of year

| J | F | M | A | M | J | J | A | S | O | N | D |

Caspian Gull

distinctive shape – long, sloping forehead, long bill, long wings & legs

white-headed, dark bill

eye small & dark

Third winter

First- winter

Adult winter

Time of year Very common ■ Common ■ Rare □ Very rare/absent □

Maps Summer □ Winter ■

121

Gulls

Glaucous Gull *Larus hyperboreus* Faoileán glas 58-69cm

A large, powerful gull. **Winter adults** show a streaked white head, white underparts, pale grey upperparts, and short white primaries. Eye shows a yellow iris, a dark pupil and a yellow orbital ring. Bill yellow with red gonys spot. Legs pink. **First-winter** birds show delicate barring on pale buff upperparts, rump and tail, creamy underparts, and short, creamy-white primaries. Birds become whiter by late winter/early spring. Heavy, pale pink bill shows a black tip. Eye dark. **Second winters** appear whiter, show a yellowish iris and a dark ring on a pink bill. **Third winters** as adult, with buff feathers on whitish wings and tail, and black markings on yellow bill. **Summer adults** show a clean, unstreaked head. Told from Iceland Gull by larger size, a heavy bill, a flat-crowned appearance, an aggressive expression and shorter primaries.

Voice & Diet Can give a deep *kyow* call and, when agitated, gives loud *gak-gak-gak* calls. Feeds on a variety of carrion, offal, fish, worms, molluscs and scraps.

Habitat and Status An uncommon but regular winter visitor from Iceland and Greenland. Found along most coastal counties, frequenting fishing ports, harbours, docklands and rubbish tips.

Iceland Gull *Larus glaucoides* Faoileán Íoslannach 50-57cm

A white-winged gull, smaller than Glaucous Gull. **Winter adults** show a streaked white head, white underparts, grey upperparts, and long, attenuated white primaries. Eye shows a yellow iris, a dark pupil and a reddish orbital ring. Bill yellow with red gonys spot. Legs pink. **First-winter** birds show delicate mottling on pale buff upperparts and tail, creamy underparts and whitish primaries. Birds become whiter by late winter/early spring. Medium-sized dark bill shows a pinkish base. Eyes dark. **Second winters** whiter, with a yellowish iris and dark ring on pink bill. **Third winters** as adult, with buff on whitish wings and tail, and black markings on yellow bill. **Summer adults** show a clean, unstreaked head. Told from Glaucous by smaller size, medium-sized bill, rounded crown, gentle expression and long primary projection. Birds from Arctic north-east Canada, known as **Kumlien's Gull**, show dark webs to the outer primaries and a darker tail band in immature plumages while adults show grey webs to white-tipped primaries.

Voice & Diet Can give shrill *kyow* and agitated *gak-gak-gak* calls. Feeds on a variety of carrion, offal, fish, worms, molluscs and scraps.

Habitat and Status Uncommon but regular winter visitor from Greenland. Found along most coastal counties, frequenting fishing ports, harbours, docklands and rubbish tips. Kumlien's Gull is a rare winter vagrant from north-east Canada.

Ivory Gull *Pagophila eburnea* Faoileán eabhartha 40-44cm

A very distinctive gull, similar in size to Common Gull but with a stocky, pigeon-like build. **Adults** show a pure white plumage, a conspicuous black eye, and shortish, black legs. Bill bluish or greenish-grey with a yellow and orange tip. Could be confused with albinistic gulls of similar size, but the colour of the bill is diagnostic and should always be checked. **First-winter** birds are unmistakable, showing a white plumage with a dusky, dirty-looking face, black-tipped primaries and tail, and varying amounts of dark spotting on the wings. Bill dark greyish with a yellowish tip. Legs blackish.

Voice & Diet Can give a harsh, tem-like *kee-ar* call. Feeds on carrion, including dead fish and mammals. Will also take fish, crustaceans, molluscs and insects.

Habitat and Status An extremely rare winter vagrant from north Greenland, Spitzbergen and other islands in the high Arctic. In winter rarely travels farther south than the Arctic Circle. Usually found in harbours and fishing ports. Can be very tame.

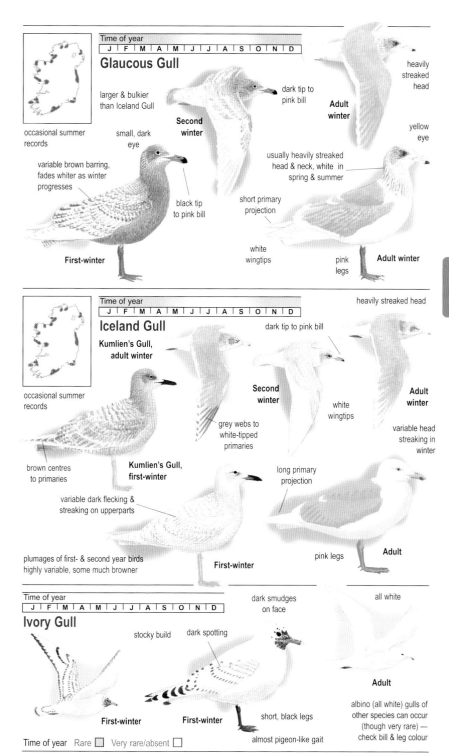

Time of year

J F M A M J J A S O N D

Glaucous Gull

larger & bulkier than Iceland Gull

occasional summer records

heavily streaked head

dark tip to pink bill

Adult winter

yellow eye

small, dark eye

Second winter

variable brown barring, fades whiter as winter progresses

usually heavily streaked head & neck, white in spring & summer

short primary projection

black tip to pink bill

white wingtips

pink legs

Adult winter

First-winter

Time of year

J F M A M J J A S O N D

Iceland Gull

Kumlien's Gull, adult winter

occasional summer records

heavily streaked head

dark tip to pink bill

Second winter

white wingtips

Adult winter

grey webs to white-tipped primaries

variable head streaking in winter

brown centres to primaries

Kumlien's Gull, first-winter

long primary projection

variable dark flecking & streaking on upperparts

plumages of first- & second year birds highly variable, some much browner

First-winter

pink legs

Adult

Time of year

J F M A M J J A S O N D

Ivory Gull

dark smudges on face

all white

stocky build

dark spotting

First-winter

First-winter

short, black legs

almost pigeon-like gait

Adult

albino (all white) gulls of other species can occur (though very rare) — check bill & leg colour

Time of year   Rare ☐   Very rare/absent ☐

Maps   Winter ▪

Gulls

Terns

Black Tern *Chlidonias niger* Geabhróg dhubh · 23-26cm

A small, compact species with short wings and a shallow fork to the tail. **Summer adults** show a black head and underparts, white undertail coverts, grey upperwings, rump and tail, grey underwings, a black bill and dark legs. **Moulting adults** can show white mottling on underparts. **Immatures** show a diagnostic black shoulder patch, white underparts and black ear coverts and crown patch. Upperwing grey with a conspicuous, dark carpal bar. Mantle grey, slightly darker than grey rump and tail. Legs pale red. Immatures of the American race *surinamensis* similar but show a grey wash on the flanks and a neater crown and ear covert patch. Flies with shallow wing beats. Does not dive like other tern species.

Voice & Diet Can give a high-pitched, squeaky *kitt* call. Feeds on a wide variety of insects which are delicately picked from the surface of lakes and marshes.

Habitat and Status A regular autumn passage migrant from Europe. Also recorded irregularly in spring and summer. Found over freshwater lakes, marshes and reservoirs, usually along coastal areas. Has been recorded inland. In autumn can be seen on passage off headlands and islands during seawatches.

White-winged Black Tern *Chlidonias leucopterus* Geabhróg bháneiteach · 21-24cm

A small, stocky tern with rounded wings, a shallow fork to the tail, and a black bill. **Summer adults** show a black head, mantle and underparts. Contrasting white upperwing shows dark outer primaries and inner secondaries. Underwing shows black coverts and grey flight feathers. Rump, tail and undertail white. **Adults** in moult can show black body and underwing mottling. Legs reddish. **Immatures** show a neat, black ear covert and crown patch, white underparts, and pale wings with a thin carpal bar. A dark mantle contrasts strongly with the grey wings and the white rump and tail. Lacks shoulder patches of immature Black Tern.

Voice & Diet Can give a high-pitched *kitt* call, similar to that of Black Tern. Feeds on a variety of insects which are picked from the surface of lakes and marshes.

Habitat and Status A rare spring and early autumn vagrant from Europe. Found feeding over freshwater lakes, marshes and reservoirs, usually along coastal areas. Has been recorded inland. In autumn can be found roosting with other tern species.

Whiskered Tern *Chlidonias hybrida* Geabhróg bhroinndubh · 23-26cm

A bulky tern with a shallow fork to a short tail and short, broad wings. **Summer adults** show a black cap, a white face which contrasts with blackish or dark grey underparts, and white undertail coverts. Mantle, wings, rump and tail grey. Bill and legs blood-red. Structure, short broad wings and the shallow fork to the tail eliminate any confusion with Arctic Tern which can show very dark underparts. **Adults in moult** can show dark mottling on the underparts. **Immatures** show white underparts, a black ear covert and crown patch, dark and pale brown barring on the mantle and scapulars, and grey wings which show brownish feathers on coverts and tertials. Rump and tail grey. Bill blackish.

Voice & Diet Can give a harsh *ky-it* call, similar to that of Black Tern. Feeds on a variety of insects which are picked from the surface of lakes and marshes.

Habitat and Status An extremely rare spring and autumn vagrant from southern and south-eastern Europe. Found on freshwater lakes, marshes and reservoirs, usually along coastal areas. Has been recorded inland.

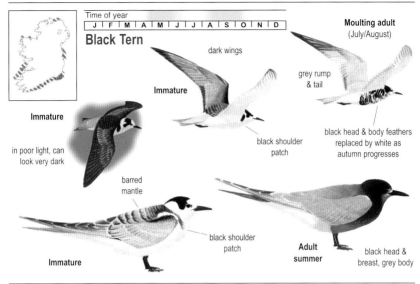

Time of year
J F M A M J J A S O N D

Black Tern

Moulting adult
(July/August)

dark wings

grey rump
& tail

Immature

black head & body feathers
replaced by white as
autumn progresses

Immature

in poor light, can
look very dark

black shoulder
patch

barred
mantle

black shoulder
patch

Adult
summer

Immature

black head &
breast, grey body

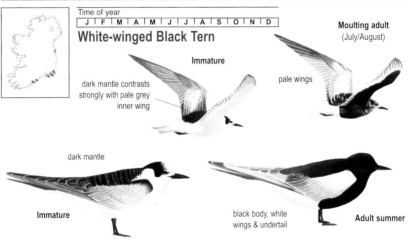

Time of year
J F M A M J J A S O N D

White-winged Black Tern

Moulting adult
(July/August)

Immature

pale wings

dark mantle contrasts
strongly with pale grey
inner wing

dark mantle

Immature

black body, white
wings & undertail

Adult summer

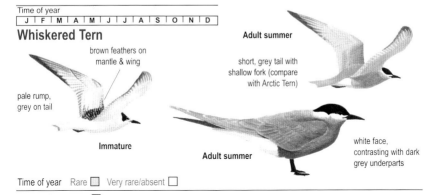

Time of year
J F M A M J J A S O N D

Whiskered Tern

Adult summer

brown feathers on
mantle & wing

short, grey tail with
shallow fork (compare
with Arctic Tern)

pale rump,
grey on tail

Immature

Adult summer

white face,
contrasting with dark
grey underparts

Time of year   Rare ☐   Very rare/absent ☐

Terns

Terns

Common Tern *Sterna hirundo* Geabhróg   30-36cm
Adults show a black cap, white cheeks and underparts, and pale grey upperparts. When perched, shows red legs, a black-tipped red bill and long wings equal to the tail length. In flight shows pale grey upperwings with a distinctive dark wedge on the mid inner primaries and dark tips to the outer primaries. Underwing grey with a dark trailing edge on outer primaries. Rump and long tail white. **Immatures** show a pale base to a dark bill, red legs, a white forehead and lores, a brownish mantle with pale edges to feathers, a dark carpal bar and dark grey secondaries and primaries. **First-summers** show white foreheads and some dark feathering on the wings.
    Voice & Diet Gives loud, grating *kee-aaar* and *kiip* calls. Immatures give hard, repeated *kik* calls. Feeds by hovering in mid-air before diving, headfirst, into water. Takes a variety of small fish.
    Habitat and Status A widespread summer visitor. Winters off West Africa. Breeds in colonies on small coastal and lake islands. Nests on the ground.

Arctic Tern *Sterna paradisaea* Geabhróg Artach   30-39cm
Adults show a rounded, black cap, white cheeks, grey-washed underparts and grey upperparts. When perched, shows short, red legs, a shortish, blood-red bill and a wing length shorter than the long tail streamers. In flight shows a plain grey upperwing with dark tips to outer primaries. Underwing white with a narrow, black trailing edge to the primaries. Rump and long tail white. **Immatures** show a dark bill, pale red legs, a white forehead and lores, pale grey upperparts, a faint carpal bar and white secondaries in flight. **First-summers** show white foreheads and some dark feathering on the wings.
    Voice & Diet Gives harsh *kee-aar* and whistling *kee-kee* calls. Immatures give harsh *kik-kik* calls. Feeds by hovering in mid-air before diving, headfirst, into water. Takes a variety of small fish.
    Habitat and Status A widespread summer visitor. Nests on the ground in colonies along coastal areas and on large inland lakes. Winters in the Antarctic.

Roseate Tern *Sterna dougallii* Geabhróg rósach   32-41cm
Adults show a black cap, white cheeks, white underparts which show a pink wash in summer, and whitish-grey upperparts. When perched shows orange-red legs, a red base to a blackish bill and long tail streamers extending well beyond the wings. In flight shows a very pale upperwing with grey outer primary wedges in late summer. White underwing lacks a dark trailing edge to the primaries. **Immatures** show a black cap with a white loral spot, a black bill and black legs. Mantle shows dark brown scalloping giving a dark, saddle-like effect in flight. Wings pale with greyish primary tips and a faint carpal bar. Underwing whitish.
    Voice & Diet Gives distinctive, high-pitched *tchu-ick* calls and loud, harsh *raaak* calls. Feeds by hovering in mid-air before diving, headfirst, into water. Takes a variety of small fish.
    Habitat and Status A scarce breeding species, found in colonies on coastal islands. Nests in hollows, under vegetation and in nest boxes. Winters off West Africa.

Forster's Tern *Sterna forsteri* Geabhróg Forster   33-36cm
Summer adults show a black tip to a reddish-orange bill, a black cap and white underparts. In flight shows pale grey upperparts, whitish inner primaries, a white rump and a pale grey tail. **Winter adults** show a black ear covert patch, a black bill and pale red legs. **Immatures** similar but show a grey wash on the nape, brownish markings on the tertials, darker primaries and lacks carpal bars.
    Voice & Diet Can give harsh, low-pitched *krarr* and *kik* calls. Feeds on a variety of small fish.
    Habitat and Status A very rare vagrant from North America. Found in coastal bays and harbours.

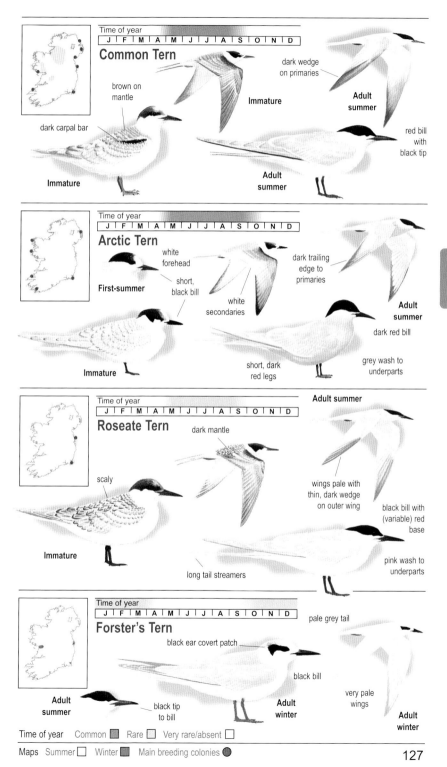

Time of year

| J | F | M | A | M | J | J | A | S | O | N | D |

Common Tern

brown on
mantle

dark carpal bar

dark wedge
on primaries

Immature

**Adult
summer**

red bill
with
black tip

Immature

**Adult
summer**

Time of year

| J | F | M | A | M | J | J | A | S | O | N | D |

Arctic Tern

white
forehead

First-summer

short,
black bill

white
secondaries

dark trailing
edge to
primaries

**Adult
summer**

dark red bill

Immature

short, dark
red legs

grey wash to
underparts

Terns

Time of year

| J | F | M | A | M | J | J | A | S | O | N | D |

Roseate Tern

dark mantle

Adult summer

scaly

wings pale with
thin, dark wedge
on outer wing

black bill with
(variable) red
base

Immature

long tail streamers

pink wash to
underparts

Time of year

| J | F | M | A | M | J | J | A | S | O | N | D |

Forster's Tern

black ear covert patch

pale grey tail

black bill

**Adult
summer**

black tip
to bill

**Adult
winter**

very pale
wings

**Adult
winter**

Time of year   Common ▨   Rare ☐   Very rare/absent ☐

Maps   Summer ☐   Winter ▨   Main breeding colonies ●

127

Terns

Sandwich Tern *Sterna sandvicensis* Geabhróg scothdhubh 38-44cm
A large tern with a slender, yellow-tipped, black bill and black legs. **Summer adults** show a black cap with a shaggy crest, white underparts and pale grey upperparts. In flight shows slender, pointed wings with dark wedges to primaries. Rump and short, forked tail white. **Winter adults** show a white forehead. **Immatures** show a slender, black bill, a black cap with white speckling on the forehead, a scalloped mantle, a dark carpal bar and dark markings on tertials and tail. Flies with strong, shallow wing beats. Hovers in mid-air and dives for fish.

Voice & Diet Gives a loud, grating *kirr-rik* call. Feeds on a variety of fish and molluscs.

Habitat and Status A common summer visitor. Found on open coastal waters and bays. Breeds in colonies on quiet, undisturbed coastal and lake islands, and on shingle beaches. Nests on the ground. Winters off West Africa.

Gull-billed Tern *Gelochelidon nilotica* Geabhróg gobdhubh 35-41cm
Like Sandwich Tern but appearing more broad-winged with a shorter, stubby, all-black bill and longer, black legs. **Summer adults** show a black cap, grey upperparts and white underparts. Rump and short, forked tail grey. In flight shows a dark trailing edge to primaries. **Immatures** show a dark eye-stripe, dark streaking on the crown, and buff mottling on the wings and back. **Winter adults** show a white head with a black eye-stripe. Does not dive but swoops to pick prey off surface of water or hawks insects in the air.

Voice & Diet Can give a deep *gur-ick* call. Feeds on a variety of insects, larvae and frogs.

Habitat and Status An extremely rare passage vagrant from southern Europe. Found on fresh-water marshes and lakes as well as coastal mudflats.

Elegant Tern *Sterna elegans* Geabhróg ghalánta 39-43cm
A slender, Sandwich Tern-sized species with a long, shaggy rear crest and a long, drooping bill which is reddish-orange at the base, fading to orange before becoming yellowish towards the tip. **Summer adults** show dark legs, a black cap, pale grey upperparts and white underparts which can show a pink wash. Rump and forked tail whitish. **Winter adults** show a white forehead contrasting with a neat dark eye patch and shaggy crest restricted to rear of crown and nape. **Immatures** show a white forehead and lores, dark markings on upperparts, dark tips to tail feathers, and pale legs. Hovers in mid-air and dives for fish.

Voice & Diet Can give a harsh *kee-rik* call. Feeds on a variety of fish.

Habitat and Status An extremely rare vagrant from the west coast of North America. Usually found with Sandwich Terns on open coastal waters and beaches or within breeding tern colonies.

Caspian Tern *Hydroprogne caspia* Geabhróg Chaispeach 47-53cm
A large tern with a heavy, thick, orange-red bill showing a dark subterminal band and a pale tip, and longish black legs. **Summer adults** show a black cap and a short, shaggy crest. Underparts white. Upperparts pale grey, with long wings showing dark tips. In flight shows a very distinctive underwing, with pale coverts, secondaries and inner primaries contrasting strongly with the blackish outer primaries. Rump and short, forked tail white. **Winter adults** show white streaking on the forehead. **Immatures** show a dark cap, a dull red bill, dark markings on mantle and wings, and dark tips to tail feathers. Appears gull-like in flight.

Voice & Diet Can give a deep, harsh *kraah* call. Feeds on a variety of fish, eggs and small birds.

Habitat and Status An extremely rare passage vagrant from southern Europe. Found on open coastal waters, brackish lagoons and freshwater lakes.

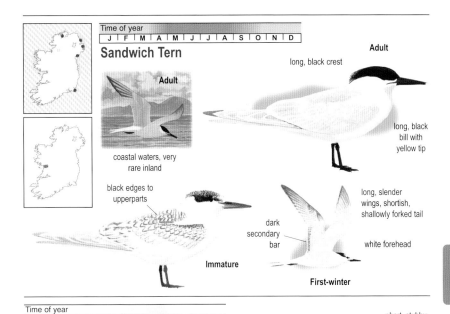

Sandwich Tern

Adult

long, black crest

Adult

coastal waters, very rare inland

long, black bill with yellow tip

black edges to upperparts

long, slender wings, shortish, shallowly forked tail

dark secondary bar

white forehead

Immature

First-winter

Terns

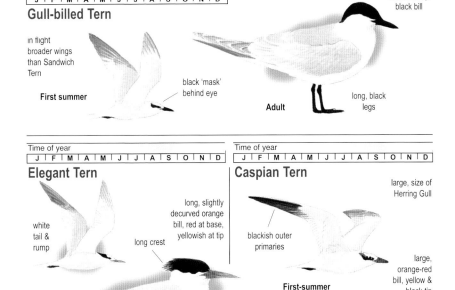

Gull-billed Tern

short, stubby, black bill

in flight broader wings than Sandwich Tern

First summer

black 'mask' behind eye

Adult

long, black legs

Elegant Tern

white tail & rump

long crest

long, slightly decurved orange bill, red at base, yellowish at tip

Adult

Caspian Tern

large, size of Herring Gull

blackish outer primaries

large, orange-red bill, yellow & black tip

First-summer

Adult

Time of year   Common ▓   Rare ▒   Very rare/absent ☐

Maps   Summer ☐   Winter ▓   Main breeding colonies ●

129

Little Tern *Sternula albifrons* Geabhróg bheag   24-27cm

A tiny, long-winged tern with a black-tipped yellow bill and orange-yellow legs. **Adults** show a white forehead patch which contrasts strongly with a black loral stripe, crown and nape. Upperparts bluish-grey with long wings. Throat, neck and underparts white. In flight the long wings show a dark leading edge to the primaries. Rump and short, forked tail white. **Immatures** show a dark, brownish bill, yellow-brown legs, a buff to white forehead and lores, a black streaked crown, and a blackish eye patch. Greyish upperparts show brown barring on the mantle and scapulars and, in flight, the wings show a complete dark leading edge. Hovers in mid-air and dives for fish.

Voice & Diet Gives loud, shrill *krii-ek* calls, a repeated, sharp *kitt* call and chattering *kirrik-kirrik-kirrik* calls. Feeds on a variety of crustaceans and small fish.

Habitat and Status A widespread but scarce summer visitor to coastal regions. Rarely found inland. Breeds in small colonies on shingle and sandy beaches. Nests on the ground.

Guillemot *Uria aalge* Foracha   40-44cm

A slim auk with a dark, pointed bill and dark legs. **Summer adults** show a dark chocolate-brown head, throat, neck and upperparts, with a thin white line on the wing formed by white tips to the secondaries. Underparts white with dark flank streaking. **Bridled Guillemots** show a white eye-ring and a white eye-stripe from behind eye. **Winter adults** have a white throat, neck and cheeks, with a thin black stripe obvious behind the eye. Crown, nape and hindneck chocolate-brown, forming a collar on sides of breast. In flight shows white sides to rump, a short, rounded tail, a white trailing edge to secondaries, whitish underwing coverts and dark axillaries. **Immatures** show less flank streaking.

Voice & Diet Extremely noisy at the breeding colonies, giving harsh, rolling *oarrr* calls. Usually silent away from the breeding colonies. Feeds by diving, swimming underwater by flapping the wings. Takes a variety of fish, marine worms, molluscs and crustaceans.

Habitat and Status A common breeding species found in summer on coastal cliffs. Breeds on sheer cliffs, laying eggs on narrow ledges. Juveniles leave the cliffs before they can fly and are fed at sea. Winters in harbours, bays and offshore waters.

Razorbill *Alca torda* Crosán   39-43cm

A stocky auk with black legs and a dark, stubby bill showing a white band and a thin white line from the eye along the upper mandible. **Summer adults** show a black head, throat, neck and upperparts, with a thin white line on the wings formed by white tips to the secondaries. Pointed tail obvious when swimming. White underparts unstreaked. **Winter adults** show a white throat and neck, with white extending behind contrastingly black ear coverts. Crown, nape and hindneck black, forming a short collar on sides of breast. In flight shows white sides to rump, a longish, pointed tail, a white trailing edge to secondaries, and clean, whitish underwing coverts. **Immatures** similar to winter adults.

Voice & Diet During the breeding season gives low, whistling and grunting calls. Adults usually silent away from the breeding colonies. Immatures give persistent peeping calls at sea in late summer and autumn. Feeds by diving, swimming underwater by flapping the wings. Feeds on fish, marine worms, molluscs and crustaceans.

Habitat and Status Common breeding species, present in summer on coastal cliffs. Nests in crevices, under boulders or on sheltered ledges. Juveniles leave the cliffs before they can fly and are fed at sea. Winters in harbours, bays and offshore waters.

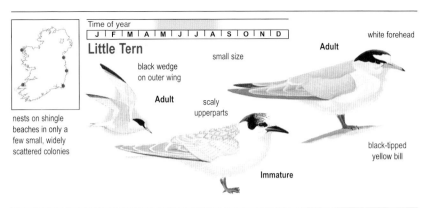

Time of year
J F M A M J J A S O N D

Little Tern

small size

black wedge
on outer wing

Adult

scaly
upperparts

Immature

white forehead

Adult

black-tipped
yellow bill

nests on shingle
beaches in only a
few small, widely
scattered colonies

Time of year
J F M A M J J A S O N D

Guillemot

thin white eye-ring & line behind eye

'Bridled'
Guillemot

dark 'armpits'
(white on Razorbill)

**Adult
summer**

Adult winter

streaking
on flanks

brown tone to
upperparts

brown tone to
upperparts

**Adult
winter**

long,
pointed

blunt tail

streaked
flanks

Adult summer

Time of year
J F M A M J J A S O N D

Razorbill

Adult summer

long tail

white line on bill
& forehead

Razorbills & Guillemots often travel
together in flocks, low over water

black
upperparts

Adult winter

blunt

unstreaked
flanks

long, pointed tail

Adult summer

Time of year   Common ▨   Rare ▨   Very rare/absent ☐

Maps   Summer ☐   Winter ▨   Main breeding colonies ●

131

Auks

Black Guillemot *Cepphus grylle* Foracha dhubh   33-36cm

A striking auk with bright red legs and a dark bill showing a bright red gape. **Summer adults** show an all sooty-black plumage with striking white wing covert patches which are very conspicuous in flight. **Winter adults** show a pale head with a dark eye patch, a greyish crown and nape, and white underparts with blackish streaking along the flanks. The blackish mantle shows broad, white edges to feathers, giving a barred and mottled appearance. The tail and wings remain blackish in winter, the large white wing covert patches being less obvious. **Immatures** similar to winter adults, but show dark barring on wing patches and duller legs.

Voice & Diet During the breeding season gives loud, whistling *spiiiiieb* calls, which can finish in trilling notes. Feeds by diving for fish, worms, molluscs and crustaceans.

Habitat and Status A widespread, resident species. Found on rocky coastal cliffs and in harbours, nesting under boulders, in caves and holes, even using crevices in walls and piers. In winter found in sheltered bays and harbours, usually remaining close to shore.

Puffin *Fratercula arctica* Puifín   29-32cm

An unmistakable, dumpy, black and white auk with a colourful bill. **Summer adults** show a triangular blue-grey, yellow and reddish-orange bill with a yellow-edged gape. Whitish face shows a greyish wash on the cheeks, and dark shading above eye extending as a thin rear eye-stripe. Crown, nape and neck black. Upperparts and tail black, contrasting with white underparts. Legs bright orange. Eye dark with a red eye-ring. **Winter adults** show a smaller, duller bill, a dusky, greyish face, and yellowish legs. **Immatures** show a stubbier bill, a dark greyish face and dusky rear flanks. Flies with rapid wing beats, showing a black upperwing and rump, and dark underwings. Stands in an upright posture.

Voice & Diet On the breeding grounds give low, moaning, growling *arr-ow-arr* calls. Usually silent at sea. Feeds on a variety of fish, worms, molluscs and crustaceans.

Habitat and Status A summer visitor to some coastal regions. Found on grassy slopes on quiet, undisturbed islands and cliffs, nesting in old rabbit and shearwater burrows. In winter disperses to the Atlantic and is seldom seen offshore.

Little Auk *Alle alle* Falcóg bheag   20-23cm

A tiny, starling-sized, black and white auk with a stubby bill and a plump, rounded, neckless appearance. In **winter** shows a black crown and cheeks, a white throat, and white extending up behind the ear coverts. A black, broken collar on the lower throat contrasts with the white underparts. Upperparts black with white tips to secondaries and short, obvious white lines on the scapulars. In **summer** shows a completely black head and throat with a thin, white crescent above eye. Flies with rapid wing beats, showing a white trailing edge to secondaries and a dark underwing. Could be mistaken for immature Puffin in flight. Legs and eyes dark. Swims buoyantly. Can be very tame and approachable.

Voice & Diet Little Auks are rarely heard in Ireland. Feeds by diving for a variety of small fish, marine invertebrates and crustaceans.

Habitat and Status A rare but regular vagrant from Arctic regions. Winters in the North Atlantic. In winter can be seen on seawatches, but also found in sheltered harbours. Following gales, 'wrecks' can occur with birds blown onto the coastline or even far inland. Occasionally recorded in early spring.

Time of year

| J | F | M | A | M | J | J | A | S | O | N | D |

Black Guillemot

overall pale, white patch on wing

Adult
summer

Adult
winter

Adult winter

Adult
summer

Adult summer

all-black plumage but for
large white patch on wing

red legs

Time of year

| J | F | M | A | M | J | J | A | S | O | N | D |

Puffin

colourful bill

Adult
summer

Adult summer

black neck
collar

stubby,
short dark
bill

dusky face

disperses well out to
sea in winter

dusky flanks

Immature, winter

orange legs

Time of year

| J | F | M | A | M | J | J | A | S | O | N | D |

Little Auk

stubby bill

small, size of Starling

dark underwing

whirring, fast wingbeats

Winter

Time of year   Common ◼   Rare ◻   Very rare/absent ☐

Maps   Summer ☐   Winter ◼   Main breeding colonies ⬤

Rock Dove *Columba livia* Colm aille   31-36cm

Wild Rock Doves are shy and unapproachable. **Adults** show a blue-grey head and neck with a green and purple neck patch. Breast, belly and undertail pale grey. Upperparts pale grey, with two broad, black wingbars across tertials and secondaries, and median coverts. Primaries dark grey. Tail blue-grey with a dark band. In flight shows a small white rump contrasting with grey upperparts, swept-back wings which show striking black bars on the secondaries and median coverts, and silvery-white under-wings. Can glide on V-shaped wings. Eye reddish-orange. Bill grey with white cere. Legs pinkish. **Immatures** duller with brownish tones. **Feral Pigeons**, the domesticated and tame city ancestor of the Rock Dove, come in an extremely wide variety of colours. Some can appear identical to wild Rock Dove but tend to show thicker bills.

Voice & Diet Gives a soft *coo-roo-coo* song occasionally associated with a strutting, fan-tailed display. Engages in display flights with slow wing beats, wing claps and long glides on V-shaped wings. Feeds on a variety of grains, seeds and, occasionally, insects.

Habitat and Status Wild Rock Doves are found on rocky sea cliffs, headlands, islands and coastal fields along Atlantic coastal regions. Nests in caves and crevices in rocks. Feral Doves are common in towns and cities as well as near grain stores and farms. Nests on ledges of buildings or in holes in ruined buildings.

Stock Dove *Columba oenas* Colm gorm   32-36cm

A stocky, compact species which lacks white in the plumage and shows a dark eye and a pale tip to a bright reddish bill. **Adults** show a blue-grey head with an emerald-green neck patch and a purple-tinged breast. Belly, undertail, mantle and rump blue-grey. Wings show two small, blackish bars on the inner coverts and tertials. The secondaries, primaries and primary coverts are dark. Short, blue-grey tail shows a very broad, dark terminal band. In flight shows a distinctive dark border to edge and rear of wings. Underwings greyish. **Immatures** show a browner plumage, a darkish bill and lack the emerald-green neck patches.

Voice & Diet Gives a deep, sharp repeated *coo-ah* call. Feeds on a variety of seeds, cereals and other plant material. Can also take small invertebrates.

Habitat and Status A locally common, widespread resident species, though largely absent from the western seaboard. Found on farmlands, woodlands, parks and along coastal cliffs and dune systems. Nests in holes in trees, old ruined buildings, cliff crevices and even rabbit burrows.

Woodpigeon *Columba palumbus* Colm coille   39-44cm

A small-headed, plump bird with a longish tail. **Adults** show a grey-blue head, a green and purple gloss on the side of the neck, and conspicuous white neck patches. Breast purplish-brown with creamy greyish-white underparts. Upperparts grey-brown, with a striking white line on bend of wing. Primary coverts and primaries dark. Rump and uppertail blue-grey with a dark tailband. Flies with swept-back wings, deep chest, head held high, showing white across middle of wing and greyish underwings. Eye yellowish. Bill orange-yellow with white cere. **Immatures** browner, lacking neck patches and showing dark eyes and duller bills.

Voice & Diet Gives a muffled, rhythmic, cooing *cooo-coo, coo, coo-cu* song, delivered from a prominent perch. Engages in display flights which involves flying steeply upwards, wing clapping and gliding downwards. Feeds on a variety of seeds, cereals and, occasionally, insects.

Habitat and Status A very common resident species. Found in a wide range of habitats, including towns, cities, parks, gardens, farmlands, woodlands and open country. Nests in trees, in hedges or on the ground.

Rock Dove

Feral Pigeon

Time of year   Rock Dove

Feral Pigeon

J | F | M | A | M | J | J | A | S | O | N | D

Rock Dove & Feral Pigeon

Rock Dove

pale grey back, double black wingbar

Rock Doves

Adult

white rump black wingbar

Feral Pigeon

Feral Pigeons come in a wide variety of colours & patterns — combinations of black, grey, white & cinnamon — some looking like Rock Doves

Time of year

J | F | M | A | M | J | J | A | S | O | N | D

Stock Dove

grey head, mantle & wings

hint of two blackish wingbars

dark eye

pinkish breast, green neck patch

black border to wings & tail

Adult

Time of year

J | F | M | A | M | J | J | A | S | O | N | D

Woodpigeon

white neck patch

conspicuous white wing crescents

yellow eye

Adult

very common, in all wooded habitats

grey head, pinkish belly

often takes flight noisily — clatter of wings

the largest of the pigeons & doves

Time of year   Very common ■   Common ■   Rare □

Maps   Resident ■

135

Collared Dove *Streptopelia decaocto* Fearán baicdhubh   29-32cm

A slim, pale, sandy-brown dove with a longish tail. **Adults** show a pinkish-brown head, with a conspicuous black and white neck collar. Breast pinkish-brown with belly and undertail pale sandy-brown. Upperparts greyish-brown, with a pale greyish bend on the wing and darker primaries. Rump and tail sandy-brown with white outer tips to tail. From below, shows a diagnostic undertail pattern of a very broad, white outer band contrasting with dark inner undertail. In flight shows rounded wings with pale grey middle, dark primaries and pale underwings. Eye dark reddish. Bill slim and dark. Legs pinkish-brown. **Immatures** lack the half-collar, appear duller and show pale edges to upperpart feathers.

    Voice & Diet Gives a deep, cooing song consisting of *coo-cooo-oo,* the emphasis being on the second syllable. In flight gives a harsh, nasal *cwurr* call. Feeds on a wide variety of grain and seeds.

    Habitat and Status A widespread, common species. First recorded in the east of the country in 1959. Now present in all counties. Found in towns, parks, gardens and farmlands, and often seen in the vicinity of mills and grainstores. Will also visit bird tables.

Turtle Dove *Streptopelia turtur* Fearán   25-29cm

A small, slender dove with a longish tail and boldly marked upperparts. **Adults** show a blue-grey head with black and white neck patches. Breast pinkish. Belly and undertail whitish. Mantle and rump grey-brown. Scapulars, lesser and median coverts, inner greater coverts and tertials rufous with black centres. Secondaries, greater and primary coverts pale greyish, contrasting with dark primaries. Tail greyish-brown with a white terminal band and a dark subterminal band. Undertail dark with a narrow white tip. In flight shows greyish underwings. Eye and legs reddish-brown. Bill dark with reddish cere. **Immatures** duller and lack prominent neck patches.

    Voice & Diet Gives a very distinctive, soft, purring *torr-r-r* song, delivered from a prominent perch. Feeds on a wide variety of seeds and grain.

    Habitat and Status A scarce passage migrant from continental Europe, found in spring and autumn. Some may over-summer, and breeding has taken place on occasions. Most frequently found on passage on coastal headlands and islands, but can occur in open country with hedgerows and small woodlands. Nests in bushes and small trees.

Nightjar *Caprimulgus europaeus* Tuirne lín   25-28cm

A distinctive, well-camouflaged, crepuscular species which flies with easy, buoyant wing beats inter-spersed with floating glides on raised wings. In flight shows long wings and tail, a broad, flattened head and a very short, wide-gaped bill. **Adult males** show a greyish-brown plumage with a compli-cated pattern of black, brown, buff and cream barring, mottling, spotting and streaking. In flight shows white spots to the three outer primaries and white tips to the outer tail feathers. **Adult females** and **immatures** are similar, but lack the white wing spots and tail tips. During the day sits still among ground vegetation or on low, horizontal branches.

    Voice & Diet The song of Nightjar is an unmistakable, rapid, rhythmical churring which rises and falls in pitch. The song can continue for long periods of time. In flight gives a sharp *quu-ic* call. On the breeding grounds can also engage in loud wing-clapping during flight displays. Feeds on a variety of insects which are caught on the wing.

    Habitat and Status Once a widespread summer visitor but now a very rare breeding species and passage migrant. Nests near felled woodland and conifer plantations with open moorland areas. On passage found in well-vegetated areas of coastal headlands and islands.

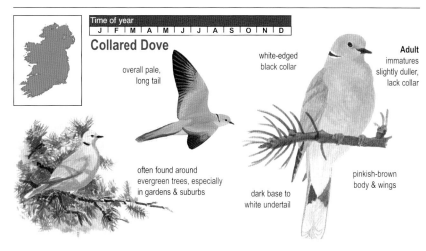

Time of year

| J | F | M | A | M | J | J | A | S | O | N | D |

Collared Dove

overall pale,
long tail

white-edged
black collar

Adult
immatures
slightly duller,
lack collar

often found around
evergreen trees, especially
in gardens & suburbs

dark base to
white undertail

pinkish-brown
body & wings

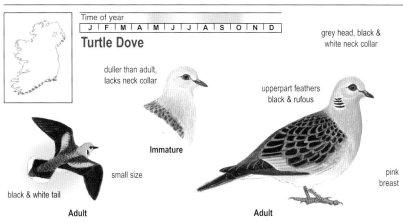

Time of year

| J | F | M | A | M | J | J | A | S | O | N | D |

Turtle Dove

grey head, black &
white neck collar

duller than adult,
lacks neck collar

upperpart feathers
black & rufous

Immature

small size

pink
breast

black & white tail

Adult

Adult

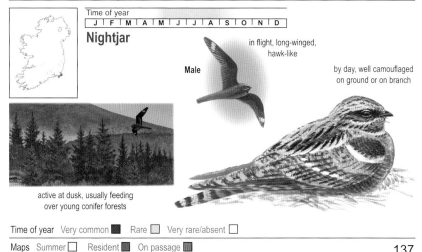

Time of year

| J | F | M | A | M | J | J | A | S | O | N | D |

Nightjar

in flight, long-winged,
hawk-like

Male

by day, well camouflaged
on ground or on branch

active at dusk, usually feeding
over young conifer forests

Time of year   Very common ■   Rare ☐   Very rare/absent ☐

Maps   Summer ☐   Resident ■   On passage ▦

Cuckoos

Cuckoo *Cuculus canorus* Cuach   32-35cm

A long-tailed, parasitic species appearing hawk-like in flight. **Adults** show a bluish-grey head, throat and upper breast with white underparts showing narrow, dark grey barring. Upperparts bluish-grey, with slightly darker wings which can be held drooped. The long, graduated, dark grey tail shows white spotting. Pointed, dark bill shows a yellowish base. Eyes yellow with a dark pupil. Legs yellow. **Females** can show brownish tones to the upperparts and a buff wash on the breast. **Immatures** show brownish upperparts with black barring, buffish-white underparts with dark barring, and distinctive white nape patches. Flies with rapid, shallow wing beats on pointed wings. Lays eggs in other species' nests, with young Cuckoos, on hatching, systematically removing all other eggs and chicks from the nest.

Voice & Diet Males give a very distinctive, far-carrying *cuc-coo* call, usually delivered from a prominent perch or on the wing. Females can give long, bubbling, chuckling calls and repeated *wah-wah* calls. Feeds on insects and larvae. The female, when laying an egg in a nest of a foster parent, will remove and eat an egg from that nest.

Habitat and Status A widespread summer migrant. Found on farmlands, moorlands, woodland edges, sand-dunes and, on passage, along coastal regions.

Great Spotted Cuckoo *Clamator glandarius* Mórchuach bhreac   35-38cm

A striking species, larger than Cuckoo and showing a long, white-edged, graduated tail. **Adults** show a crested grey cap, greyish-brown upperparts with bold white spots on the wings, creamy underparts and a yellowish throat. **Immatures** show a black crown, a yellowish throat, smaller wing spots and warm rufous on the primaries, very obvious in flight.

Voice & Diet Can give loud, rattling-type calls. Feeds on a variety of insects and larvae.

Habitat and Status A very rare passage migrant from southern Europe. Found in open country on coastal islands and headlands.

Yellow-billed Cuckoo *Coccyzus americanus* Cuach ghob-bhuí   28-32cm

A slim, secretive, long-tailed bird showing a curved bill with a striking, yellow lower mandible. **Adults** show a greyish crown and ear coverts, with greyish-brown upperparts contrasting with rufous wing patches. The wing patches are especially obvious in flight or when the wings are drooped. The long, graduated, blackish tail shows bold white tips, very striking from below. Underparts white. Shows a dark eye, a yellow orbital ring and greyish legs. **Immatures** similar, but show a dark grey tail with broad but more diffuse white tips. Flies with fast, shallow wing beats.

Voice & Diet Usually silent when found in Ireland. Feeds on a variety of insects, berries and fruit.

Habitat and Status An extremely rare autumn vagrant from North America. Frequents areas of scrub, dense bushes and well-vegetated gardens on coastal headlands and islands.

Black-billed Cuckoo *Coccyzus erythrophthalmus* Cuach ghobdhubh   28-32cm

A slim, secretive, long-tailed bird appearing very similar to Yellow-billed Cuckoo, but shows little or no rufous on the wings, has paler undertail feathers with smaller, more diffuse white tips, and shows a dark bill. **Adults** show a completely black bill, a dark eye and a red orbital ring. **Immatures** show a grey base to a dark bill and a pale yellow-buff orbital ring. Flies with fast, shallow wing beats. Can be easily overlooked, sitting still in deep cover or moving quietly through dense vegetation.

Voice & Diet Usually silent when found in Ireland. Feeds on a variety of insects, berries and fruit.

Habitat and Status An extremely rare autumn vagrant from North America. Frequents areas of scrub, dense bushes and well-vegetated gardens on coastal headlands and islands.

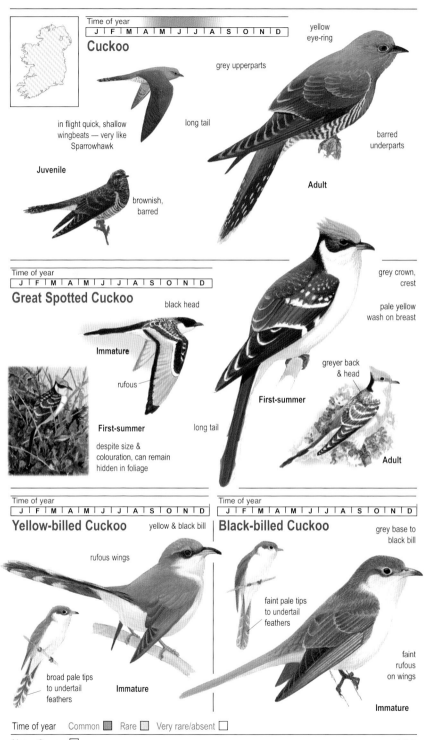

Time of year

| J | F | M | A | M | J | J | A | S | O | N | D |

Cuckoo

yellow eye-ring

grey upperparts

long tail

in flight quick, shallow
wingbeats — very like
Sparrowhawk

barred
underparts

Juvenile

brownish,
barred

Adult

Time of year

| J | F | M | A | M | J | J | A | S | O | N | D |

Great Spotted Cuckoo

grey crown,
crest

pale yellow
wash on breast

black head

Immature

rufous

greyer back
& head

First-summer

First-summer

long tail

despite size &
colouration, can remain
hidden in foliage

Adult

Time of year

| J | F | M | A | M | J | J | A | S | O | N | D |

Yellow-billed Cuckoo

yellow & black bill

rufous wings

broad pale tips
to undertail
feathers

Immature

Time of year

| J | F | M | A | M | J | J | A | S | O | N | D |

Black-billed Cuckoo

grey base to
black bill

faint pale tips
to undertail
feathers

faint
rufous
on wings

Immature

Time of year   Common ■   Rare ▨   Very rare/absent □

Barn Owl *Tyto alba* Scréachóg reilige 32-36cm

A distinctive species showing black eyes set in a white, heart-shaped face. Crown, mantle, wings, rump and tail orange-buff with varying amounts of grey speckling. Underparts white. **Females** generally show more buff on neck sides, wings and tail than **males**, and have variable, small, dark flecks on the breast. **Immatures** similar. When perched appears upright with a large head and longish legs. Flies with slow, deep wing beats. Can hover briefly when hunting.

Voice & Diet Gives an eerie, drawn-out screech, often delivered in flight. At, and around the nest, adult females and young give loud snoring and hissing calls. Feeds on small mammals such as rats, mice and shrews. Will also take small birds, particularly in winter, and occasionally bats, frogs and toads.

Habitat and Status A scarce, but widely distributed, resident breeding species, with the majority of breeding pairs now confined to the south-west. Has suffered a serious decline in recent years. Found in mainly lowland areas, hunting over open areas of rough grassland, hedgerow and forest edge. Nests in old, undisturbed buildings, ruins, farms and church towers, occasionally in suburban areas. Will also occasionally nest in hollows in trees. Slightly more widespread in winter.

Long-eared Owl *Asio otus* Ceann cait 34-37cm

A slim, upright, nocturnal species with striking, long tufts on the head. Greyish-brown crown contrasts with an orangy face which shows pale eyebrows and striking, black vertical lines from the tufts to the bill. Eyes bright orange. Pale buffish-white underparts show dark streaking to belly and onto flanks. Upperparts greyish-brown with fine barring and streaking. In flight shows an orangy upperwing with mottling on the coverts, barring on the secondaries and primaries, and a distinctive orangy primary patch. Underwing white with fine barring on the tip and a dark carpal patch. Tail shows indistinct barring. Flies with deep wing beats interspersed with glides.

Voice & Diet In spring gives a low, muffled, repeated *oo* call. Can also give a variety of wheezes, barks and screams as well as a call resembling the flight call of Collared Dove. Young birds can give a far-carrying, squeaking call. During display flights engages in wing-clapping. Feeds on mice, rats, shrews, birds and insects.

Habitat and Status A widespread, but uncommon, resident breeding species. Found in woodlands, nesting in old crow nests, squirrel dreys and occasionally on the ground. Autumn passage migrants from Europe can be found roosting in small trees or in hedgerows on coastal headlands and islands.

Short-eared Owl *Asio flammeus* Ulchabhán réisc 36-40cm

A stocky owl usually seen during daylight hours. A pale, sandy-buff crown shows two indistinct tufts, while a pale face shows bright yellow eyes set in black eye-rings. Dark streaking on pale buffish-white underparts usually confined to the breast, with faint flank streaking. Upperparts pale sandy-buff with dark, heavy blotching. In flight shows a pale buff upperwing with heavy mottling on coverts, strong barring on primaries and secondaries, a white trailing edge, a dark carpal patch, and a striking, pale primary patch. Underwing white with a solid dark tip and carpal patch. Tail strongly barred. Flies with slow, deep wing beats. Glides on raised wings.

Voice & Diet Gives a shrill, barking *kwock* call. Can also give a low-pitched *bo-bo-bo* call near the nest. During display flights engages in wing-clapping. Feeds on rats, mice and, where available, voles. Will also take small birds and insects.

Habitat and Status A scarce passage and winter visitor to Ireland from Iceland, northern Europe, Scotland and northern England. Breeding has occurred. Found on the ground or perched on posts close to rough vegetation, usually in coastal marshes or dunes as well as stubble fields, bogs and moorlands. Nests on the ground in heather, grass or gorse.

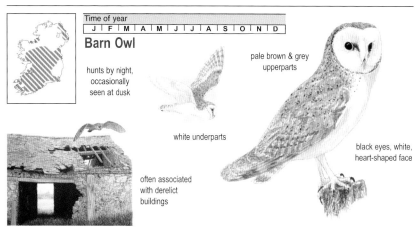

Time of year

| J | F | M | A | M | J | J | A | S | O | N | D |

Barn Owl

hunts by night, occasionally seen at dusk

pale brown & grey upperparts

white underparts

black eyes, white, heart-shaped face

often associated with derelict buildings

Time of year

| J | F | M | A | M | J | J | A | S | O | N | D |

Long-eared Owl

hunts by night

orange eyes & face

prominent 'ear tufts'

indistinct carpal patch

streaked brown underparts

remains well hidden in foliage by day

Time of year

| J | F | M | A | M | J | J | A | S | O | N | D |

Short-eared Owl

hunts by day

yellow eyes, whitish face

'ear tufts' barely noticable

distinct carpal patch

streaked brown underparts

Time of year Common ■ Rare ▨ Very rare/absent □

Maps Summer □ Winter ■ Resident ■

Owls

Snowy Owl *Bubo scandiacus* Ulchabhán sneachtúil   54-66cm

An enormous, diurnal owl with yellow eyes and long, broad, rounded wings. **Adult males** are pure white with scattered dark spots. **Adult females** are larger and show a white face and dark spotting on the crown. Upperparts show extensive dark barring on the back and coarse spotting on the wings. Underparts white with narrow dark barring. Breast centre white. **Immature males** like females but are considerably smaller and show finer barring and spotting on the upper and underparts. **Immature females** like adult female but show heavier barring on the upper and underparts highlighting the white face and breast centre, and show greyish wash on tertials. Shows densely feathered white feet and a short, dark bill.

    Voice & Diet Gives a harsh, *crek-crek* call as well as drawn-out mewing calls. Feeds on a wide range of small mammals and birds.

    Habitat and Status A rare passage vagrant and winter visitor from northern Europe and Iceland. Has also bred on a number of occasions. Nests in a scrape on the ground. Found on open areas of rocky moorland and bogs as well as on coastal headlands and islands.

Scop's Owl *Otus scops* Ulchabhán scopach   19-21cm

A tiny, slim and upright owl, smaller than Little Owl. Shows a greyish-brown, cryptically patterned plumage with delicate black streaking on the crown and underparts. Paler face shows a blackish border while the streaked upperparts show pale buff spotting and white braces. When relaxed appears rotund and shows small ear-tufts. When alert becomes more upright and flattened in appearance and shows long ear-tufts. Eyes yellow.

    Voice & Diet Song is a repetitive, short, low, whistling *tuub*. Feeds on small insects.

    Habitat and Status A very rare passage vagrant from southern Europe. Found in gardens on coastal islands and headlands.

Little Owl *Athene noctua* Ulchabhán beag   23-28cm

A small, squat owl with a large, rounded head and bright yellow eyes. Head and upperparts brownish with extensive white streaking and spotting. Underparts whitish with broad dark streaking. From behind the pale nape shows two dark patches creating 'false eyes'. Diurnal and crepuscular in behaviour, perching on posts and poles.

    Voice & Diet Gives a distinctive, sharp *kee-ew* call. Feeds on variety of insects, worms, small mammals, small amphibians and birds.

    Habitat and Status A rare vagrant from Europe. Found around open farmland, parks and open woodland.

Time of year

| J | F | M | A | M | J | J | A | S | O | N | D |

Snowy Owl

large size

Adult male
white plumage,
with only a few
dark spots

hunts by day on
open moorland

Immature female
white plumage, heavily barred grey,
greyish tertials

Adult female
white plumage
lightly barred grey

Owls

Time of year

| J | F | M | A | M | J | J | A | S | O | N | D |

Scop's Owl

yellow eyes

small

streaked, pale
grey plumage

nocturnal, remaining well
hidden by day

Time of year

| J | F | M | A | M | J | J | A | S | O | N | D |

Little Owl

yellow eyes

dark brown,
large white spots
on mantle

small

hunts by day, often perching prominently
in open country

Time of year   Rare ☐   Very rare/absent ☐

Swifts

Swift *Apus apus* Gabhlán gaoithe   16-18cm

A large, agile, all-dark bird with long, scythe-like wings and a short, forked tail. **Adults** show a small, inconspicuous pale throat patch which can contrast with the sooty-brown head, upperparts and underparts. The sooty-brown tail is short and shows a deep fork, although this is not always obvious as the tail can be closed to a point. **Immatures** show a slightly larger throat patch and appear browner. Small bill, eye and legs dark. Flies on stiff wings with rapid wing beats and skilful glides. Highly adapted to an aerial life, eating, sleeping and mating on the wing. Only lands during the breeding season. Highly gregarious, occasionally forming large, noisy flocks.

Voice & Diet Gives a long, loud, shrill, piercing screech, often delivered during rapid aerial chases around rooftops. Takes a variety of flying insects which are caught on the wing. Can store food items in the throat, which can give the throat a bulging appearance.

Habitat and Status A very common passage and summer visitor from wintering grounds in Africa. Found over towns, villages, cliffs, lakes, marshes and open country. Breeds in colonies, nesting in holes in eaves, under roof tiles, church towers and cliffs.

Alpine Swift *Apus melba* Gabhlán Alpach   20-23cm

A very large, brown and white swift with long, broad-based, scythe-like wings and a short, forked tail which can appear pointed when closed. Head, upperparts, rump and tail brown. A small, white throat patch contrasts with a brown breast band. Striking white belly conspicuous against brownish flanks and undertail. Upperwing uniform brown, with underwing showing contrasting, darker lesser and median coverts. Flight appears more lazy than Swift, with longer wings producing slower wing beats.

Voice & Diet Rarely heard in Ireland, but can give loud, trilling screeches. Feeds on a variety of insects which are caught on the wing.

Habitat and Status A very rare passage vagrant from southern Europe. Highly aerial, birds can be found almost anywhere, with sightings over towns, lakes, marshes, rivers and at coastal headlands and islands.

Pallid Swift *Apus pallidus* Gabhlán bánlíoch   16-18cm

Very similar in size and shape to Swift but shows a browner plumage and slightly broader wings. In flight shows a pale brown head with a thin, dark eye mask, a large, whitish throat patch, and pale-fringed brownish underparts. Underwings show a strong contrast between darker wing coverts and pale secondaries and inner primaries. Outer primaries dark. Upperwing shows similar pattern. From above shows a dark 'saddle' on the mantle contrasting with paler rump and head. Brown tail shows a shallow fork.

Voice & Diet Gives a long, loud, shrill, piercing screech similar to, but lower pitched than, Swift. Feeds on flying insects which are caught on the wing.

Habitat and Status A very rare spring and autumn passage vagrant from southern Europe. Found over towns, lakes, marshes and rivers near coastal headlands or islands.

Chimney Swift *Chaetura pelagica*   13-14cm

A small, compact, all-dark swift showing broad wings and a short, squared tail which, on very close view, shows thin spines. Shows an all-dark, brown plumage with paler throat and breast. In flight appears bat-like with fast, fluttering wingbeats and glides.

Voice & Diet Rarely heard in Ireland, but can give hard, chipping and twittering calls. Feeds on insects which are caught on the wing.

Habitat and Status An extremely rare autumn vagrant from North America. Most reports refer to birds seen over coastal headlands and islands.

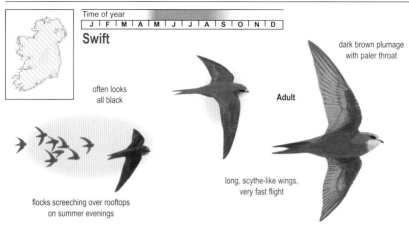

Time of year

| J | F | M | A | M | J | J | A | S | O | N | D |

Swift

often looks
all black

dark brown plumage
with paler throat

Adult

long, scythe-like wings,
very fast flight

flocks screeching over rooftops
on summer evenings

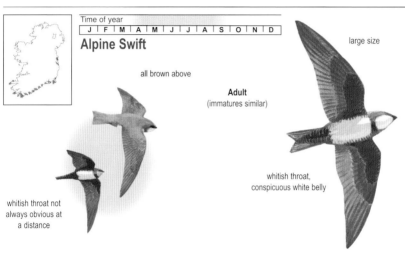

Time of year

| J | F | M | A | M | J | J | A | S | O | N | D |

Alpine Swift

all brown above

Adult
(immatures similar)

large size

whitish throat,
conspicuous white belly

whitish throat not
always obvious at
a distance

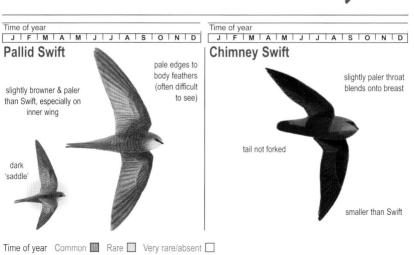

Time of year

| J | F | M | A | M | J | J | A | S | O | N | D |

Pallid Swift

slightly browner & paler
than Swift, especially on
inner wing

pale edges to
body feathers
(often difficult
to see)

dark
'saddle'

Time of year

| J | F | M | A | M | J | J | A | S | O | N | D |

Chimney Swift

slightly paler throat
blends onto breast

tail not forked

smaller than Swift

Time of year   Common ■   Rare ■   Very rare/absent □

Maps   Summer □   On passage ■

Kingfisher, Bee-eater & Roller

Kingfisher *Alcedo atthis* Cruidín   15-17cm

A small, brightly-coloured, short-winged bird with a long, dagger-like bill. **Adults** show a bright blue-green crown and moustachial stripe with pale barring and spotting. Nape dark blue-green. Dark loral stripe contrasts with bright orange-chestnut loral spot and ear coverts. Throat and neck patch white. Underparts bright orange-chestnut. Mantle to rump pale turquoise. Short, green-blue wings show pale spotting on the scapulars and coverts. Short tail bright blue. Bill dark with an orange-red base, more extensive on **females**. **Immatures** greener with paler underparts. Legs orange-red. Eye dark. Flies rapidly with whirring wing beats, the bright turquoise mantle and rump being very conspicuous.

Voice & Diet Gives a shrill, harsh *chee* or *chrii* call both in flight and when perched. The song is seldom heard and consists of a short trill. Feeds on a wide variety of small fish and aquatic insects. Dives into the water from an overhanging branch or open perch, opening wings on impact.

Habitat and Status A common resident bird found in all counties. Found along rivers and streams, and on lakes, canals and marshes. In winter can occur on coastal estuaries and bays, occasionally found feeding on channels on tidal marshes. Nests in excavated tunnels on banks of rivers, streams and canals.

Bee-eater *Merops apiaster* Beachadóir Eorpach   27-30cm

A brightly-coloured bird with a long, curved bill and long central tail feathers. **Adults** show a chestnut crown and nape, a white and blue forehead and supercilium, and black lores and ear coverts. A bright yellow throat shows a thin, black lower border. Underparts bright turquoise. Mantle pale chestnut. Upperwing very colourful with pale yellow scapulars, greenish lesser coverts, chestnut secondaries, median and greater coverts and blue primaries. Black tips to primaries and secondaries form a trailing edge to wings. Tail greenish-blue with long central feathers. **Immatures** similar, but show greenish upperparts and a shorter tail. Curved bill long and blackish. Eye brown. Flight graceful with rapid wing beats and glides.

Voice & Diet Gives a very distinctive bubbling, rolling, liquid *prruip* call which is loud, far-carrying and often repeated. Occasionally, when feeding or passing high overhead, can be heard clearly but not seen. Feeds on a wide variety of large flying insects such as bees and dragonflies which are caught on the wing.

Habitat and Status An extremely rare spring and autumn vagrant from southern Europe. Found in open country, usually with scattered trees for perching. Many sightings in Ireland refer to coastal headlands and islands.

Roller *Coracias garrulus* Rollóir   30-33cm

A large, brightly-coloured bird with a thick, dark, pointed bill. **Summer adults** show a bright turquoise head, a black eye-stripe, a chestnut mantle, dark blue and turquoise wing coverts, and blackish primaries and secondaries. Breast, belly, flanks and undertail bright turquoise. Rump bluish. Tail dark greenish-blue with pale turquoise edges and black tips to outer feathers. **Winter adults** and **immatures** show a dull brownish-green head and breast, and a duller mantle. In flight shows a dramatic wing pattern, with the dark blue leading edge and turquoise wing coverts contrasting strongly with the blackish primaries and secondaries. The undulating flight appears lazy.

Voice & Diet Gives a deep, harsh, crow-like *krr-rak* call. Can also give chattering-type calls. Feeds in a shrike-like manner, swooping down on large insects from a prominent perch on trees, wires or fences.

Habitat and Status An extremely rare passage vagrant from southern and central Europe. Found in open country with scattered trees, although when seen in Ireland may be close to coastal areas or on islands and headlands.

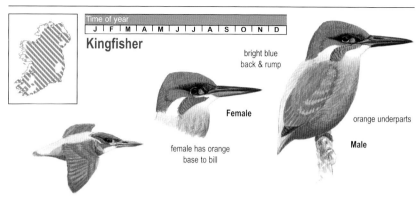

Time of year

| J | F | M | A | M | J | J | A | S | O | N | D |

Kingfisher

bright blue
back & rump

Female

orange underparts

female has orange
base to bill

Male

Time of year

| J | F | M | A | M | J | J | A | S | O | N | D |

Bee-eater

brightly coloured

Adult

Kingfisher, etc

Time of year

| J | F | M | A | M | J | J | A | S | O | N | D |

Roller

distinctive blue &
brown plumage

large size

Adult

Time of year   Common ■   Rare ■   Very rare/absent □

Maps   Resident ■   On passage ■

Hoopoe *Upupa epops* Húpú   26-28cm

An exotic species with a bold plumage and a long, curved bill. Crown shows a long, pinkish-brown, black-tipped crest. This can be fanned, but is usually depressed, giving the head a hammer-like profile. Apart from a thin, dark eye-stripe, the face, nape, throat, mantle and scapulars are pinkish-brown, contrasting with the bold black and white pattern of the wings. Breast pinkish-brown, fading to white on the belly, flanks and undertail. Tail black with a white central band. Flight appears lazy and undulating, the wings closing following each wing beat. In flight the striking wing pattern and the boldly patterned rump and tail are obvious.

Voice & Diet The distinctive, low *poo-poo-poo* song is rarely heard in Ireland. On occasions gives a quiet, chattering alarm call. Feeds on the ground in a methodical fashion, probing soft earth or sand for worms, larvae and insects.

Habitat and Status A scarce but annual passage vagrant from southern Europe. Found in a variety of habitats including farmland, coastal pastures, sand-dunes, parklands and gardens. On passage occurs on coastal islands and headlands. Has been recorded in winter.

Great Spotted Woodpecker *Dendrocopos major* Mórchnagaire breac   23-25cm

A striking pied woodpecker with a thick, pointed, dark bill, a dark eye and dark legs. **Adult males** show a black crown contrasting with a pale forehead, white cheeks and red and white nape patches. A black moustachial stripe joins a black stripe from the lower nape and continues down side of neck. Lower nape and upperparts black, with large, white oval shoulder patches. Wings blackish with white barring. Throat and underparts white, with a bright red undertail extending onto lower belly. Tail black with white-notched outer feathers. **Females** do not show a red nape patch. **Immatures** show a reddish crown, thinner moustachial stripes and faint barring on the white shoulder patches. Flight fast and undulating.

Voice & Diet Gives a loud, explosive *kiick* call. In early spring males declare their territories by loud but brief drumming on old tree trunks. Feeds on a wide range of insects, larvae, seeds and nuts. Will also take eggs and nestlings.

Habitat and Status Formerly a rare winter vagrant from northern Europe but now a rare breeding species. Nests in holes in trees. Found in open woodland. In winter will visit gardens and bird feeding stations.

Wryneck *Jynx torquilla* Cam-mhuin   15-16cm

A shy species with a complex plumage pattern. **Adults** and **immatures** alike, showing a brownish central crown stripe extending down nape and onto brownish mantle. Sides of crown greyish, continuing down to form a greyish V on mantle. Brown eye-stripe extends down side of neck. Pale supercilium visible behind eye. Fine barring present on whitish chin and buffish throat. Underparts grey-buff, with dark barring and arrowhead markings. Brownish wings show black, white and grey barring and spots. Rump and long tail greyish, with fine barring and dark bands on tail. Short, greyish, pointed bill. Legs brownish. Feet show two toes forward and two behind. Eye brownish with dark pupil. Flies with long glides on closed wings.

Voice & Diet Rarely heard in Ireland. On the breeding grounds gives shrill, falcon-like calls. Feeds chiefly on ants which are licked up from the ground, from old walls or from tree trunks. When feeding on the ground, hops with raised tail but can perch, woodpecker-like, when feeding on tree trunks.

Habitat and Status A rare but regular passage vagrant from northern and central Europe. On passage found on coastal headlands and islands, usually feeding along old walls, perching along hedgerows, or feeding in quiet, well-vegetated gardens.

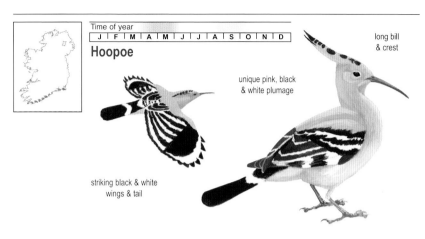

Time of year

| J | F | M | A | M | J | J | A | S | O | N | D |

Hoopoe

long bill
& crest

unique pink, black
& white plumage

striking black & white
wings & tail

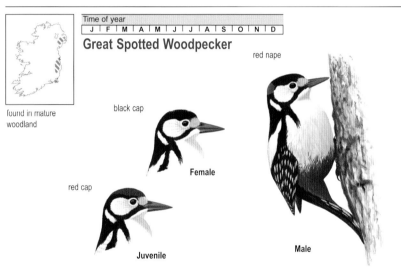

Time of year

| J | F | M | A | M | J | J | A | S | O | N | D |

Great Spotted Woodpecker

red nape

found in mature
woodland

black cap

Female

red cap

Juvenile

Male

Woodpeckers

Time of year

| J | F | M | A | M | J | J | A | S | O | N | D |

Wryneck

cryptic plumage
barred underparts

Time of year   Rare ▢   Very rare/absent ▢

Maps   Resident ▢   On passage ▢

149

Larks

Skylark *Alauda arvensis* Fuiseog   17-19cm

A large lark showing a long, streaked crest which can be raised or flattened on the head. Face appears plain, with a creamy supercilium, a thin eye-stripe behind the eye and thin streaking on brownish cheeks. Heavy streaking on the buffish breast extends as a malar stripe onto the paler throat. Underparts creamy. Upperparts brown with heavy blackish streaking. Flight undulating, showing a white trailing edge to the wings and white edges to the long tail. Pale bill thick and pointed. Legs pinkish. Shows a very long hindclaw. **Immatures** appear scaly with a short crest.

Voice & Diet Song consists of loud, clear, warbling notes delivered from high in the air. Also sings during fluttery display flights. Can sing from posts or trees. In flight gives a rippling *chirrup* call. Feeds on a variety of seeds, worms, insects and larvae.

Habitat and Status A widespread, resident breeding species. Found in a variety of habitats, including moorlands, farmlands, rough pastures and sand-dunes. Also found on stubble fields in autumn. Nests on the ground.

Short-toed Lark *Calandrella brachydactyla* Fuiseog ladharghearr   13-14cm

A dumpy, sparrow-like lark with a thick, pale bill and pale legs. Streaked, sandy-brown crown can show a short crest. Creamy supercilium contrasts with a dark eye-stripe behind the eye. Cheeks show faint streaking. Upperparts pale sandy-brown with thin streaking. Dark-centred median coverts show as a bar across the wing. Short primaries usually hidden under the long tertials. Underparts whitish, with dark patches on the sides of the breast. In flight shows a plain wing and white edges to the tail.

Voice & Diet Gives chirruping *tchi-tchirrp* and drawn-out *tee-oo* calls. Feeds on seeds and insects.

Habitat and Status A rare spring and autumn passage vagrant from southern Europe. Usually found on areas of open sandy or stony ground, short grassy areas and stubble fields at coastal locations.

Woodlark *Lullula arborea* Fuiseog choille   13-15cm

Like Skylark, but shows a shorter tail, an ill-defined crest, a striking whitish supercilium which almost meets on the nape, and unstreaked, warm, rufous-brown ear coverts. Crown and upperparts brownish, with heavy, dark streaking. Whitish underparts show a buff-washed breast with clear, dark spotting. In flight the wings show two black and white patches on the leading edge, but lack a white trailing edge. Short tail shows brown sides and conspicuous white tips.

Voice & Diet Gives a soft *thewee* call. Song is a series of warbling notes delivered during display flights. Feeds on seeds and insects.

Habitat and Status Formerly a common breeding species but now an extremely rare vagrant from Europe. Usually found on areas of open ground on coastal islands and headlands.

Shore Lark *Eremophila alpestris* Fuiseog adharcach   16-18cm

A large lark showing a striking, pale yellowish face, a black loral stripe extending onto the cheeks, and a dark eye-stripe behind eye. Rear cheeks yellowish. Pale yellow supercilium is bordered above by a black stripe which forms short horns on the side of the head. The pale yellowish throat contrasts with a black gorget across the breast. Nape and upperparts pinkish-brown with dark streaking. Underparts whitish with buff streaking on flanks. In **summer** shows longer horns and a bright yellow face and throat. Wings plain. Tail shows white outer edges. Bill greyish. Legs dark.

Voice & Diet Gives pipit-like *tsee-tsi* and whistling-type *tsiu* calls. Feeds on seeds and insects.

Habitat and Status An extremely rare vagrant from northern Europe with most records referring to winter months. Found on coastal, stony shingle or sandy beaches and stubble fields.

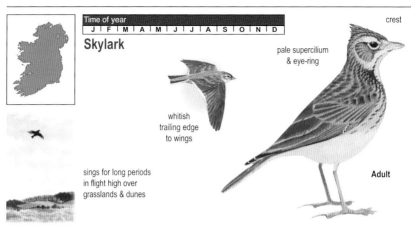

Time of year

| J | F | M | A | M | J | J | A | S | O | N | D |

Skylark

crest

pale supercilium & eye-ring

whitish trailing edge to wings

sings for long periods in flight high over grasslands & dunes

Adult

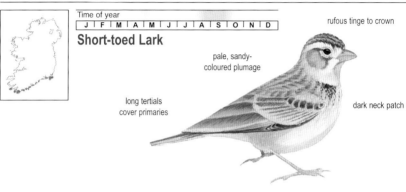

Time of year

| J | F | M | A | M | J | J | A | S | O | N | D |

Short-toed Lark

rufous tinge to crown

pale, sandy-coloured plumage

long tertials cover primaries

dark neck patch

Time of year

| J | F | M | A | M | J | J | A | S | O | N | D |

Woodlark

rufous cheeks

white supercilium meets on nape

Time of year

| J | F | M | A | M | J | J | A | S | O | N | D |

Shore Lark

Adult summer

small 'horns' on crown (can be hard to see)

distinctive black & yellow face pattern

found on gravel or stony areas, usually near coast

Adult winter

Larks

Time of year   Very common ■   Rare □   Very rare/absent □

Maps   Resident ■   On passage ▨

Swallows & Martins

Swallow *Hirundo rustica* Fáinleog   16-22cm

Adults show a glossy bluish head, a dark red forehead and throat patch, a dark bluish breast band, and long tail streamers. Underparts creamy white. Upperparts and rump dark glossy blue. Wings browner. White subterminal patches on the central tail feathers form a distinctive white band on the undertail and narrow white markings on the uppertail. Tail streamers longest on males. **Immatures** show shorter tail streamers and buffish throat and forehead patches. Short legs and bill dark.

Voice & Diet Gives a high, tinkling *vitt* call. Song combines various twittering, warbling and trilling notes. Feeds on insects which are caught on the wing.

Habitat and Status A common summer visitor from wintering grounds in southern Africa. Builds a nest of mud pellets under rafters, and on ledges and under eaves of old sheds and barns. Faithful to nest sites. Found on farmlands, in suburbs, and over lakes and rivers. Will roost in reedbeds.

House Martin *Delichon urbicum* Gabhlán binne   12-14cm

A compact bird with a forked tail and a large, conspicuous white rump. **Adults** show a metallic dark blue head and upperparts. Throat and underparts white. Wings browner. Large white rump contrasts strongly with the dark upperparts and the dark, metallic blue forked tail which lacks long tail streamers. **Immatures** show a brownish wash on the breast, duller upperparts and white tips to the tertials. Wings more triangular in shape than Swallow. Bill dark. Legs and feet feathered white.

Voice & Diet Gives clear *tchirrrip* and sharp *tseep* calls. Song consists of weak, chirruping, twittering notes. Feeds on insects which are caught on the wing.

Habitat and Status A common summer visitor from wintering grounds in Africa. Found in towns, villages, farms and around cliffs. Nests in colonies. Builds a nest made of mud pellets under eaves of houses, on bridges or on cliffs.

Sand Martin *Riparia riparia* Gabhlán gainimh   11-13cm

A small brown and white species with a short tail and a brown breast band. **Adults** show a dull brown crown, nape and ear coverts. Chin and throat white, contrasting with a broad, brown breast band. Underparts white. Upperparts brown. Brown tail is short and shows a very shallow fork. **Immatures** show pale edges to wing and upperpart feathers, creating a scaly appearance. In flight shows brownish underwings. Short legs and bill dark.

Voice & Diet Gives a short, sharp, dry, repeated *tchrrip* call. Song consists of weak, harsh twittering. Feeds on insects which are caught on the wing.

Habitat and Status A common summer visitor from wintering grounds in southern Africa. Found in areas close to water. Breeds in colonies, digging and nesting in tunnels in sand or earth banks.

Red-rumped Swallow *Cecropis daurica* Fáinleog ruaphrompach   16-19cm

A stocky bird with long, broad tail streamers and a striking, pale buff rump. **Adults** show a metallic blue crown, with a chestnut-buff nape and supercilium and pale buff face. Mantle, scapulars and tertials metallic blue, with remainder of wings brownish. Underparts pale buff with thin streaking. In flight shows a striking warm-to-pale-buff rump which can appear two-toned, and a long black tail with no white spots or markings. The upper and undertail coverts are also black, making the tail appear extremely long and broad-based. **Immatures** show a paler neck collar and rump, and shorter tails. Short legs and bill dark.

Voice & Diet Gives a short, rasping *tschirrit* call. Feeds on insects caught on the wing.

Habitat and Status A rare spring and late autumn visitor from southern Europe. Usually found over open country, marshes, lakes and rivers at coastal locations.

152

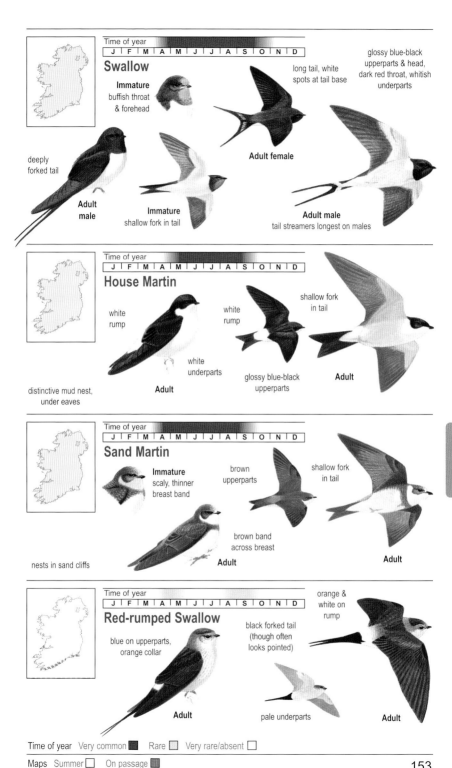

Time of year

J F M A M J J A S O N D

Swallow

Immature
buffish throat & forehead

long tail, white spots at tail base

glossy blue-black upperparts & head, dark red throat, whitish underparts

deeply forked tail

Adult male

Immature
shallow fork in tail

Adult female

Adult male
tail streamers longest on males

Time of year

J F M A M J J A S O N D

House Martin

white rump

white rump

shallow fork in tail

white underparts

glossy blue-black upperparts

Adult

distinctive mud nest, under eaves

Adult

Time of year

J F M A M J J A S O N D

Sand Martin

Immature
scaly, thinner breast band

brown upperparts

shallow fork in tail

brown band across breast

nests in sand cliffs

Adult

Adult

Time of year

J F M A M J J A S O N D

Red-rumped Swallow

blue on upperparts, orange collar

black forked tail (though often looks pointed)

orange & white on rump

Adult

pale underparts

Adult

Time of year Very common ▮ Rare ▢ Very rare/absent ▢

Maps Summer ▢ On passage ▮

153

Swallows

Pipits

Meadow Pipit *Anthus pratensis* Riabhóg mhóna   14-15cm
A small, active pipit, similar to Tree Pipit. **In spring** shows streaked brownish upperparts and crown. A pale supercilium fades behind the eye while a faint eye-stripe behind the eye gives the face a plain appearance. Underparts show a dark malar and heavy streaking extending down as heavy flank streaking. Whitish underparts show a faint buffish wash on the breast. **In autumn** upperparts brighter with a yellowish-buff wash to underparts. Rump unstreaked. Tail shows white outer feathers. Legs pink-orange with a long hindclaw. Bill pale with a dark tip.

   Voice & Diet Gives a thin, repeated *tsip* call. Song is a series of accelerated, thin, piping notes given during a display flight, ending in a glide and giving a rapid, musical trill. Feeds on a variety of insects and larvae, as well as seeds in the autumn.

   Habitat and Status A common, widespread, resident species. Frequents rough pastures, farmland, sand-dunes, moorlands and offshore islands. Nests in a shallow depression on the ground.

Tree Pipit *Anthus trivialis* Riabhóg choille   14-15cm
A small pipit, similar to Meadow Pipit. **In spring** shows streaked, greenish upperparts and crown. Supercilium strong behind the eye, contrasting with a dark eye-stripe which may extend across the lores. Pale spot often present on rear ear coverts. Underparts show a dark malar and heavy streaking on breast, becoming thinner on the flanks. Underparts show a strong orange-buff wash on the breast contrasting with whiter belly. **In autumn** breast can show a creamy wash. Rump unstreaked. Tail shows white outer feathers. Legs pinkish with a short hindclaw. Bill pale with dark tip.

   Voice & Diet Gives a buzzing *tzeep* call and also a soft *sip* call. Song is a loud, accelerated series of notes given during a display flight, and ending with repeated *seea* notes given during a descending glide. Feeds in a slow, methodical manner, taking a variety of small insects.

   Habitat and Status A scarce but annual spring and autumn passage migrant from Europe. Usually found feeding with other pipits on open pastures on coastal islands and headlands.

Red-throated Pipit *Anthus cervinus* Riabhóg phíbrua   15-16cm
In autumn resembles a cold-plumaged Meadow Pipit. Brownish upperparts show two pale tramlines contrasting with dark streaking and a streaked rump. Tail shows white outer feathers. Pale supercilium contrasts with a streaked crown and dark eye-stripe. Creamy-white underparts show a dark malar meeting heavy breast streaking which extends onto flanks. **In summer** shows a red throat and face. Legs pale pinkish. Bill pale with a dark tip.

   Voice & Diet Gives a distinctive, explosive, thin *prseeeee* call. Feeds on insects, larvae and seeds.

   Habitat and Status A very rare passage vagrant from northern Europe and Scandinavia. Found on coastal headlands and islands, feeding on open rough pastures and farmland.

Olive-backed Pipit *Anthus hodgsoni* Riabhóg dhroimghlas   14-15cm
Similar to Tree Pipit. Olive-green upperparts and crown show very faint streaking. Facial pattern very striking, showing a strong, pale supercilium contrasting with a dark lateral crown stripe and a dark eye-stripe. Rear of the ear coverts show a whitish teardrop-shaped spot and a dark border. Underparts show an orange-buff wash on the breast contrasting with whiter belly, a dark malar stripe, and heavy breast streaking, becoming thinner on the flanks. Rump unstreaked. Tail shows white outer feathers. Bill pale. Legs pale pinkish. Persistently pumps tail when feeding.

   Voice & Diet Gives a thin, hoarse, repeated *tseep* call. Feeds on a variety of insects.

   Habitat and Status An extremely rare autumn vagrant from north-eastern Russia and Asia. Found on rough pastures, farmlands and well-vegetated gardens on coastal headlands and islands.

Meadow Pipit

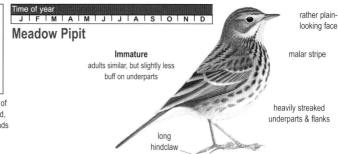

rather plain-looking face

malar stripe

Immature
adults similar, but slightly less buff on underparts

a very common bird of grasslands, moorland, fields, open grasslands

heavily streaked underparts & flanks

long hindclaw

Tree Pipit

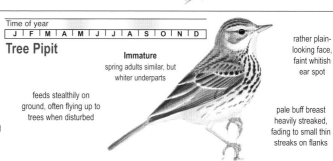

rather plain-looking face, faint whitish ear spot

Immature
spring adults similar, but whiter underparts

feeds stealthily on ground, often flying up to trees when disturbed

on passage not necessarily associated with trees

pale buff breast heavily streaked, fading to small thin streaks on flanks

---

Red-throated Pipit

brick red breast & face

whitish lines on mantle

whitish lines on mantle

dark streaking on white breast

Adult summer
this plumage very rare in Ireland

lacking buff tones

Immature

Pipits

Olive-backed Pipit

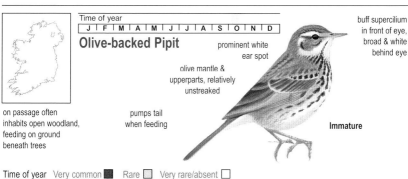

buff supercilium in front of eye, broad & white behind eye

prominent white ear spot

olive mantle & upperparts, relatively unstreaked

pumps tail when feeding

on passage often inhabits open woodland, feeding on ground beneath trees

Immature

Time of year   Very common ▓   Rare ▒   Very rare/absent ☐

Maps   Resident ▓   On passage ▒

Pipits

Rock Pipit *Anthus petrosus* Riabhóg chladaigh 15-17cm

A rather drab pipit, slightly larger and taller than Meadow Pipit. Upperparts dull olive-grey with dark streaking and showing inconspicuous, creamy-buff wingbars. Rump dull greyish-brown. Shows a faint, pale supercilium and a thin, dark eye-stripe which highlights a narrow, pale eye-ring. Ear coverts show a dark lower border. Dull creamy underparts show a dark malar stripe and heavy brown streaking on the breast and flanks which may extend onto the paler belly. In flight appears long-winged. Unlike other pipits, the darkish tail shows greyish outer feathers. Long, dagger-like bill is pale with a dark tip. Legs blackish but can show a dull pinkish hue. **Scandinavian race** *littoralis,* identical in winter but in spring can show pinkish tones to underparts, reduced streaking on breast and paler outer tail-feathers.

Voice & Diet Gives a loud, full, harsh *pseep* call. Song is similar to that of Meadow Pipit but is a louder, more musical series of accelerated notes given during a rising display flight. The song finishes with a loud, strong trill given during a descending glide. Feeds on a variety of insects, larvae, molluscs and seeds.

Habitat and Status A common, resident breeding species found in all coastal counties. Rarely found inland. Frequents areas of rocky coastline and islands, occasionally occurring on mudflats and estuaries in winter. Nests in holes or crevices in rocks or cliffs.

Water Pipit *Anthus spinoletta* Riabhóg uisce 15-17cm

A timid pipit, similar to Rock Pipit but showing a more contrasting plumage. In **winter** shows plain greyish-brown upperparts with faint streaking and contrasting whitish wingbars and edges to the tertials. Greyish-brown crown shows dark streaking and contrasts with a white supercilium which tapers to a point towards the nape. Nape usually appears paler than mantle. Underparts whitish, with dark streaking on the breast becoming diffuse on the flanks. Unlike Rock Pipit, shows striking, white outer tail-feathers. In **summer** shows a bluish-grey head, a white supercilium and whitish underparts with a pale pink wash on the breast and faint streaking on the flanks. Pale, pointed bill shows a dark tip. Legs dark.

Voice & Diet Gives a *fist* call which, although similar to Rock Pipit, sounds thinner and shorter. Feeds on a wide range of insects, larvae and worms. Will occasionally take seeds.

Habitat and Status A rare but regular passage and winter visitor from Europe. Found on flooded fields, marshes, saltmarshes or along the fringes of small lakes, usually close to coastal locations. Not approachable, flushing easily.

Buff-bellied Pipit *Anthus rubescens* Riabhóg tharr-dhonnbhuí 15-16cm

Initially similar to Water Pipit but is smaller and more compact while the plain, unmarked lores can give the species a more Meadow Pipit-like appearance. In **autumn** and **winter** shows a greyish brown crown and mantle with faint streaking and dull pale wingbars. Shows a neat, whitish eye-ring and a pale buff supercilium, often with warmer tones on the lores. Ear coverts greyish-brown with a dark lower border. Underparts show warm buff tones with a well-defined malar stripe and heavy breast streaking becoming more diffuse on the flanks. Tail shows white outer feathers. In **summer** shows greyish upperparts, and orange-buff underparts with faint streaking. Bill pale with a dark tip. Legs dark.

Voice & Diet Gives a single, high, Meadow Pipit-like *tsipp* call. Feeds on a variety of insects, larvae and seeds.

Habitat and Status A very rare autumn vagrant from North America. Found along rocky coast-lines and beaches. Often found with Rock Pipits foraging for insects on exposed seaweed.

Littoralis Rock Pipit

J	F	M	A	M	J	J	A	S	O	N	D

Rock Pipit

Rock Pipit rarely strays inland

Littoralis Rock Pipit

greyish crown & mantle

pink flush on breast (variable)

Adult summer *Littoralis* or 'Scandinavian Rock Pipit'

faint supercilium

drab overall, pale wingbars

heavily streaked underparts

Adult (immatures similar)

dark legs

Time of year

J	F	M	A	M	J	J	A	S	O	N	D

Water Pipit

found on freshwater margins, occasionally washed-up seaweed on beaches

greyish head

paler underparts & wingbars

Adult, summer

pale pinkish wash to breast (variable)

Adult winter (immatures similar)

Time of year

J	F	M	A	M	J	J	A	S	O	N	D

Buff-bellied Pipit

found on coast, often on washed-up seaweed on beaches

very similar to Meadow Pipit & Rock Pipit but more buff on breast & head

buff supercilium

buff wash to underparts

Immature autumn

dark legs

Time of year   Very common ■   Rare ☐   Very rare/absent ☐

Maps   Winter ■   Resident ■   On passage ▥

Pipits

Pipits & Pied Wagtail

Richard's Pipit *Anthus richardi* Riabhóg Richard   17-19cm
A large, bulky pipit with brownish upperparts showing heavy, dark streaking and dark centres to wing feathers. Nape and crown streaked. Broad, creamy supercilium contrasts with a dark eye-stripe behind the eye. Lores pale. Ear coverts appear pale-centred and show a dark moustachial stripe. A thick, dark malar stripe ends with a large dark spot where it meets the diffuse streaking on the breast. Underparts buff, especially on the flanks. Long, dark tail shows white outer feathers. Pale, thick bill shows a dark tip. Long, orangy legs show a long hindclaw. Sometimes hovers before perching.
    Voice & Diet Gives a distinctive, sharp, explosive *schreep* call. Feeds on insects, larvae and seeds.
    Habitat and Status A rare autumn vagrant from Siberia. Also recorded in winter. Usually found on rough pastures on coastal headlands and islands.

Tawny Pipit *Anthus campestris* Riabhóg dhonn   16-18cm
A large, slender, wagtail-like, pale, sandy-coloured pipit. Sandy upperparts, nape and crown either lacks streaking or shows very faint streaking. Dark centres to median coverts create a striking bar on the plain wing. Pale supercilium contrasts with a dark eye-stripe and lores. Ear coverts sandy with a dark moustachial stripe. Thin, darkish malar stripe fades into faint streaking on the breast. Can lack breast streaking. Underparts creamy. Long tail shows creamy-buff outer feathers. Shows a pale, thin bill. Long, orangy legs show a short hindclaw.
    Voice & Diet Gives soft, *tseeup* and loud, *chirrup* calls. Feeds on insects, larvae and worms.
    Habitat and Status A rare spring and autumn passage vagrant from southern Europe. Found on short grass, rough pastures and farmlands, usually at coastal locations.

Pied Wagtail *Motacilla alba yarrellii* Glasóg shráide   17-19cm
A black and white bird with a long, constantly wagging tail. **Summer males** show a white face and forehead, with a black crown and nape meeting a black bib. Back, wings and rump black. Wings show white bars and white-edged tertials. Tail black with white outer edges. Underparts white with dark grey flanks. **Summer females** show a blackish-grey back. **Winter adults** show a white throat, a black, crescent-shaped breast band and a blackish-grey back. **Juveniles** show a brownish-grey crown and back, a black rump, a buff-tinged face and throat, a messy breast band and greyish flanks. **First-winter** birds similar to winter adults, but show greyish upperparts.

Birds of the race *alba*, known as **White Wagtails**, differ with **summer males** showing a white face and forehead, with a black crown and nape which do not meet the black bib. Back ash-grey, contrasting with crown and blackish wings which show whitish bars and white-edged tertials. Greyish rump contrasts with black, white-edged tail. Underparts white with clean flanks. On **summer females** grey of back extends onto nape. **Winter adults** differ by showing a white throat and a black, crescent-shaped breast band. **Immatures** show a grey crown, back and rump, paler wings with fainter bars, a thin, messy breast band and clean flanks. Can show pale yellow tones to face and throat. Legs and thin, pointed bill black on both races.

    Voice & Diet Both races give a loud, shrill *tchissick* call with an abrupt *tchik* call given in alarm. Song consists of twitters and warbles. Feeds on a wide variety of insects and seeds.
    Habitat and Status A widespread and common species. Found around towns, farms and shorelines. Nests in holes in walls, in sheds and under plants. White Wagtail is an uncommon spring and autumn passage migrant from Iceland and continental Europe.

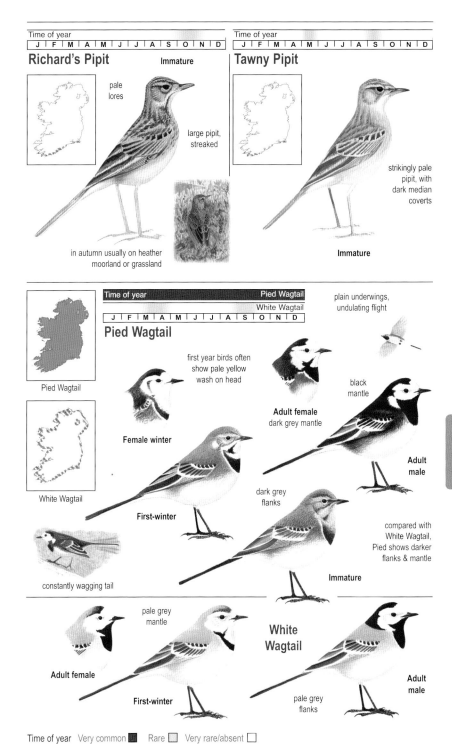

Richard's Pipit

Immature

pale lores

large pipit, streaked

in autumn usually on heather moorland or grassland

Tawny Pipit

strikingly pale pipit, with dark median coverts

Immature

Pied Wagtail

plain underwings, undulating flight

Pied Wagtail

first year birds often show pale yellow wash on head

Female winter

Adult female
dark grey mantle

black mantle

Adult male

White Wagtail

First-winter

dark grey flanks

constantly wagging tail

Immature

compared with White Wagtail, Pied shows darker flanks & mantle

pale grey mantle

Adult female

First-winter

White Wagtail

pale grey flanks

Adult male

Pipits, wagtails

Time of year   Very common ■   Rare □   Very rare/absent □

Maps   Resident ■   On passage ▨

159

Wagtails

Grey Wagtail *Motacilla cinerea* Glasóg liath   18-20cm

A bright bird with a long, constantly wagging tail. **Summer males** show a grey head and mantle, a white supercilium, a black throat and white sub-moustachial stripes. Wings darker, with white-edged tertials. Tail black with white edges. Rump bright yellowish-green. Breast, undertail and centre of belly bright yellow. Flanks white. **Females** differ by showing a whitish throat, buffish supercilium, greenish tones to ear coverts and a paler breast. **Winter males** similar to females, but show a buff-yellow breast. **Immatures** similar to winter adults, but upperparts greyish-brown. Legs pinkish. Bill thin and dark. Appears slim and long-tailed in flight, with a white wingbar and dark underwing coverts.

    Voice & Diet Gives a sharp, abrupt, loud *stzit* or *stzitzi* call. Song consists of a twittering, trilling warble. Feeds on a wide variety of insects, larvae and even molluscs.

    Habitat and Status A common, widespread, resident species. Usually found along fast-moving rivers and streams. Can also occur in cities, feeding along dockland areas and around park ponds. Nests in holes or on ledges under bridges, walls or old buildings near water.

Yellow Wagtail *Motacilla flava* Glasóg bhuí   16-17cm

A slender, long-tailed species with a thin, pointed, dark bill and dark legs. **Spring males** show bright yellow underparts, throat and supercilium which contrast with a yellow-green crown, ear coverts and upperparts. Dark wings show two narrow white bars and thin white edges to the tertials. Rump greenish. Tail dark with white outer feathers. **Females** show brownish-green upperparts with a pale, yellow-washed supercilium, throat, breast and undertail. **Immatures** similar to females with a pale supercilium and chin, and can show a dark malar stripe and breast band. Blue-headed, Ashy-headed, Grey-headed and Black-headed races can occur and the males of these races show distinctive head patterns.

    Voice & Diet Gives a very distinctive, thin, *tsweep* call both on the ground when feeding and in flight. Song is a series of short, warbling, thin *tsip-tsip* notes. Feeds on a wide range of small insects and larvae. Often found close to cattle, flitting suddenly into the air to catch insects disturbed by the feeding animals.

    Habitat and Status A scarce but regular spring and autumn passage migrant and a rare breeding species. On passage found at coastal locations, feeding on rough pastures, marshes and short turf. In summer frequents lowland rough pastures, farmlands, marshes and wet meadows. Nests on the ground in cover of grass tussocks or crops. Other races are scarce to very rare vagrants from Europe, with Blue-headed Wagtails recorded annually. Blue-headed has also bred.

Citrine Wagtail *Motacilla citreola* Glasóg chiotrónach   15-17cm

A striking wagtail with a heavy, black, pointed bill and a long, black, white-edged tail. **Adult males** show a bright yellow head and underparts with white undertail coverts. A black half-collar contrasts with pale grey upperparts. Blackish wings show two broad white wingbars and white edges to tertials. **Females** show a greyish-brown crown and ear coverts, a grey nape, a yellow supercilium and throat, and diffuse yellow underparts with a whitish undertail. **Immatures** show a greyish crown and nape, with a whitish supercilium continuing around pale grey ear coverts and onto sides of breast. The whitish breast can show diffuse spots forming an indistinct gorget. Upperparts and rump grey with wings showing two broad white wingbars and white tertial edges as on adults. Underparts whitish. Undertail-coverts white. Legs dark.

    Voice & Diet Gives a very distinctive, loud Yellow Wagtail-like *tsreep* flight call. Feeds on a wide range of insects and larvae.

    Habitat and Status A rare passage vagrant from eastern Europe and Asia. Found at coastal locations, feeding in rough, wet pastures, in marshes and on short turf.

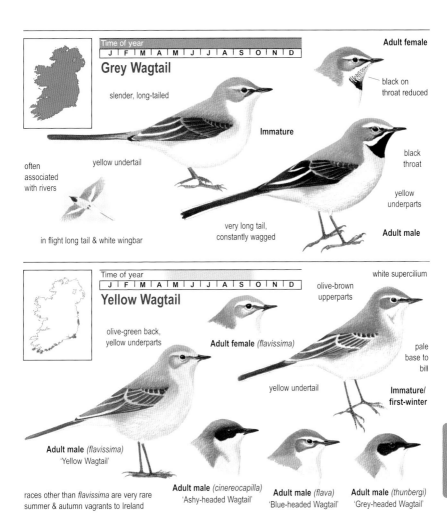

Grey Wagtail

slender, long-tailed

Adult female

black on throat reduced

often associated with rivers

yellow undertail

Immature

black throat

yellow underparts

in flight long tail & white wingbar

very long tail, constantly wagged

Adult male

Yellow Wagtail

olive-green back, yellow underparts

Adult female (*flavissima*)

white supercilium

olive-brown upperparts

pale base to bill

yellow undertail

Immature/ first-winter

Adult male (*flavissima*)
'Yellow Wagtail'

races other than *flavissima* are very rare summer & autumn vagrants to Ireland

Adult male (*cinereocapilla*)
'Ashy-headed Wagtail'

Adult male (*flava*)
'Blue-headed Wagtail'

Adult male (*thunbergi*)
'Grey-headed Wagtail'

Wagtails

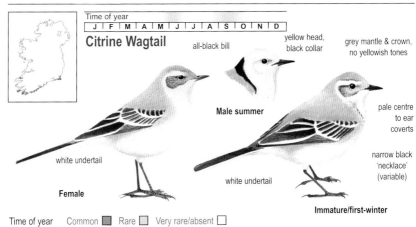

Citrine Wagtail

all-black bill

yellow head, black collar

grey mantle & crown, no yellowish tones

Male summer

pale centre to ear coverts

white undertail

narrow black 'necklace' (variable)

white undertail

Female

Immature/first-winter

Time of year   Common ▪   Rare ▫   Very rare/absent ☐

Maps   Resident ▪   On passage ▨

161

Waxwing, Dipper & Wren

Waxwing *Bombycilla garrulus* Síodeiteach   17-19cm

A tame, colourful species. **Adults** show a pinkish-brown head with a long crest, a black eye mask, a black bib which is sharply defined on males, and a white line from the bill onto the face. The cheeks are pinkish-brown but show warm chestnut tones. Upperparts greyish-brown. Wings show white and yellow V-tips to the black primaries, white and bright red waxy tips to the secondaries and white-tipped primary coverts. Rump grey. Tail shows a black subterminal band and a bright yellow tip. Underparts pinkish-brown with deep rufous-brown undertail coverts. Short, dark bill slightly hooked. **Immatures** show paler, duller wings. In flight appears very Starling-like, showing a short tail and triangular wings.

  Voice & Diet Gives a very distinctive, weak, trilling *sirrrrr* call. Feeds on a variety of berries and buds in winter. Will also eat fruit. In spring can sometimes be seen fly-catching.

  Habitat and Status An uncommon to rare winter visitor from Scandinavia, found in very small numbers annually. In some years can occur in large numbers known as 'irruptions'. Usually reported in town and city gardens.

Dipper *Cinclus cinclus* Gabha dubh   17-19cm

A plump, short-tailed species with a striking white throat and breast. Seen along fast-flowing rivers, perching on rocks and bobbing continuously before plunging into the water. **Adults** show a dark brown head, a blackish mantle, wings, rump and tail, and a white throat and breast. This white gorget is bordered below by a dull chestnut band which fades into the blackish belly and flanks. Short bill dark. Legs greyish. When perched, flashes a white eyelid when blinking. **Immatures** show a dark greyish head and upperparts, and a dirty, off-white gorget. Flight fast and direct, usually low over the water. Continental European birds lack the chestnut lower border to the white gorget.

  Voice & Diet Gives a loud, sharp *zit-zit* call, usually in flight. Can also give a hard *klink* note. The song is a series of warbling and grating notes. Feeds by walking along the bottom of a stream or swimming on or below the surface of the water, searching for a variety of aquatic insects. Also takes molluscs, crustaceans, small fish, worms and tadpoles.

  Habitat and Status A scarce but widely distributed resident breeding species. Found along fast-flowing streams and rivers. Builds a domed nest on walls, on ledges, under bridges or among tree roots, always nesting above or close to water. The Black-bellied, European race is a rare winter vagrant to Ireland.

associated exclusively with
fast-running streams

Wren *Troglodytes troglodytes* Dreoilín   9-10cm

A tiny, active species which shows very short, rounded wings and a stubby, cocked tail. **Adults** show a rufous-brown head and a striking, pale buff supercilium. Upperparts and short wings rufous-brown with dark barring. Short, cocked, rufous-brown tail also shows thin, dark bars. Underparts pale buff with dark brown barring on the flanks and white spots on the undertail. Thin, pointed, dark bill is slightly curved. **Immatures** similar, but show mottling on the crown and throat, a fainter super-cilium, and lack spots on undertail. Flight is fast and straight, with rapid, whirring wing beats.

  Voice & Diet Gives harsh, loud, repeated *tic* calls when alarmed. The song is very loud and consists of harsh, rattling, shrill, warbling notes, followed by a rapid trill. Feeds on a wide variety of small insects and spiders. Will also take some seeds.

  Habitat and Status An extremely common, widespread, resident breeding species. Found in a wide range of habitats, including gardens, parks, farmland, woodlands, upland scrub and moorlands. Builds a domed nest in ivy, hedgerows, old buildings and walls.

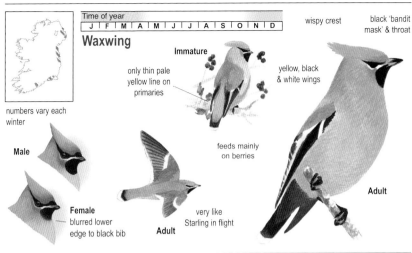

Time of year

J F M A M J J A S O N D

Waxwing

numbers vary each winter

wispy crest

black 'bandit mask' & throat

Immature

only thin pale yellow line on primaries

yellow, black & white wings

feeds mainly on berries

Male

Female
blurred lower edge to black bib

very like Starling in flight

Adult

Adult

Time of year

J F M A M J J A S O N D

Dipper

feeds underwater

grey, scaly plumage

Immature

Adult

white breast & throat contrasting strongly with dark brown body

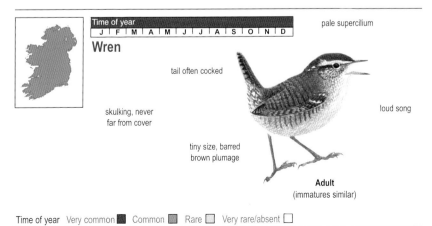

Time of year

J F M A M J J A S O N D

Wren

pale supercilium

tail often cocked

skulking, never far from cover

loud song

tiny size, barred brown plumage

Adult
(immatures similar)

Time of year   Very common ■   Common ■   Rare ☐   Very rare/absent ☐

Maps   Winter ■   Resident ■

Dunnock, Robin & Nightingale

Dunnock *Prunella modularis* Donnóg   14-15cm
A small, rather drab, grey and brown bird with a dark, slender, pointed bill. **Adults** show a grey head with brownish crown and ear coverts. Mantle rufous-brown with blackish streaks. The rufous-brown wings show dark centres to the feathers, adding to the streaked appearance of the upperparts. Rump and tail greyish-brown. The breast, belly, flanks and undertail are grey, with brown streaking present on the flanks. Eye deep reddish-brown. **Immatures** show a browner head with a white throat, dark streaking on buffish breast and flanks, and less rufous upperparts.
    Voice & Diet Gives a high, piping *tseep* call. The song is a hurried, high, broken jingle. Sings from a prominent perch. Feeds on a variety of small insects and seeds.
    Habitat and Status A very common, widespread, resident species. Found in areas with good cover and undergrowth. Present in towns and cities, being found in parks and gardens. In country areas, found along hedgerows and woodland fringes. Nests in dense cover in bushes and small trees.

Robin *Erithacus rubecula* Spideog   13-14cm
A cheeky, rotund bird with a bright orange-red breast. **Adults** unmistakable, with an olive-brown crown, nape and upperparts. The lores, ear coverts and breast are bright orange-red, with a grey border from behind eye to the sides of the breast. Belly and undertail white. **Juveniles** show a brownish head and wings, with the mantle, face and breast strongly spotted buff. **Immatures** are similar to adults, but can show brighter tips to greater coverts. Eye appears large and rounded. Bill dark, thin and pointed. Legs thin and blackish. Hops along the ground, frequently pausing in an upright stance with flicks of the tail and wings. A highly territorial species, usually solitary.
    Voice & Diet Gives a sharp, harsh, repeated *tic* call. Also gives softer *tsiip* and *tsee* calls. Song is a variety of short, high, liquid, warbling phrases. Feeds on a wide selection of small insects, worms and seeds. Will frequently visit bird tables.
    Habitat and Status A very common and widespread resident species found in all counties. In spring and autumn some vagrants from Europe may occur. Found in gardens, parks, hedgerows and woodlands. Nests in holes in walls, in trees, or on ledges. Occasionally found nesting in unusual places such as old kettles or watering cans.

Nightingale *Luscinia megarhynchos* Filiméala   16-17cm
A sturdy, rather plain, skulking species with a deep chestnut-red, rounded tail. **Adults** show a warm brown crown, nape and upperparts, with slightly paler ear coverts. The longish wings can occasionally be drooped, emphasising the chestnut-red tail which can be held cocked. Underparts buff-brown with a whitish throat and belly. Can occasionally show a greyish wash along the flanks. **Immatures** show pale tips to greater coverts and tertials. The dark eye is conspicuous in the plain face and shows a white eye-ring. The pointed bill is horn-coloured. Legs brownish. An extremely skulking species, moving and feeding in deep cover.
    Voice & Diet As Nightingale is only a passage vagrant, the beautiful, rich song for which this species is renowned is rarely heard in Ireland. On passage can give loud *tac* calls. Feeds on a wide variety of insects, worms and larvae. Will also take berries.
    Habitat and Status An extremely rare spring and autumn passage vagrant from Europe. Most records refer to coastal islands and headlands. A skulking species found in areas of dense cover in gardens, in bramble patches or along hedgerows.

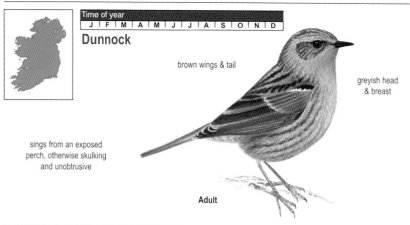

Time of year

| J | F | M | A | M | J | J | A | S | O | N | D |

Dunnock

brown wings & tail

greyish head & breast

sings from an exposed perch, otherwise skulking and unobtrusive

Adult

Time of year

| J | F | M | A | M | J | J | A | S | O | N | D |

often tame & inquisitive

Robin

can show a buff wingbar

buff spots

red-orange breast & face

this plumage can be seen from April to August

Immature

Adult

Time of year

| J | F | M | A | M | J | J | A | S | O | N | D |

pale eye-ring

Nightingale

rufous tail & rump

skulking, usually in deep cover

pale underparts, buffish wash

against light, tail looks bright orange

Immature
(adults similar)

pinkish legs

Time of year Very common ■ Rare □ Very rare/absent □

Maps   Resident ■

Chats

Bluethroat *Luscinia svecica* Gormphíb   14-15cm

Males and **females** of this skulking, Robin-like bird show a brownish crown, nape and ear coverts, a whitish supercilium, a dark coronal stripe, and brownish upperparts. Brownish tail shows rufous patches on the base. Underparts whitish. **Adult males** show a bright blue throat and breast with a red or white central patch (depending on the race), and a black, white and rufous lower border. **Females** show whitish sub-moustachial stripes, a buff-white throat and breast which can show blue and chestnut tones, and a black malar stripe meeting a broken black breast band. **Immatures** resemble females. Pointed bill dark. Eye dark. Has a Robin-like stance, with drooped wings and cocked tail.

    Voice & Diet Gives a sharp *tac* call and can also give a softer *wheet* call. Feeds in a chat-like fashion, taking a wide variety of small insects, berries and seeds.

    Habitat and Status A very rare spring and autumn passage vagrant from northern and central Europe. Both the Red-spotted race from northern Europe and the White-spotted race from central Europe have occurred. Very skulking on passage, seeking deep cover and undergrowth on coastal islands and headlands.

(Common) Redstart *Phoenicurus phoenicurus* Earrdheargán   14-15cm

A slim bird which shows a striking orange-red tail and rump in flight. **Summer males** show a black throat and ear coverts, a white forehead and supercilium, orange-red underparts and a blue-grey crown, nape and mantle. Undertail pale. Wings brownish. **Autumn** and **first-winter males** show pale mottling on underparts and throat, with immatures being browner above with a faint supercilium. **Adult females** are warm brown above and creamy-buff below, usually with a white chin. Can show a peach wash on breast and flanks. **Immature females** similar. All plumages show an orange-red rump and tail with dark central tail feathers. Eye dark with a pale eye-ring. Thin, pointed bill dark. Legs dark.

    Voice & Diet Gives a Willow Warbler-like *hooweet* call, occasionally preceded by *tchuc* calls. The song consists of hurried warbling notes and twitters, and ends weakly. The song can recall a mixture between Chaffinch and Robin. Feeds on a wide variety of insects. Will also take berries.

    Habitat and Status A very rare breeding species, and an uncommon but regular spring and autumn migrant. In summer occurs in mature deciduous woodland. Nests in holes in trees or old walls. On migration can be found in gardens and areas with good cover on coastal headlands and islands.

Black Redstart *Phoenicurus ochruros* Earrdheargán dubh   14-15cm

A dark bird which shows a conspicuous, bright orange-red tail and rump in flight. **Winter adult males** have a blackish-grey crown, nape and mantle, with blackish wings showing white patches. Cheeks and throat blackish, extending onto breast. Belly and undertail pale greyish. **Suummer males** show black upperparts, throat and breast. **Females** are greyish-brown on upperparts and on the underparts from the chin to the belly. Undertail paler. **Immatures** similar to adult females. In all plumages the rump and tail are orange-red with dark central tail feathers. The tail can sometimes be flicked. Bill thin, dark and pointed. Legs blackish. Dark eye shows a very thin eye-ring.

    Voice & Diet The scratchy, hissing song is rarely heard in Ireland. Usually silent on passage but wintering birds can occasionally give a short, soft *tsit* call. Feeds on a wide range of insects. Will also take berries.

    Habitat and Status An uncommon winter visitor from central Europe. Also a regular spring and autumn passage migrant. Wintering birds are usually found at coastal locations like rocky beaches and piers and around old, ruined buildings. Tends to perch prominently.

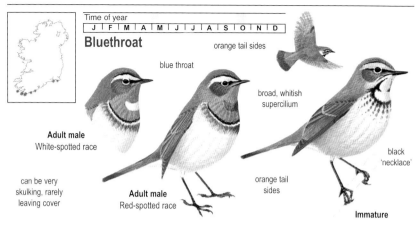

Time of year
| J | F | M | A | M | J | J | A | S | O | N | D |

Bluethroat

orange tail sides

blue throat

broad, whitish
supercilium

Adult male
White-spotted race

black
'necklace'

can be very
skulking, rarely
leaving cover

orange tail
sides

Adult male
Red-spotted race

Immature

Time of year
| J | F | M | A | M | J | J | A | S | O | N | D |

(Common) Redstart

warm brown upperparts,
pale underparts

upright stance,
often twitches
tail

oak forest in
summer, hedges &
coastal scrub on
migration

orange outer
tail, rump &
undertail

Immature male
(autumn)

striking
plumage

Female/immature

Male summer

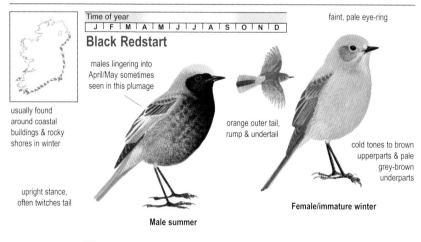

Time of year
| J | F | M | A | M | J | J | A | S | O | N | D |

Black Redstart

faint, pale eye-ring

males lingering into
April/May sometimes
seen in this plumage

usually found
around coastal
buildings & rocky
shores in winter

orange outer tail,
rump & undertail

cold tones to brown
upperparts & pale
grey-brown
underparts

upright stance,
often twitches tail

Female/immature winter

Male summer

Chats

Time of year   Rare ▨   Very rare/absent ☐

Maps   Summer ☐   Winter ▦   On passage ▧

Chats

Whinchat *Saxicola rubetra* Caislín aitinn   12-14cm

Summer males show a blackish crown and ear coverts, a white supercilium and dark-streaked brownish upperparts and rump. Wings dark with white inner wing coverts and primary coverts. Underparts buff, with a white border to cheeks and a whitish belly and undertail. **Females** show a brown crown and cheeks, a creamy supercilium, and paler buff breast and flanks which can show spotting. Upperparts fawn, with white tips to dark-centred feathers. Wings show a small white covert patch and a pale tertial panel. **Autumn males** and **immatures** similar to females. In all plumages the short tail shows whitish patches on the base. Pointed bill, eye and legs dark.

Voice & Diet Gives short, sharp, repeated *stic-stic* or *tu-stic-stic* calls and a low churring-type call. Song is a brief, twittering, variable warble. Feeds on a wide variety of insects and larvae.

Habitat and Status A scarce summer visitor and regular passage migrant. Frequents areas of rough pasture, mountain valleys and young conifer plantations. On passage found on open coastal areas. Nests in grass tussocks and, occasionally, at the base of small trees.

Stonechat *Saxicola torquatus* Caislín cloch   12-14cm

Summer males show a black head and throat, a reddish-orange breast and striking white neck patches. Belly and undertail whitish. Mantle blackish with brown streaking. Wings dark with white inner covert patches. Rump whitish and can show some dark streaking. Tail dark. In winter shows buffish tips to upperpart feathers, mottling on throat and a duller breast. **Adult females** show a brown head and throat, a faint supercilium, pale sides to neck, and streaked, brown upperparts with white wing patches. Breast reddish-buff. **Immatures** similar. Eye, bill and legs dark. **Siberian race** (Eastern Stonechat) show an unstreaked white or pale rump, slightly longer wings with males showing large white neck patches. **Females** and **immatures** show a pale plumage and a pale throat.

Voice & Diet Gives sharp, repeated *tsack-tsack* or *weet-tsack-tsack* calls which sound like stones clicked together. Song is a variety of repeated, high-pitched phrases. Feeds on a variety of insects, worms and larvae. Also takes seeds on occasions.

Habitat and Status A common resident species. Frequents rough pasture, young forestry plantations and mountain valleys, usually in areas with gorse, heather or bracken. In winter moves to low-lying areas and coastal locations. A small number also migrate to Europe in autumn. Nests in gorse or in thick cover. Eastern Stonechat is an extremely rare autumn vagrant, found on coastal headlands and islands.

Wheatear *Oenanthe oenanthe* Clochrán   14-16cm

A distinctive species showing a white rump and a black inverted T on a short, white tail. **Summer males** show a greyish crown and mantle, a white supercilium, and a black eye mask with white lower cheeks. Wings blackish. Breast buffish. Belly and undertail white. **Autumn males** show brownish-grey upperparts and buff-edged wing feathers. **Adult females** show a brownish mask, a creamy supercilium, brownish-grey upperparts, brownish wings and a buffish breast. **Autumn females** show browner upperparts and buff-edged wing feathers. **Immatures** have brownish upperparts, a creamy supercilium, buff-edged wing feathers and sandy-buff underparts. Eye, pointed bill and legs dark. Birds of the Greenland race tend to appear larger and show darker tones to underparts.

Voice & Diet Gives harsh *chack* or *weet-chack* calls. Song consists of harsh *chack*-type phrases combined with whistles, warbles and wheezing notes. Feeds on a wide range of insects.

Habitat and Status A common summer visitor and passage migrant. Found on mountains, on moorlands and at coastal locations. Frequents areas of low grass, rough pastures and dunes. Feeds on open ground and perches prominently. Nests in holes in walls, rocks or even old rabbit burrows. On passage found on coastal shingle banks, beaches, islands and headlands.

Time of year

| J | F | M | A | M | J | J | A | S | O | N | D |

Whinchat

white supercilium

pale buff supercilium

orange breast

orange breast, white 'moustache'

Female/ immature

small white patch at base of primaries

white at side of tail base

Male

small area of white at side of tail base

Time of year

| J | F | M | A | M | J | J | A | S | O | N | D |

Stonechat

buff rump

Female

small white patch on wing

orange breast

pale supercilium

black head, white collar

pale rump

orange breast

Immature 'Siberian Stonechat' (very rare)

Male

Time of year

| J | F | M | A | M | J | J | A | S | O | N | D |

Wheatear

black ear coverts

buff supercilium

grey back

white rump, black tip to tail

scaly upperparts, barred breast

buff breast

Juvenile

Male

Female/immature

Chats

Thrushes

Ring Ouzel *Turdus torquatus* Lon creige   23-26cm

Like Blackbird but appears long-winged and shows a conspicuous white crescent-shaped patch on the breast. **Males** are black, with silvery edges to the wing feathers, long primaries and a pure white breast patch. The shorter, thicker bill is lemon-yellow. Males also lack the yellow eye-ring of male Blackbird. **Females** are dark blackish-brown and show a pale breast patch. **Immatures** are dark brown and lack the white breast patch, although this can appear as a pale brownish patch on some young males. Best separated from immature Blackbirds by silvery-white edges to the wing feathers, clearly visible even in flight, and by the long primaries.

Voice & Diet Can give a loud, harsh, hollow, chattering *chak-chak* call. The song is a series of lonely piping notes, often finished with chattering notes. Sings from a prominent perch. Feeds on worms, slugs, insects, seeds and berries.

Habitat and Status A rare summer breeding bird of mountainous scree slopes. Nests in grass on steep, rocky outcrops. Recorded on migration in spring and autumn. Has occurred in winter. On migration occurs in fields and along hedgerows on coastal islands and headlands.

Blackbird *Turdus merula* Lon dubh   24-28cm

Male shows an all-black plumage which contrasts with a bright orange-yellow bill and yellow eye-ring. **Female** dull brown with a pale throat, and slightly paler underparts which can often show indistinct spotting. Bill dark with a dull yellowish base. **Immature females** are slightly paler than adults. **Immature males** are dark blackish-brown with paler underparts, and differ from adult males by lacking an orange bill and yellow eye-ring. The short wings which lack pale edges help identify immature Blackbirds from immature Ring Ouzels. Runs along ground, frequently pausing with tail and head in the air.

Voice & Diet Gives loud, strong *chuck, chuck* alarm calls which usually end in an excited series of high notes. In flight can give a *tsee* call, thinner than that of Redwing. Song is loud and fluty, with a variety of melodic notes, usually delivered from a prominent perch. Feeds on worms, slugs, snails, insects, as well as berries and fallen fruit such as apples.

Habitat and Status A very common bird of gardens, towns, farmlands and woodlands. Nests in bushes and hedgerows as well as in trees, old walls and out-houses. In winter populations increase with the arrival of birds from Europe.

Fieldfare *Turdus pilaris* Sacán   24-28cm

A large, striking thrush with contrasting upperparts and heavily spotted underparts. **Adults** show a grey head and nape, a thin pale supercilium, a blackish eye-stripe and a dark border to the lower ear coverts. Mantle chestnut-brown, with brownish-grey wings showing dark centres to the tertials and primaries. Rump grey, contrasting strongly with the black tail. Throat white with dark malar stripe and spotting. Breast yellow-buff with very heavy inverted arrowhead spotting, fading onto whitish flanks and belly. **Immatures** show brownish tones to nape and dull yellow breast. Bill pale yellow with a dark tip. Eye and legs dark. In flight shows a whitish underwing. Usually seen in large, mixed thrush flocks.

Voice & Diet In flight gives a soft *tsee* call, similar to but not as drawn-out as that of Redwing. Also gives a harsh, chattering *chik-chak-chak* call. Feeds on insects, worms, slugs and berries as well as windfall fruit.

Habitat and Status A common winter visitor from northern Europe. Found on open fields and open woodlands, moving in large flocks which often include Redwings. During hard weather will visit town gardens to feed on berries. On migration found along hedgerows and in fields on coastal islands and headlands.

Time of year

J F M A M J J A S O N D

Ring Ouzel

very rare winter visitor

in summer breeds on the highest peaks

Immature
(autumn)

faint crescent on breast, scaly wing & breast feathers

Adult male

silvery white edges to wings

Adult male

broad white crescent on breast

Time of year

J F M A M J J A S O N D

Blackbird

one of the commonest birds in Ireland

dull yellow eye-ring & bill

orange-yellow bill & eye-ring

Immature male
much duller eye-ring & bill

dark brown, slightly pale throat, indistinct spotting

Female

Male

Time of year

J F M A M J J A S O N D

Fieldfare

grey head, faint pale supercilium

chestnut-brown mantle

Adult
immatures similar

dark border to lower edge of ear coverts

yellow-buff breast, heavily spotted

pale grey rump, black tail

Time of year   Very common ■   Common ■   Rare □   Very rare/absent □

Maps   Summer □   Winter ■   Resident ■   On passage ▨

171

Thrushes

Thrushes

Song Thrush *Turdus philomelos* Smólach ceoil   22-24cm

A small, shy thrush with warm brown upperparts and heavily spotted underparts. The black eye is not conspicuous in the warm yellow-buff face. **Adults** show dark borders to the ear coverts while the spotting on the throat forms a malar stripe. Breast and flanks yellow-buff with arrowhead spotting, heaviest on the breast. Crown, nape, mantle, wings and tail warm brown. Wings show pale buff edges to coverts. Upperparts appear relatively uniform and lack the contrasting upperpart plumage of Mistle Thrush. **Immatures** like adults but show pale spotting on the mantle. In flight shows an orange-buff underwing. Bill brownish, with pale base to lower mandible. Legs pale. Rarely seen in flocks.

Voice & Diet Gives a soft *tsip* call, often heard in flight. When alarmed gives a sharp *chi-chip-chip* call. The song is loud and wandering, consisting of sharp, melodic notes which are repeated. Feeds on worms, slugs, insects and berries. Also feeds on snails by smashing the shells on a favourite 'anvil' stone.

Habitat and Status A common bird of gardens, parks and woodlands. In winter populations increase with the arrival of birds from Europe. Feeds in areas of dense cover. Nests in trees or hedges and occasionally in old out-houses.

Mistle Thrush *Turdus viscivorus* Liatráisc   26-29cm

A large, pot-bellied thrush with heavy spotting on the underparts, and long wings and tail. Large, black eye conspicuous in a rather pale face. **Adults** show a dark ear covert border and dark spots on a pale throat. Breast and flanks pale buff with heavy, broad, wedge-shaped spotting. Crown, nape and mantle greyish-brown with contrasting wings due to white tips on median and greater coverts and dark centres to the tertials and primaries. Long tail greyish-brown with diagnostic white tips to the outer-tail feathers. In flight shows a whitish underwing. **Immatures** similar, but show pale edges to upperpart feathers. Legs pale. Bill horn-coloured.

Voice & Diet When alarmed gives a diagnostic, repeated, rattling *prrr-rr-rr~rr* call. Song quite Blackbird-like but with the melodic phrases uttered in a faster and sharper tone. Sings from a prominent perch. Feeds on insects, worms, fruit and berries. Will occasionally take young birds and eggs from nests.

Habitat and Status A common resident bird of parks, woodlands, towns and mountains. Feeds in the open. Nests in trees. In late summer and winter can form large flocks. Populations increase in winter with the arrival of birds from Europe.

Redwing *Turdus iliacus* Deargán sneachta   20-23cm

A striking, dark brown thrush with a striking white supercilium and heavy underpart streaking. **Adults** show dark brown crown and nape and a broad white supercilium and sub-moustachial stripe. Ear coverts brown. Mantle, tail and wings uniform dark brown, with **immatures** showing pale tips to greater coverts and tertials. Underparts creamy white, with heavy breast streaking extending onto throat as a malar stripe, and fading onto flanks. Shows a striking red patch on the flanks. In flight shows a reddish underwing. Eye dark. Legs pale. Bill dark with a yellow base. Usually seen in large, mixed thrush flocks.

Voice & Diet The call is a soft, long *tseee*, often heard at night in late autumn and winter as flocks pass overhead on migration. Can also give a sharp *chich-up* call. Feeds on berries, insects and worms.

Habitat and Status A common winter visitor from northern Europe and Iceland. Found in large flocks on open fields or open woodlands. In autumn can be found on coastal islands and headlands. Also visits town gardens to feed on berries.

Time of year

J F M A M J J A S O N D

Song Thrush

warm brown
upperparts

heavy spotting on
buff underparts

orange-buff underwing

Adult
sexes similar

Time of year

J F M A M J J A S O N D

Mistle Thrush

a large thrush,
rather pale overall

heavy spotting
on underparts

white corners to tail

Adult

Time of year

J F M A M J J A S O N D

Redwing

distinct, white supercilium

overall dark
above

heavily streaked
underparts

red flanks

dark red flanks &
inner underwing

Adults
immature similar

Thrushes

Time of year Very common ■ Common ■ Rare □ Very rare/absent □

Maps Winter ■ Resident ■

173

Rare thrushes

Swainson's Thrush *Catharus ustulatus* Smólach Swainson   16-18cm

A small, shy species, very similar to Grey-cheeked Thrush. Shows a warm, olive-brown crown, nape and upperparts. Warm brown ear coverts highlight a large, pale buff eye-ring and a pale buff supercilium before the eye, forming a loral stripe. The warm buff throat shows a malar stripe extending as spotting onto a warm buff upperbreast. This spotting becomes more diffuse and fades into the whitish-grey underparts. Bill dark with a pale yellowish base. Legs pale. In flight shows a striking dark and white pattern on underwing. Call: Gives a sharp *chip* call. Range: North America.

Grey-cheeked Thrush *Catharus minimus* Smólach glasleicneach   15-17cm

An elusive, small thrush very similar to Swainson's Thrush. Shows a cold greyish-brown crown, nape and upperparts, greyish ear coverts, and a diffuse, pale eye-ring. Spotting on the throat fades into the greyish-white underparts. Breast can show a faint buff wash but often lacks any buff tones. Dark bill shows a pinkish-yellow base. Legs pale. In flight shows a striking dark and white pattern on underwing. Call: Can give a high-pitched *quuer* call in flight. Range: North America.

Hermit Thrush *Catharus guttatus* Smólach díthreabhach   15-17cm

A small, shy species, similar in size to Swainson's Thrush. Shows a warm brown head and cheeks, a striking white eye-ring, pale lores, warm brown upperparts and, in flight, a distinctive reddish-brown tail. The tail is often held raised. Underparts whitish with bold black spotting and streaking on the breast and a greyish-buff wash on the breast sides and flanks. Wings show a rusty tinge to secondaries, creating a panel on the closed wings. Bill pinkish with a dark tip. Legs pink. In flight shows a striking dark and white pattern on underwing. Call: Gives a soft *chup* call. Range: North America.

American Robin *Turdus migratorius* Smólach imirce   22-25cm

A bright, Blackbird-sized thrush. **Males** show a blackish head contrasting with a broken white eye-ring, a white loral spot, a black-streaked, whitish throat, and bluish-grey upperparts. Underparts are brick-red with white on the rear belly. White undertail shows black spotting. Dark bluish-grey tail shows white tips to outer feathers. **Females** similar, but shows paler, brown-tinged upperparts, a browner head and paler red underparts. Bill yellow with a dark tip but is darker in winter. Legs dark. **Immatures** like females but tend to show a dark bill. Call: Gives a Blackbird-like *chup* call. Range: North America.

Rock Thrush *Monticola saxatilis* Smólach aille   17-20cm

A striking species showing a dark-centred, chestnut tail. **Summer males** show a pale bluish head and throat, deep chestnut underparts and dark bluish upperparts with a white patch on lower back. Long, dark brown wings show chestnut underwing coverts and axillaries. Bill, eye and legs dark. **Females/immatures** show barring on the brownish head, upperparts and warm brown underparts. **Winter males** like females but show some white on the back and bluish tones on the crown. Call: Gives a short *chaak* call. Range: Southern Europe.

White's Thrush *Zoothera dauma* Smólach White   28-31cm

A shy, elusive species, slightly bigger than Mistle Thrush. Pale brown head shows a dark rear border to the ear coverts and extensive barring on the crown, nape and throat continuing as large, dark crescents onto the pale buff-tinged breast and white underparts. Upperparts and rump also show extensive barring. In flight shows black and white bands on the underwing and buff wingbars on dark upperwings. Tail shows striking white outer tips set against dark inner tail feathers and pale brown central feathers. Bill dark with pale base. Legs pinkish. Call: Usually silent but can give a soft *zeee* call. Range: Siberia.

Time of year

| J | F | M | A | M | J | J | A | S | O | N | D |

Swainson's Thrush

buff eye-ring & lores

buff wash on spotted breast

Immature (autumn)

in flight, Swainson's, Grey-cheeked & Hermit thrushes all show a broad white wingbar on the underwing

Time of year

| J | F | M | A | M | J | J | A | S | O | N | D |

Grey-cheeked Thrush

pale half eye-ring

grey wash to head & nape

Immature (autumn)

Time of year

| J | F | M | A | M | J | J | A | S | O | N | D |

Hermit Thrush

whitish eye-ring & lores

distinct spotting on breast

rufous wash on tail

Immature (autumn)

Time of year

| J | F | M | A | M | J | J | A | S | O | N | D |

American Robin

black head with white spots above & below eye

grey back

rufous breast

Immature

Time of year

| J | F | M | A | M | J | J | A | S | O | N | D |

Rock Thrush

scaly, pale edges to wing feathers

unique pattern of orange & blue, dark wings, white rump

orange wash on flank & undertail

Adult male

Immature (autumn)

Time of year

| J | F | M | A | M | J | J | A | S | O | N | D |

White's Thrush

long bill

a large thrush, slender

scaly underparts

pink legs

Immature (autumn)

Time of year   Rare ▨   Very rare/absent ☐

175

Warblers

Grasshopper Warbler *Locustella naevia* Ceolaire casarnaí   12-13cm

A shy, skulking, heavily streaked, olive-brown warbler. Adults and immatures similar, showing olive-brown upperparts with heavy streaking on the crown, mantle and rump, a faint supercilium and brownish cheeks. Wings show dark centres to feathers and short, curved primaries. Rounded tail can be held cocked. Underparts buffish-white with a whitish throat and yellow-buff sides to breast and flanks. Breast and flanks can show thin streaking. Undertail coverts show dark streaking. Legs pale pink or orange. Bill shows a dark upper and a pinkish lower mandible. Heavy streaking eliminates confusion with Savi's Warbler.

Voice & Diet The distinctive song is a far-carrying, single, long, reeling note which may recall the winding of an angler's reel. Sings both night and day. Also gives a short, sharp *twhick* call. Feeds on a variety of insects and spiders.

Habitat and Status A common breeding species found in areas of marshland with scattered trees and bushes, moorlands with bushes and gorse, neglected hedgerows, and young conifer plantations. Nests on or just above the ground in grass tussocks or undergrowth. On passage found on coastal headlands and islands.

Sedge Warbler *Acrocephalus schoenobaenus* Ceolaire cíbe   12-13cm

A pale brown warbler with streaked upperparts and a creamy-white supercilium. **Adults** show pale brown upperparts with dark streaking, heaviest on the crown. A broad, creamy-white supercilium is bordered by a dark lateral crown-stripe and a dark eye-stripe. Cheeks brownish. Clean underparts creamy, with a yellow-buff wash on sides of breast and flanks along with fine streaking. Wings long with pale edges to dark-centred feathers. Unstreaked rump warm buff, contrasting with upperparts in flight. Tail feathers pale brown and rounded. **Immatures** similar, but show a paler plumage, a pale buff central crown-stripe and spotting on breast. Bill dark with a paler base. Gape bright orange-red. Legs brownish.

Voice & Diet Gives short, loud *tuc* and *chirr* calls. Song is a loud, fast sequence of harsh, grating, chattering notes mixed with musical and trilling notes. Also mimics other species. Can sing from dense cover or perched prominently on top of reeds or sedges as well as during short display flights. Feeds on a variety of insects, larvae and berries.

Habitat and Status A common summer visitor found in a wide range of habitats, including reed-beds, marshes, hedgerows and bushes close to ditches or wetlands, and dense vegetation near water. Nests in reeds, sedges or bushes above shallow water. On passage can be found along hedgerows or in gardens on coastal headlands and islands.

Aquatic Warbler *Acrocephalus paludicola* Ceolaire uisce   12-13cm

A skulking, streaked, yellow-buff warbler resembling Sedge Warbler. **Adults** show a dark crown with a well-defined yellow-buff crown-stripe unlike the thin, messy crown-stripe of immature Sedge Warbler. Broad supercilium yellowish-buff. with a broad, dark eye-stripe confined to rear of eye. Some adults can show dark lores. Cheeks pale brown. Heavily streaked upperparts yellow-buff with two conspicuous lines on mantle. Rump yellow-buff and streaked. Pointed tail feathers give a spiky appearance in flight. Pale cream underparts can show a varied amount of streaking on the breast and flanks. **Immatures** similar but show a brighter plumage with distinctly pale lores and no streaking on the underparts. Bill appears thicker and paler than Sedge Warbler. Legs pink.

Voice & Diet Gives short, loud *tuc* and *churr* calls, almost identical to those of Sedge Warbler but delivered in a deeper tone. Feeds on a wide variety of insects.

Habitat and Status A very rare passage vagrant from central Europe. Usually found in open reed-beds, sedges and areas of damp, tangled vegetation.

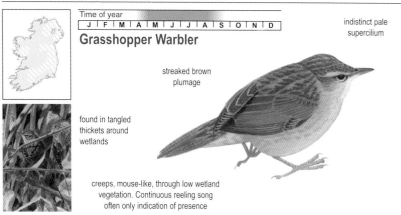

Time of year

| J | F | M | A | M | J | J | A | S | O | N | D |

Grasshopper Warbler

indistinct pale
supercilium

streaked brown
plumage

found in tangled
thickets around
wetlands

creeps, mouse-like, through low wetland
vegetation. Continuous reeling song
often only indication of presence

Time of year

| J | F | M | A | M | J | J | A | S | O | N | D |

Sedge Warbler

striking, white supercilium

faint pale central
crown stripe

dark
lores

found in reed-beds,
sedges, tangled
hedgerows &
wetland margins

dark
lores

bright red gape
when singing

Immature
(July/August)

immatures can show
faint streaking on
upper breast

Adult summer

Warblers

Time of year

| J | F | M | A | M | J | J | A | S | O | N | D |

Aquatic Warbler

broad, white central
crown stripe

striking, whitish
supercilium

pale lores

conspicuous pale
lines down mantle

unstreaked breast

compared with immature
Sedge Warbler, much
more contrasting,
obvious, pale mantle
stripes & crown stripe

Immature autumn

pale pinkish
legs

Time of year   Common ▨ Rare ☐ Very rare/absent ☐

Maps   Summer ☐

177

Warblers

Savi's Warbler *Locustella luscinioides* Ceolaire Savi 13-15cm

A large, dull brown species similar to Reed Warbler. **Adults** and **immatures** similar, showing a dull brown, rounded head with a distinct, thin supercilium and a pale, narrow eye-ring. Upperparts dull brown with short wings showing curved primaries. Lacks the warmer tones and straight primaries of Reed Warbler. Rump dull brown. Brown tail can be held cocked and appears rounded in flight. Underparts dull buff with a white throat. Undertail coverts warm buff with paler buff tips. Long bill shows dark upper and yellowish lower mandibles. Legs brownish or pinkish.

Voice & Diet Song is similar to the reeling song of Grasshopper Warbler, but is shorter, lower-pitched and more buzzing. Also gives a quiet Robin-like *tsck* call. Feeds on insects.

Habitat and Status A very rare summer and passage vagrant from Europe. Found in reed-beds.

Reed Warbler *Acrocephalus scirpaceus* Ceolaire giolcaí 12-14cm

A plain, warm brown warbler with shortish, pointed wings and a rounded tail. **Adults** show a warm brown head and a short, faint supercilium. Upperparts and wings warm brown, with dark centres to tertials and pale edges to primaries. Rump shows rufous tones. Underparts white with warm buff wash on sides of breast and flanks, highlighting a white throat. Undertail clean white. **Immatures** similiar but show warmer tones on the upperparts and rump. Long, slender bill pinkish-yellow with a darker upper edge. Legs brownish-grey with yellowish feet.

Voice & Diet Gives low *chee* and harsh *tchurr* calls. Song consists of repeated *jac-jac-jac, cerr-cerr-cerr* notes, interspersed with more liquid notes. Song similar to Sedge Warbler but is lower pitched and slower. Feeds on insects and on berries in autumn.

Habitat and Status An uncommon summer breeding species and passage migrant. Found in reed-beds, sedges and vegetation close to water. Nests in reeds. On passage can be found along hedgerows or in gardens on coastal headlands and islands.

Marsh Warbler *Acrocephalus palustris* Ceolaire corraigh 13-15cm

Very like Reed Warbler, but shows paler brown upperparts, lacking warm brown tones on the rump. Shows a short, pale supercilium and a conspicuous, pale eye-ring. Underparts creamy-white with a faint buff wash. Wings appear more contrasting than on Reed Warbler, showing pale edges to darker tertials and long, dark primaries showing striking pale tips. Alula often darker than the wing coverts. Legs pale yellowish-pink. Shows pale claws. Bill shorter than Reed Warbler.

Voice & Diet Gives Reed Warbler-like calls. Song is a series of fast notes with extensive mimicry. Usually sings from dusk to dawn. Feeds on insects and larvae.

Habitat and Status A very rare summer and passage vagrant from south-eastern and central Europe. Found along ditches and scrub, often close to reed-beds. On passage found along hedgerows or in gardens on coastal headlands and islands.

Blyth's Reed Warbler *Acrocephalus dumetorum* Ceolaire Blyth 12-14cm

Very similar to Reed Warbler, but shows a more greyish-brown head and upperparts and lacks the warm tones to the rump. Short wings lack contrastingly dark centres to tertials or pale edges to primaries. Shows a whitish supercilium, more prominent before the eye and an inconspicuous, whitish eye-ring. Underparts off-white with a greyish-buff wash on the breast and flanks. Long bill shows a dark tip to a pale lower mandible. Legs dark.

Voice & Diet Gives a clear, sharp *zheck* call, often likened to the call of Lesser Whitethroat. Feeds on a variety of insects and larvae.

Habitat and Status A very rare autumn vagrant from north-eastern Europe and Asia. Very skulking. On passage found along hedgerows or in gardens on coastal headlands and islands.

Time of year
| J | F | M | A | M | J | J | A | S | O | N | D |

Savi's Warbler

blunt-looking wingtips,
rounded wings

found exclusively in
large *phragmites*
reed-beds

faintly barred
undertail coverts

Adult

loud, reeling song

Time of year
| J | F | M | A | M | J | J | A | S | O | N | D |

Reed Warbler

faint pale
supercilium

plain, rufous-brown plumage

Immature autumn
adults slightly less rufous

in summer found in large *phragmites* reed-beds.
On migration can be found in tangled
hedgerows & wetland margins

Time of year
| J | F | M | A | M | J | J | A | S | O | N | D |

Time of year
| J | F | M | A | M | J | J | A | S | O | N | D |

Marsh Warbler

slightly longer
wings than Reed
Warbler, with whiter
wingtips

Blyth's Reed Warbler

shows shorter, plainer wings
than Reed Warbler, slightly
less contrasting wing
feathers, especially
tertials

usually
dark tip to
lower mandible

Marsh & Blyth's Reed
Warbler very difficult
to separate from
Reed Warbler

Immature autumn
adults have slightly
yellower underparts

dark legs

**Immature
autumn**

Warblers

Time of year   Rare ▢   Very rare/absent ▢

Maps   Summer ▢   On passage ▨

179

Warblers

Icterine Warbler *Hippolais icterina* Ceolaire ictireach   13-14cm
A sturdy, slim, long-winged warbler similar to Melodious Warbler. Shows a long, sloping forehead and a plain-faced appearance. Lacks dark stripe between the eye and bill. Shows a very faint supercilium. In **autumn** shows a pale, greyish-green head and upperparts. Pale edges to the tertials and secondaries create a panel on the closed wing, while the primary projection is about equal to the length of the tertials. Can also show pale edges to greater coverts. Tail square-ended. Underparts creamy, with a pale yellow wash on the chin and throat. Long, wide, orange bill shows a dark culmen. Legs bluish-grey. **Spring adults** show brighter upperparts and yellowish underparts.
> **Voice & Diet** Can give brief, hard *teck* calls, not unlike those of *Sylvia* warblers. Feeds on a wide variety of insects and larvae as well as ripe fruit and berries.
> **Habitat and Status** A rare but regular passage migrant from northern and eastern Europe. Found in gardens and hedgerows on coastal headlands and islands.

Melodious Warbler *Hippolais polyglotta* Ceolaire binn   12-13cm
A rounded, short-winged warbler similar to Icterine Warbler. Like Icterine, appears plain-faced, lacking a dark stripe between the eye and bill, and showing a faint supercilium. However, head shape appears more rounded. In **autumn** head and upperparts olive-green. Wings appear plain, lacking the pale wing panel of Icterine while the greater coverts lack pale edges. Primary projection short, being about half the length of the tertials with the primaries appearing bunched. Tail square-ended. Underparts yellowish, brightest on the throat and upper breast. Long, wide, orange bill shows a dark culmen. Legs brownish. **Spring adults** show brighter upperparts and yellower underparts. Feeds in a slow, methodical manner.
> **Voice & Diet** Can occasionally give a brief, House Sparrow-like chattering call. Feeds on a wide variety of insects and larvae as well as ripe fruit and berries.
> **Habitat and Status** A rare but regular passage migrant from southern and south-western Europe. Found in gardens and hedgerows on coastal headlands and islands. Tends to be more skulking than Icterine. Could be overlooked in dense cover.

Booted Warbler *Hippolais caligata*   11-13cm
A small, plain warbler which resembles a *Phylloscupus* warbler rather than a *Hippolais* warbler. Shows a sloping forehead and short, thick bill which has a pinkish-brown base and a dark tip. Shows a dark eyestripe and a pale supercilium which extends beyond the eye. Upperparts greyish brown with a short primary projection. Underparts whitish with buff tones on the flanks. Legs brownish-pink with dark toes.
> **Voice & Diet** Can give a brief, hard *chrec* call. Feeds on a variety of insects and larvae.
> **Habitat and Status** An extremely rare autumn vagrant from north-eastern Europe. Found in low vegetation on coastal headlands and islands.

Eastern Olivaceous Warbler *Hippolais pallida* Ceolaire bánlíoch   12-14cm
A plain warbler which initially resembles Booted Warbler. Shows a more sloped forehead, a longer, slender bill with a bright yellow lower mandible, and olive tones to a greyish-buff crown and upperparts. Also shows a faint supercilium and eye-ring on a plain face. Supercilium does not extend beyond the eye. Lores dark. Underparts whitish with greyish-buff wash. Appears longer winged than Booted Warbler. Legs bluish-grey. When feeding, often dips the tail downwards.
> **Voice & Diet** Can give a hard *chack* call not unlike that of Blackcap. Feed on insects and larvae.
> **Habitat and Status** An extremely rare passage vagrant from south-eastern Europe. Found in gardens and hedgerows on coastal headlands and islands.

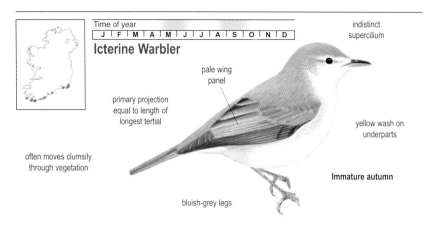

Time of year
J F M A M J J A S O N D

Icterine Warbler

indistinct
supercilium

pale wing
panel

primary projection
equal to length of
longest tertial

yellow wash on
underparts

often moves clumsily
through vegetation

Immature autumn

bluish-grey legs

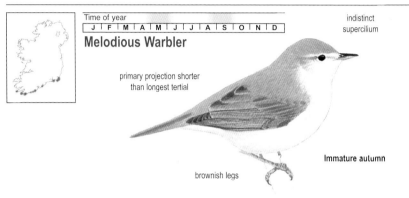

Time of year
J F M A M J J A S O N D

Melodious Warbler

indistinct
supercilium

primary projection shorter
than longest tertial

Immature autumn

brownish legs

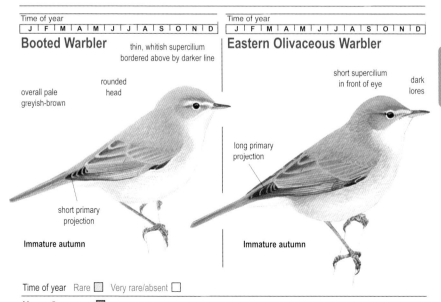

Time of year
J F M A M J J A S O N D

Booted Warbler

thin, whitish supercilium
bordered above by darker line

rounded
head

overall pale
greyish-brown

short primary
projection

Immature autumn

Time of year
J F M A M J J A S O N D

Eastern Olivaceous Warbler

short supercilium
in front of eye

dark
lores

long primary
projection

Immature autumn

Time of year Rare ☐ Very rare/absent ☐

Maps On passage ▨

Warblers

Blackcap *Sylvia atricapilla* Caipín dubh　　　　　　　　　　　　　13-15cm
A very striking warbler with a distinctive black or chestnut crown, a longish tail and a thin, long bill. **Adult males** show a glossy black cap extending down to eye level, greyish cheeks, nape and mantle, and brownish-grey wings. Rump and tail greyish. Throat, neck and breast pale grey, with flanks and belly showing a greyish wash. Undertail whitish. **Adult females** show a bright chestnut cap and are more greyish-brown upperparts with buff-tinged whitish underparts. **Immature males** show brownish flecks on black cap, while **immature females** appear more yellow-brown on crown. Black eye shows a thin, whitish orbital ring. Bill black. Can be skulking in summer.

Voice & Diet Gives a hard, repeated *tacc* and harsh, churring calls. Song contains a rich variety of melodic, soft, clear, warbling notes and usually starts with squeaky or scratchy notes. Sings from deep in cover. Feeds on a wide range of insects in summer, taking berries in autumn and winter. Will also visit gardens to feed on windfall apples.

Habitat and Status A common breeding species and a regular passage migrant. Birds from eastern Europe winter in small numbers. In summer frequents mixed woodland with good undergrowth. On passage found along hedgerows and gardens at coastal locations. In winter a regular garden visitor. Nests in hedges and brambles.

Whitethroat *Sylvia communis* Gilphíb　　　　　　　　　　　　　　13-15cm
A large, slim, long-tailed warbler with pinkish legs. **Adult males** show a grey crown, ear coverts and nape, a brownish mantle and brownish wings with bright, conspicuous, rufous edges to secondaries and tertials. Rump brown. Long tail grey-brown with narrow, white outer-tail feathers. White throat contrasts with greyish-white underparts which can show a pinkish-buff wash on breast and flanks. **Adult females** and **immatures** similar, showing brownish heads, with immatures also showing buff-white edges to tail. Eyes pale and show a broken, narrow, white orbital ring. Bill greyish.

Voice & Diet Gives loud, harsh *teak* and hoarse *tchar* calls as well as quiet *whet, whet, whit-whit-whit* calls. Song consists of short, rapid, scratchy, warbling notes given from a prominent perch or during aerial display flights. Feeds on a variety of insects in summer and berries in autumn.

Habitat and Status A widespread summer visitor and passage migrant. Found in open areas with hedges and scrub. Often found on woodland edges. On migration found along hedgerows and in gardens on coastal headlands and islands. Nests low in dense cover.

Lesser Whitethroat *Sylvia curruca* Gilphíb bheag　　　　　　　　13-14cm
A compact, short-tailed warbler with steel-grey legs. **Adults** show a grey forehead, crown and nape, and darker lores and ear coverts which can appear as a dark mask. Upperparts dark greyish-brown and lack rufous edges to the wing feathers. Rump grey. Short tail greyish-brown with white outer-tail feathers. Throat white, with underparts greyish-white, occasionally showing a pinkish-buff wash on breast and flanks. In autumn adults can appear paler grey on the upperparts. Dark eye shows no orbital ring. **Immatures** show greyish-brown heads, pale brownish tones on the upperparts, creamy white throats and buffish tones on breast and flanks. Tail shows off-white outer-tail feathers. Short, dark greyish bill.

Voice & Diet Gives loud, abrupt, harsh *tcack* and *charr* calls. Song consists of soft warbling notes followed by a fast, far-carrying, single-note rattle. Feeds on a wide variety of insects, taking berries in autumn.

Habitat and Status An extremely rare breeding species, but a regular passage migrant from Europe. Frequents areas of dense vegetation with brambles, bushes and small trees. On passage found along hedgerows on coastal headlands and islands. Nests in dense hedges and bushes.

Blackcap

black cap

Male

chestnut cap

Female

First-winter male

chestnut flecks on black crown

pale greyish-brown underparts

Whitethroat

grey head

rufous wings

white throat contrasts with underparts

often sings in flight

Female/immature

Male

Male

Lesser Whitethroat

faint pale supercilium

dark grey-brown upperparts

blackish ear coverts

Adult

Immature

dark legs

dark legs

Warblers

Time of year   Common ▩   Rare ▢   Very rare/absent ▢

Maps   Summer ▢   Winter ▨   On passage ▩

Warblers

Garden Warbler *Sylvia borin* Ceolaire garraí   13-15cm

A stocky featureless warbler with a thick, greyish bill and grey legs. **Adults** show an olive-brown head with a faint, pale supercilium, a thin eye-ring and a greyish area on the side of neck. A large, dark eye is conspicuous in a plain face. Tail and upperparts plain olive-brown with tertials showing darker centres. Short, olive-brown tail is unmarked. Underparts whitish with breast and flanks showing a buff wash. **Immatures** show warmer olive-brown upperparts and buffish flanks.

Voice & Diet Gives hard *tchack* and repeated *churr* calls. Song is a prolonged, soft, melodic warbling. Sings from deep in cover. Feeds on a variety of insects and berries.

Habitat and Status An uncommon breeding species and a regular passage migrant. Found in woodland with dense undergrowth. Nests in low brambles and bushes. On passage found along hedgerows on coastal headlands and islands.

Barred Warbler *Sylvia nisoria* Ceolaire barrach   14-16cm

Resembles a large Garden Warbler at first glance. **Immatures** show a pale grey head, a plain face with a thin, dark eye-stripe, and a narrow, pale eye-ring. Upperparts pale sandy-grey. Wings show whitish tips to median coverts, pale grey edges to greater coverts, and pale tips and edges to primaries and tertials. Long, greyish tail shows narrow, white outer-tail feathers. Underparts white with a buffish wash along the flanks. Flanks and undertail can also show faint barring. Eye pale brown. Hefty dark bill shows a pale grey base on lower mandible. Legs grey. Can be very skulking. **Summer adults** show strong barring on the underparts and a pale eye.

Voice & Diet Gives a loud, harsh *tchack* call. Can also give low churring and grating calls. Feeds on a variety of insects and berries in autumn.

Habitat and Status A rare but regular autumn vagrant from central and eastern Europe. Found in areas of dense vegetation on coastal headlands and islands.

Dartford Warbler *Sylvia undata* Ceolaire fraoigh   12-14cm

A small, dark, skulking warbler with a long tail which is often held cocked. **Males** show grey upperparts and wings, a dark grey head, and a plum-coloured throat and breast with small white spots on the throat. Belly whitish. Long tail greyish-brown with a narrow white border. **Females** show paler brown upperparts with a brownish-grey head. Underparts pale plum or pinkish-buff with white spots on throat and a whitish belly. Eye and orbital ring reddish-orange. Legs bright yellow-orange. Bill long, pointed and dark with a yellow-orange base. **Immatures** similar to female, but show dark eyes with a duller orbital ring and duller legs.

Voice & Diet Gives sharp, metallic *tchirr* and short, hard *tic* calls. Feeds on a variety of insects.

Habitat and Status An extremely rare passage vagrant from Europe. On passage found in areas of dense coastal vegetation.

Subalpine Warbler *Sylvia cantillans* Ceolaire Fo-Alpach   12-13cm

A small warbler with a red eye, a reddish eye-ring, a dark-tipped pale bill and orange legs. **Adult males** show a blue-grey head, thin, white moustachial stripes, and bright pinkish or orange-brown throat, breast and flanks. Upperparts blue-grey with browner wings. Tail greyish with white outer feathers. Belly and undertail whitish. **Females** similar, but show washed-out pinkish-buff underparts and fainter moustachial stripes. **Immature males** similar to drab adult males. **Immature females** show pale sandy-grey upperparts, whitish underparts with buff flanks and a pale eye-ring. Immatures show buffish-white edges to tail.

Voice & Diet Gives a sharp, quiet *tec* call. Feeds on a variety of insects.

Habitat and Status A rare passage vagrant from southern Europe. On passage found along hedgerows on coastal headlands and islands.

Time of year

J F M A M J J A S O N D

Garden Warbler

pale grey behind
ear coverts

rather featureless

plain, grey-brown
plumage

Adult/immature

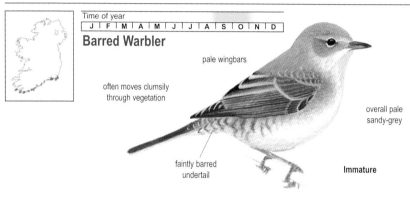

Time of year

J F M A M J J A S O N D

Barred Warbler

pale wingbars

often moves clumsily
through vegetation

overall pale
sandy-grey

faintly barred
undertail

Immature

Time of year

J F M A M J J A S O N D

Dartford Warbler

red eye-ring

Male

white spots
on throat

**Female/
immature**

overall, very
dark, long-tailed

dull pinkish
underparts

Time of year

J F M A M J J A S O N D

Subalpine Warbler

white moustachial
stripe

red eye-ring

Male

bright
orange
throat &
breast

dark eye, faint
pale eye-ring

Immature

overall pale

Time of year Common ▨ Rare ▢ Very rare/absent ▢

Maps Summer ▢ On passage ▨

Warblers

Willow Warbler *Phylloscopus trochilus* Ceolaire sailí   10-12cm

A small warbler, very similar to Chiffchaff but showing pale legs and a pale orangy base to a thin, dark, pointed bill. Long wings give Willow Warbler an attenuated, slim appearance. **Spring adults** show pale green upperparts, a well-defined, yellowish supercilium, a strong eye-stripe and blotchy ear coverts. Pale panel obvious on closed wing. Underparts show a bright yellow wash on the throat and breast, and a clean whitish belly and undertail. **Immatures** show green upperparts and a lemon-yellow supercilium and underparts. Unlike Chiffchaff, does not flick the tail when feeding. In flight appears long-winged.

Voice & Diet Distinctive song consists of thin liquid notes which are delivered softly at first, but which grow louder before the notes descend and fade away. Also gives a loud *hoo-eet* call. Feeds on a wide range of small insects and spiders. Occasionally eats berries.

Habitat and Status An extremely common summer visitor as well as a spring and autumn passage migrant. Rarely seen in winter. Frequents woodlands, hedgerows, copses and any areas with bushes and scrub. Nests in good cover on or near the ground. On passage found in gardens and hedgerows on islands, headlands and coastal stretches.

Chiffchaff *Phylloscopus collybita* Tiuf-teaf   10-12cm

A small warbler, very similar to Willow Warbler but showing dark legs and a thin, dark, pointed bill with very little orange on the base. Short wings give Chiffchaff a rotund appearance. When feeding, constantly flicks the tail. **Spring adults** show dull, olive-green upperparts, a short, yellowish super-cilium, and a dark eye-stripe with pale crescents obvious above and below the eye. Plain wings show blackish alula. Underparts olive-yellow and can show buffish tones. **Immatures** show olive-green upperparts and buffish underparts. Chiffchaffs of the Siberian race *tristis* show beige upperparts, whitish underparts, a pale supercilium and can show a short, pale wingbar.

Voice & Diet Diagnostic song consists of repeated *chiff-chaff* notes. Also gives a sharp, short *hweet* call, similar to the call of Willow Warbler. Feeds on small insects and spiders.

Habitat and Status An extremely common summer visitor as well as a spring and autumn passage migrant. Small numbers occur each winter. Found in open woodland and in mature hedgerows, brambles and scrub. Nests in deep cover above the ground. On passage found along hedgerows and gardens at coastal locations. The Siberian race *tristis* is a rare late autumn vagrant, usually found on coastal headlands and islands.

Wood Warbler *Phylloscopus sibilatrix* Ceolaire coille   12-13cm

A very striking, brightly-coloured warbler, larger and more slender and attenuated in appearance than Willow Warbler. Upperparts very bright green, with very long wings showing conspicuous green edges to dark-centred feathers. Green crown and dark eye-stripe both contrast with the striking, bright yellow supercilium, ear coverts and throat. Rump and tail bright green. Underparts are frosty, silky white and contrast strongly with the bright yellow throat. The yellow of the throat fades into the white of the upper breast but can appear very clear-cut. Legs pale. Bill shows a pale, orangy base. When feeding does not flick the tail but can droop the long wings.

Voice & Diet Distinctive song consists of repeated *tseep-tseep* notes, followed by a fast, shivering trill. Song often delivered during gliding display flights. Also gives a plaintive *tseu* call. Feeds on a wide variety of small insects and spiders. Will occasionally eat berries.

Habitat and Status A rare summer visitor and breeding species. Found in mature deciduous forests, building a domed nest in cover on the ground. Occasionally found on passage, feeding in gardens and trees on coastal headlands and islands.

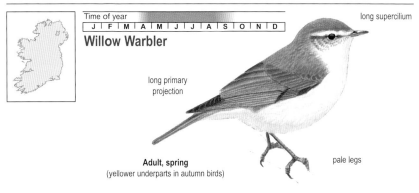

Time of year
J F M A M J J A S O N D

Willow Warbler

long supercilium

long primary projection

pale legs

Adult, spring
(yellower underparts in autumn birds)

Time of year
J F M A M J J A S O N D

Chiffchaff

small, pale crescent under eye

shortish supercilium

Immature, autumn
can have buffish wash to plumage

buffish wash

dark legs

in autumn, some eastern race birds are even paler, with a hint of a pale wingbar

often 'dips' tail

short primary projection

dark legs

Adult, spring

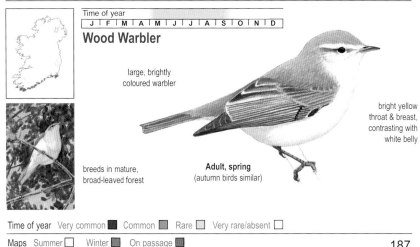

Time of year
J F M A M J J A S O N D

Wood Warbler

large, brightly coloured warbler

bright yellow throat & breast, contrasting with white belly

breeds in mature, broad-leaved forest

Adult, spring
(autumn birds similar)

Warblers

Time of year Very common ■ Common ■ Rare □ Very rare/absent □

Maps Summer □ Winter ■ On passage ▨

Warblers

Greenish Warbler *Phylloscopus trochiloides* Ceolaire scothghlas   11-12cm
An active warbler similar to the Siberian *tristis* race of Chiffchaff. Flicks the wings when feeding. Shows a greyish-green crown with a long white or yellowish supercilium which broadens behind the eye and contrasts with a dark eye-stripe. Upperparts greyish-green with bright edges to wing feathers and a clear-cut white or yellowish greater covert bar. Can occasionally show a fainter median covert bar. Tail greenish with bright edges. Underparts whitish. Bill yellowish or pinkish-yellow with a dark culmen and tip. Legs brownish. *Tristis* Chiffchaffs differ by showing a duller plumage, a diffuse, less clear-cut wingbar and a dark bill.
   Voice & Diet Gives a soft, distinctive *soo-wee* call which can sound similar to a softer version of the call of Pied Wagtail. Feeds on small insects and spiders.
   Habitat and Status A very rare autumn vagrant from north-eastern and eastern Europe. Found in well-vegetated gardens, hedgerows and trees on coastal headlands and islands.

Arctic Warbler *Phylloscopus borealis* Ceolaire Artach   12-13cm
A chunky warbler similar to, but larger than, Greenish Warbler. Shows a greenish crown with a very long, whitish supercilium which kinks upwards as it extends beyond the ear coverts. A dark eye-stripe contrasts with pale mottling on the ear coverts, which also show a dark border. Greenish upperparts show a whitish greater covert bar and can frequently show a median covert bar. Underparts whitish. Legs orange-yellow. Yellowish bill longer and heavier than Greenish Warbler with a dark culmen and tip. Greenish Warbler differs by showing a shorter supercilium, usually only one wingbar, a slimmer, shorter bill, and darker legs.
   Voice & Diet Gives a distinctive, short, hard, metallic *zik* call, quite unlike that of Greenish Warbler. Feeds on a variety of insects, larvae and spiders.
   Habitat and Status An extremely rare autumn vagrant from northern Europe. On passage found in well-vegetated gardens, along hedgerows and in trees on coastal headlands and islands.

Yellow-browed Warbler *Phylloscopus inornatus* Ceolaire buímhalach   9-11cm
A small, bright warbler showing show a bright olive-green crown, nape and upperparts, and greyish-white underparts which can show a faint yellowish wash along the flanks. Pale greenish ear coverts show faint blotches. A bright creamy-yellow supercilium appears upcurved behind the eye and contrasts with a dark eye-stripe. Darker wings show two creamy-yellow wingbars on the greater and median coverts, and pale whitish-yellow edges to dark tertials. Short tail and rump olive-green. Legs pale. Thin, pale bill shows a dark tip.
   Voice & Diet Calls frequently, giving a strong, sharp, loud *swe-eet* call, with the second phrase higher pitched. Feeds on a variety of small insects and spiders.
   Habitat and Status A rare but regular late autumn vagrant from northern Siberia. Usually found along hedgerows or in well-vegetated gardens on coastal headlands and islands.

Hume's Warbler *Phylloscopus humei* Ceolaire Hume   9-11cm
Very similar to Yellow-browed Warbler but appears duller with greyish-green crown, nape and upperparts. Long supercilium pale yellowish but shows buff tones before the eye and a buffish wash on the ear coverts. Underparts greyish-white. Wings show a prominent pale wingbar on the greater coverts and a weaker median covert wingbar. Pale greyish tertials show whitish-yellow edges. Short tail and rump greyish-green. Legs and bill dark.
   Voice & Diet Gives a loud, strong, whistling *dssewo* call quite unlike the call of Yellow-browed Warbler. Feeds on a variety of small insects and spiders.
   Habitat and Status An extremely rare late autumn/early winter vagrant from northern Siberia. Found in well-vegetated gardens on coastal headlands and islands.

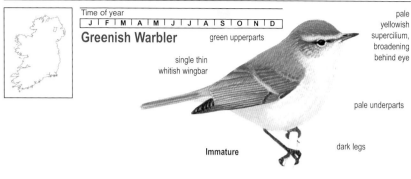

Time of year

| J | F | M | A | M | J | J | A | S | O | N | D |

Greenish Warbler

green upperparts

single thin
whitish wingbar

pale
yellowish
supercilium,
broadening
behind eye

pale underparts

dark legs

Immature

Time of year

| J | F | M | A | M | J | J | A | S | O | N | D |

Arctic Warbler

green upperparts

can show two
wingbars

prominent,
long, yellow
supercilium

large bill

pale underparts,
greyish wash on flanks

Immature

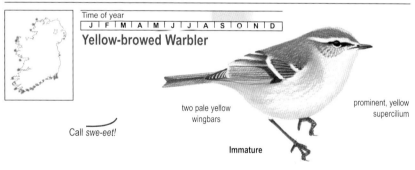

Time of year

| J | F | M | A | M | J | J | A | S | O | N | D |

Yellow-browed Warbler

two pale yellow
wingbars

Call *swe-eet!*

prominent, yellow
supercilium

Immature

Warblers

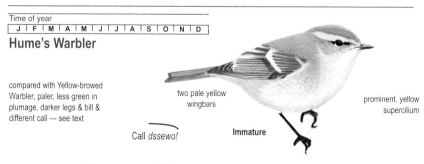

Time of year

| J | F | M | A | M | J | J | A | S | O | N | D |

Hume's Warbler

compared with Yellow-browed
Warbler, paler, less green in
plumage, darker legs & bill &
different call — see text

two pale yellow
wingbars

Call *dssewo!*

prominent, yellow
supercilium

Immature

Time of year   Rare ▨   Very rare/absent ☐

Maps   On passage ▨

189

Warblers

Radde's Warbler *Phylloscopus schwarzi* Ceolaire Radde   12-13cm

A chunky, brownish warbler, heavier in appearance than Chiffchaff and showing a heavy, pale, pinkish-orange bill and thick, pale, yellowish legs. Shows a brownish crown with a dark upper border to a prominent supercilium which is broader and buffish before the eye, becoming creamy behind the eye. Thick, dark eye-stripe contrasts with pale mottling on the ear coverts. Upperparts brownish, with olive tones on wings, rump and tail. Underparts creamy-yellow with a buff wash on sides of breast and along flanks. Undertail coverts usually warm rusty-buff. Can be skulking, moving heavily through low cover or feeding on the ground.

Voice & Diet Gives a distinctive, soft, but sharp *tchwet* call, usually delivered from deep cover. This can occasionally be repeated to give a staggered *tchwet-tet-tet* call. Feeds on a wide variety of insects, larvae and spiders.

Habitat and Status An extremely rare autumn vagrant from Siberia. Frequents areas of dense scrub, thick hedgerows and gardens on coastal headlands and islands.

Dusky Warbler *Phylloscopus fuscatus* Ceolaire breacdhorcha   10-12cm

A Chiffchaff-like warbler showing dark brown upperparts and crown, and greyish-white underparts with a buff wash along the flanks. Shows a conspicuous, rust-tinged, whitish supercilium extending behind the eye but appearing paler before the eye. Ear coverts pale brown. Thin, fine bill shows a pale base and dark tip. Legs pale flesh coloured. Tends to be extremely skulking and feeds close to the ground. Can be confused with Radde's Warbler but key differences shown by Radde's include a thicker, heavier and paler bill, yellowish legs, more yellowish-buff tones to the underparts, a broader, buff and cream supercilium, and mottled ear coverts. Radde's Warbler also appears quite heavy and slow-moving by comparison to Dusky Warbler.

Voice & Diet Gives a very loud *thek* call from deep in cover. Feeds on the ground or in low cover and takes a wide variety of insects, larvae and spiders.

Habitat and Status An extremely rare autumn vagrant from Siberia. Frequents areas of dense scrub, thick hedgerows and gardens on coastal headlands and islands.

Western Bonelli's Warbler *Phylloscopus bonelli* Ceolaire Bonelli   11-12cm

A pale warbler, slightly larger than Chiffchaff and showing a large black eye in a plain face. Pale greenish-grey head shows pale lores and lacks a prominent eye-stripe and supercilium. Underparts white and can show a pale buff wash. Pale greenish-grey upperparts contrast with green edges to the wing feathers which form a bright green panel on the closed wing. Tertials also striking, showing dark centres and pale greenish edges. In flight shows a striking, pale yellow rump and a dark green central tail with bright green edges. Pointed bill shows a dark upper mandible and a pale orange-pink cutting edge and lower mandible. Legs greyish-brown. Lack of a prominent eye-stripe and supercilium eliminates possible confusion with any unusually pale *Phylloscopus* warblers.

Voice & Diet Gives a very loud, far-carrying *boo-eet* call which, although similar to that of Willow Warbler, rises sharply on the second phrase. An active feeder taking a variety of insects and spiders.

Habitat and Status An extremely rare autumn vagrant from southern and central Europe. Usually found in well-vegetated gardens with trees and bushes.

Time of year

J F M A M J J A S O N D

Radde's Warbler

prominent supercilium, paler to rear, buffish in front of eye

yellowish wash on underparts

Immature

rusty-buff undertail

pale legs

Time of year

J F M A M J J A S O N D

Dusky Warbler

supercilium paler in front of eye

plain, dark brown upperparts

pale underparts

Immature

flesh-coloured legs

Time of year

J F M A M J J A S O N D

Western Bonelli's Warbler

plain looking face

plain, greyish-green upperparts

pale lores, no prominent eyestripe, faint supercilium

pale underparts

Immature

pale green edges to tail & wing feathers

dark legs

Warblers

Time of year   Rare ▣   Very rare/absent ☐

Warblers

Pallas's Warbler *Phylloscopus proregulus* Ceolaire Pallas   9-10cm

A tiny, active, brightly-coloured warbler, similar to Yellow-browed Warbler but showing a bright yellow rump. Shows an olive-green crown with a contrasting creamy-yellow central crown-stripe, a broad creamy-yellow supercilium and a dark eye-stripe. Upperparts bright olive-green, with darker wings showing two bright yellow wingbars formed by tips to the greater and median coverts. Dark tertials show broad white edges. Frosty-white underparts often show a yellow wash on the sides of the breast and flanks. Frequently hovers when feeding, revealing the bright yellow rump. Thin, pointed bill dark. Legs pale. Moves in a Goldcrest-like manner but can be extremely skulking.

Voice & Diet A usually silent species, Pallas's can give a faint, quiet *chu-ee* call. Feeds actively in cover, taking a wide range of small insects and spiders. Also catches insects on the wing. During feeding hovers, can delicately pick insects from the surface of leaves.

Habitat and Status An extremely rare, late autumn vagrant from southern Siberia. Usually seen along hedgerows and in well-vegetated gardens on coastal headlands and islands.

Goldcrest *Regulus regulus* Cíorbhuí   8-9cm

This tiny, warbler-like bird is Ireland's smallest species. **Males** show a black-edged, orange-yellow crown, and a dull greenish nape and upperparts. Wings show two white bars, white edges to the tertials and a dark wing panel. A large pale area around the dark eye gives the face a plain, open expression. The rump and short, forked tail are dull greenish. Underparts dull whitish, occasionally showing a greenish wash across the breast or along flanks. **Females** similar, but show a pure yellow, black-edged crown. **Juveniles** appear brownish on the head, lacking the yellow crown, and showing darkish crown edges. Small, thin, pointed bill dark. Legs pale.

Voice & Diet Gives soft, high-pitched, repeated *zii* calls. The song is also very soft and high-pitched, consisting of repeated *ziida-ziida* notes and ending in a short twitter. Feeds in a busy, active manner, taking a wide variety of spiders and small insects. In recent winters has taken to visiting nut-feeders in gardens.

Habitat and Status A common breeding species found in all counties. In autumn and spring, occurs as a passage migrant on coastal headlands and islands. In winter numbers may increase with the arrival of birds from Britain and northern Europe. Found in a variety of habitats, including deciduous and coniferous woodland, and in gardens with good vegetation. Nests under thick cover in conifers or, occasionally, in ivy.

Firecrest *Regulus ignicapilla* Lasairchíor   9-10cm

A tiny, active, warbler-like species similar to Goldcrest but showing a striking head pattern and a very bright plumage. Like Goldcrest, **males** show a black-edged, orange-yellow crown but differ by showing a broad, white supercilium and a dark eye-stripe. The ear coverts are greyish-green and highlight a small, pale crescent below the dark eye. The upperparts appear bright green with distinctive bronze-tinged greenish-yellow patches on the shoulders. The wings show two narrow white wingbars. Rump and short, forked tail greenish. Underparts whitish, appearing cleaner than on Goldcrest. **Females** similar, but show a yellowish crown. Small, thin, pointed bill dark. Legs pale.

Voice & Diet Gives a repeated *zit* call, which, although similar to Goldcrest, is lower-pitched and delivered in a quieter, less persistent manner. Feeds actively, taking a wide range of small insects and spiders.

Habitat and Status A scarce but regular annual passage migrant from Europe. Most records refer to birds seen in autumn, with small numbers occurring in spring. There are also several winter records. On passage found in gardens and trees on coastal headlands and islands.

Time of year

| J | F | M | A | M | J | J | A | S | O | N | D |

Pallas's Warbler

yellow crown stripe & supercilium

lemon-yellow rump

two yellow wingbars

Immature

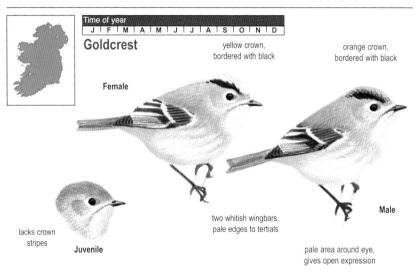

Time of year

| J | F | M | A | M | J | J | A | S | O | N | D |

Goldcrest

yellow crown, bordered with black

orange crown, bordered with black

Female

lacks crown stripes

Juvenile

two whitish wingbars, pale edges to tertials

Male

pale area around eye, gives open expression

Time of year

| J | F | M | A | M | J | J | A | S | O | N | D |

Firecrest

yellow crown

white supercilium, black eyestripe, white crescent under eye

orange crown

Female

Male

bronze-tinged shoulder patch (more prominent on males)

Warblers

Time of year   Very common ■   Rare ☐   Very rare/absent ☐

Maps   Resident ■   On passage ▨

193

Flycatchers

Spotted Flycatcher *Muscicapa striata* Cuilire liath   13-15cm

An upright, rather drab bird, usually seen chasing insects in mid-air, hovering and twisting before returning to an open perch. Plain, grey-brown upperparts show dark streaking confined to the steep forehead. Wings show pale edges to the tertials, greater coverts and long primaries. A habit of drooping and repeatedly flicking the wings exposes the grey-brown tail. The tail, which can be pumped slowly, does not show white edges or basal patches. Greyish-white underparts show brown streaking on the breast and diffuse streaking on the pale throat. Sexes alike. Thin, pointed bill black. Legs dark. **Immatures** show pale buff spots on upperparts.

Voice & Diet Call is a soft, scratchy *tsee* or *tsee-tuc*. The song is short, containing thin scratchy *tsip-tsic* notes repeated at intervals. Song is delivered from a perch. As the name suggests, feeds on all forms of insects, usually caught on the wing.

Habitat and Status A bird of open wooded areas including parks and gardens. Prefers areas with open ground where fly-catching flights can be made easily. An uncommon, but widespread, summer visitor. Spotted Flycatcher is usually one of the last migrants to arrive. Nests in holes of trees, in walls, buildings or creeping plants such as ivy. On passage found on coastal headlands and islands.

Red-breasted Flycatcher *Ficedula parva* Cuilire broinnrua   11-13cm

A small, rotund bird similar in shape to Pied Flycatcher. **Autumn adults** show a grey-brown head and upperparts, and creamy, buff-washed underparts. Plain wings are usually held drooped, allowing white patches on the base of the black tail to be seen easily. Tail often held cocked, showing a pure white undertail. A large, black eye and a broad, white orbital ring give an innocent facial expression. **Immatures** similar, but show pale edges to wing coverts. **Summer males** show an orange-red throat patch. Legs dark and bill blackish. Although feeds like other flycatchers, Red-breasted can be quite skulking and warbler-like in behaviour.

Voice & Diet Call is a short wren-like *trr-trr*, delivered as a soft, low trill. Can also give a sharp *chic* call. Feeds on insects caught both on the wing or picked, warbler-like, off foliage.

Habitat and Status Rare but regular vagrant from eastern Europe, usually occurring in late autumn. Normally found frequenting gardens or well-vegetated areas on coastal headlands and islands.

Pied Flycatcher *Ficedula hypoleuca* Cuilire alabhreac   12-13cm

Very similar to Spotted Flycatcher, but appears smaller and more rotund. **Summer males** show a black head with a small, white forehead patch, bold white patches on black wings, and white edges to a black tail. Underparts white. **Females** show grey-brown upperparts, white wing patches, blackish tails with white edges and whitish underparts. **Autumn males** similar to females, but retain the white forehead patch. **Immatures** similar to females, but can show a thin pale wingbar on the median coverts and can lack a whitish primary base patch. Holds wings drooped and flicks the wings and tail often. Thin, pointed bill black. Legs dark.

Voice & Diet Call is a sharp *whiit* or, on occasions, a shorter *tik*. These calls can often be combined to give a *whiit-tik*. The song can often be confused with Redstart and consists of strong, repeated *zee-iit* notes, often mingled with more scratchy, liquid notes. Feeds on insects, usually caught on the wing.

Habitat and Status An extremely rare Irish breeding bird of deciduous woodlands. Nests in holes of trees and walls. Will also use nest boxes. A regular passage migrant with most records referring to autumn. On passage found in gardens and along hedgerows on coastal headlands and islands.

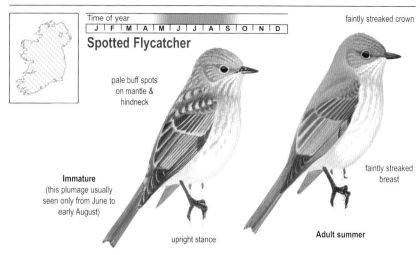

Time of year

| J | F | M | A | M | J | J | A | S | O | N | D |

Spotted Flycatcher

faintly streaked crown

pale buff spots
on mantle &
hindneck

Immature
(this plumage usually
seen only from June to
early August)

upright stance

faintly streaked
breast

Adult summer

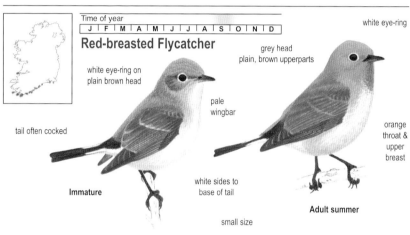

Time of year

| J | F | M | A | M | J | J | A | S | O | N | D |

Red-breasted Flycatcher

white eye-ring

grey head
plain, brown upperparts

white eye-ring on
plain brown head

pale
wingbar

tail often cocked

orange
throat &
upper
breast

white sides to
base of tail

Immature

small size

Adult summer

Time of year

| J | F | M | A | M | J | J | A | S | O | N | D |

Pied Flycatcher

white edges to
base of tail

white wingbar &
tertial edges

Immature
Adult female very
similar

Adult male

distinctive, black
& white plumage

Time of year   Common ▪   Rare ▪   Very rare/absent ▫

Maps Summer ▫   On passage ▪

Flycatchers

Coal Tit *Periparus ater* Meantán dubh   10-12cm

A small, active bird. **Adults** show a black head and chin contrasting with striking, yellowish-white cheeks and nape patch. Underparts yellowish-white with buff tones on flanks. Upperparts greyish olive-buff with slightly darker wings showing two whitish wingbars. Rump olive-buff. Forked tail dark buff-grey. Small, stubby bill blackish. Legs dark. **Immatures** show browner upperparts with yellower cheeks, nape and underparts. Ireland has a specific race of Coal Tit. British race birds show whiter cheeks and underparts, and more olive-grey upperparts.

Voice & Diet Gives a variety of calls, including high-pitched, piping *tsuu* and thin *tzee-tzee-tzee* notes. Song is a repeated, high-pitched *teecho-teecho-teecho*. Feeds on insects, spiders and seeds. In winter, a common visitor to garden feeding stations, taking seeds and nuts.

Habitat and Status An extremely common and widespread resident breeding species. Frequents woodlands, parks and gardens. Nests in holes using old tree stumps, walls and rocks. British race occurs widely in winter. Continental race rare.

Blue Tit *Cyanistes caeruleus* Meantán gorm   11-12cm

An active, colourful bird with a short, stubby, black bill and dark legs. **Adults** show a pale blue crown, with a white lower border and cheeks contrasting with a black bib and eye-stripe. Dark blue collar and nape highlight a small, white nape patch. Underparts bright yellow, with a dark line down the centre of the belly. Upperparts green, with one white wingbar on bright blue wings. Rump green. Short, forked tail blue. **Immatures** show a greenish-brown crown and hindneck, yellowish cheeks, crown border and nape patch, a diffuse black bib and more olive-green upperparts.

Voice & Diet Gives a wide range of calls, including a rapid *tzee-tzee-tzee-tzit* and harsh churring notes. The song begins with two or three *tzee* notes followed by a fast, liquid trill. Feeds on a wide variety of insects, spiders, fruit, seeds, berries and grain. A common visitor to garden feeding stations taking nuts and seeds.

Habitat and Status An extremely common and widespread resident breeding species. Frequents deciduous woodlands, parks, gardens, hedgerows and ditches. Nests in holes in trees or walls, and will frequently use nest boxes. In winter very common in suburban gardens. Also found in areas of reeds in winter. Occasionally associates with other tit species to form large roving parties.

Great Tit *Parus major* Meantán mór   13-15cm

A larger, striking species with a dark, pointed bill and dark greyish legs. **Adult males** show a shining blackish-blue head and throat with white cheeks and a pale yellowish nape spot. Bright yellow underparts show a black central band from the throat onto the whitish undertail coverts. Band thickest on centre of belly. Upperparts olive-green, with bluish-grey wings showing a white wingbar and obvious white edges to the tertials. Forked, bluish-grey tail shows distinctive, white outer edges. **Adult females** similar, but show a narrower black band on the underparts. **Immatures** appear duller overall, with yellowish cheeks and brownish tones to upperparts.

Voice & Diet Gives a very large range of loud calls including a Chaffinch-like *tzink*, a fast, repeated, short *tui,* and thin, high-pitched *tzee-tzee-tzee* notes as well as harsh churring calls. Song repeated, loud *teecho-teecho-teecho* notes. Feeds on a variety of insects, spiders, worms, fruit, seeds and berries. A common visitor to nut and seed feeders.

Habitat and Status An extremely common and widespread resident breeding species. Frequents woodlands, parks, gardens and hedgerows. Nests in holes in trees and, less frequently, in walls. Like Blue Tits, will frequently use nest boxes. In winter extremely common in suburban gardens. Occasionally associates with other tit species to form large roving parties.

Coal Tit

black crown, white cheeks

white nape patch

grey-olive upperparts, tail & wings with two whitish wingbars

Adult

Adult

some lack yellow tones

underparts (& usually cheeks) washed pale yellow

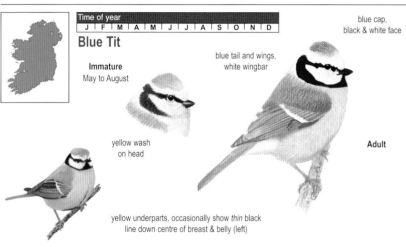

Blue Tit

blue cap, black & white face

Immature
May to August

blue tail and wings, white wingbar

Adult

yellow wash on head

yellow underparts, occasionally show *thin* black line down centre of breast & belly (left)

Great Tit

black crown, white cheeks

blue-grey tail & wings, white wingbar

Adult female

Adult male

female has paler yellow underparts & thinner black line down centre of belly

yellow underparts, thick black line down centre of breast & belly

Tits

Time of year   Very common ▓

Maps   Resident ▓

Tits & Treecreeper

Long-tailed Tit *Aegithalos caudatus* Meantán earrfhada   13-15cm
A tiny, active bird with a small black bill, a rounded, fluffed-up body, and an extremely long tail. **Adults** show a white head with a black stripe from above eye onto side of neck and meeting black mantle. Throat and breast whitish, with belly, flanks and undertail showing a pinkish wash. Pinkish scapulars contrast with mantle. Wings dark, showing striking white edges. Rump dark. The long, graduated tail is black with white outer edges. **Immatures** show dark cheeks, a shorter tail, browner upperparts with whitish scapulars, and whitish underparts. Flight appears weak and undulating, with long tail conspicuous. A highly gregarious species.
   Voice & Diet Gives a variety of calls including a distinctive, low *tsupp,* a trilling *tsrrup* and a repeated *tsee-tsee-tsee* call. Song consists of a mixture of call notes. Feeds in an acrobatic manner, taking small insects and spiders.
   Habitat and Status A common resident species found in woodlands, hedgerows, parklands and gardens. In winter can often associate with other tit species, forming large, roving flocks. Prolonged hard winter weather can sometimes reduce populations. Nests in thorny bushes or high in trees, building an oval, mossy nest.

Bearded Reedling/Bearded Tit *Panurus biarmicus* Meantán croiméalach 16-17cm
A distinctive, tit-like bird with a long tail. **Adult males** show a pale grey head with black lores and moustaches, a short, orange bill and an orange-yellow eye. Underparts pinkish-grey with black undertail coverts. Mantle and rump tawny-brown. Short wings show black centres to feathers with broad white and buff edges. Long, graduated, tawny-brown tail shows narrow white edges. **Females** show a tawny head lacking black moustaches, a greyish breast, pale undertail coverts and a duller bill and eye. Legs blackish. **Immatures** similar to females but show black down centre of back and on sides of tail. **Immature males** show black lores. Flight low and weak.
   Voice & Diet Gives a distinctive, pinging, *tching* call, sometimes followed by a trilling *tirr* call. Also gives a range of *tick* notes and squeaky calls. Feeds on insects and seeds.
   Habitat and Status An extremely rare vagrant from Europe. Bearded Reedling has bred in Ireland. The last recorded breeding occurred in the east and south-west during the early 1980s. Severe winters reduced the populations drastically and it became extinct as a breeding species by the end of the 1980s. Found in large, extensive reed-beds.

Treecreeper *Certhia familiaris* Snag   12-14cm
A small, brown and white bird which moves up trees in a mouse-like, spiralling fashion. **Adults** show a thin, down-curved bill, a whitish supercilium, and streaked brownish crown and cheeks. Throat, breast, belly and undertail white with pale buff flanks. Mantle and wings show a complicated pattern of brown with pale buff and dark streaking and pale wingbars. Rump rufous-brown. Tail brown with stiff, pointed feathers which are pressed against the tree trunk for support. **Immatures** show brown flecks on breast and flanks, duller white underparts and colder brown upperparts. Climbs up trees in a jerky manner before dropping down to the base of another to begin again. Usually solitary.
   Voice & Diet Gives a thin, high-pitched *tzeu* call and a softer *tset*. Song almost Goldcrest-like, consisting of *tzee-tzee-tzee-tsizzi-tzee,* starting slowly but accelerating towards the finish. Feeds on a wide variety of insects.
   Habitat and Status A common resident species. Found in deciduous and coniferous woodlands, parks and gardens. Tends to feed on trees with gnarled bark. Nests behind bark, in ivy or in crevices in trees.

Long-tailed Tit

long, black & white tail

Adult

black, white & pink plumage

Immature
late May to July

ear coverts dark, pale pink eye-ring

weak flight, whirring wings, long tail. Often in small groups

J F M A M J J A S O N D

Bearded Reedling or Bearded Tit

yellow iris & bill

pale brown head

black, white & chestnut wing pattern

found exclusively in large reed-beds

Male

black 'moustache', grey head, black undertail

Female

long, orange tail with white outer tail feathers

Time of year
J F M A M J J A S O N D

Treecreeper

decurved bill

moves up tree trunk, often in a spiral, before flying to base of next tree

streaked brown plumage, white underparts

Adult
immatures slightly browner on underparts

Tits, etc

Time of year   Common ■   Very rare/absent ☐

Golden Oriole *Oriolus oriolus* Óiréal órga   23-26cm

A shy, slender, Starling-sized bird with a striking plumage and a pinkish-red bill. **Males** show a bright sulphur-yellow head, mantle and underparts contrasting with a black loral patch and black wings. In flight shows conspicuous, yellow primary coverts and bright yellow outer tips to a black tail. **Females** appear duller, with a yellow-green head and upperparts, browner wings, and paler underparts with faint brown streaking. Tail dark, with rump and outer-tail tips pale yellow. Some older females can appear as bright as males, but show greyish lores and green tones to upperparts. **Immatures** similar to females. Flight strong and undulating.

Voice & Diet Both sexes can occasionally give harsh, scratching, Jay-like calls. Song consists of loud, clear, fluty notes. Feeds on insects, berries and fruit.

Habitat and Status A rare but regular spring passage migrant from Europe. Extremely rare in autumn. Most are found in mature or well-vegetated gardens on coastal headlands and islands. A skulking and often elusive species. Has been recorded in suitable woodland breeding habitat in summer.

Great Grey Shrike *Lanius excubitor* Mórscréachán liath   22-25cm

Large, long-tailed, grey, black and white shrike with a thick, dark bill. **Adult males** show a pale grey forehead, crown and nape extending onto mantle, a black mask from base of bill through eye onto ear coverts and a thin, white supercilium meeting over the bill. Short, black wings show a small area of white on the base of the primaries forming a small white patch on the open wing. Also shows white tips to the tertials and a conspicuous, white scapular stripe. Rump grey. Long, black tail shows white outer-tail feathers with white tips to outermost feathers. Underparts white. **Females** similar, but show faint barring on the underparts. **Immatures** like females but show a duller face mask and can show pale tips to wing-coverts creating a thin wingbar. Legs dark.

Voice & Diet Gives a harsh, angry, falcon-like *shikk-shikk* call. Feeds on small mammals, birds and insects. Occasionally creates a store of prey items by impaling them on thorns to be consumed at leisure. This practice lends shrikes their other name, 'Butcher-birds'.

Habitat and Status A very rare late autumn and winter visitor from northern Europe. Normally found in open areas with scattered trees and telegraph poles and wires, and hunting from prominent perches.

Lesser Grey Shrike *Lanius minor* Mioncréachán liath   19-21cm

Resembles a small, long-winged, short-tailed Great Grey Shrike. **Adults** unmistakable, showing a broad, black face patch from over the forehead to behind the eye. The whitish underparts show a delicate, salmon-pink wash on the breast and upper belly. **Immatures** can be more easily confused with Great Grey Shrike, as the black face mask does not extend over the forehead. However, Lesser Grey lacks a white supercilium, shows longer wings with obvious pale tips and edges to the primaries, has an inconspicuous, white scapular stripe but a larger white primary patch. Lesser Grey also shows a smaller, stubbier bill. Adults lacks white tips to tertials which can be present on immatures.

Voice & Diet Can give a harsh *tsche-tsche* call. Feeds on small mammals, birds and insects.

Habitat and Status A very rare passage vagrant from southern, central and eastern Europe. Found in open country with scattered trees and wires, usually along coastal locations.

Time of year

| J | F | M | A | M | J | J | A | S | O | N | D |

Golden Oriole

Male

pinkish-red bill

Female

green upperparts,
yellow rump

striking black
& yellow
plumage

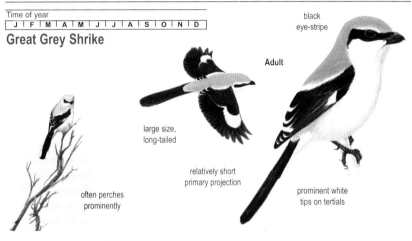

Time of year

| J | F | M | A | M | J | J | A | S | O | N | D |

Great Grey Shrike

black
eye-stripe

Adult

large size,
long-tailed

relatively short
primary projection

often perches
prominently

prominent white
tips on tertials

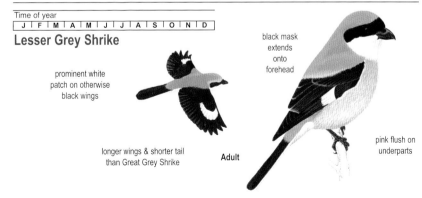

Time of year

| J | F | M | A | M | J | J | A | S | O | N | D |

Lesser Grey Shrike

black mask
extends
onto
forehead

prominent white
patch on otherwise
black wings

longer wings & shorter tail
than Great Grey Shrike

Adult

pink flush on
underparts

Shrikes

Time of year   Rare ☐   Very rare/absent ☐

Shrikes

Red-backed Shrike *Lanius collurio* Scréachán droimrua   16-18cm
Males show a grey head, a black mask through eye onto ear coverts, a white supercilium, and a rust-red mantle and wing coverts, with the remaining wing feathers darker brown. Rump grey. A black tail shows broad white patches at the base. White underparts can show a peach wash on the breast. **Females** rufous-red on upperparts and head, with a dark brown eye mask and a white supercilium. Tail dark with white edges. Rump grey-brown. Underparts white with faint barring. **Immatures** similar to females, with crescent-shaped barring on sides of breast and flanks, and barring on the upperparts. Rump and tail brown. Bill dark, with females showing a paler base. Legs dark.

Voice & Diet Can give a sharp, falcon-like *che-ek* call. Feeds on small birds and insects. Like other shrikes, can impale prey items on thorns.

Habitat and Status A rare passage vagrant from Europe. On passage usually found in areas of open ground with convenient perches on coastal headlands and islands. Prefers prominent perches such as telegraph wires or bushes where prey can be easily spotted.

Isabelline Shrike *Lanius isabellinus*   16-18cm
Similar in size and shape to Red-backed Shrike with a striking, orange-red uppertail. **Immatures** differ from immature Red-backed Shrike by appearing paler overall, with a bright orange-red tail, a paler eye mask and lack barring on the upperparts. Underparts show faint barring on the flanks. Thick, hooked bill shows a dark tip and a pinkish base. **Adults** show sandy, greyish-brown upperparts, white underparts with a buff wash on the flanks, a small white patch on the primaries and a narrow, black eye-mask. Sexes similar. Bill usually darker on adults.

Voice & Diet Can give a sharp, falcon-like *chi-ek* call. Feeds on small birds and insects.

Habitat and Status An extremely rare passage vagrant from central Asia and southern Siberia. Usually found in areas of open ground with prominent perches, on coastal headlands and islands.

Woodchat Shrike *Lanius senator* Scréachán coille   16-18cm
Adult males show a deep chestnut crown and nape which extends as far as the black mantle. A broad black mask runs from the forehead through the eye and onto the ear coverts. Wings black, with white scapulars forming large, white wing patches. White base to primaries obvious in flight. Black tail shows broad white edges and contrasts with the white uppertail coverts and pale rump. Underparts white. **Females** show duller colours, faint crescents on breast and flanks, and pale edges to wing feathers. **Immatures** greyish-brown on head and upperparts, with barring on upper and underparts. White centres to scapulars, white tips to median coverts and a whitish rump help separate immature Woodchat Shrikes from immature Red-backed Shrikes. Birds of the race *badius* from the western Mediterranean islands lack a prominent white base to the primaries and show less black on the forehead. Bill dark. Legs dark.

Voice & Diet Can give harsh, chattering calls. Feeds on insects or small birds. Like other shrikes, can occasionally impale prey on thorns.

Habitat and Status A rare passage vagrant from central and southern Europe. Usually found on coastal headlands and islands where they perch on bushes or small trees. Can be easily overlooked as they do not always sit on prominent perches like other shrikes.

Time of year

J | F | M | A | M | J | J | A | S | O | N | D

rufous & black wings, grey rump

Red-backed Shrike

warm brown
upperparts & tail,
scaly underparts

**Adult
female**

rufous back,
grey head

can perch
prominently

white sides to base of tail

immature

Adult male

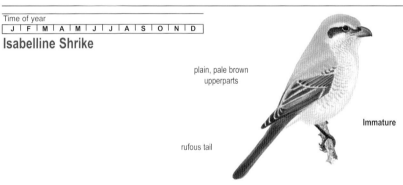

Time of year

J | F | M | A | M | J | J | A | S | O | N | D

Isabelline Shrike

plain, pale brown
upperparts

Immature

rufous tail

Time of year

J | F | M | A | M | J | J | A | S | O | N | D

rufous & black
head pattern

Woodchat Shrike

pale rump

white on scapulars,
scaly underparts &
upperparts

Immature

**Adult
female**

brown tail

prominent
white scapulars

Adult male

Shrikes

Time of year   Rare ☐   Very rare/absent ☐

Crows

Magpie *Pica pica* Snag breac 42-51cm

A boldly-patterned, cheeky bird with a long, wedge-shaped tail. **Adults** initially appear black and white but, when seen well, show an elaborate variety of colours. Head, mantle and breast black with a bluish-purple gloss. The wings are black with blue and green sheens, but show white scapulars and white, black-edged primaries. Undertail and rump black. Long tail appears black, but shows green, purple and bronze sheens. Flies with long trailing tail and white scapulars and primaries contrasting strongly with otherwise black upperparts. Belly and flanks white. **Immatures** show a duller plumage and shorter tail. Shows a stout, pointed dark bill. Legs and eyes dark.

Voice & Diet Very vocal, giving loud, chattering *chacka-chacka-chack* calls both in flight and when alarmed. Feeds on insects, slugs and seeds, but also steals eggs and nestlings.

Habitat and Status A very common resident species found in towns, cities, parks and open farmland. Often seen alone or in pairs, although sometimes forms small parties. Walks in a deliberate manner while searching for food. Builds a large nest in trees or bushes. Can often remain faithful to the same nesting site.

Jackdaw *Corvus monedula* Cág 32-35cm

A small, compact crow with a glossy black plumage. **Adults** show a pale ash-grey nape creating a black-capped appearance and glossy black upper and underparts. The dark, pointed bill is considerably shorter than in other crow species. Legs dark. Eye whitish-grey with a dark pupil. **Immatures** lack the pale grey nape and show darker eyes. In flight has pointed wings and a short tail. On the ground hops cheekily and is highly inquisitive. A gregarious species, Jackdaws are usually found in large flocks, often associating with Rooks. **Scandinavian race** birds show a bright white neck collar.

Voice & Diet Gives a characteristic *jak-jak* call, often repeated. Will also frequently give a *kee-yaw* call which is flatter and shorter than the similar calls of Chough. Feeds on a wide variety of food, including slugs, insects and berries. Will occasionally take eggs and nestlings.

Habitat and Status An abundant resident bird found in woodlands, parks, towns, cities, farmland and quarries. Nests in holes in trees and cliffs, or occasionally in chimney pots. Often seen on open land in large flocks. Scandinavian race birds are rare winter visitors.

Chough *Pyrrhocorax pyrrhocorax* Cág cosdearg 36-42cm

An absolute acrobat of the air, this Jackdaw-sized, glossy black crow is easily identified by the long, thin, decurved red bill, red legs and distinctive *chauuh* call. **Adults** show a bluish gloss to an all-black plumage. **Immatures** duller and show a pale orange bill and paler legs. The long, pointed bill is used for probing and can sometimes appear stained as a result. In flight the wings appear rounded with long primary fingers while the short tail is slightly rounded. Flies with easy, buoyant wing beats interspersed with swoops on closed wings. On the ground walks or hops in a sideways manner. Sometimes associates with other crows, particularly Jackdaws.

Voice & Diet Gives a distinctive, loud, high-pitched *chauuh* call which, although similar to that of Jackdaw, is delivered in a more explosive manner. Feeds on worms, slugs, insects and larvae. Will also take grain.

Habitat and Status An uncommon bird of rugged headlands and islands. Feeds in sand-dune areas, in coastal moorland and short-cropped grass known as machair. Nests in coastal cliff holes or caves.

Time of year
J F M A M J J A S O N D

Magpie

striking black & white plumage

long tail
(longest in adult males)

Adult

distinctive, domed nest

Time of year
J F M A M J J A S O N D

Jackdaw

pale eye

black plumage, ash-grey nape

black, triangular-shaped bill

Adult

commonly nests in ruined or derelict buildings, often in chimneys

Time of year
J F M A M J J A S O N D

Chough

long, decurved red bill

family party on clifftop grass

Immatures (centre two birds)
pale orange bill, paler legs

broad wings, flamboyant flight

Adult

often in flocks

red legs

Crows

Time of year Very common ■ Common ■

Crows

Rook *Corvus frugilegus* Rúcach   43-47cm

A common, scraggy-looking crow with a long, pointed, grey bill and a whitish face patch. Forehead steep and, despite the rounded crown, often appears flat-headed. **Adults** have a glossy black plumage showing a purple sheen. Shaggy belly feathers cover the upper legs, creating a baggy-trousers effect which is useful when separating **immature** birds, which lack the pale bill and face patch, from Carrion Crows. In flight has narrow wings and a long, slightly rounded tail.

Voice & Diet A very noisy species, especially when roosting at dusk. Gives a sharp, repeated, grumpy *kaarg* call. Feeds on root crops, berries, insects, worms and slugs.

Habitat and Status An extremely common resident bird found on farmland, parks, towns and cities. Feeds in large, often mixed flocks on open land. Nests in the very tops of trees in large colonies called rookeries.

Hooded Crow *Corvus cornix* Caróg liath   45-50cm

An unmistakable grey and black crow with a dark, thick-set, blunt bill. **Adults** show a black head, breast, wings and tail contrasting with a grey mantle and underparts. In flight shows black, rounded wings and a short, black, square tail. **Immatures** are duller grey, often with dark mantle markings, and with brownish wings and tails. Usually solitary, but can occur in small parties, often with Rooks and Jackdaws.

Voice & Diet Gives a loud, harsh *kaaw,* flatter in tone than Rook. Will also give a honking nasal-type *kraa* call. Takes a wide variety of food, including carrion, small birds and mammals, eggs, insects and grain. Along the coast can occasionally be seen to drop molluscs onto hard surfaces in an attempt to crack open the shells.

Habitat and Status A common resident bird found in a wide variety of habitats, including woodland, farmland, towns and mountains. Nests in trees, on cliffs or in old buildings.

Carrion Crow *Corvus corone* Caróg dhubh   45-50cm

Adults show an all-black glossy plumage and a dark, thick-set, blunt bill. Separated from immature Rooks by the blunt, thicker bill and tidier leg feathers, thus lacking the the baggy-trousers effect of Rook. In flight shows rounded wings and a short, black, square tail. **Immatures** duller. Usually solitary, but often seen with Hooded Crows and can hybridise with that species.

Voice & Diet Gives loud, harsh *kaaw* and honking, nasal-type *kraa* calls like Hooded Crows. Feeds on carrion, small birds and mammals, eggs, insects and grain.

Habitat and Status An uncommon visitor from Britain and Europe. Can occur at any time of the year, with most records referring to autumn and winter. Usually seen at coastal locations.

Raven *Corvus corax* Fiach dubh   60-68cm

The largest member of the crow family. **Adults** show a purple or green sheen to an all-black glossy plumage, a thick, heavy, dark bill and shaggy throat feathers. In flight the long wings have obvious primary fingers. The thick bill, along with the shaggy throat, give a large-headed profile in flight, while the diagnostic long, wedge-shaped tail is easy to see. When soaring can look like a large raptor. Usually seen alone, in pairs or in small family parties. **Immatures** appear duller.

Voice & Diet Gives a very distinctive, deep, loud, honking *prruc-pruc* call and a variety of softer, quieter, croaking calls. Feeds on carrion but will kill weak or injured small mammals and birds. Also feeds on eggs, slugs, worms, insects and grain.

Habitat and Status A common resident bird of mountain glens and coastal cliffs. Nests are built on cliff outcrops or in trees. Can nest as early as January or February.

Time of year
J F M A M J J A S O N D

Rook

Adult

Immature

whitish face patch

Adult

nests commonly in large, noisy colonies in large trees

more slender bill than Carrion Crow

Time of year
J F M A M J J A S O N D

Hooded Crow

grey & black

black hood

often perches conspicuously

Adult

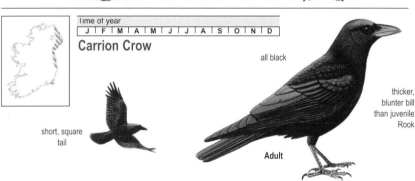

Time of year
J F M A M J J A S O N D

Carrion Crow

all black

thicker, blunter bill than juvenile Rook

short, square tail

Adult

Time of year
J F M A M J J A S O N D

Raven

glossy black plumage

shaggy throat

large size

large, long-winged, wedge-shaped tail

Adult

Crows

Time of year   Very common ■   Common ■   Rare □

Jay *Garrulus glandarius* Scréachóg 33-37cm

A stocky, skulking species with a stout, dark bill. **Adults** show a black-streaked, whitish crown, a broad, black moustachial stripe, a white throat and purplish-brown cheeks, nape and mantle. Black wings show a bright blue and black barred wing patch, a conspicuous white panel formed by white bases to the secondaries, and deep chestnut inner edges to the tertials. Underparts pinkish-brown, fading to white on the centre of the belly. Undertail coverts white. In flight a white rump contrasts strongly with a black tail. Jays in Ireland belong to a specific race.

Voice & Diet Gives very harsh, loud *skkaaaa* and loud, barking *kaa* calls. Can also give a subdued, mewing-type note. Feeds on fruit, berries, nuts and acorns. Known to bury food in the autumn, utilising hidden stores during hard winter periods. Also feeds on insects, worms, slugs, eggs, nestlings and small mammals.

Habitat and Status A widely distributed, resident breeding species. Frequents deciduous and coniferous woodlands, open mature parklands and, occasionally in winter, orchards and suburban gardens. Nests in trees or large, mature bushes.

Starling *Sturnus vulgaris* Druid 20-23cm

A common species showing a long, pointed bill, a short tail and triangular wings in flight. **Summer males** show a purple and green gloss to a blackish head and underparts, buff edges to mantle and wing feathers, and a grey base to a yellow bill. **Females** similar, but show some pale underpart spots and a pink base to the bill. **Winter males** show buff spotting on the upperparts, white spotting on the head and underparts, and a brown bill. **Winter females** show larger underpart spotting. Legs pinkish. **Immatures** greyish-brown with a white throat, dark lores, a dark bill and dark legs. Immatures in moult show a mixture of immature and adult winter plumages.

Voice & Diet Gives a variety of calls including harsh, grating *tzheerr* and thin, whistling *tzoo-ee* notes. Song a rambling selection of warbling, whistling and clicking. Some mimicry may be included. Feeds on the ground in noisy flocks, probing with open bills in search of insects, worms and slugs. Also feeds on grain, fruit, berries, scraps and insects.

Habitat and Status A common, widespread breeding species. Found in a wide range of habitats including cities, farmland, woodland and shorelines. Nests in holes in trees or buildings, usually in loose colonies. In late autumn birds arrive from northern and central Europe. Can form huge winter roosting flocks, usually in reed-beds, woodlands, on buildings or cliffs.

Rose-coloured Starling *Pastor roseus* Druid rósach 20-22cm

A stocky species with a shorter and stubbier bill than Starling. **Adults** show a black head, breast, wings and tail contrasting with a pink mantle, rump and belly. Crown shows elongated rear feathers. Bill and legs pink. In winter pink is obscured by buff fringes. **Immatures** appear similar to immature Starling, but show pale lores, a sandy-grey head and upperparts, darker wings with buff edges to the feathers, pale buff underparts and rump, and a white throat. Unlike immature Starling, the stubbier bill is pale yellow with a reddish tip, and the legs are pale pink. Immatures usually occur when immature Starlings are in an adult-like plumage.

Voice & Diet Gives grating *tzheerr* and whistling *tzoo-ee* calls, similar to Starling but delivered in a higher-pitched, harsher tone. Feeds on insects, worms, slugs, grain, fruit and berries.

Habitat and Status A rare vagrant from south-eastern Europe. Has occurred in summer but most records refer to autumn when birds are found with Starling flocks on coastal islands and headlands.

Time of year

| J | F | M | A | M | J | J | A | S | O | N | D |

Jay

white rump, blue
wing patches

black
'moustache'

distinctive
plumage

Adult
immatures are
similar

Time of year

| J | F | M | A | M | J | J | A | S | O | N | D |

Starling

large flocks
gather at dusk in
autumn & winter

triangular-shaped
wings

yellow bill

glossy black
plumage

Adult summer

plain brown,
black bill &
'mask'

dark bill

Immature

black with white
spotting

Adult winter

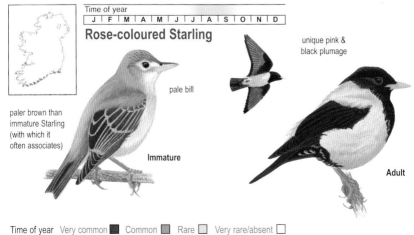

Time of year

| J | F | M | A | M | J | J | A | S | O | N | D |

Rose-coloured Starling

unique pink &
black plumage

pale bill

paler brown than
immature Starling
(with which it
often associates)

Immature

Adult

Crows, etc

House Sparrow *Passer domesticus* Gealbhan binne   14-16cm

Summer males show a grey forehead and crown, a brownish-grey nape, a black throat and chin patch, black lores and pale cheeks. Underparts greyish-white. Chestnut upperparts show broad dark streaks and contrast with a grey rump and uppertail coverts. **Winter males** show a small black chin patch but a greyish throat. Head colours appear more diffuse with dusky grey forehead and crown. **Females** appear duller, with streaked, paler upperparts, and show a brownish crown and a pale supercilium. Underparts greyish-white. **Immatures** like females with young males showing traces of black chin patch by late summer. Shows a thick, short bill. A highly gregarious species, feeding and roosting in noisy flocks. Can occasionally take communal dust baths.

Voice & Diet Gives a loud, repeated *chirrp* or *chirp* call. Flight call is a short *zwit.* Feeds on a variety of seeds, nuts, scraps and, during the breeding season, worms and larvae.

Habitat and Status A widespread, resident town and city species, usually found close to human habitation. Nests in holes and cavities, often under roof tiles. Can nest in trees and bushes, constructing a dome-shaped nest with a side entrance.

Tree Sparrow *Passer montanus* Gealbhan crainn   13-15cm

Tree Sparrows are slightly smaller and more colourful than the very similar House Sparrow. **Males** and **females** are identical, showing a striking head pattern with a deep chestnut crown and a distinctive black spot on white cheeks. The black throat and chin patch are neater than House Sparrow. Shows a white neck collar and streaked chestnut upperparts. Tail and rump warm brown. Underparts greyish-white. Thick bill short and dark. **Immatures** show a brownish-grey tinge to the centre of the crown, buffish-grey underparts and a yellowish base to the bill.

Voice & Diet Gives a distinctive, sharp, repeated *tek* call. When perched, can also give a loud *tritt* call. Feeds on a wide variety of seeds, cereals and, occasionally, insects.

Habitat and Status A widespread but scarce resident species. Found on open farmland. Breeds in widely scattered colonies, nesting in holes in trees and old buildings.

Red-eyed Vireo *Vireo olivaceus* Gláséan súildearg   13-14cm

Adults and **immatures** show a blue-grey crown bordered by a black lateral crown-stripe, and a whitish supercilium contrasting strongly with a dark eye-stripe. Ear coverts pale olive-green. Upperparts olive-green. Wings and tail slightly darker. Underparts silky white but can show a yellowish wash on the flanks and undertail. The strong, darkish bill shows a hooked tip. Legs bluish-grey. Immatures show a brownish iris, while adults can show a brighter red iris.

Voice & Diet Can give a short, sharp, scolding *chew* call. Feeds in a deliberate manner, taking a wide range of insects. Will also feed on berries.

Habitat and Status A very rare autumn vagrant from North America. Found in gardens and along hedgerows on coastal islands and headlands.

Philadelphia Vireo *Vireo philadelphicus* Gláséan Philadelphia   12-14cm

Initially similar to Red-eyed Vireo, but is smaller and has a more rounded crown. Shows a bluish-grey crown and nape, a dark eye-stripe and a whitish supercilium. Shows a whitish crescent below the eye. Upperparts olive-green and contrast with bright, yellowish underparts. Shows a short, stout greyish bill, a dark eye and bluish-grey legs.

Voice & Diet Can give a short, nasal *cheef* call. Feeds on a variety of insects and berries.

Habitat and Status An extremely rare autumn vagrant from North America. Recorded at coastal locations.

Time of year
J | F | M | A | M | J | J | A | S | O | N | D

House Sparrow

grey forehead & crown

usually in small flocks

pale streaked upperparts

black bill, throat & breast

dominant males have most black on breast

Female

Male

Time of year
J | F | M | A | M | J | J | A | S | O | N | D

Tree Sparrow

black spot on white cheeks

chestnut crown

Sexes alike

Time of year
J | F | M | A | M | J | J | A | S | O | N | D

Red-eyed Vireo

blue-grey crown white supercilium

bright greenish upperparts

whitish underparts

Time of year
J | F | M | A | M | J | J | A | S | O | N | D

Philadelphia Vireo

white supercilium & crescent under eye

olive-green upperparts, faint wingbar

yellow underparts

Time of year   Very common ▧   Rare ☐   Very rare/absent ☐

Maps   Resident ▧   On passage ▨

Sparrows

Finches

Chaffinch *Fringilla coelebs* Rí rua   14-16cm

Summer males show a dark forehead patch contrasting with a blue-grey crown and nape, a pinkish breast and cheeks, and a chestnut-coloured mantle. Dark wings show double white wingbars and white bases to the primaries. Primaries and tertials also show olive-green edges. Forked tail shows white outer feathers. Rump olive-green. **Winter males** duller. **Females** show similar wing markings, but the upperparts and head are greyish-brown. The centre of the crown and the nape are paler, creating dark lines from side of neck onto sides of crown. Underparts pale greyish-brown. **Immatures** similar to females. Thick bill blue-grey. Legs pale.

Voice & Diet Calls frequently, giving a loud *pinnk* call and a *chip* flight call. In spring and summer males can be heard to give a *whiit* call. Song consists of scratchy, chipping-type notes finished rapidly with a *ptsse-eeo* note. Feeds on seeds, berries, fruit and occasionally insects.

Habitat and Status A common, widespread species. Frequents gardens, parklands, hedgerows and woodland. In winter found in farmyards and on open fields when resident birds are joined by birds from northern Europe. Nests in bushes and low trees.

Brambling *Fringilla montifringilla* Breacán   14-15cm

A colourful finch with a black and orange plumage and a white rump. **Winter males** show a mottled brown head and mantle, and grey from behind eye onto nape and sides of neck. A bright orange shoulder patch and two buff wingbars are obvious on blackish wings. Upper breast orange, fading to a white lower breast, belly and undertail. Shows diffuse spotting on flanks. Deeply notched blackish tail contrasts with the white rump. Bill yellow with a dark tip. **Females** similar, but show a paler head and shoulder patch, and an orange wash on the breast. **Summer males** show a black head and mantle, and orange on the throat, breast and scapulars. Bill black on summer males. Legs pale.

Voice & Diet Calls include a Chaffinch-like *chick* in flight and a *tsueek* when on the ground. Feeds on seeds and berries. Often found feeding on beechmast.

Habitat and Status An uncommon but regular winter visitor from northern Europe. Found in mixed finch flocks on farmlands, open fields and beech woodland. In late autumn occurs on coastal headlands and islands. Numbers can fluctuate from winter to winter, with flocks of several hundred occasionally recorded.

Goldfinch *Carduelis carduelis* Lasair choille   14-15cm

A colourful finch showing striking head and wing markings. Sexes alike. **Adults** show a bright red forehead and chin, black before eye, and white cheeks and throat. Crown and sides of neck black. Mantle buff-brown, extending onto lower throat, sides of breast and along flanks. Underparts white. Wings black with a bright yellow wingbar, yellow bases to primaries and white tips to primaries, secondaries and tertials. Rump white. The black, notched tail shows white tips. **Immatures** show a greyish-brown head and mantle, and duller wing markings. Bill whitish-grey and pointed. Legs pale. Flight undulating.

Voice & Diet The twittering, chattering *ptswit-wit-wit* flight call is unmistakable. Can also give a loud *ee-uu* call. The song consists of trilling, twittering notes. Feeds on a variety of seeds and is often found feeding on thistles. Also takes small insects.

Habitat and Status A common finch found on open ground such as parks, gardens and woodland edges as well as waste ground where thistles are likely to grow. A resident species but numbers can increase in winter with birds arriving from Europe. Nests in bushes and trees.

Time of year

| J | F | M | A | M | J | J | A | S | O | N | D |

Chaffinch

one of Ireland's commonest birds

white tail sides

double white wingbars

grey head, pink underparts

white wingbars

Female

Male

Time of year

| J | F | M | A | M | J | J | A | S | O | N | D |

Brambling

numbers vary each winter

white rump

white rump

black & orange plumage

Female winter

Male winter
shows an all-black head in summer

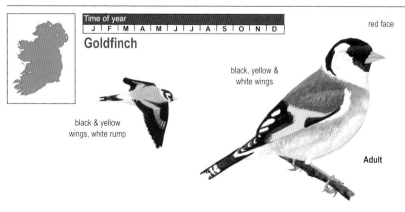

Time of year

| J | F | M | A | M | J | J | A | S | O | N | D |

Goldfinch

red face

black, yellow & white wings

black & yellow wings, white rump

Adult

Finches

Time of year   Very common ■   Rare □   Very rare/absent □

Maps   Winter ■   Resident ■

Finches

Greenfinch *Carduelis chloris* Glasán darach 14-16cm

A chunky finch with bright yellow wing and tail flashes, a thick, pale bill and pale legs. **Summer males** show an olive-green head and upperparts, and bright yellow-green underparts. Greyish wings show a bright yellow flash on the primaries. Rump yellow-green. Dark, forked tail shows yellow flashes at base. **Winter males** show brown tones to upperparts and head. **Adult females** show a faintly streaked, greyish-brown head and upperparts with yellow-tinged, whitish underparts and dull yellow wing and tail flashes. **Immatures** show streaked brownish heads and upperparts, pale, streaked underparts, a brownish rump and pale yellow wing and tail flashes.

Voice & Diet In flight gives a distinctive, soft, repeated, trilling *chit* call. In spring males can give a long, drawn-out, nasal *tsueee* note. The twittering song consists of a variety of call notes and is delivered from a prominent perch or during a slow, wing-flapping, bat-like flight display. Feeds on a variety of berries, seeds, fruit and occasionally insects.

Habitat and Status A widespread, resident species. Found in a wide range of habitats, nesting in hedgerows, bushes and trees in gardens, parks, woodland edges and farmland. In winter can be found on arable fields and coastal saltmarshes. A common winter visitor to nut and seed feeders in city and town gardens.

Siskin *Carduelis spinus* Siscín 11-13cm

An agile finch which shows two bright yellow wingbars, a pointed, pale bill and dark legs. **Adult males** show a black crown and chin, olive-green ear coverts, and a yellowish supercilium, throat and breast. Upperparts olive-green with faint streaking. Yellow-edged, black wings show two broad yellow wingbars. Yellow-green rump unstreaked. Short, dark, forked tail shows yellow base. Underparts white with dark streaking along flanks. **Adult females** show heavily streaked greyish-green upperparts and head. Wings similar to males. Underparts whitish with heavier streaking. **Immatures** like females, but show browner upperparts and a greyish rump.

Voice & Diet Gives distinctive, loud, shrill *tseu* or more extended *tseu-eet* calls. Song consists of a combination of call notes and more warbling, twittering notes. The song can be delivered from a prominent perch or during display flights. Feeds on a wide range of seeds.

Habitat and Status A common, widespread, resident species. In summer frequents conifer plantations and mixed woodlands. Nests high in conifers. In winter found in areas with alder, birch and larch trees and is a regular visitor to seed and nut feeders in town and city gardens. In autumn regularly seen at coastal headlands and islands. In winter numbers increase with the arrival of birds from Europe.

Serin *Serinus serinus* Seirín 11-12cm

A small, dumpy finch with a short, stubby bill. **Males** show a bright yellow forehead, supercilium, throat and breast. Crown and ear coverts dull greenish with light streaking. Ear coverts also show a bright yellow lower patch and crescent below the eye. Underparts white with heavy dark streaking on sides of breast and flanks. Dull green upperparts show dark streaking, thin pale wingbars and a bright yellow rump. **Females** appear duller, showing a faint yellow wash on the face and breast, heavily streaked whitish underparts and streaked dull greenish upperparts. **Immatures** like females but lack yellow wash to plumage.

Voice & Diet Gives a buzzing *sir-rr-il* call as well as a clearer *ch-eu* call. Song is a series of fast, sharp, jingling notes. Feeds on a variety of seeds.

Habitat and Status An extremely rare spring and autumn passage migrant from Europe. When found, usually seen in well-vegetated gardens on coastal headlands and islands.

Greenfinch

large, pale bill

green &
yellow

bright yellow patches
in wings & tail

Female
duller, less green

Male

Siskin

yellow rump & tail sides,
yellow wing stripe

black cap
& chin

yellow wingbars
& rump

often on peanut
feeders in
winter

Female

Male

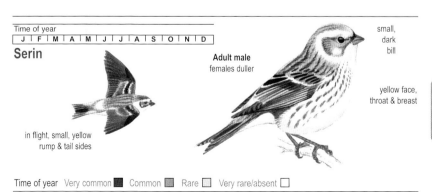

Serin

Adult male
females duller

small,
dark
bill

yellow face,
throat & breast

in flight, small, yellow
rump & tail sides

Finches

Time of year   Very common ■   Common ■   Rare □   Very rare/absent □

Maps   Summer □   Winter ■   Resident ■

215

Finches

Linnet *Carduelis cannabina* Gleoiseach   13-14cm

Summer males show a bright red forehead and breast, a grey head, a pale throat and whitish underparts. Warm brown upperparts show faint streaks and a faint wingbar. Dark primaries show white flashes on outer feathers. Forked tail shows white edges. Bill greyish. **Winter males** show a streaked grey head and faint streaking on buff breast and flanks. **Females** like winter males, but show a browner head. **Immatures** show a pale-buff face and less underpart streaking.

    Voice & Diet In flight gives twittering, musical *tret-tret-terret* and drawn-out *tsweet* calls. Song is a variety of twittering, trilling, fluty notes. Feeds on seeds and some insects.

    Habitat and Status A widespread breeding species. Found on farmlands, rough pastures, waste ground, coastal pastures and young plantations. Nests in dense cover on the ground or in brambles and bushes.

Twite *Carduelis flavirostris* Gleoiseach sléibhe   13-14cm

Summer males show a warm buff face, throat and breast, and streaked, brownish ear coverts, nape and crown. Underparts whitish with heavy streaking. Brownish upperparts show heavy streaking, striking pale wingbars and a pinkish rump. Forked tail shows white sides. Bill dark. **Winter males** show a pale yellow bill, a buffish rump and streaked, buff flanks. **Females** show a streaked buffish rump.

    Voice & Diet In flight gives nasal, metallic *tchweek* calls. Also gives soft *tseee* calls. Song consists of a range of twittering, trilling, musical notes. Feeds on seeds and some insects.

    Habitat and Status An uncommon resident species. Nests among heather and gorse or in old walls. Found on moorlands and pastures. In winter found on coastal stubble fields and saltmarshes.

(Lesser) Redpoll *Carduelis flammea* Deargéadan   11-13cm

Summer males show a bright red forehead, a black chin and pinkish tones on chin and breast. Underparts whitish with dark flank streaking. Crown and upperparts brown with heavy streaking. Wings show two whitish-buff wingbars. Rump streaked. Forked, brownish tail lacks white sides. Undertail white with a broad, dark centre to the longest undertail covert. **Winter males** duller. **Females** show heavier underpart streaking. **Immatures** similar to females. Bill yellow with a black tip. Legs dark. Scandinavian birds (**Mealy Redpolls**) show whiter underparts, more red on the forehead, white wingbars, white-edged wing feathers, a streaked white rump and white 'tramlines' on the mantle. Greenland birds are bigger, darker and show heavy underpart streaking.

    Voice & Diet In flight gives a twittering, rhythmic, repeated *chei-chei-chei* call. Can also give a drawn-out *tsweeck* call. Song consists of a variety of trilling notes. Feeds on a wide range of seeds, particularly those of birch and alder. Will also take some insects.

    Habitat and Status A widespread breeding species. In summer found in woodlands, nesting in high bushes and young conifers. In autumn and winter leaves mountainous areas. Also visits gardens in winter. Scandinavian and Greenland birds are rare autumn and winter vagrants.

Arctic Redpoll *Carduelis hornemanni* Deargéadan Artach   12-14cm

Similar to Mealy Redpoll but show a brighter, crisper plumage. White underparts show streaking on the sides of the breast, becoming thinner or absent on the flanks. Pale head shows dark crown streaking and red on the forehead. Also shows an unstreaked white rump and broad white 'tramlines' on the mantle. Undertail can be pure white or can show a very narrow dark centre to the longest undertail covert. Shows a small, yellow bill contrasting with black on the chin and lores. Legs black.

    Voice & Diet Gives twittering, Redpoll-like *chei-chei-chei* calls. Feeds on seeds and insects.

    Habitat and Status A very rare autumn vagrant from Scandinavia and Greenland. Found on coastal headlands and islands.

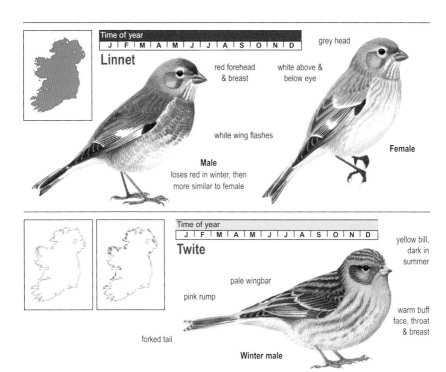

Time of year

| J | F | M | A | M | J | J | A | S | O | N | D |

grey head

Linnet

red forehead & breast

white above & below eye

white wing flashes

Female

Male
loses red in winter, then
more similar to female

Time of year

| J | F | M | A | M | J | J | A | S | O | N | D |

yellow bill, dark in summer

Twite

pale wingbar

pink rump

warm buff face, throat & breast

forked tail

Winter male

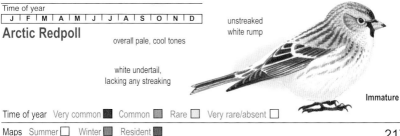

Time of year

| J | F | M | A | M | J | J | A | S | O | N | D |

(Lesser) Redpoll

Male

pink wash on breast

faint wingbars

red forehead, black face

'Mealy' Redpoll, male

Female/ immature

larger, colder tones on upperparts, red breast

Time of year

| J | F | M | A | M | J | J | A | S | O | N | D |

unstreaked white rump

Arctic Redpoll

overall pale, cool tones

white undertail, lacking any streaking

Immature

Time of year Very common ■ Common ■ Rare □ Very rare/absent □

Maps Summer □ Winter ■ Resident ■

Finches

Finches

Crossbill *Loxia curvirostra* Crosghob   16-17cm

Stocky, large-headed finch with long wings, a short, deeply-forked tail and a large bill which is crossed at the tip. This bill shape is an adaptation for extracting seeds from the cones of coniferous trees. **Males** show an orange-red head, upperparts and underparts, and a brighter, orange-red rump. **Females** are dull greyish-green with a bright yellow-green rump. The wings of both sexes are brownish. **Immatures** are pale greyish-green and heavily streaked. Eye and legs blackish. Highly gregarious, often moving in large, noisy flocks. Flight strong and undulating.

   Voice & Diet Gives a short, sharp *chip*. Song consists of a series of trills and high pitched *tir-ee* notes. Feeds mainly on conifer seeds, although will take berries and occasionally insects.

   Habitat and Status An uncommon breeding bird and regular passage migrant. Found in coniferous forests. Nests early in the year. Populations can fluctuate with the arrival of birds from Europe. On passage found on coastal headlands and islands.

Bullfinch *Pyrrhula pyrrhula* Corcrán coille   14-16cm

Plump, thick-necked finch with a short, blackish-grey, thickset bill. **Males** show a black crown and upper nape, continuing down below the eye and onto the chin. Cheeks, throat, breast and upper belly bright pink-red and contrasting with white lower belly and undertail. Mantle blue-grey. Black wings show a broad, pale wingbar. Black tail appears square-ended. In flight shows a broad, white rump. Duller **females** show pinkish-buff cheeks, breast and upper belly, a greyish-brown mantle and a duller black crown. **Immatures** similar but lack a black cap. Legs dark.

   Voice & Diet Gives a soft *dieu* call. The song is a quiet variety of creaking notes. Feeds on seeds, berries, fruit buds and, occasionally, insects.

   Habitat and Status A common resident species found in open parkland, woods, orchards and well-developed gardens. Builds nests in bushes or brambles. Rarely seen in large flocks.

Hawfinch *Coccothraustes coccothraustes* Glasán gobmhór   16-17cm

A bull-necked, secretive finch with a very large, bluish-grey bill. **Adult males** show a warm brown crown and ear coverts, a black bib and lores, and a grey hindneck. Mantle and scapulars rich dark brown. Glossy bluish-black wings show a white covert patch. Rump and white-tipped tail warm brown. Underparts pinkish-brown with white undertail. In flight shows a striking white wing patch and a whitish, transparent band on the primaries. Bill paler in winter. Eye brown with a black pupil. **Adult females** appear duller.

   Voice & Diet Gives explosive *tzik* and thin *tzriip* calls. Feeds on a variety of seeds, berries and beechmast. Also feeds on insects in summer.

   Habitat and Status A very rare breeding species and vagrant from Europe. Found in open woodlands and mature parks. On passage found in gardens on coastal headlands and islands.

Common Rosefinch *Carpodacus erythrinus* Rósghlasán coiteann   14-15cm

Stout, thick-billed finch, usually found in the drab female or immature plumages. **Immatures** and **females** are extremely nondescript with greyish-brown upperparts and head, paler underparts showing faint streaking and an inconspicuous malar stripe. Brownish wings show two diagnostic pale wingbars on the median and greater coverts. Large, black, beady eye prominent in a plain face. **Summer males** show a bright pink-red head and breast, often extending down onto the whitish belly and flanks. Upperparts streaked greyish-brown. Rump pinkish-red. Notched tail greyish-brown. The thick, short bill is dark horn-coloured. Legs brownish.

   Voice & Diet Can give a quiet *teu-ic* call. Song consists of loud *teu-teu* notes. Feeds on seeds.

   Habitat and Status A rare but regular vagrant from eastern Europe. Found in stubble fields, in gardens or along hedgerows on coastal islands and headlands. Often associates with other finches.

Time of year
J F M A M J J A S O N D

bright red

Crossbill

crossed mandibles usually only visible at close range

greenish

usually confined to pine forests, eating only pine cone seeds

Male

Female/immature

Time of year
J F M A M J J A S O N D

conspicuous white rump

Bullfinch

often seen in pairs

black cap, white wingbar on black wing

pinkish red

Adult female

black tail

Adult male

Time of year
J F M A M J J A S O N D

large bill

Hawfinch

often inconspicuous, despite colourful plumage

Adult male
females slightly duller

in flight large-billed, short-tailed

white wing patches & tail tip

Time of year
J F M A M J J A S O N D

beady eye, plain head

Common Rosefinch

stout, dark bill

two pale wingbars

red head & breast

Adult male, spring

Immature/female

Time of year   Very common ■   Common ■   Rare □   Very rare/absent □

Maps   Winter ■   Resident ■   On passage ■

Finches

219

Buntings

Yellowhammer *Emberiza citrinella* Buíóg   16-17cm

A colourful species, with **summer males** showing a yellow head and underparts with olive-brown head streaking, a chestnut ear covert border and moustachial stripe, a diffuse chestnut breast band, and dark streaking on chestnut-washed flanks. Chestnut upperparts show dark streaking. Chestnut rump unstreaked. Tail shows white outer edges. **Winter males** show heavier head and underpart streaking, and darker head markings. **Females** show a pale yellow head with olive-brown ear covert border, moustachial and malar stripes. Underparts yellowish with brown breast and flank streaking. Upperparts as male. **Immatures** duller than females with finer streaking. Bill greyish. Legs pinkish.

Voice & Diet Gives a sharp, loud, metallic *tzwik* call. The song is a distinctive combination of repeated, high-pitched, tinkling notes finishing in a drawn-out, wheezy *chueee* note. This song is traditionally transcribed as *a little-bit-of-bread-and-no-cheese*, the emphasis being on the *cheese*. Feeds on seeds, grain, berries and fruit. In summer takes insects, spiders and worms.

Habitat and Status An uncommon, but widespread, resident species. Frequents hedgerows on arable farmland, woodland edges, overgrown scrub and gorse slopes, and young conifer plantations. Nests on or near the ground in overgrown bases of hedges and brambles.

Lapland Bunting *Calcarius lapponicus* Gealóg Laplannach   14-16cm

A long-winged bunting with a short, yellowish bill and dark legs. **Winter males** and **females** show a buff crown, a black lateral crown-stripe, and buff lores, ear coverts and supercilium. Black eye-stripe forms a thick border to ear coverts and continues as a moustachial stripe. Nape chestnut or warm buff. White tips to median and greater coverts, and chestnut greater coverts, contrast with streaked, buff upperparts. Creamy underparts show a dark malar stripe and streaking on breast and flanks. **Winter males** tend to be brighter with dark blotching on the breast. **Immatures** show a duller head and nape. **Summer males** show a black head and throat with white from eye to sides of breast.

Voice & Diet In flight or when flushed gives a very distinctive, dry, rattling *trickitick* call which can often be followed by a softer, descending *teuu* note. Feeds on a wide range of seeds and will occasionally take insects.

Habitat and Status A scarce but regular autumn and winter visitor. On passage found on coastal islands and headlands, frequenting crop and stubble fields, pastures and moorland. In winter found along coastal counties. Can be very tame.

Snow Bunting *Plectrophenax nivalis* Gealóg shneachta   16-18cm

A striking, tame bunting with a yellowish bill and dark legs. **Winter males** show a warm buff crown, cheeks and breast sides, and a pale buff nape. Underparts white. Dark-streaked, pale buff upperparts contrast with white inner wings and black primaries. In flight shows white sides to black tail. **Females** show dull buff upperparts, crown, cheeks and sides of breast with streaking on nape and upperparts. Wings show browner primaries with dark bars across the base of the secondaries and on the wing coverts. Underparts creamy with buff flanks. **Immatures** very dull, showing a very small area of white on the wings. **Summer males** show a black and white plumage and a black bill.

Voice & Diet In flight or when flushed gives a rippling, musical *tirrirrirrip* call. Also gives a plaintive *teu* call. Feeds on seeds, grain and insects.

Habitat and Status An uncommon but regular autumn passage migrant and winter visitor from Iceland and Scandinavia. On passage found on coastal headlands and islands, frequenting pastures and moorlands. In winter found on coastal shingle banks, dunes, stubble and crop fields, piers and harbours. Can also winter inland, usually on mountains and high moorlands.

Time of year

| J | F | M | A | M | J | J | A | S | O | N | D |

Yellowhammer

Female
(immatures slightly duller)

bright yellow & black head pattern

Adult male

male sings from prominent perch

largely confined to grain-growing areas

feeds on seeds, grain, etc

Time of year

| J | F | M | A | M | J | J | A | S | O | N | D |

Lapland Bunting

yellow bill, dark tip

chestnut & black wings

buff & black head

Immature

Summer male
this plumage very rare in Ireland

Male, winter

black legs

Time of year

| J | F | M | A | M | J | J | A | S | O | N | D |

Snow Bunting

white patches on wing & tail

Female winter

buff head, yellow bill

black legs

this plumage rarely seen in Ireland

Male winter

Male summer

more white on wings

Time of year   Common ▦   Rare ▢   Very rare/absent ▢

Maps   Summer ▢   Winter ▦

221

Buntings

Buntings

Reed Bunting *Emberiza schoeniclus* Gealóg ghiolcaí   14-16cm

A striking species with a long, white-edged tail. **Summer males** show a black head and throat contrasting with a white moustachial stripe and neck collar. Upperparts rufous with black streaking and centres to wing feathers. Underparts whitish with flank streaking. In winter black on head and throat obscured by buffish tips. **Adult females** and **immatures** show a brownish crown with a thin, dark, lateral crown-stripe and buff supercilium. Ear coverts and lores brownish, with a dark eye-stripe from behind eye forming a dark ear covert border and a moustachial stripe meeting the bill. Creamy throat shows a malar stripe. Breast and flanks streaked. Bill greyish. Legs brownish.

Voice & Diet Song consists of repeated, hurried *tzik-tzik-tzik-tzizzizik* notes. Gives loud, shrill *tswee* and harsh *chink* calls. Feeds on a wide range of insects and larvae in summer, taking seeds and grain in winter.

Habitat and Status A common, widespread, resident species. Found in a wide range of habitats, including reed-beds, marshes, hedgerows, sand-dunes and young conifer plantations. Nests on or near the ground in tussocks, rank vegetation or bushes. In winter leaves mountainous regions in favour of low-lying arable or coastal habitats.

Little Bunting *Emberiza pusilla* Gealóg bheag   13-14cm

A small bunting with a striking head pattern. **Adult males, females** and **immatures** similar, showing a warm brown crown, a black lateral crown-stripe, a buff supercilium behind eye, chestnut lores and ear coverts, and a pale spot on rear ear coverts. Eye shows a pale orbital ring. Eye-stripe behind eye forms a dark border to rear of ear coverts, Lacks a moustachial stripe. Thin malar stripe does not meet bill. White underparts show breast and flank streaking. Upperparts buff with black streaking. Whitish median covert tips form a wingbar. Greater coverts can show pale tips. Outer tail feathers white. Short bill greyish with a straight culmen. Legs pinkish.

Voice & Diet On passage can give very distinctive, Robin-like *tick* or thrush-like *tsip* calls which are unlike the calls given by Reed Bunting. Feeds on the ground in a low, crouched manner, taking a variety of seeds and, occasionally, insects.

Habitat and Status A very rare vagrant from northern Scandinavia and Siberia. Most records refer to autumn, although reported both in spring and winter. Found on coastal headlands and islands in rough pastures, crop fields and short grass.

Rustic Bunting *Emberiza rustica* Gealóg thuathúil   14-15cm

Autumn adults and **immatures** show white underparts, with chestnut breast streaking extending and broadening onto flanks. Pale nape patch contrasts with a streaked brown crown which can appear crested. Supercilium buff before eye, creamy-buff and prominent behind eye. Lores and ear coverts brownish with a pale buff rear spot. Dark stripe behind eye forms ear covert border and thin moustachial stripe. Pale throat shows malar stripe. Dark-streaked chestnut upperparts show wingbars formed by pale median and greater covert tips. Outer tail feathers white. **Summer males** show a black crown and cheeks, and a white supercilium and nape patch. Bill pinkish with a grey tip. Legs pinkish-brown.

Voice & Diet On passage can give a hard, sharp, repeated, Robin-like *tsip* call. Feeds on the ground, taking a variety of seeds, grain and, occasionally, insects.

Habitat and Status A very rare vagrant from northern Scandinavia and Siberia. Most records refer to autumn, although has been recorded in spring. Found on coastal headlands and islands in rough pastures, crop fields and short grass. Often perches in the open on top of low bushes, wires or fence posts.

Time of year
J F M A M J J A S O N D

Reed Bunting

Male in winter

blackish malar stripe

distinctive black & white
head pattern

chestnut on wings,
grey rump

Adult female

Adult male

Time of year
J F M A M J J A S O N D

Little Bunting

chestnut lores & ear
coverts, black lateral
crown stripe

greyish bill with
straight culmen

Immature
(adults similar)

Time of year
J F M A M J J A S O N D

Rustic Bunting

rufous nape
& breast

distinctive
head
pattern

pale spot on
ear coverts

rufous flanks
& streaking

Summer male

Immature

Buntings

Buntings

Ortolan Bunting *Emberiza hortulana* Gealóg gharraí   16-17cm

A long-winged bunting showing a pale orbital ring and pale, reddish-pink bill and legs. **Adult males** show a greyish-olive head, nape and upper breast, and a pale yellow throat and moustachial stripe. Underparts orange-buff. Warm brown upperparts show dark streaking and two pale wingbars. **Adult females** similar, but show brownish tones to head and breast, thin breast streaking and paler underparts. **Immatures** like females, but show a brownish head, a pale throat and moustachial stripe, a streaked grey-buff breast, thin streaking on pale underparts and streaked, brownish upperparts.

Voice & Diet Gives a soft, liquid *tsip* call as well as harder *twick,* and sharper *tseu* calls. Feeds on a wide range of seeds, occasionally taking insects.

Habitat and Status A rare passage migrant from continental Europe found on stubble and crop fields on coastal islands and headlands.

Black-headed Bunting *Emberiza melanocephala* Gealóg cheanndubh   16-18cm

Summer males show a black crown and cheeks, bright yellow sides of neck and underparts, and a bright chestnut nape, sides of breast and upperparts. Dark wings show two whitish bars. **Females** show a greyish-brown head and upperparts, with a faint chestnut tinge on the mantle and sides of the breast. Underparts pale washed-out yellow. **Immatures** show a pale brown, streaked head and upperparts, and pale wingbars. Pale yellowish underparts show a very faint malar stripe, dark streaking on the breast fading onto the flanks and a bright yellow undertail. In all plumages does not show white on the tail. Bill greyish.

Voice & Diet Gives short *chuuh* and *tzit* calls. Feeds on a variety of seeds and, occasionally, insects.

Habitat and Status A very rare vagrant from south-eastern Europe. Found on stubble and crop fields on coastal islands and headlands.

Yellow-breasted Bunting *Emberiza aureola* Gealóg bhroinnbhuí   14-16cm

Summer males show a deep brown head and upperparts, a black face and throat, a white carpal patch and a white wingbar. Bright yellow underparts show a dark breast band and flank streaking. **Females** show a brown-streaked crown with a pale buff central crown and supercilium. A dark eyestripe forms a border to the brownish ear coverts which show a pale rear patch. Lores pale. Underparts pale yellow with streaking on breast sides and flanks. Can show a faint malar stripe. Upperparts pale buff with dark streaking. Wings show two pale bars. Brown rump appears heavily streaked. **Immatures** like females, but show paler underparts and heavier breast and flank streaking. Legs and bill pinkish.

Voice & Diet Gives a *tzick* call. Feeds on a variety of seeds, grain and insects.

Habitat and Status A very rare vagrant from northern Europe. Found on stubble and crop fields on coastal islands and headlands.

Corn Bunting *Emberiza calandra* Gealóg bhuachair   17-19cm

A large species showing a thick, yellowish bill. **Summer adults** show a streaked brownish crown and a broad, dark border to heavily-streaked ear coverts. Underparts whitish with a broad malar stripe and heavy streaking on the sides of the breast and flanks. Upperparts greyish-brown with heavy dark streaking on the mantle, and dark centres to the wing feathers. Long brownish tail does not show white outer feathers. **Winter adults** and **immatures** appear duller. Legs pinkish.

Voice & Diet Gives a low, sharp *tikk* call. Song a fast, complicated jingle of rattles and chirps, often described as sounding like rattling keys. Feeds on a variety of seeds and insects.

Habitat and Status Formerly a scarce breeding species but now a rare winter and passage migrant from Europe. Found on coastal farmland and open country. Nests on the ground.

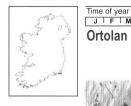

Time of year

| J | F | M | A | M | J | J | A | S | O | N | D |

Ortolan Bunting

greyish head, yellow moustachial stripe & throat

Adult

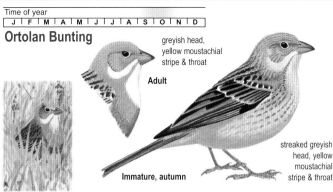

feeds on the ground

streaked greyish head, yellow moustachial stripe & throat

Immature, autumn

Time of year

| J | F | M | A | M | J | J | A | S | O | N | D |

Black-headed Bunting

darkish head, streaked

Female/immature

yellowish underparts

black head, yellow nape & underparts

Summer male

Time of year

| J | F | M | A | M | J | J | A | S | O | N | D |

Yellow-breasted Bunting

dark lateral crown stripe, pale central crown stripe

pale lores, pinkish bill

whitish spot on ear coverts

streaked upperparts

Immature

yellowish underparts, lightly streaked

Time of year

| J | F | M | A | M | J | J | A | S | O | N | D |

Corn Bunting

streaked brown plumage

heavy, pale bill

pale eyering

darkish lower edge to ear coverts

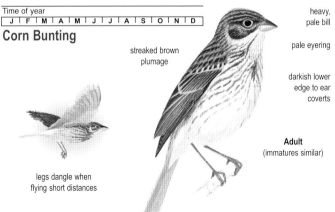

former resident, now presumed extinct as a breeding species in Ireland. Now occurs as a migrant/vagrant

legs dangle when flying short distances

Adult
(immatures similar)

Buntings

Time of year   Rare ☐   Very rare/absent ☐

Rare North American Passerines

The majority of North American passerines found in Ireland are immature birds blown across the Atlantic Ocean by storms during their autumn migration. For that reason, the birds described and illustrated here are mostly in immature plumage. See also Black-billed and Yellow-billed Cuckoos on page 138, Buff-bellied Pipit on page 156, Hermit, Swainson's and Gray-cheeked Thrushes on page 174 and Red-eyed and Philadelphia Vireo on page 210.

Northern Parula *Parula americana* Parúl tuaisceartach　　　　10-12cm
Immature males show a bluish face, a greenish crown, and a bright yellow throat and breast broken by a bluish band. The breast can also show bright red flecks. Belly and undertail white. Upperparts and wings bluish with a yellowish-green mantle, two prominent white wingbars, and greenish edges to wing feathers. Rump and short tail bluish. **Immature females** similar but lack the band and rufous patches on the breast and show more greenish-blue upperparts. Call: Usually silent but can give a sharp *chip* call.

Yellow-rumped Warbler *Dendroica coronata* Ceolaire buíphrompach　　　　12-14cm
Immature males show a dull brownish head with a faint, pale supercilium and, occasionally, a yellowish crown patch. Shows a white throat, creamy underparts, bright yellow patches on the breast sides and streaking from sides of breast onto flanks. Brownish upperparts show dark streaking. Rump bright yellow. Blue-grey wings show two whitish wingbars and white edges to tertials. Greyish tail shows white spots on the outermost two or three feathers, conspicuous from below. **Immature** females appear duller. Call: Gives a clear, hard *chikk* call.

Blackpoll Warbler *Dendroica striata* Ceolaire dubhéadanach　　　　12-13cm
Immatures show a dull olive-green crown, ear coverts and upperparts, a pale yellow-buff supercilium, faint streaking on the mantle, two white wingbars and white edges to tertials. Pale underparts show faint streaking from the breast onto flanks. Undertail white. Undertail shows white spots towards the tips of the outer-tail feathers. Legs pale. Call: Gives a clear *chip* call.

Yellow Warbler *Dendroica petechia* Ceolaire buí　　　　11-13cm
Adult males show a dark eye and bill, a bright yellow face and underparts with reddish streaking on the breast and flanks. Upperparts bright yellow-green with yellow tail spots visible on spread tail. Legs pale reddish. **Females** slightly duller and lack breast and flank streaking. **Immatures** duller than females with greenish-brown upperparts, pale, yellow-washed underparts and a pale eye-ring and loral area. Can be very skulking. Call: Gives a clear *tzip* call.

American Redstart *Setophaga ruticilla* Earrdheargán Meiriceánach　　　　13-14cm
Immature males show a bluish-grey head with a pale supercilium before the eye, and narrow white eye crescents. Pale greyish underparts show an orange-yellow patch on the sides of the breast. Upperparts brownish-green with a bright yellow wing patch. The long, blackish tail is often held cocked to reveal bright yellow patches at the base. **Immature females** similar but show a yellow patch on the sides of the breast and can lack a yellow wing patch. Call: Gives a squeaky *chik* and thin *tsit* calls.

Black-and-white Warbler *Mniotilta varia* Ceolaire dubh is bán　　　　11-13cm
Adult males show a black crown with a white central stripe, a white supercilium, and black ear coverts and throat. Upperparts black with white streaks. White underparts show black streaking extending from throat onto breast, flanks and undertail. **Females** and **immatures** show a whitish throat, a pale supercilium and buff-washed rear flanks. Legs dark. Pointed bill shows a pale base. When feeding moves along branches and tree trunks like a Treecreeper. Call: Gives a sharp *stic* call.

Northern Parula

white eye-ring

tiny size, bright
yellow, green & blue

prominent white
wingbars

Immature female

Yellow-rumped Warbler

yellow on flanks
& crown

yellow rump

Immature male

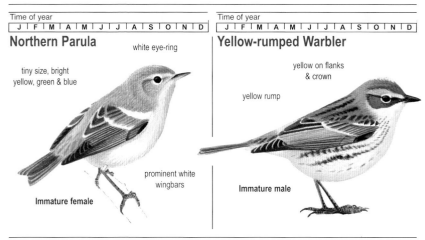

Blackpoll Warbler

bright green above,
yellow throat & breast

white wingbars
& tertial edges

**Autumn
Adult/immature**

Yellow Warbler

pale eye-ring
& lores

dark eye
& bill

bright yellow
& green

Female

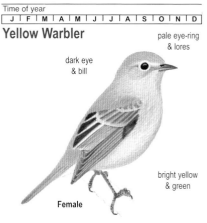

American Redstart

Immature male

black & yellow tail,
frequently fanned

orange on side
of breast, yellow
wingbar

Time of year   Rare ☐   Very rare/absent ☐

Black-and-white Warbler

black & white
stripes & streaking

Immature

often creeps along
tree trunks

Rare

227

Northern Waterthrush *Seiurus noveboracensis* Smólach uisce tuaisceartach   13-15cm
Immatures shows a dull olive-brown crown and ear coverts, a dark eye-stripe, and a very long, yellowish-buff supercilium. Upperparts and tail plain dull olive-brown. Whitish underparts show heavy black streaking from the throat to the flanks and belly. Flanks can show a yellowish-buff wash. **Adults** similar but show a paler supercilium. Legs pinkish. Dark bill shows a pinkish base. Feeds on the ground, usually close to water and constantly bobs tail. Call: A loud *stwik*.

Scarlet Tanager *Piranga olivacea* Tanagair scarlóideach   15-17cm
A large, finch-like species with a thick, pale bill. **Immatures** show greenish upperparts with brownish wings and yellowish underparts. **Immature males** can show black on the scapulars and on some wing feathers. Underwing coverts whitish. Call: Can give a harsh *chik-burr* call.

Baltimore Oriole *Icterus galbula*   17-19cm
A large species with a long, pointed bill. **Immatures** show a pale orange head, a dark crown, an orange throat and breast and a whitish belly. Upperparts brownish with a pale orange rump and edges to the tail. Dark wings show two whitish bars. Call: A clear *pioo-li*.

Bobolink *Dolichonyx oryzivorus* Bobóilinc   16-18cm
A large bunting-like species. **Immatures** show a striking, yellow-buff crown, a blackish lateral crown-stripe, and a broad, yellow-buff supercilium. Cheeks and lores pale buff, with a dark eye-stripe from behind the eye forming a border to the rear of the ear coverts. Streaked, pale brown upperparts show yellow-buff braces, and whitish wingbars and edges to tertials. Brownish tail shows pointed feathers. Underparts yellow-buff with faint streaking. Call: A short *bink*, in flight.

Rose-breasted Grosbeak *Pheucticus ludovicianus* Gobach mór broinnrósach 18-20cm
A stocky bird showing a huge, pale bill. **Immature males** show a dark brown crown with a pale central stripe, a white supercilium, dark ear coverts and streaked brown upperparts. Wings show whitish bars and primary bases, and pale-tipped tertials. Underwing coverts pinkish. Pale underparts heavily streaked on yellowish-buff breast and flanks. Can show pink on breast and throat. **Immature females** lack pink on underparts and show yellow underwing coverts. Call: A hard *chik*.

White-throated Sparrow *Zonotrichia albicollis* Gealbhan píbgheal   15-17cm
A striking species showing a thick, greyish bill. **Adults** show a white central crown-stripe, a black lateral crown-stripe and eye-stripe, and a conspicuous supercilium, bright yellow before the eye, and white above and behind the eye. A white throat shows a thin malar stripe. Cheeks and underparts greyish, fading to buff on the flanks which also show faint streaking. Undertail white. Upperparts brown with dark streaking. Brown wings show dark centres to the feathers and two white bars. **Immatures** show a buffish central crown-stripe and supercilium, a thicker, darker malar stripe and streaking on the breast. Legs pale. Call: A sharp *chinc* call.

Northern Waterthrush

striking, long supercilium

constantly
bobs tail

heavily streaked
underparts

feeds on ground,
usually near water

Immature

Scarlet Tanager

dark wings, black
on scapulars on
young males

thick,
pale
bill

yellowish
underparts

**Immature
male**

Baltimore Oriole

unmistakable
orange-yellow,
with black &
white wings

pointed bill

Immature

Bobolink

blackish crown with
buff central stripe

pinkish
bill

heavily streaked
upperparts

buff underparts,
faintly streaked

pointed tail
feathers

Immature

Rose-breasted Grosbeak

striking head
pattern

heavy,
pinkish bill

Immature male

White-throated Sparrow

distinctive head pattern

Adult

black
border to
white
throat

Rare

Time of year   Rare ☐   Very rare/absent ☐

Rare Vagrants

The following species are considered extremely rare vagrants to Ireland. We have included English, scientific and, where possible, the Irish names of each species in this section. Some species have only been recently added to the Irish list and, as a result, Irish names have yet to be assigned to them.

Lesser White-fronted Goose

Anser erythropus Mionghé bhánéadanach   56-65cm
Appears very similar to White-fronted Goose, but is smaller and daintier, with a shorter neck and a rounded head. Shows a diagnostic yellow eye-ring at all ages. Adult plumage as White-fronted, but shows more extensive white on the face extending as a point onto the forehead. Tends to show less black barring on the belly. Pinkish bill appears short and triangular. Legs orange-yellow. Immatures lack the white face patch and black barring on the belly. Told by the yellow eye-ring, structure and the short, pinkish bill. Range: Northern Europe.

Ruddy Shelduck

Tadorna ferruginea Seil-lacha rua   59-70cm
A large, goose-like duck with a short, black bill and dark legs. Males show an orange-brown body, dark wing tips and tail, a pale yellow-buff head, a creamy face and a black neck collar. Females similar, but show a whiter face and lack the black neck collar. In flight, shows a striking white forewing, a dark green speculum and dark wing tips. Behaviour as Shelduck. Range: Southern and south-eastern Europe, North Africa.

Baikal Teal

Anas formosa   40-43cm
A dabbling duck, larger than Teal. Males show a striking face pattern with a brown crown, a thin white supercilium, a black vertical stripe from the eye down the cheek and onto the chin, a yellow face and a green nape. Breast pinkish-brown contrasting with greyish rear neck and flanks, and a striking white vertical stripe on the side of the breast. Rear flanks show a white stripe which contrasts with a blackish stern. Greyish upperparts show white-edged, elongated scapulars. In flight shows a broad, white trailing edge to a blackish-green speculum, a reddish upper edge to the speculum, and whitish underwing coverts. Adult

females may recall female Garganey appearing greyish-brown overall with a face pattern showing a dark crown, a dark eye-stripe, a dark cheek stripe and a dark-bordered, whitish loral spot. In flight shows a wing pattern similar to males. Immatures like females but show warmer reddish brown tones on the breast and a paler, less striking face pattern. Bill greyish. Range: North and east Siberia.

Redhead

Aythya americana   43-50cm
A diving duck appearing very similar to Pochard. Males show a more rounded crown than Pochard and an orange-red eye. Head chestnut orange, contrasting with a black breast, pale grey upperparts and flanks, and a black stern. Best told by bill pattern which is pale grey with a white subterminal band and a black tip. Females like female Pochard but again show a more rounded crown and a grey bill with a narrow, pale subterminal band and a black tip. In flight shows pale greyish secondaries and primaries, contrasting with upperwing coverts. Range: North America.

Bufflehead

Bucephala albeola   32-38cm
A small, Teal-sized duck. Males very distinctive showing a glossy black head with a large, white patch on the rear of the head, white underparts and black and white upperparts. Females and immatures show a brownish-grey head with a striking, white oval patch on the rear of the cheek, dark brownish upperparts and greyish underparts. Bill, short, pale grey in males, darker in females. Range: North America.

Barrow's Goldeneye

Bucephala islandica   42-52cm
Very similar to Goldeneye but appears darker and slightly larger. Males show a domed, bluish-black head with a striking white crescent spot before the eye. This face spot extends as a point above the eye. Breast and flanks white with a dark stripe on sides of upper breast. Stern dark. Upperparts blackish with white scapular spots. Eye yellow. Bill dark. In flight shows a black and white inner wing contrasting with a dark outer wing. Females very similar to female Goldeneye but are larger and show a more domed head as well as more extensive yellow on the dark bill. Head dark

brown contrasting with a pale neck, and greyish breast, flanks and upperparts. In flight shows white secondaries and dark-tipped greater coverts contrasting with a dark upperwing. Immatures like females but show a dark bill. Range: Iceland, Greenland and North America.

Hooded Merganser

Mergus cucullatus Síolta chochaill   42-50cm
A striking species, smaller than Red-breasted Merganser and showing a long, narrow bill. Males show an erectile fan crest on a black head and a long white stripe behind the eye which, when the crest is raised, appears as a striking white patch. The white breast shows two black stripes, while the blackish upperparts with diagnostic white shafts to the tertials contrast with the orange-brown flanks. Narrow bill black. Iris yellow. Females show a brownish head with a fuller crest than female Red-breasted Merganser, The breast and flanks are brownish, with darker upperparts showing white shafts to the tertials. Dark bill shows a yellowish base. Iris brownish. Range: North America.

Capercaillie

Tetrao urogallus Capall coille   55-88cm
A very large gamebird extinct in Ireland since the eighteenth century. Males show a blackish-grey head, breast and tail, a brown mantle and wings, white shoulder patches, and white on the belly, undertail and tail. Males also show a striking red wattle above the eye and a whitish bill. Females are heavily barred and show an orange-buff head, breast and tail, brownish upperparts and wings, and whitish under- parts. Range: Scotland; central and northern Europe.

Pacific Diver

Gavia pacifica   59-68cm
Very similar to Black-throated Diver but appears slightly smaller, shows a shorter bill and, most impor- tantly, lacks a white flank/thigh patch. Adult winters show more extensive dark on the face and a more rounded crown than Black-throated. From the side, the hind-neck appears more rounded and 'inflated', creating a unique head profile. Chin, throat and breast white. Can show a black throat strap but it should be noted that some Black-throated Divers can also show a narrow black stripe on the throat. Upperparts dark. Underparts white and, in flight, shows a dark strap across the ventral area. Immatures similar but show pale edges to upperpart feathers. Adult summers show a blackish-grey face, grey hindneck, a black throat and chin, and white stripes on the side of the

neck. Upperparts black with extensive white spots on the mantle. Range: North America.

Bulwer's Petrel

Bulweria bulwerii Peadairín Bulwer   25-28cm
A large species, intermediate in size between petrels and shearwaters. Shows an all-dark plumage, with long wings showing pale upperwing bars. The long, tapering tail appears wedge-shaped when spread. Flies with swooping wing beats interspersed with glides over the water. Range: Azores and Madeira.

Swinhoe's Petrel

Oceanodroma monorhis   18-21cm
All all-dark petrel, very similar in size and shape to Leach's Petrel. Shows long, angled wings with a contrasting pale panel on the upperwing, pale shafts to the primary feathers which are almost impossible to see in the field, and dark underwings. Unlike Leach's Petrel, shows an all-dark rump. Tail shows a shallow fork. Range: Eastern Asia.

Madeiran Petrel

Oceanodroma castro Guairdeall Maidéarach 19-21cm
A white-rumped petrel very similar to both Leach's and Wilson's Petrels. Shows a shallow fork to the tail, a dark body, long, broad, angled wings and a pale upperwing bar. Unlike Wilson's, the toes do not project past the tail. Differs from Leach's by showing a less conspicuous wingbar, and more extensive white on the rump which extends onto the sides of the rear flanks and undertail coverts. Flies with quick, shallow wing beats. Range: Azores, Madeira and Portugal.

Red-billed Tropicbird

Phaethon aethereus   44-50cm
An exotic, tern-like species showing a white wedge- shaped tail with extremely long, white central tail streamers. Adults show a bright red, pointed bill and a white head with a black stripe through the eye extending onto the rear crown. Underparts white. Upperparts and rump white with extensive dark barring. In flight shows dark outer wings. Immatures lack the long tail streamers and show yellowish bills. Range: West Africa.

Double-crested Cormorant

Phalacrocorax auritus Broigheall clusach   76-88cm
Similar but smaller than Cormorant with bright orange lores, chin and bill. Adults show a glossy black plumage with pale-edged wing feathers and wispy crests in summer plumage. Immatures appear dark brown above with a pale brown foreneck and breast,

and a dark belly and undertail. This plumage is the opposite to that shown in immature Cormorant where the neck and upper breast is dark and the belly white. Immature Double-crested also show the striking orange lores, chin and bill. Range: North America.

Magnificent Frigatebird

Fregata magnificens   92-113cm
An enormous seabird with long, angled wings and a long, forked tail. Adult males show an all-dark plumage with a red throat patch. Adult females differ by showing a whitish breast patch and a pale upperwing bar. Immatures similar to females, but show a whitish head and more extensive white on the underparts. Very skilled in the air, flying with slow wing beats and long glides. Often soars to great heights. Rarely lands on the water, picking food from the surface in flight. Will also steal food from other seabirds. Range: Tropical Atlantic and east Pacific.

American Bittern

Botaurus lentiginosus Bonnán Meiriceánach 58-70cm
Very similar to but smaller than Bittern. Differs by showing a brown crown and forehead, a dark eye-stripe, a black stripe from the base of the bill along the side of the neck, broad brown stripes on the foreneck and no barring on the sides of the neck. The long, greenish-yellow bill tends to show a dark culmen. Unlike Bittern, the primary coverts and flight feathers do not show any barring and appear uniformly dark in flight. Range: North America.

Green Heron

Botaurus virescens   40-46cm
A small, short-necked heron. Adults show a dark crown with a rufous face, sides of neck and breast, narrow, pale yellow neck and breast stripes and a pale chin. Upperparts greyish-green with a short, dark tail. Underparts bluish-grey. Long, dark bill shows a yellow lower mandible. Legs yellowish. Immatures show a dark crown, a brownish face, neck and breast with extensive dark streaking, and broad, pale stripes extending from the throat onto the breast. Upperparts dark with pale edges to feathers. Underparts greyish with dark streaking. Bill yellowish-green. Legs yellow. Range: North America.

Little Blue Heron

Egretta caerulea   58-62cm
A Little Egret-like heron. Immatures best told from Little Egret by the thicker neck, a shorter, thicker bill with a greyish base and dark tip, pale green legs and

greyish-green lores. Overall plumage white but shows small dark tips to primaries and, as the bird matures, more extensive greyish mottling on upper and underparts. Adults very distinctive with a dark plum-toned bluish-grey head, and dark bluish-grey upper and underparts. Bill shows a bluish base and dark tip. Legs green. Range: North America.

Black Stork

Ciconia nigra Storc dubh   92-105cm
A large, striking species, similar in size to White Stork. Adults show a glossy black head, upper breast and upperparts, and white underparts. Long, dagger-like bill and legs scarlet-red. In flight shows dark under-wings which contrast with white axillaries and under-parts. Soars on long, broad wings and with neck extended. Immatures show a greyish-brown head and upper breast, brownish-black upperparts, and greyish-green legs and bill. Range: South-western and eastern Europe.

Honey Buzzard

Pernis apivorus Clamhán riabhach   52-60cm
Similar in size to Buzzard, showing longer, slender wings and a small protruding head. Upperparts greyish-brown with a greyish head and nape and three unevenly spaced bands on the brownish uppertail. Underparts and underwing coverts show heavy barring, with conspicuous dark bands on the flight feathers and tail. Unlike Buzzard, tends to soar and glide on flat wings while the wing beats appear deeper and more elastic. Range: Great Britain and Europe.

Bald Eagle

Haliaeetus leucocephalus Iolar maol   80-94cm
A large, Golden Eagle-sized raptor. Adults very distinctive showing a large, yellow bill, brown wings, and brown upper and underparts contrasting strongly with a striking white head, tail and undertail. Juveniles appear dark brown overall with a dark bill, white axillaries and whitish centres to the tail feathers. Immature birds show white patches on the head, tail, breast and wing feathers, as well as a distinctive white triangle on the back. The bill gradually turns yellow as the bird matures which can take up to four years. Range: North America.

Griffon Vulture

Gyps fulvus Bultúr gríofa   96-109cm
An enormous raptor with a featherless, greyish head, very broad, long wings and a short tail. In flight shows sandy-brown upperparts and upperwing coverts

contrasting with dark flight feathers and tail. Underparts streaked brown with pale brown underwing coverts. In flight shows very long wings held in an acute V when soaring. Range: Southern Europe.

Spotted Eagle

Aquila clanga Iolar breac   59-69cm
A large raptor, smaller than Golden Eagle. Adults show a uniformly dark brown plumage, no barring on the flight feathers and tail, and a pale U on the uppertail coverts. Immatures similar, but show white spotting on the scapulars and upperwing coverts, and a larger, more conspicuous U on the uppertail coverts. In flight wings appear broad and are held slightly bowed when soaring. Range: Eastern and north-eastern Europe.

Lesser Kestrel

Falco naumanni Mionphocaire gaoithe   28-33cm
A smaller, slimmer falcon than Kestrel with narrower wings and a wedge-tipped tail. Adult males show a blue-grey head without moustachials, chestnut upperparts which show no spotting or barring, and a blue-grey tail with white tips and a black subterminal band. Underparts buffish with light spotting. In flight shows chestnut and blue-grey upperwing coverts, while the underwings are whitish with faint spotting on the coverts and dark trailing edges and tips. Females appear similar to female Kestrel, but show thinner barring on the upperparts, a diffuse moustachial and paler, lightly spotted underparts. Lesser Kestrels show whitish claws, unlike the black claws of Kestrel. Hawks for insects on the wing, tending to hover less frequently. Range: Southern Europe.

Sora

Porzana carolina Gearr sora   19-23cm
A very distinctive rail, with adults showing a black face-mask and throat, a black-centred, unstreaked chestnut crown, bluish-grey cheeks, neck and breast, broad barring on the flanks, and buff-white undertail coverts. The warm brown upperparts show dark centres to the mantle feathers, scapulars and tertials. Bill yellow. Legs greenish. Immatures similar, but show a creamy supercilium and throat, warm-buff cheeks and breast, and a duller yellowish-green bill. Resembles Spotted Crake, but shows no red base to the bill or white spots on the neck and breast. Range: North America.

Little Crake

Porzana parva Gearr beag   17-19cm
A very small, shy crake. Males show a blue-grey face and underparts with faint, whitish barring on lower flanks, bolder barring on the undertail, and an olive-brown crown. Upperparts olive-brown with diffuse whitish streaking. Bill greenish with a red base. Legs green. Females similar, but show a pale grey face, a whitish throat and pale buff underparts with diffuse white barring on greyish flanks. Immatures resemble females, but can show grey and buff barring extending from the flanks onto the sides of the breast, whitish spotting on the scapulars and wing coverts, and a dull greenish bill. Range: Eastern and central Europe.

Baillon's Crake

Porzana pusilla Gearr Baillon   16-18cm
A very shy crake similar to, but smaller than, Little Crake. Adults show a dark blue-grey face and underparts, with very heavy black and white barring on the flanks extending onto the undertail. Crown and upperparts rufous-brown, with white and black spotting and streaking on the mantle and wings. Bill olive-green. Legs pale brownish or greyish-green. Immatures show pale brown underparts, with brown barring on the sides of the breast becoming black and white on the flanks and undertail. Bill brownish. Range: Southern and south-eastern Europe.

American Coot

Fulica Americana
Cearc cheannann Mheiriceánach   36-40cm
Very similar to Coot, but shows a dark band on the white bill, a reddish-brown top to the white shield, and white sides to the undertail coverts. Head and neck appear black, and contrast slightly with the greyish body. Range: North America.

Sandhill Crane

Grus canadensis Grús Ceanadach   98-104cm
A tall species similar to, but smaller than, European Crane. Adults show a bright red forehead patch, a pale grey plumage which can show brown staining, and a long, pointed dark bill. Legs greyish. Immatures lack the red forehead patch of adults and show a rufous-brown head and neck, and rufous tips to the wing feathers. Bill dark brownish. Range: North America.

Little Bustard

Tetrax tetrax Bustard beag   40-45cm
A duck-sized, stocky, thick-necked species showing a short bill. Males show a sandy-brown crown, a blue-grey face and throat, a striking black and white neck

patch, fine dark barring on sandy-brown upperparts, and whitish underparts. Females show fine dark barring on a sandy-brown head, neck and upperparts, and whitish underparts. In flight black primary coverts and wing tips contrast strongly with the extensive white on the wings. Glides on bowed wings in a grouse-like manner. Range: Southern and south-eastern Europe.

Great Bustard

Otis tarda Bustard mór   90-104cm
A very heavy, stocky, thick-necked species similar in size to a large goose. Males show a greyish head with long, white whiskers on the sides of the white throat, a rufous breast band and white underparts. Upperparts rufous-brown with black barring and a prominent, white secondary panel. Tail rufous-brown with black barring. Bill short and thick. Females similar, but appear smaller and lack the rufous breast band. In flight shows a broad white panel across the upper primaries and secondaries contrasting with a black trailing edge. Range: Southern, central and south-eastern Europe.

Cream-coloured Courser

Cursorius cursor Rasaí bánbhuí   24-28cm
A sandy-coloured, plover-like species with a short, dark, decurved bill and long, creamy legs. Adults show a striking white supercilium extending onto nape which is bordered below by a broad black eye-stripe from behind eye. Rear of sandy crown shows a bluish-grey tinge. Underwings black. White-tipped tail shows a black subterminal band. Immatures show less defined head markings. Range: North Africa and Middle East.

Collared Pratincole

Glareola pratincola Pratancól muinceach   24-28cm
A long-winged, tern-like wader which shows a greyish-buff head, upperparts and sides of breast, a white belly and a creamy, black-bordered throat. Short, dark bill shows a red base. In flight shows a dark, white-edged, forked tail, and a white rump and uppertail coverts. Upperwing shows darker outer primaries, a paler inner wing and a white trailing edge to the second-aries. Underwing shows reddish-brown axillaries and coverts, but can appear black at a distance. Range: Southern Europe.

Black-winged Pratincole

Glareola nordmanni Pratancól dubheiteach 24-28cm
Very similar to Collared Pratincole, showing a black-bordered, creamy throat, a white belly, a white-edged,

dark, forked tail, and a white rump and uppertail coverts. However, head, upperparts and sides of breast appear darker and the short, dark bill shows a smaller red base. In flight does not show any contrast between outer and inner wings, and lacks a white trailing edge to secondaries. Underwing coverts and axillaries black. Range: Eastern Europe.

Semipalmated Plover

Charadrius semipalmatus   16-18cm
Very similar to Ringed Plover but is smaller, more slender and shows a shorter, thicker bill. Adults appear slightly darker than Ringed Plover and show a thinner breast band. Face pattern similar to Ringed Plover with a black and white forehead, and dark ear coverts and lores. However, usually lacks a prominent supercilium behind the eye and shows a thin yellow orbital ring. Underparts white. Crown, nape and upperparts greyish brown. Bill shows an orange base and a dark tip. Legs orange with partial webbing between all toes. Immatures very similar to immature Ringed Plover but again appears smaller, more slender and show a thinner, unbroken breast band. Crown and cheeks dark greyish brown with a striking white forehead and supercilium, and a thin, yellowish orbital ring. Importantly, usually shows a thin white line over the gape creating a white stripe above the bill and below the lores. Upperparts pale greyish brown with pale fringes to upperpart feathers. Bill dark with an orange base to lower mandible. Legs dull yellow-orange with partial webbing between all toes. Gives a distinctive, fast, whistling *cheewee* call. Range: North America.

Sociable Plover

Chettusia gregarious Pilibín ealtúil   27-30cm
An upright plover, similar in size to Lapwing. In winter plumage shows a striking white supercilium contrasting with a dark crown and eye-stripe, greyish brown upperparts and breast, and a pale belly and undertail. In summer plumage shows a black crown, yellow-buff cheeks, and a black and deep chestnut belly patch. In flight the broad, rounded wings show black primaries, white secondaries and greyish-brown coverts and scapulars. This striking upperwing pattern shows a strong resemblance to that of Sabine's Gull. White tail shows a broad, black subterminal band. Can associate with Lapwing flocks. Range: South-eastern Russia.

Great Knot

Calidris tenuirostris   24-28cm
Very similar to Knot but appearing slightly larger with

a longer, more decurved bill, a smaller headed appearance and longer wings. Adult summers show extensive head streaking and dark, broad spotting and 'arrowhead' markings on breast and flanks. Upperparts show pale-edged, dark feathering contrasting with warm, reddish-brown scapulars. Immatures and adult winters similar to Knot but show more extensive spotting on the breast. Legs greenish in colour. Range: North-east Siberia.

Western Sandpiper
Calidris mauri Gobadáinín iartharach   14-17cm
Like Semipalmated Sandpiper but shows a longer, slightly decurved bill. Juveniles show a greyish crown. Upperparts show contrasting rufous edges to upper scapulars. Underparts white. Sides of breast streaked. Face plainer than juvenile Semipalmated. Summer adults show 'arrowhead' streaking on breast and flanks, warm buff crown, rufous ear coverts and rufous and black scapulars. Shows small webbing between toes. Legs black. Range: North America.

Red-necked Stint
Calidris ruficollis   13-16cm
Similar in size and structure to Little Stint, but tends to appear longer-winged and also shows a shorter bill. Summer adults show a reddish-orange upper breast, throat and cheeks, extending onto supercilium and crown which shows black streaking. Underparts white with black breast streaking extending onto sides of breast as distinctive arrowhead markings. Upperparts greyish with some rufous, black-tipped scapulars. May also be confused with summer plumaged Sanderling which appear bigger overall, show a longer bill, more extensive reddish-orange colouring on the breast sides and upperparts, and also lack a hind toe. Juvenile Red-necked Stint appear similar to juvenile Little Stint but show greyish wing-coverts, indistinct white 'braces' on the mantle and a brown wash across the breast. Range: North-east Siberia.

Long-toed Stint
Calidris subminuta Gobadáinín ladharfhada 14-16cm
A very small wader which tends to stand upright and tall, recalling a miniature Wood Sandpiper in structure and stance. Summer adults show a warm brown, dark-streaked crown, a white supercilium which does not reach the base of the bill and warm brown cheeks. Shows rufous fringes to the mantle feathers, scapulars and tertials. Underparts white with dark streaking on sides of breast. Bill long, dark and pointed with a pale base to the lower mandible. Legs yellowish-green with long toes that extend beyond the tail in flight.

Juveniles similar but show white mantle 'braces' and rufous scapulars and tertials which contrast with greyish wing coverts. In all plumages resembles Least Sandpiper which differs from Long-toed Stint by showing a supercilium that reaches the bill base, shorter legs, toes that do not extend beyond tail in flight, warm rufous fringes to both scapulars and coverts in juvenile plumage, and overall shape and stance. Range: Siberia.

Least Sandpiper
Calidris minutilla Gobadáinín bídeach   12-14cm
Tiny wader with short, dark bill and yellowish legs, recalling a miniature Pectoral Sandpiper. Juveniles show a warm brown, streaked crown and ear coverts, a dark smudge on the lores and a white supercilium. Breast streaked. Underparts white. Upperpart feathers show dark centres with rufous and white edges. Summer adults show heavy streaking on breast and head, and rufous and white edges to upperpart feathers. Range: North America.

Sharp-tailed Sandpiper
Calidris acuminata Gobadán carr-rinneach 17-21cm
Very like Pectoral Sandpiper but lacks sharply defined breast band. Summer adults show a rufous, dark streaked crown, a white supercilium prominent behind eye, and a white stripe below dark ear coverts. Underparts show heavy streaking on breast extending as dark, arrowhead markings onto sides of breast, flanks and to undertail. Upperpart feathers show black centres and whitish edges. Bill dark with a paler base. Legs greenish-yellow. Juveniles show an unstreaked, orange-buff breast with streaking confined to the breast sides. Range: Eastern Siberia.

Stilt Sandpiper
Micropalama himantopus
Gobadán scodalach   19-23cm
A tall, upright wader with long, yellow-green legs and a long, dark, slightly decurved bill. Summer adults show a warm buff crown, a white supercilium and chestnut ear coverts. Heavy streaking on neck continues as dark barring on breast, belly and undertail. Dark upperparts show buff and white edges to scapulars. Winter adults grey above, white below. Juveniles show a dark crown, a pale supercilium, a dark eye-stripe and streaking on neck, breast and flanks. Upperparts show warm buff edges to upper scapulars. In flight shows a whitish rump, uniform wings and long legs projecting beyond tail. Range: North America.

Wilson's Snipe

Gallinago delicata   25-27cm
Very similar to Snipe but shows colder and darker plumage tones. Shows a thin, white central crown stripe contrasting with a broad, black lateral crown stripe. Pale buff supercilum bulges before the eye and contrasts with dark eyestripe. Ear coverts pale with a dark lower border. Throat streaked extending as heavy barring onto the breast. Flanks extensively barred. Breast and flanks lack the buff tones as shown on Snipe. Upperparts very dark with broad white mantle and scapular stripes. In flight upperwing shows a very narrow secondary bar and can show pale tips to greater and primary coverts. Underwings appear more evenly coloured than Snipe, lacking the two pale underwing stripes shown by that species. Axillaries also appear barred. Outer-tail feathers also show three or four clearly defined dark bars on a white background, creating a crisper outer-tail pattern than that shown by Snipe. Bill long and dark with a dull olive base. Legs greenish. Range: North America.

Great Snipe

Gallinago media Naoscach mhór   26-30cm
A stocky species, slightly larger than Snipe with a shorter bill. Rarely calls when flushed and does not zig-zag in flight. Rounded wings and body give a Woodcock-like profile. Differs from Snipe by showing a more heavily-barred belly, two distinctive white borders to darker greater coverts, and white outer-tail feathers. Range: Northern and north-eastern Europe, and Siberia.

Upland Sandpiper

Bartramia longicauda Gobadán sléibhe   28-32cm
A distinctive species with a long, slender neck, a small head and a long, wedge-shaped tail. Thin, straight, yellow bill shows a black tip. Legs yellow. Crown shows dark streaking and highlights an inconspicuous, pale supercilium. Brown-buff neck and breast shows heavy streaking fading to barring on whiter belly and flanks. Dark upperpart feathers show paler edges. In flight shows uniformly dark wings and a contrastingly dark back, rump and uppertail coverts. Range: North Amenca.

Marsh Sandpiper

Tringa stagnatilis Gobadán corraigh   22-25cm
Like an elegant, small Greenshank. Shows a long, fine, dark bill and long, greenish legs. Summer adults show a pale supercilium with streaking on crown, cheeks and breast extending as spots on flanks. Upperparts grey with heavy, dark spotting. Winter adults grey

above, white below. Juveniles show dark grey upperpart feathers with white fringes, dark streaking on crown and sides of breast, a white supercilium, and dark ear coverts. In flight shows a white rump extending as wedge up back. Range: Eastern Europe.

Terek Sandpiper

Xenus cinereus Gobadán Terek   22-25cm
Like a large Common Sandpiper with a long, dark, upcurved bill and short, yellow-orange legs. Summer adults show grey upperparts with a black stripe on upper scapulars, a dark carpal area, a greyish crown and a white supercilium. Underparts white. Breast shows a grey wash and light streaking. Juveniles similar but show darker upperparts and duller legs. In flight shows a white trailing edge to wings and a grey tail and rump. Range: Northern Europe and Siberia.

Thayer's Gull

Larus thayeri   54-60cm
Initially recalling Iceland Gull in structure. First-winters show dark coffee-coloured heads and under-parts with pale barring on the undertail. Upperparts dark with pale fringes. Tertials appear quite plain with dark centres and pale edges. Tertials do not appear coarsely marked. Primaries appear dark with pale edges. Bill dark. Legs pink. Eye dark. In flight shows dark outer edges and pale inner edges to primaries, dark secondaries and a broad darkish tailband. Underwing appears pale with pale under primaries and underwing coverts. Second winters show a streaked, white head and breast with brownish tones to breast and belly. Mantle greyish contrasting with pale brown wing feathers which can show traces of pale grey. Primaries dark brown with pale outer edges but some individuals can show blacker primaries. Bill shows dark tip and pinkish base. Legs pink. Eye dark. Third winters show heavy dark streaking on a white head and breast, and white belly and undertail. Upperparts grey with white scapular and tertial steps, and white-edged secondaries. Primaries dark with pale edges. Bill pale yellow with dark subterminal band. Legs pink. Eye dark. Adult winters show extensive dark streaking on the white head and breast, white underparts and dark grey upperparts. Primaries blackish with white outer edges. In flight shows white underwings with small blackish tips to outer primaries. Eye usually dark with a purple orbital ring. Bill pale yellowish-green with a small red gony's spot. Legs deep pink. Adult summers like adult winters but lack head and breast streaking, and show brighter yellow bills with a red gony's spot. Range: North America.

Sooty Tern

Onychoprion fuscatus   42-46cm

Very similar to Bridled Tern showing a thick, black bill and legs. However, appears slightly larger and darker. Adults show blackish upperparts, wings, rump and forked tail. Underwings white with a broad dark trailing edge to the secondaries and primaries. Underparts white. A black cap contrasts with a striking white forehead which does not extend beyond the eye. Immatures show a dark head, breast and upper belly, off-white lower belly and flanks, and dark upperparts with pale fringes to wing feathers. Range: Red Sea, Persian Gulf and West Indies.

Bridled Tern

Onychoprion anaethetus   38-42cm

Very similar to Sooty Tern showing a thick, black bill and legs. Adults show greyish-brown upperparts, wings, rump and forked tail. Underwings white with a narrow, dark trailing edge to the secondaries and primaries. Underparts white. A black cap contrasts with a striking white forehead which extends as a white supercilium above and behind eye. Also shows a narrow, white neck band. Immatures show a less distinctive head pattern and pale fringes to upperpart feathers. Range: North-west Africa and the Red Sea.

Royal Tern

Sterna maxima   43-49cm

A large, heavy tern with a thick, orange-yellow bill. Summer adults show dark legs, a black cap with a short, shaggy rear crest, pale grey upperparts and white underparts. Rump and forked tail whitish. Winter adults show a white forehead and crown. Immatures show a white forehead and lores, brown markings on upperparts, dark tips to tail feathers, and pale legs. Could be confused with Caspian Tern, but shows white tips to the under-primaries. Range: North America and north-west Africa.

Lesser Crested Tern

Sterna bengalensis

Miongheabhróg chíorach   33-40cm

A large, Sandwich Tern-sized bird showing dark grey upperparts and white underparts. Like Sandwich Tern, shows a shaggy crest to the black crown but differs by having a long, bright orange-yellow bill which is broad at the base. In flight shows a greyish rump and tail centre. Tail is also short and distinctly forked. Legs black. In winter shows a white forehead. Immatures show a winter adult-like head, a more yellowish bill and dark centres to the coverts, tertials and scapulars. Range: North and north-west Africa.

Brünnich's Guillemot

Una lomvia Foracha Brünnich   40-44cm

Very similar to Guillemot, but shows a thicker, stubbier bill with a distinctive white stripe on the base of the upper mandible. Brünnich's Guillemot also lacks flank streaking and shows a steep forehead. In winter black of the crown extends down to cover the ear coverts. Therefore does not show the black eyestripe of winter-plumaged Guillemot. Short tail may be held cocked. Range: Iceland and Arctic regions.

Pallas's Sandgrouse

Syrrhaptes paradoxus

Gaineamhchearc Pallas   27-32cm

A dove-like species with a short, stubby bill and a long, pointed tail. Males show a grey and rufous head, a grey breast, pale buff underparts and a black belly patch. Brownish upperparts show heavy barring. Wings show grey outer primaries, black inner primaries and secondaries, and pale buff coverts. Females appear duller and show more extensive barring on the wing coverts and head. Range: Central Asia.

Mourning Dove

Zenaida macroura   29-31cm

A small, long-tailed dove. Adults show a bluish crown and nape, contrasting with a pinkish-buff face, breast and upperparts. Face also shows a small spot on lower cheeks. Upperparts greyish-brown with darker primaries and also showing distinctive dark spots on the wings. Belly pale. In flight the long, tapered tail shows white outer tips and black subterminal bands, creating a very striking pattern. Dark eye shows a bluish orbital. Bill short and dark. Legs reddish. Immatures show pale spotting on the breast and pale edges to upperpart feathers. Range: North America.

Common Nighthawk

Chordeiles minor   23-25cm

Very similar to, but slightly smaller than Nightjar showing a cryptic combination of finely barred, greyish upperparts and barred underparts. Dark, greyish crown finely barred with pale cheeks showing dark streaking. In flight shows long, pointed wings with all dark primaries and strongly contrasting white primary patches. Flies with slow wing beats and frequent glides. Rump grey with dark barring. Dark tail forked. Adults show a white throat patch which is duller, or lacking, on immatures. Range: North America.

White-throated Needletail
Hirundapus caudacutus
Gabhlán earrspíonach   19-21cm
A large swift with swept-back wings. Shows a dark plumage with a white forehead, throat and upper breast, and a diagnostic white U-shaped patch on the undertail. Dark upperparts show a pale greyish patch on the back. Short tail is square-ended. Could be confused with semi-albinistic Swifts. Range: Asia.

Little Swift
Apus affinis Gabhlán beag   12-14cm
A small, all-dark swift with a conspicuous, square, white rump patch, and a whitish forehead and throat patch. Tail almost square-ended. Wings short and broad. Flight is slower than Swift, and appears almost bat-like. Range: Africa and Asia.

Belted Kingfisher
Megaceryle alcyon Cruidín creasa   31-35cm
A very large kingfisher with a long, dagger-like, dark bill. Males show a blue-grey head with a shaggy crest on the rear crown, a white loral spot, neck collar and throat, and blue-grey upperparts with small whitish spots on the wing feathers. White underparts show a broad, blue-grey breast band and flank markings. Long, blue-grey tail shows white barring. Females similar, but show a second, lower, bright rufous breast band, and some rufous along the flanks. Range: North America.

Green Woodpecker
Picus viridis Cnagaire glas   31-36cm
A large, brightly coloured woodpecker with a strong, pointed dark bill and a bright yellowish rump. Males have a bright red crown, a black face mask and black moustachials which show a red central stripe. Upperparts dull green with dark, barred flight feathers. Underparts pale greyish-green with barring on the ventral region. Short, graduated, dark tail shows faint barring. Females similar, but lack the red central stripe to the black moustachials. Range: Continental Europe.

Yellow-bellied Sapsucker
Sphyrapicus varius Súdhiúlaí tarrbhuí   21-25cm
A brightly-marked woodpecker with a red crown, a bold black and white face pattern, and black upperparts showing white barring and a large white wing patch. Males show a black-bordered, red throat patch. Whitish underparts show a lemon-yellow wash and black barring on the flanks and vent. Rump white. Females similar, but show a diffuse red crown patch,

and a black-bordered white throat patch. On immatures, dark brown mottling replaces the black of the head pattern and flanks. Upperparts blackish with pale, yellow-washed barring on the back, and a bright white wing patch. Underparts also show a lemon-yellow wash. Immature males show a diffuse, reddish throat patch. Immature females show a whitish throat. Range: North America.

Northern Flicker
Colaptes auratus   29-33cm
A medium-sized woodpecker showing a plain, greyish head with a small, red nape patch and buff-brown face and throat. Males show a distinctive, black malar stripe which is lacking on females. Upperparts pale buff with black barring and spotting. Pale underparts show a black breast patch, and extensive black spotting. Tail dark and contrasts strongly with a white rump, especially obvious in flight. Underwings show a bright yellow wash. Bill long, dark and pointed. Range: North America.

Brown Shrike
Lanius cristatus   17-20cm
A Red-backed Shrike-sized bird, showing short, dark wings and a long, rounded, brown tail. Adults show brown upperparts contrasting with a black eye mask, a white supercilium and a brownish-grey crown. Shows a white throat and chin, and pale underparts with a strong yellow-buff wash on the breast and flanks. Immatures show a fainter eye mask and some barring on the sides of the breast and flanks. Bill long, hooked and dark tipped. Range: Siberia and East Asia.

Marsh Tit
Poecile palustris Meantán lathaí   11-13cm
Initially similar to Coal Tit in size and structure. Shows an all-black, glossy crown, a small black bib, white cheeks and brownish upperparts. The wings appear plain, lacking wingbars. The underparts are greyish-white with buffish flanks. Short, stubby bill and legs dark. Tail shows inconspicuous, white edges. Range: Continental Europe.

American Cliff Swallow
Petrochelidon pyrrhonota Fáinleog aille   13-15cm
A House Martin-like species showing a pale orange rump and a dark, square tail which lacks streamers. Adults show a bluish-black crown contrasting with a whitish forehead and reddish cheeks and sides of neck. Nape pale reddish-grey, forming a distinctive collar. Chin, throat and upper breast black. Underparts whitish. Upperparts bluish-black with

239

some white streaking. Wings dark and broad. Can appear similar to Red-rumped Swallow but lacks the tail streamers and dark ventral area of that species. Immatures appear duller overall. Range: North America.

Cetti's Warbler

Cettia cetti Ceolaire Cetti   13-14cm
A sturdy, skulky warbler showing a dull chestnut-brown crown, upperparts and wings, a whitish super-cilium, and pale greyish-white underparts. Shows a broad, rounded chestnut-brown tail, very striking in flight. Tends to be very elusive and difficult to see. Range: Continental Europe.

Sardinian Warbler

Sylvia melanocephala Ceolaire Sairdíneach 13-14cm
A Whitethroat-sized warbler with males showing a very striking plumage of a black head with a white throat, a bright red orbital and eye-ring, grey upper-parts with dark-centred tertials and whitish under-parts showing a grey wash across the breast and flanks. Long, dark tail shows white edges and white tips to all but central feathers, forming a very distinctive tail pattern. Legs pinkish. Females show a greyish head with a white throat and a pale brownish eye-ring and a thin, reddish orbital ring. Underparts whitish, with a brownish wash on breast and flanks. Upperparts pale brown with brown-edged, black tertials. Both sexes show a thin, dark, pointed bill with a distinctive grey base to the lower mandible. Range: southern and Eastern Europe.

Pallas's Grasshopper Warbler

Locustella certhiola Ceolaire casarnaí Pallas 13-14cm
A very shy, skulking species which resembles Grasshopper Warbler. Shows a heavily streaked, greyish-brown crown, a prominent, whitish super-cilium, and streaked, rufous-brown upperparts. Tertials show small, whitish tips or spots on inner webs. Underparts creamy-buff, occasionally showing a rufous wash on the breast, flanks and undertail. Breast shows diffuse spotting. Unlike Grasshopper Warbler, the undertail coverts lack dark streaks. Pallas's Grasshopper Warbler also shows a distinctive undertail pattern with brown fading to black towards the tip, and showing pale, whitish tips on all but the central feathers. Uppertail appears more rufous-brown. Range: Asia.

Skyes's Warbler

Hippolais rama   11-13cm
Very similar to both Booted and Eastern Olivaceous Warblers. Shows a long, sloping forehead and a long bill which has a pale yellow lower mandible with a faint dark tip. Head and upperparts pale greyish-brown. Unlike Booted Warbler, lacks a strong super-cilium behind the eye. Lores dark. Tertials appear quite plain. Primary projection very short. Lacks white tips to secondaries. Tail appears long. Can flick the tail but does not pump tail downwards like Eastern Olivaceous. Underparts off-white, lacking the buff tones on the flanks as shown on Booted. Legs darkish. Gives a sharp *chec* call. Range: Central Asia.

Paddyfield Warbler

Acrocephalus agricola Ceolaire gort ríse   12-14cm
A stocky, short-winged warbler similar to Reed Warbler and showing a brown crown and upperparts, greyish-brown sides to the neck, a warm rufous-brown rump, and long, rounded tail. Pale whitish underparts show a warm buff wash on the flanks. Unlike Reed Warbler, shows a conspicuous, whitish supercilium, broadening behind the eye, bordered below by a dark eye-stripe and above by a darkish coronal stripe. The short, dark bill shows a yellowish base to the lower mandible. Range: Eastern Europe.

Great Reed Warbler

Acrocephalus arundinaceus
Mórcheolaire giolcaí   16-20cm
A large, long-tailed bird resembling a huge Reed Warbler. Shows a warm brown crown, upperparts, rump and tail. The long wings show contrasting dark centres and pale edges to the feathers, while the primaries show pale tips. Shows a prominent white supercilium and greyish-brown ear coverts. Underparts greyish-white with a warm buff wash on the flanks. Shows a large, heavy bill with a pale base to the lower mandible, and thick, dark legs. Range: Continental Europe.

Fan-tailed Warbler

Cisticola juncidis Ceolaire earrfheanach   10-11cm
A small, short-winged warbler with a short tail often held cocked to reveal the conspicuous black and white tips. Crown and upperparts pale buff with heavy, dark streaking. Shows a pale buff supercilium and a beady dark eye set in a plain face. Throat whitish, fading onto a warm buff breast and flanks. Fast, active species, difficult to observe. Flight weak and undulating. Flight call is a hard, repeated *chit*. Range: Southern Europe and North Africa.

Cedar Waxwing

Bombycilla cedrorum   16-18cm
Smaller and less colourful than Waxwing. In all plumages show pale undertail coverts. Adults show a buff-brown head with a short crest, a black eye mask showing a white upper border, a small smudgy black bib and a white line from bill onto face. Upperparts greyish-brown with plain greyish wings showing red waxy tips to secondaries. Tertials show white inner edges. Uppertail greyish with a broad yellow tip and dark subterminal band. Underparts greyish-brown with a whitish undertail. Legs and bill dark. First-winters similar but lack red tips to secondaries. Immatures show a greyish crown and upperparts, plain grey wings with white inner edges to tertials and a small dark eye mask. Throat and upper breast greyish, with remainder of underparts whitish and showing extensive, broad, greyish smudges and streaking. Undertail coverts pale. Uppertail greyish with narrow, yellowish tip. Bill appears paler than adults and first-winters. Call a thin, high-pitched *sreee*. Range: North America.

Gray Catbird

Dumetella carolinensis Catéan liath   20-22cm
A very distinctive, thrush-like species with a longish tail. Adults show an all-bluish-grey plumage with a neat black cap and striking rufous undertail coverts. Adults also show a brownish-red iris. Immatures similar but show brownish tones to the wing feathers and a duller iris. Range: North America.

Siberian Thrush

Zoothera sibirica Smólach Sibéarach   20-22cm
A Song Thrush-sized species which shows distinctive black and white bands on the underwing. Adult males show a dark bill, a dark bluish-grey plumage with a bold white supercilium, a whitish rear belly, and black spotting on a whitish undertail. Immature males similar, but show a creamy supercilium and throat, and pale grey mottling on dark underparts. Females show a creamy supercilium, a brown crown, ear coverts and upperparts, a dark malar stripe on a pale throat, and brown barring and spotting on pale under-parts. Range: Siberia.

Rufous Bush Robin

Cercotrichas galactotes
Torspideog ruadhonn   15-17cm
A slim, chat-like species with a long, graduated, rufous tail showing striking black and white tips. Shows a clear, whitish supercilium, a dark eye-stripe, plain, whitish ear coverts, a rufous-brown crown and upper-

parts, and whitish underparts. When perched, often cocks or fans the bright tail. Range: Southern Europe and North Africa.

Thrush Nightingale

Luscinia luscinia Filiméala smólaigh   15-17cm
Very similar to Nightingale, but tends to appear slightly darker on the upperparts and shows a darker, less rufous tail. The whitish underparts also show faint mottling on the grey-washed breast which can continue to form a diffuse malar stripe. Range: Eastern Europe.

Red-flanked Bluetail

Tarsiger cyanurus   13-14cm
A colourful, Robin-like species. Females and first-winters show an olive-grey crown, face and upper-parts with a striking blue tail. Shows a greyish face with dark lores and a faint supercilium before eye. Also shows a neat, white bib on throat and a whitish eye ring. Breast greyish-brown, fading to pale greyish-white on belly and undertail. Flanks show orange patches. Adult summer males very striking showing a greyish-blue crown, nape and upperparts, a bright blue tail and a darkish face showing dark lores and a whitish supercilium before the eye. Throat white with a greyish-blue smudge extending from side of neck onto side of breast. Undeparts pale with extensive orange-red wash on sides of breast and flanks. Winter males similar to females but show a stronger face pattern with a more clearly defined white supercilium and throat, more orange-red tones on flanks and greyish-blue shoulder patches. Short bill and legs dark. Often flicks tail downwards. Range: Northern Scandinavia and Asia.

Isabelline Wheatear

Oenanthe isabellina Clochrán gainimh   15-17cm
A slim, pale, upright species very similar to female Wheatear. On Isabelline Wheatear the wings never appear darker than the upperparts and show pale centres to the wing coverts which contrast with the darker alula. Also shows a broad, creamy supercilium and a shorter tail with a broader, black tail-band. Underwing coverts and axillaries are also white. Range: South-eastern Europe and Middle East.

Pied Wheatear

Oenanthe pleschanka Clochrán alabhreac   14-16cm
Smaller and slimmer than Wheatear, showing a larger white rump and more white on the tail due to a narrower, black tail-band. Summer males shows a white crown and nape contrasting with black face

mask, back and wings. Underparts whitish-buff, with white undertail coverts. Females appear quite dark, showing a greyish throat and upper breast, a dark, greyish-brown head with an inconspicuous supercilium, uniformly dark, greyish-brown upperparts, and whitish underparts. Immature females similar, but show buff fringes to wing feathers and buffish underparts. Immature males show pale fringes to a blackish face mask, a dark greyish-brown crown and upperparts, buff fringes to the wing feathers and a buffish wash on the breast. Range: South-eastern Europe.

Black-eared Wheatear

Oenanthe hispanica Clochrán cluaisdubh   14-16cm
A smaller, slimmer species than Wheatear, showing a very narrow, black tail-band. Some inner tail feathers are almost pure white but show small black spots on the tips. Adult males show a pale buff crown and mantle, a black eye mask, and either a black or whitish throat. Wings black. Rump white. Underparts show buffish tones on the breast fading to white on the belly and undertail. Females show either dark brownish upperparts with a greyish-brown throat and a dark eye mask, or paler buffish upperparts with a pale throat. Underparts creamy with a warm buff wash on the breast. Range: Southern Europe.

Desert Wheatear

Oenanthe deserti Clochrán fásaigh   14-16cm
A small wheatear showing an almost wholly black tail and a narrow, buff-tinged white rump. Adult males show a creamy-buff crown and upperparts, with a striking black throat and ear coverts which meet the black wings. Wings can show a white stripe on the scapulars. Underparts pale creamy-buff. First-year males similar, but show pale fringes to blackish throat feathers, buff edges to wing feathers and appear duller above and below. Females show a pale buff crown and upperparts, darker ear coverts, pale buff fringes to wing feathers and creamy-buff underparts. Range: North Africa and Middle East.

Pechora Pipit

Anthus gustavi Riabhóg Pechora   14-15cm
Very similar to immature Red-throated Pipit. In all plumages shows an olive-brown, heavily streaked crown, a diffuse, pale supercilium, pale cheeks and a weak dark smudge on lores. Nape shows fine streaking. Upperparts olive-brown with dark streaking and broad, white mantle stripes. Wings show broad, white wingbars formed by white tips on greater and median coverts. Dark-centred tertials are short and, as a result, Pechora Pipit shows a short primary projection beyond the tertails. Rump and uppertail streaked. Tail shows off-white edges. Throat white with dark malar stripe not reaching bill base. Malar forms a dark breast spot which extends as heavy streaking onto breast and flanks. Breast shows a buff wash contrasting with white belly, flanks and undertail. Shows a heavier bill than Red-throated Pipit with a pinkish or brownish base. Legs pale. Can be elusive and difficult to flush. Gives a short, harsh *dseep* call. Range: Asia.

Two-barred Crossbill

Loxia leucoptera Crosghob báneiteach   14-16cm
Very similar to Crossbill, but shows two broad white wingbars and prominent white tips to the tertials. Many Crossbills may also have similar markings, but never show such broad wingbars widening on the inner coverts, or well-defined white tertial tips. Two-barred Crossbill is smaller than Crossbill, and usually shows a slimmer bill. Males also show a pinker, paler plumage than Crossbill and can have pale edges to brownish scapulars. Females of both species show similar colourations. Range: Northern Europe.

Indigo Bunting

Passerina cyanea Gealóg phlúiríneach   11-13cm
A small bunting with large pale bill. Summer males show a bright blue plumage with blackish centres to the wing feathers. In winter the blue is partially obscured by brownish fringes to the feathers. Females appear very drab, showing a brown head and upperparts, and pale buff underparts with faint streaking on the breast and flanks. Females show faint bluish tones to the tail and wings. Immatures appear similar to females, but can show paler tips to the greater coverts which form an indistinct wing bar. Immature males can also show some bluish feathers on the mantle and underparts. Range: North America.

Fox Sparrow

Passerella iliaca Gealbhan sionnagh   15-16cm
A large bunting with a thick, pale bill. Shows a grey and blotched rufous crown, a grey supercilium and sides of neck, and bright chestnut ear coverts. White throat and underparts show a thick chestnut malar stripe and streaking, extending onto the flanks. The streaking may form a chestnut patch on the sides of the breast. Mantle olive-brown with a rufous wash and dark streaking. The wings are chestnut and show two thin, pale wingbars and darker centres to the feathers. Rump and long tail bright chestnut, very conspicuous in flight. Range: North America.

White-crowned Sparrow

Zonotrichia leucophrys   15-16cm
A long-tailed species with a striking head pattern. Adults show a white central crown stripe contrasting with a blackish lateral crown stripe which in turn contrasts with a broad, white supercilium. Also shows a dark eyestripe from behind the eye. Cheeks, nape, neck, breast and belly pale grey with warm brownish tones to flanks. Throat and undertail pale. Upperparts greyish-brown with broad, dark streaks. Wings show two white wingbars, with dark centres and warm rufous edges to wing feathers. Rump and long tail greyish brown. Bill pink. Legs pale. Immatures show a pale buff central crown stripe, brown lateral crown stripes and eyestripes, a pale buff supercilium and a pale brown wash on the face. Range: North America.

Dark-eyed Junco

Junco hyemalis Luachairín shúildubh   13-15cm
A distinctive bunting with a thick, pale, pinkish-white bill. Males show a slate-grey head, breast, flanks and upperparts contrasting with a white belly and undertail. Long, slate-grey tail shows broad, conspicuous, white outer edges. Females appear more greyish-brown on the head and upperparts. Immatures similar to adults, but show stronger brownish fringes to mantle and flanks, and browner wing feathers. The bill on immatures can also appear slightly darker. Range: North America.

Pine Bunting

Emberiza leucocephalos Gealóg phéine   16-18cm
A Yellowhammer-sized bunting with summer males showing a striking head pattern including a black-bordered white crown and ear coverts, and an orange-brown supercilium and throat. Underparts white with streaked, rufous-washed breast and flanks. Nape greyish brown with warmer brown upperparts showing black streaking. Wings show dark centres to feathers with warm brown edges and thin white tips to coverts, and white-edged primaries. Rump warm red-brown similar to Yellowhammer. Winter males appear greyish brown on the head but still show black-bordered, white ear coverts. Females show a paler brown supercilium, dark-bordered whitish ear coverts, a white throat and a dark malar stripe meeting dark breast streaking. Immatures appear very similar to immature Yellowhammer but differ by showing streaked, white underparts with no yellowish wash, and white edges to the primaries (yellowish on Yellowhammer). Bill conical in shape with a pale grey lower mandible and a dark upper mandible. Legs pinkish. Range: Siberia.

Cirl Bunting

Emberiza cirlus   15-17cm
A Yellowhammer-like species. Summer adult males show a dark streaked crown, a bright yellow supercilium contrasting with a black eyestripe and yellow cheeks. Chin and throat black, extending to below cheeks and highlighting a narrow yellow band on upper breast/lower throat. Nape greyish-green, extending as a band across upper breast. Lower breast, belly and undertail pale yellow with rufous wash to sides of breast extending as brownish streaking on flanks. Upperparts brown with dark streaking. Wings show dark centres and pale brown edges to feathers with white-tipped median coverts creating a small, white wingbar. Rump olive-grey. Tail dark with pale edges. Legs pinkish-orange. Bill grey. Winter males show a more diffuse face pattern. Females show a dark crown, a pale yellow supercilium, a dark eyestripe from behind eye, pale lores and pale cheeks. A dark lower border to the ear coverts contrasts with a pale yellowish submoustachial stripe. Dark malar extends down as heavy streaking on yellow-washed underparts which also show warm rufous tones on sides of breast and flanks. Immatures like females but lack yellow tones on face and underparts with supercilium, cheeks and submoustachials pale buff. Unlike immature Yellowhammer, shows fine streaking on flanks. Range: Europe.

Blue-winged Warbler

Vermivora pinus   11-12cm
An extremely striking species showing bright yellow underparts and crown. Adults show a dark bill, a contrasting black eyestripe, olive-green nape and back, and two broad white wingbars on bluish-grey wings. Rump olive, tail bluish with white outer feathers, and undertail contrastingly white. Immatures similar but show a more olive crown with a yellow forehead, a dark eyestripe, narrower, duller wingbars and a pale bill. Very active and tit-like when feeding, constantly flicking tail. Range: North America.

Ovenbird

Seiurus aurocapilla Éan oighinn   13-15cm
A very skulking species which moves along the ground, usually in cover. Shows a bright olive-green head and upperparts with a striking, black-bordered, orange central crown-stripe. The large black eye shows conspicuous white eye-rings. White underparts show heavy black streaking, fading on the buff-washed flanks. White throat also shows a strong black malar stripe. Legs pale pinkish. Dark bill shows a pinkish base. Range: North America.

Common Yellowthroat

Geothlypis trichas   12-13cm

A skulking species showing a plain, olive-green crown and upperparts. Immature males show a brownish forehead, a dark face patch and lores, and a bright yellow throat contrasting with olive-brown breast and flanks. Undertail yellow. Tail olive-green. Immature females lack the dark face and lores of males, and show paler, creamy-yellow throats and undertails. Adult summer males show a black face, lores and forehead with a white upper border, bright yellow on throat, breast and undertail, and olive-green upperparts. Belly and flanks olive-brown. Adult summer females similar to immature females but show brighter yellow tones on throat and undertail. Bill darkish with paler base. Legs pinkish. Range: North America.

Canada Warbler

Wilsonia Canadensis   12-13cm

A very striking, colourful species which shows a complete white eye-ring surrounding a dark eye which creates a large-eyed appearance to the face. Immatures show a pale greyish-blue crown, fading to pale yellow on the forehead. Cheeks pale greyish with darkish lores. Upperparts and tail plain greyish-blue. Throat, breast, belly and flanks bright yellow with a greyish wash on the sides of the breast and dark smudges on the lower breast. Undertail white. Legs pinkish. Bill dark with pale lower mandible. Adult summer males show a dark greyish-blue crown and upperparts with black on the forehead and lores extending onto the lower cheeks and sides of breast. Supercilium bright yellow before the eye. Throat, breast, belly and flanks bright yellow with black streaking across breast. Undertail white. Adult summer females like immatures but show dark streaking on breast, and brighter yellow on throat, breast, belly and flanks. Range: North America.

Footnotes to Rare Species Accounts

The following species have been recorded in Ireland but are considered to have escaped, been released from captivity or were not specifically identified.

Red-breasted Goose *Branta ruficollis*
Greater Flamingo *Phoenicopterus ruber*
Booted Eagle *Hieraaetus pennata*
Red-legged Partridge *Alectoris rufa*
Black Wheatear/White-crowned Black Wheatear
Oenanthe leucura/Oenanthe leucopyga
House Crow *Corvus splendens*
Red-headed Bunting *Emberiza bruniceps*

The following species have been recorded in Ireland but are now extinct worldwide.
Great Auk *Pinguinus impennis*
Eskimo Curlew *Numenius borealis*

The Irish List

The **Species** column gives the English and Latin names.

The **Race**, or Subspecies, column includes the Latin name of any race or subspecies (the terms are interchangeable). '—' indicates where there are none, i.e. the species is monotypic. The symbol > indicates race/subspecies.

The **Category** column is represented by the following:

Category A Species that have been recorded in an apparently natural state in Ireland at least once since January 1950.

Category B Species that have been recorded in an apparently natural state in Ireland at least once up to 31 December 1949, but have not been recorded subsequently.

Category C1 Species that, although originally introduced by man, have established feral breeding populations in Ireland which apparently maintain themselves without necessary recourse to further introductions.

Category C2 Species that have occurred, but are considered to have originated from established naturalised populations outside Ireland.

Category D1 Species that would otherwise appear in Categories A or B, except that there is a reasonable doubt that they have ever occurred in a natural state.

Category D2 Species that have arrived through ship or other human assistance.

Category D3 Species that have only ever been found dead on the tideline.

Category D4 Species that would otherwise appear in Category C1, except that their feral populations may or may not be self-supporting.

Category E Species that have been recorded as introductions, transportees or escapes from captivity.

Species

English & Latin name	Race	Category
❑ Mute Swan *Cygnus olor*	—	A,C1
❑ Bewick's Swan *Cygnus columbianus*	*bewickii*	A
> Tundra Swan	*columbianus*	—
❑ Whooper Swan *Cygnus cygnus*	—	A
❑ Bean Goose *Anser fabalis*	*fabalis*	A
> Tundra Bean Goose	*rossicus*	—
❑ Pink-footed Goose *Anser brachyrhynchus*	—	A
❑ White-fronted Goose *Anser albifrons*	*flavirostris*	A,D1
> Russian White-fronted Goose	*albifrons*	—
❑ Lesser White-fronted Goose *Anser erythropus*	—	A
❑ Greylag Goose *Anser anser*	*anser*	A / C1
❑ Snow Goose *Anser caerulescens*	*caerulescens*	A
> Greater Snow Goose	*atlanticus*	—
❑ Cackling Goose *Branta hutchinsii*	*hutchinsii*	A
❑ Canada Goose *Branta canadensis*	*canadensis*	A / C1
❑ Barnacle Goose *Branta leucopsis*	—	A / C1

❏	Brent Goose *Branta bernicla*	*brota*	A
	> Dark-bellied Brent Goose	*bernicla*	—
	> Black Brant	*nigricans*	—
❏	Ruddy Shelduck *Tadorna ferruginea*	—	B / D1
❏	Shelduck *Tadorna tadorna*	—	A
❏	Mandarin Duck *Aix galericulata*	—	C1
❏	Wigeon *Anas penelope*	—	A
❏	American Wigeon *Anas americana*	—	A
❏	Gadwall *Anas strepera*	—	A
❏	Teal *Anas crecca*	*crecca*	A
❏	Green-winged Teal *Anas carolinensis*	—	A
❏	Baikal Teal *Anas formosa*	—	A
❏	Mallard *Anas platyrhynchos*	*platyrhynchos*	A / C1
❏	American Black Duck *Anas rubripes*	—	A
❏	Pintail *Anas acuta*	*acuta*	A
❏	Garganey *Anas querquedula*	—	A
❏	Blue-winged Teal *Anas discors*	—	A
❏	Shoveler *Anas clypeata*	—	A
❏	Red-crested Pochard *Netta rufina*	—	A
❏	Pochard *Aythya ferina*	—	A
❏	Redhead *Aythya americana*	—	A
❏	Ring-necked Duck *Aythya collaris*	—	A
❏	Ferruginous Duck *Aythya nyroca*	—	A
❏	Tufted Duck *Aythya fuligula*	—	A
❏	Scaup *Aythya marila*	*marila*	A
❏	Lesser Scaup *Aythya affinis*	—	A
❏	Eider *Somateria mollissima*	*mollissima*	A
❏	King Eider *Somateria spectabilis*	—	A
❏	Long-tailed Duck *Clangula hyemalis*	—	A
❏	Common Scoter *Melanitta nigra*	—	A
❏	Surf Scoter *Melanitta perspicillata*	—	A
❏	Velvet Scoter *Melanitta fusca*	—	A
❏	Bufflehead *Bucephala albeola*	—	A
❏	Barrow's Goldeneye *Bucephala islandica*	—	A
❏	Goldeneye *Bucephala clangula*	*clangula*	A
❏	Hooded Merganser *Lophodytes cucullatus*	—	A / D1
❏	Smew *Mergellus albellus*	—	A
❏	Red-breasted Merganser *Mergus serrator*	—	A
❏	Goosander *Mergus merganser*	*merganser*	A
❏	Ruddy Duck *Oxyura jamaicensis*	*jamaicensis*	C1 / C2
❏	Red Grouse *Lagopus lagopus*	*scotica*	A
❏	Capercaillie *Tetrao urogallus*	*urogallus*	B
❏	Grey Partridge *Perdix perdix*	*perdix*	A / C1
❏	Quail *Coturnix coturnix*	*coturnix*	A
❏	Pheasant *Phasianus colchicus*	*colchicus*	C1
❏	Red-throated Diver *Gavia stellata*	—	A
❏	Pacific Diver *Gavia pacifica*	—	A
❏	Black-throated Diver *Gavia arctica*	*arctica*	A
❏	Great Northern Diver *Gavia immer*	—	A

❑	White-billed Diver *Gavia adamsii*	—	A
❑	Black-browed Albatross *Thalassarche melanophris*	*melanophris*	A
❑	Fulmar *Fulmarus glacialis*	*glacialis*	A
❑	Fea's / Zino's Petrel *Pterodroma feae / madeira*	n/a	A
❑	Bulwer's Petrel *Bulweria bulwerii*	—	A
❑	Cory's Shearwater *Calonectris diomedea*	*borealis*	A
❑	Great Shearwater *Puffinus gravis*	—	A
❑	Sooty Shearwater *Puffinus griseus*	—	A
❑	Manx Shearwater *Puffinus puffinus*	—	A
❑	Balearic Shearwater *Puffinus mauretanicus*	—	A
❑	Macaronesian Shearwater *Puffinus baroli*	*baroli*	A
❑	Wilson's Petrel *Oceanites oceanicus*	*exasperatus*	A
❑	Storm Petrel *Hydrobates pelagicus*	—	A
❑	Leach's Petrel *Oceanodroma leucorhoa*	*leucorhoa*	A
❑	Swinhoe's Petrel *Oceanodroma monorhis*	—	A
❑	Madeiran Petrel *Oceanodroma castro*	—	B
❑	Red-billed Tropicbird *Phaethon aethereus*	not determined	A
❑	Gannet *Morus bassanus*	—	A
❑	Cormorant *Phalacrocorax carbo*	*carbo*	A
	> Continental Cormorant	*sinensis*	—
❑	Double-crested Cormorant *Phalacrocorax auritus*	not determined	A
❑	Shag *Phalacrocorax aristotelis*	*aristotelis*	A
❑	Frigatebird sp. *Fregata* sp.	n/a	A
❑	Bittern *Botaurus stellaris*	*stellaris*	A
❑	American Bittern *Botaurus lentiginosus*	—	A
❑	Little Bittern *Ixobrychus minutus*	*minutus*	A
❑	Night Heron *Nycticorax nycticorax*	*nycticorax*	A
❑	Green Heron *Butorides virescens*	--	A
❑	Squacco Heron *Ardeola ralloides*	—	A
❑	Cattle Egret *Bubulcus ibis*	*ibis*	A
❑	Little Blue Heron *Egretta caerulea*	—	A
❑	Little Egret *Egretta garzetta*	*garzetta*	A
❑	Great White Egret *Ardea alba*	*alba*	A
❑	Grey Heron *Ardea cinerea*	*cinerea*	A
❑	Purple Heron *Ardea purpurea*	*purpurea*	A
❑	Black Stork *Ciconia nigra*	—	A
❑	White Stork *Ciconia ciconia*	*ciconia*	A
❑	Glossy Ibis *Plegadis falcinellus*	—	A
❑	Spoonbill *Platalea leucorodia*	*leucorodia*	A
❑	Pied-billed Grebe *Podilymbus podiceps*	not determined	A
❑	Little Grebe *Tachybaptus ruficollis*	*ruficollis*	A
❑	Great Crested Grebe *Podiceps cristatus*	*cristatus*	A
❑	Red-necked Grebe *Podiceps grisegena*	*grisegena*	A
❑	Slavonian Grebe *Podiceps auritus*	*auritus*	A
❑	Black-necked Grebe *Podiceps nigricollis*	*nigricollis*	A
❑	Honey Buzzard *Pernis apivorus*	—	A
❑	Black Kite *Milvus migrans*	*migrans*	A
❑	Red Kite *Milvus milvus*	*milvus*	A / C2
❑	White-tailed Eagle *Haliaeetus albicilla*	—	A / C2 / D4

List

❏ Bald Eagle *Haliaeetus leucocephalus*	not determined	A
❏ Griffon Vulture *Gyps fulvus*	*fulvus*	B
❏ Marsh Harrier *Circus aeruginosus*	*aeruginosus*	A
❏ Hen Harrier *Circus cyaneus*	*cyaneus*	A
❏ Montagu's Harrier *Circus pygargus*	—	A
❏ Goshawk *Accipiter gentilis*	*gentilis*	A
❏ Sparrowhawk *Accipiter nisus*	*nisus*	A
❏ Buzzard *Buteo buteo*	*buteo*	A
❏ Rough-legged Buzzard *Buteo lagopus*	*lagopus*	A
> Rough-legged Hawk	*sanctijohannis*	—
❏ Spotted Eagle *Aquila clanga*	—	B
❏ Golden Eagle *Aquila chrysaetos*	*chrysaetos*	A / D4
❏ Osprey *Pandion haliaetus*	*haliaetus*	A
❏ Lesser Kestrel *Falco naumanni*	—	B
❏ Kestrel *Falco tinnunculus*	*tinnunculus*	A
❏ Red-footed Falcon *Falco vespertinus*	—	A
❏ Merlin *Falco columbarius*	*aesalon*	A
> Taiga Merlin	*columbarius*	—
❏ Hobby *Falco subbuteo*	*subbuteo*	A
❏ Gyr Falcon *Falco rusticolus*	—	A
❏ Peregrine *Falco peregrinus*	*peregrinus*	A
❏ Water Rail *Rallus aquaticus*	*aquaticus*	A
❏ Spotted Crake *Porzana porzana*	—	A
❏ Sora *Porzana carolina*	—	A
❏ Little Crake *Porzana parva*	—	B
❏ Baillon's Crake *Porzana pusilla*	*intermedia*	B
❏ Corncrake *Crex crex*	—	A
❏ Moorhen *Gallinula chloropus*	*chloropus*	A
❏ Coot *Fulica atra*	*atra*	A
❏ American Coot *Fulica americana*	not determined	A
❏ Crane *Grus grus*	—	A
❏ Sandhill Crane *Grus canadensis*	*canadensis*	B
❏ Little Bustard *Tetrax tetrax*	—	B
❏ Great Bustard *Otis tarda*	*tarda*	B
❏ Oystercatcher *Haematopus ostralegus*	*ostralegus*	A
❏ Black-winged Stilt *Himantopus himantopus*	*himantopus*	A
❏ Avocet *Recurvirostra avosetta*	—	A
❏ Stone Curlew *Burhinus oedicnemus*	*oedicnemus*	A
❏ Cream-coloured Courser *Cursorius cursor*	not determined	A
❏ Collared Pratincole *Glareola pratincola*	*pratincola*	A
❏ Black-winged Pratincole *Glareola nordmanni*	—	A
❏ Little Ringed Plover *Charadrius dubius*	*curonicus*	A
❏ Ringed Plover *Charadrius hiaticula*	*hiaticula*	A
❏ Semipalmated Plover *Charadrius semipalmatus*	—	A
❏ Killdeer *Charadrius vociferus*	*vociferus*	A
❏ Kentish Plover *Charadrius alexandrinus*	*alexandrinus*	A / E
❏ Dotterel *Charadrius morinellus*	—	A
❏ American Golden Plover *Pluvialis dominica*	—	A
❏ Pacific Golden Plover *Pluvialis fulva*	—	A

❏ Golden Plover *Pluvialis apricaria*	–	A
❏ Grey Plover *Pluvialis squatarola*	–	A
❏ Sociable Plover *Vanellus gregarius*	–	A
❏ Lapwing *Vanellus vanellus*	–	A
❏ Great Knot *Calidris tenuirostris*	–	A
❏ Knot *Calidris canutus*	*islandica*	A
> Siberian Knot	*canutus*	–
❏ Sanderling *Calidris alba*	–	A
❏ Semipalmated Sandpiper *Calidris pusilla*	–	A
❏ Western Sandpiper *Calidris mauri*	–	A
❏ Red-necked Stint *Calidris ruficollis*	–	A
❏ Little Stint *Calidris minuta*	–	A
❏ Temminck's Stint *Calidris temminckii*	–	A
❏ Long-toed Stint *Calidris subminuta*	–	A
❏ Least Sandpiper *Calidris minutilla*	–	A
❏ White-rumped Sandpiper *Calidris fuscicollis*	–	A
❏ Baird's Sandpiper *Calidris bairdii*	–	A
❏ Pectoral Sandpiper *Calidris melanotos*	–	A
❏ Sharp-tailed Sandpiper *Calidris acuminata*	–	A
❏ Curlew Sandpiper *Calidris ferruginea*	–	A
❏ Stilt Sandpiper *Calidris himantopus*	–	A
❏ Purple Sandpiper *Calidris maritima*	–	A
❏ Dunlin *Calidris alpina*	*alpina*	A
> Schiøler's Dunlin	*artica*	–
> Schinz's Dunlin	*schinzii*	–
❏ Broad-billed Sandpiper *Limicola falcinellus*	*falcinellus*	A
❏ Buff-breasted Sandpiper *Tryngites subruficollis*	–	A
❏ Ruff *Philomachus pugnax*	–	A
❏ Jack Snipe *Lymnocryptes minimus*	–	A
❏ Common Snipe *Gallinago gallinago*	*gallinago*	A
❏ Wilson's Snipe *Gallinago delicata*	–	A
❏ Great Snipe *Gallinago media*	–	A
❏ Short-billed Dowitcher *Limnodromus griseus*	not determined	A
❏ Long-billed Dowitcher *Limnodromus scolopaceus*	–	A
❏ Woodcock *Scolopax rusticola*	–	A
❏ Black-tailed Godwit *Limosa limosa*	*limosa*	A
> Icelandic Black-tailed Godwit	*islandica*	–
❏ Bar-tailed Godwit *Limosa lapponica*	*lapponica*	A
❏ Eskimo Curlew *Numenius borealis*	–	B
❏ Whimbrel *Numenius phaeopus*	*phaeopus*	A
> Hudsonian Whimbrel *hudsonicus*	–	
❏ Curlew *Numenius arquata*	*arquata*	A
❏ Upland Sandpiper *Bartramia longicauda*	–	A
❏ Terek Sandpiper *Xenus cinereus*	–	A
❏ Common Sandpiper *Actitis hypoleucos*	–	A
❏ Spotted Sandpiper *Actitis macularius*	–	A
❏ Green Sandpiper *Tringa ochropus*	–	A
❏ Solitary Sandpiper *Tringa solitaria*	not determined	A
❏ Spotted Redshank *Tringa erythropus*	–	A

List

249

❏ Greater Yellowlegs *Tringa melanoleuca*	—	A
❏ Greenshank *Tringa nebularia*	—	A
❏ Lesser Yellowlegs *Tringa flavipes*	—	A
❏ Marsh Sandpiper *Tringa stagnatilis*	—	A
❏ Wood Sandpiper *Tringa glareola*	—	A
❏ Redshank *Tringa totanus*	*totanus*	A
❏ Turnstone *Arenaria interpres*	*interpres*	A
❏ Wilson's Phalarope *Phalaropus tricolor*	—	A
❏ Red-necked Phalarope *Phalaropus lobatus*	—	A
❏ Grey Phalarope *Phalaropus fulicarius*	—	A
❏ Pomarine Skua *Stercorarius pomarinus*	—	A
❏ Arctic Skua *Stercorarius parasiticus*	—	A
❏ Long-tailed Skua *Stercorarius longicaudus*	*longicaudus*	A
❏ Great Skua *Stercorarius skua*		A
❏ Ivory Gull *Pagophila eburnea*	—	A
❏ Sabine's Gull *Xema sabini*	—	A
❏ Kittiwake *Rissa tridactyla*	*tridactyla*	A
❏ Bonaparte's Gull *Chroicocephalus philadelphia*	—	A
❏ Black-headed Gull *Chroicocephalus ridibundus*	—	A
❏ Little Gull *Hydrocoloeus minutus*	—	A
❏ Ross's Gull *Rhodostethia rosea*	—	A
❏ Laughing Gull *Larus atricilla*	not determined	A
❏ Franklin's Gull *Larus pipixcan*	—	A
❏ Mediterranean Gull *Larus melanocephalus*	—	A
❏ Common Gull *Larus canus*	*canus*	A
❏ Ring-billed Gull *Larus delawarensis*	—	A
❏ Lesser Black-backed Gull *Larus fuscus*	*graellsii*	A
> Baltic Lesser Black-backed Gull	*fuscus*	—
> Continental Lesser Black-backed Gull	*intermedius*	—
❏ Herring Gull *Larus argentatus*	*argenteus*	A
> Scandinavian Herring Gull	*argentatus*	—
❏ Yellow-legged Gull *Larus michahellis*	*michahellis*	A
> Atlantic Gull	*atlantis*	—
❏ Caspian Gull *Larus cachinnans*	—	A
❏ American Herring Gull *Larus smithsonianus*	—	A
❏ Iceland Gull *Larus glaucoides*	*glaucoides*	A
> Kumlien's Gull	*kumlieni*	—
❏ Thayer's Gull *Larus thayeri*	—	A
❏ Glaucous Gull *Larus hyperboreus*	*hyperboreus*	A
❏ Great Black-backed Gull *Larus marinus*	—	A
❏ Sooty Tern *Onychoprion fuscatus*	not determined	A
❏ Little Tern *Sternula albifrons*	*albifrons*	A
❏ Gull-billed Tern *Gelochelidon nilotica*	*nilotica*	A
❏ Caspian Tern *Hydroprogne caspia*	—	A
❏ Whiskered Tern *Chlidonias hybrida*	*hybrida*	A
❏ Black Tern *Chlidonias niger*	*niger*	A
> American Black Tern	*surinamensis*	—
❏ White-winged Black Tern *Chlidonias leucopterus*	—	A
❏ Sandwich Tern *Sterna sandvicensis*	*sandvicensis*	A

❏ Elegant Tern *Sterna elegans*	—	A
❏ Royal Tern *Sterna maxima*	not determined	A
❏ Lesser Crested Tern *Sterna bengalensis*	not determined	A
❏ Forster's Tern *Sterna forsteri*	—	A
❏ Common Tern *Sterna hirundo*	*hirundo*	A
❏ Roseate Tern *Sterna dougallii*	*dougallii*	A
❏ Arctic Tern *Sterna paradisaea*	—	A
❏ Guillemot *Uria aalge*	*albionis*	A
❏ Brünnich's Guillemot *Uria lomvia*	not determined	A
❏ Razorbill *Alca torda*	*islandica*	A
❏ Great Auk (extinct) *Pinguinus impennis*	—	B
❏ Black Guillemot *Cepphus grylle*	*arcticus*	A
❏ Little Auk *Alle alle*	*alle*	A
❏ Puffin *Fratercula arctica*	—	A
❏ Pallas's Sandgrouse *Syrrhaptes paradoxus*	—	A
❏ Rock Dove / Feral Pigeon *Columba livia*	*livia*	A
❏ Stock Dove *Columba oenas*	*oenas*	A
❏ Woodpigeon *Columba palumbus*	*palumbus*	A
❏ Collared Dove *Streptopelia decaocto*	*decaocto*	A
❏ Turtle Dove *Streptopelia turtur*	*turtur*	A
❏ Mourning Dove *Zenaida macroura*	not determined	A
❏ Great Spotted Cuckoo *Clamator glandarius*	—	A
❏ Cuckoo *Cuculus canorus*	*canorus*	A
❏ Black-billed Cuckoo *Coccyzus erythrophthalmus*	—	B
❏ Yellow-billed Cuckoo *Coccyzus americanus*	—	A
❏ Barn Owl *Tyto alba*	*alba*	A
❏ > Dark-breasted Barn Owl	*guttata*	—
❏ Scops Owl *Otus scops*	*scops*	A
❏ Snowy Owl *Bubo scandiacus*	—	A
❏ Little Owl *Athene noctua*	*vidalli*	A / C2
❏ Long-eared Owl *Asio otus*	*otus*	A
❏ Short-eared Owl *Asio flammeus*	*flammeus*	A
❏ Nightjar *Caprimulgus europaeus*	*europaeus*	A
❏ Common Nighthawk *Chordeiles minor*	not determined	A
❏ Chimney Swift *Chaetura pelagica*	—	A
❏ White-throated Needletail *Hirundapus caudacutus*	not determined	A
❏ Swift *Apus apus*	*apus*	A
❏ Pallid Swift *Apus pallidus*	not determined	A
❏ Alpine Swift *Apus melba*	*melba*	A
❏ Little Swift *Apus affinis*	not determined	A
❏ Kingfisher *Alcedo atthis*	*ispida*	A
❏ Belted Kingfisher *Megaceryle alcyon*	—	A
❏ Bee-eater *Merops apiaster*	—	A
❏ Roller *Coracias garrulus*	*garrulus*	A
❏ Hoopoe *Upupa epops*	*epops*	A
❏ Wryneck *Jynx torquilla*	*torquilla*	A
❏ Green Woodpecker *Picus viridis*	*viridis*	B
❏ Yellow-bellied Sapsucker *Sphyrapicus varius*	—	A
❏ Great Spotted Woodpecker *Dendrocopos major*	*major*	A

List

❏	Philadelphia Vireo *Vireo philadelphicus*	—	A
❏	Red-eyed Vireo *Vireo olivaceus*	not determined	A
❏	Golden Oriole *Oriolus oriolus*	*oriolus*	A
❏	Brown Shrike *Lanius cristatus*	not determined	A
❏	Isabelline Shrike *Lanius isabellinus*	*isabellinus*	A
❏	Red-backed Shrike *Lanius collurio*	*collurio*	A
❏	Lesser Grey Shrike *Lanius minor*	—	A
❏	Great Grey Shrike *Lanius excubitor*	*excubitor*	A
❏	Woodchat Shrike *Lanius senator*	*senator*	A
	> Balearic Woodchat Shrike	*badius*	—
❏	Chough *Pyrrhocorax pyrrhocorax*	*pyrrhocorax*	A
❏	Magpie *Pica pica*	*pica*	A
❏	Jay *Garrulus glandarius*	*hibernicus*	A
❏	Jackdaw *Corvus monedula*	*spermologus*	A
	> Eastern Jackdaw	*soemmerringii* or *monedula*	—
❏	Rook *Corvus frugilegus*	*frugilegus*	A
❏	Carrion Crow *Corvus corone*	*corone*	A
❏	Hooded Crow *Corvus cornix*	*cornix*	A
❏	Raven *Corvus corax*	*corax*	A
❏	Goldcrest *Regulus regulus*	*regulus*	A
❏	Firecrest *Regulus ignicapilla*	*ignicapilla*	A
❏	Blue Tit *Cyanistes caeruleus*	*obscurus*	A
❏	Great Tit *Parus major*	*newtoni*	A
❏	Coal Tit *Periparus ater*	*hibernicus*	A
	> British Coal Tit	*britannicus*	—
	> Continental Coal Tit	*ater*	—
❏	Marsh Tit *Poecile palustris*	not determined	A
❏	Bearded Tit *Panurus biarmicus*	not determined	A
❏	Short-toed Lark *Calandrella brachydactyla*	*brachydactyla*	A
❏	Woodlark *Lullula arborea*	*arborea*	A
❏	Skylark *Alauda arvensis*	*arvensis*	A
❏	Shore Lark *Eremophila alpestris*	*flava*	A
❏	Sand Martin *Riparia riparia*	*riparia*	A
❏	Swallow *Hirundo rustica*	*rustica*	A
❏	House Martin *Delichon urbicum*	*urbicum*	A
❏	Red-rumped Swallow *Cecropis daurica*	*rufula*	A
❏	American Cliff Swallow *Petrochelidon pyrrhonota*	not determined	A
❏	Cetti's Warbler *Cettia cetti*	not determined	A
❏	Long-tailed Tit *Aegithalos caudatus*	*rosaceus*	A
❏	Greenish Warbler *Phylloscopus trochiloides*	*viridanus*	A
❏	Arctic Warbler *Phylloscopus borealis*	not determined	A
❏	Pallas's Warbler *Phylloscopus proregulus*	—	A
❏	Yellow-browed Warbler *Phylloscopus inornatus*	—	A
❏	Hume's Warbler *Phylloscopus humei*	*humei*	A
❏	Radde's Warbler *Phylloscopus schwarzi*	—	A
❏	Dusky Warbler *Phylloscopus fuscatus*	not determined	A
❏	Western Bonelli's Warbler *Phylloscopus bonelli*	—	A
❏	Wood Warbler *Phylloscopus sibilatrix*	—	A
❏	Chiffchaff *Phylloscopus collybita*	*collybita*	A
	> Scandinavian Chiffchaff	*abietinus*	—

> Siberian Chiffchaff	*tristis*	—
❏ Willow Warbler *Phylloscopus trochilus*	*trochilus*	A
> Northern Willow Warbler	*acredula*	—
❏ Blackcap *Sylvia atricapilla*	*atricapilla*	A
❏ Garden Warbler *Sylvia borin*	*borin*	A
❏ Barred Warbler *Sylvia nisoria*	not determined	A
❏ Lesser Whitethroat *Sylvia curruca*	*curruca*	A
> Siberian Lesser Whitethroat	*blythi*	—
❏ Whitethroat *Sylvia communis*	*communis*	A
❏ Dartford Warbler *Sylvia undata*	*dartfordiensis*	A
❏ Subalpine Warbler *Sylvia cantillans*	*cantillans*	A
❏ Sardinian Warbler *Sylvia melanocephala*	not determined	A
❏ Pallas's Grasshopper Warbler *Locustella certhiola*	not determined	A
❏ Grasshopper Warbler *Locustella naevia*	*naevia*	A
❏ Savi's Warbler *Locustella luscinioides*	not determined	A
❏ Eastern Olivaceous Warbler *Hippolais pallida*	not determined	A
❏ Booted Warbler *Hippolais caligata*	—	A
❏ Sykes's Warbler *Hippolais rama*	—	A
❏ Icterine Warbler *Hippolais icterina*	—	A
❏ Melodious Warbler *Hippolais polyglotta*	—	A
❏ Aquatic Warbler *Acrocephalus paludicola*	—	A
❏ Sedge Warbler *Acrocephalus schoenobaenus*	—	A
❏ Paddyfield Warbler *Acrocephalus agricola*	—	A
❏ Blyth's Reed Warbler *Acrocephalus dumetorum*	—	A
❏ Marsh Warbler *Acrocephalus palustris*	—	A
❏ Reed Warbler *Acrocephalus scirpaceus*	*scirpaceus*	A
❏ Great Reed Warbler *Acrocephalus arundinaceus*	*arundinaceus*	A
❏ Fan-tailed Warbler *Cisticola juncidis*	not determined	A
❏ Cedar Waxwing *Bombycilla cedrorum*	—	A
❏ Waxwing *Bombycilla garrulus*	*garrulus*	A
❏ Treecreeper *Certhia familiaris*	*britannica*	A
❏ Wren *Troglodytes troglodytes*	*indigennus*	A
❏ Grey Catbird *Dumetella carolinensis*	—	A
❏ Starling *Sturnus vulgaris*	*vulgaris*	A
❏ Rose-coloured Starling *Pastor roseus*	—	A
❏ Dipper *Cinclus cinclus*	*hibernicus*	A
> Black-bellied Dipper	*cinclus*	—
❏ White's Thrush *Zoothera dauma*	*aurea*	A
❏ Siberian Thrush *Zoothera sibirica*	not determined	A
❏ Hermit Thrush *Catharus guttatus*	not determined	A
❏ Swainson's Thrush *Catharus ustulatus*	*swainsoni*	A
❏ Grey-cheeked Thrush *Catharus minimus*	not determined	A
❏ Ring Ouzel *Turdus torquatus*	*torquatus*	A
❏ Blackbird *Turdus merula*	*merula*	A
❏ Fieldfare *Turdus pilaris*	—	A
❏ Song Thrush *Turdus philomelos*	*clarkei*	A
❏ Redwing *Turdus iliacus*	*iliacus*	A
❏ Mistle Thrush *Turdus viscivorus*	*viscivorus*	A
❏ American Robin *Turdus migratorius*	not determined	A
❏ Spotted Flycatcher *Muscicapa striata*	*striata*	A

List

	Species	Subspecies	Status
❑	Rufous Bush Robin *Cercotrichas galactotes*	*galactotes*	A
❑	Robin *Erithacus rubecula*	*melophilus*	A
❑	Thrush Nightingale *Luscinia luscinia*	—	A
❑	Nightingale *Luscinia megarhynchos*	*megarhynchos*	A
❑	Bluethroat *Luscinia svecica*	*svecica*	A
	> White-spotted Bluethroat	*cyanecula*	—
❑	Red-flanked Bluetail *Tarsiger cyanurus*	not determined	A
❑	Black Redstart *Phoenicurus ochruros*	*gibraltariensis*	A
❑	Common Redstart *Phoenicurus phoenicurus*	*phoenicurus*	A
❑	Whinchat *Saxicola rubetra*	—	A
❑	Stonechat *Saxicola torquatus*	*hibernans*	A
	> Eastern Stonechat	*maurus* or *stejnegeri*	—
❑	Isabelline Wheatear *Oenanthe isabellina*	—	A
❑	Wheatear *Oenanthe oenanthe*	*oenanthe*	A
	> Greenland Wheatear	*leucorrhoa*	—
❑	Pied Wheatear *Oenanthe pleschanka*	—	A
❑	Black-eared Wheatear *Oenanthe hispanica*	*hispanica*	A
❑	Desert Wheatear *Oenanthe deserti*	not determined	A
❑	Black Wheatear sp. *Oenanthe luecura / leucopyga*	n/a	A
❑	Rock Thrush *Monticola saxatilis*	—	A
❑	Red-breasted Flycatcher *Ficedula parva*	—	A
❑	Pied Flycatcher *Ficedula hypoleuca*	*hypoleuca*	A
❑	Dunnock *Prunella modularis*	*hebridium*	A
❑	House Sparrow *Passer domesticus*	*domesticus*	A
❑	Tree Sparrow *Passer montanus*	*montanus*	A
❑	Yellow Wagtail *Motacilla flava*	*flavissima*	A
	> Blue-headed Wagtail	*flava*	—
	> Ashy-headed Wagtail	*cinereocapilla*	—
	> Grey-headed Wagtail	*thunbergi*	--
	> Black-headed Wagtail	*feldegg*	—
❑	Citrine Wagtail *Motacilla citreola*	not determined	A
❑	Grey Wagtail *Motacilla cinerea*	*cinerea*	A
❑	Pied Wagtail *Motacilla alba*	*yarrellii*	A
	> White Wagtail	*alba*	—
❑	Richard's Pipit *Anthus richardi*	—	A
❑	Tawny Pipit *Anthus campestris*	not determined	A
❑	Olive-backed Pipit *Anthus hodgsoni*	not determined	A
❑	Tree Pipit *Anthus trivialis*	*trivialis*	A
❑	Pechora Pipit *Anthus gustavi*	not determined	A
❑	Meadow Pipit *Anthus pratensis*	*whistleri*	A
❑	Red-throated Pipit *Anthus cervinus*	—	A
❑	Rock Pipit *Anthus petrosus*	*petrosus*	A
	> Scandinavian Rock Pipit	*littoralis*	—
❑	Water Pipit *Anthus spinoletta*	*spinoletta*	A
❑	Buff-bellied Pipit *Anthus rubescens*	*rubescens*	A
❑	Chaffinch *Fringilla coelebs*	*gengleri*	A
❑	Brambling *Fringilla montifringilla*	—	A
❑	Serin *Serinus serinus*	—	A
❑	Greenfinch *Carduelis chloris*	*chloris*	A

❏	Goldfinch *Carduelis carduelis*	*britannica*	A
❏	Siskin *Carduelis spinus*	—	A
❏	Linnet *Carduelis cannabina*	*cannabina*	A
❏	Twite *Carduelis flavirostris*	*pipilans*	A
❏	Redpoll *Carduelis flammea*	*cabaret*	A
	> Mealy Redpoll	*flammea*	—
	> Greenland Redpoll	*rostrata*	—
❏	Arctic Redpoll *Carduelis hornemanni*	not determined	A
❏	Two-barred Crossbill *Loxia leucoptera*	*bifasciata*	B
❏	Crossbill *Loxia curvirostra*	*curvirostra*	A
❏	Common Rosefinch *Carpodacus erythrinus*	not determined	A
❏	Bullfinch *Pyrrhula pyrrhula*	*pileata*	A
	> Northern Bullfinch	*pyrrhula*	—
❏	Hawfinch *Coccothraustes coccothraustes*	*coccothraustes*	A
❏	Snow Bunting *Plectrophenax nivalis*	*nivalis*	A
❏	Lapland Bunting *Calcarius lapponicus*	*lapponicus*	A
❏	Scarlet Tanager *Piranga olivacea*	—	A
❏	Rose-breasted Grosbeak *Pheucticus ludovicianus*	—	A
❏	Indigo Bunting *Passerina cyanea*	—	A
❏	Fox Sparrow *Passerella iliaca*	*iliaca*	A
❏	White-crowned Sparrow *Zonotrichia leucophrys*	not determined	A
❏	White-throated Sparrow *Zonotrichia albicollis*	—	A
❏	Dark-eyed Junco *Junco hyemalis*	not determined	A
❏	Pine Bunting *Emberiza leucocephalos*	not determined	A
❏	Yellowhammer *Emberiza citrinella*	*caliginosa*	A
❏	Cirl Bunting *Emberiza cirlus*	—	A
❏	Ortolan Bunting *Emberiza hortulana*	—	A
❏	Rustic Bunting *Emberiza rustica*	not determined	A
❏	Little Bunting *Emberiza pusilla*	—	A
❏	Yellow-breasted Bunting *Emberiza aureola*	not determined	A
❏	Reed Bunting *Emberiza schoeniclus*	*schoeniclus*	A
❏	Black-headed Bunting *Emberiza melanocephala*	—	A
❏	Corn Bunting *Emberiza calandra*	*clanceyi*	A
❏	Bobolink *Dolichonyx oryzivorus*	—	A
❏	Baltimore Oriole *Icterus galbula*	—	A
❏	Black-and-white Warbler *Mniotilta varia*	—	A
❏	Blue-winged Warbler *Vermivora pinus*	—	A
❏	Northern Parula *Parula americana*	—	A
❏	Yellow Warbler *Dendroica petechia*	not determined	A
❏	Yellow-rumped Warbler *Dendroica coronata*	not determined	A
❏	Blackpoll Warbler *Dendroica striata*	—	A
❏	American Redstart *Setophaga ruticilla*	—	A
❏	Ovenbird *Seiurus aurocapilla*	not determined	A
❏	Northern Waterthrush *Seiurus noveboracensis*	—	A
❏	Common Yellowthroat *Geothlypis trichas*	not determined	A
❏	Canada Warbler *Wilsonia canadensis*	—	A

List

Species included in category D. These species do not form part of the Irish List

Red-breasted Goose *Branta ruficollis*	—	D1
Red-legged Partridge *Alectoris rufa*	not determined	D4
Greater Flamingo *Phoenicopterus ruber*	—	D1
Booted Eagle *Hieraaetus pennata*	—	D1
Bridled Tern *Onychoprion anaethetus*	*melanoptera*	D3
Northern Flicker *Colaptes auratus*	*auratus*	D2
House Crow *Corvus splendens*	not determined	D2
Purple Martin *Progne subis*	not determined	D1
American Goldfinch *Carduelis tristis*	not determined	D1
Red-headed Bunting *Emberiza bruniceps*	—	D1

Irish Bird Names

This list includes the official names of all the species in the Irish language as published by the Irish Rare Birds Committee (IRBC 1998). The names were standardised by An Coiste Téarmaíochta (the Terminology Committee) of the Department of Education in Ireland.

For well-known species, the names tend to reflect traditional usage; for the more inconspicuous and rarer species, they have been devised in conjunction with An Coiste Téarmaíochta.

Mute Swan **Eala bhalbh**
Bewick's Swan **Eala Bewick**
Whooper Swan **Eala ghlórach**
Bean Goose **Síolghé**
Pink-footed Goose **Gé ghobghearr**
White-fronted Goose **Gé bhánéadanach**
Lesser White-fronted Goose
  Mionghé bhánéadanach
Greylag Goose **Gé ghlas**
Snow Goose **Gé shneachta**
Canada Goose **Gé Cheanadach**
Barnacle Goose **Gé ghiúrainn**
Brent Goose **Cadhan**
Ruddy Shelduck **Seil-lacha rua**
Shelduck **Seil-lacha**
Mandarin Duck **Lacha mhandrach**
Wigeon **Rualacha**
American Wigeon **Rualacha Mheiriceánach**
Gadwall **Gadual**
Teal **Praslacha**
Green-winged Teal **Praslacha ghlaseiteach**
Mallard **Mallard**
American Black Duck **Lacha chosrua**
Pintail **Biorearrach**
Garganey **Praslacha shamhraidh**
Blue-winged Teal **Praslacha ghormeiteach**
Shoveler **Spadalach**
Red-crested Pochard **Póiseard cíordhearg**
Pochard **Póiseard**
Ring-necked Duck **Lacha mhuinceach**
Ferruginous Duck **Póiseard súilbhán**
Tufted Duck **Lacha bhadánach**
Scaup **Lacha iascán**
Lesser Scaup **Mionlacha iascán**
Eider **Éadar**

King Eider **Éadar taibhseach**
Long-tailed Duck **Lacha earrfhada**
Common Scoter **Scótar**
Surf Scoter **Scótar toinne**
Velvet Scoter **Sceadach**
Goldeneye **Órshúileach**
Hooded Merganser **Síolta chochaill**
Smew **Síolta gheal**
Red-breasted Merganser **Síolta rua**
Goosander **Síolta mhór**
Ruddy Duck **Lacha rua**
Red-throated Diver **Lóma rua**
Black-throated Diver **Lóma Artach**
Great Northern Diver **Lóma mór**
White-billed Diver **Lóma gobgheal**
Pied-billed Grebe **Foitheach gob-alabhreac**
Little Grebe **Spágaire tonn**
Great Crested Grebe **Foitheach mór**
Red-necked Grebe **Foitheach píbrua**
Slavonian Grebe **Foitheach cluasach**
Black-necked Grebe **Foitheach píbdhubh**
Black-browed Albatross
  Albatras dú-mhalach
Fulmar **Fulmaire**
Bulwer's Petrel **Peadairín Bulwer**
Cory's Shearwater **Cánóg Cory**
Great Shearwater **Cánóg mhór**
Sooty Shearwater **Cánóg dhorcha**
Manx Shearwater **Cánóg dhubh**
Mediterranean Shearwater **Cánóg Bhailéarach**
Macaronesian Shearwater **Cánóg bheag**
Wilson's Petrel **Guairdeall Wilson**
Storm Petrel **Guairdeall**
Leach's Petrel **Guairdeall gabhlach**
Madeiran Petrel **Guairdeall Maidéarach**

Gannet **Gainéad**
Cormorant **Broigheall**
Double-crested Cormorant
   Broigheall cluasach
Shag **Seaga**
Bittern **Bonnán**
American Bittern **Bonnán Meiriceánach**
Little Bittern **Bonnán beag**
Night Heron **Corr oíche**
Squacco Heron **Corr scréachach**
Cattle Egret **Éigrit eallaigh**
Little Egret **Éigrit bheag**
Great White Egret **Éigrit mhór**
Grey Heron **Corr réisc**
Purple Heron **Corr chorcra**
Black Stork **Storc dubh**
White Stork **Storc bán**
Glossy Ibis **Íbis niamhrach**
Spoonbill **Leitheadach**
Honey Buzzard **Clamhán riabhach**
Black Kite **Cúr dubh**
Red Kite **Cúr rua**
White-tailed Eagle **Iolar mara**
Bald Eagle **Iolar maol**
Griffon Vulture **Bultúr gríofa**
Marsh Harrier **Cromán móna**
Hen Harrier **Cromán na gcearc**
Montagu's Harrier **Cromán liath**
Goshawk **Spioróg mhór**
Sparrowhawk **Spioróg**
Buzzard **Clamhán**
Rough-legged Buzzard **Clamhán lópach**
Spotted Eagle **Iolar breac**
Golden Eagle **Iolar fíréan**
Osprey **Coirneach**
Lesser Kestrel **Mionphocaire gaoithe**
Kestrel **Pocaire gaoithe**
Red-footed Falcon **Fabhcún cosdearg**
Merlin **Meirliún**
Hobby **Fabhcún coille**
Gyr Falcon **Fabhcún mór**
Peregrine Falcon **Fabhcún gorm**
Red Grouse **Cearc fhraoigh**
Capercaillie **Capall coille**
Grey Partridge **Patraisc**
Quail **Gearg**
Pheasant **Piasún**

Water Rail **Rálóg uisce**
Spotted Crake **Gearr breac**
Sora **Gearr sora**
Little Crake **Gearr beag**
Baillon's Crake **Gearr Baillon**
Corncrake **Traonach**
Moorhen **Cearc uisce**
Coot **Cearc cheannann**
American Coot
   Cearc cheannann Mheiriceánach
Crane **Grús**
Sandhill Crane **Grús Ceanadach**
Little Bustard **Bustard beag**
Great Bustard **Bustard mór**
Oystercatcher **Roilleach**
Black-winged Stilt **Scodalach dubheiteach**
Avocet **Abhóiséad**
Stone Curlew **Crotach cloch**
Cream-coloured Courser **Rásaí bánbhuí**
Collared Pratincole **Pratancól muinceach**
Black-winged Pratincole
   Pratancól dubheiteach
Little Ringed Plover **Feadóigín chladaigh**
Ringed Plover **Feadóg chladaigh**
Killdeer **Feadóg ghlórach**
Kentish Plover **Feadóigín chosdubh**
Dotterel **Amadán móinteach**
American Golden Plover
   Feadóg bhuí Mheiriceánach
Pacific Golden Plover **Feadóg bhuí Áiseach**
Golden Plover **Feadóg bhuí**
Grey Plover **Feadóg ghlas**
Sociable Plover **Pilibín ealtúil**
Lapwing **Pilibín**
Knot **Cnota**
Sanderling **Luathrán**
Semipalmated Sandpiper
   Gobadáinín mionbhosach
Western Sandpiper **Gobadáinín iartharach**
Little Stint **Gobadáinín beag**
Temminck's Stint **Gobadáinín Temminck**
Long-toed Stint **Gobadáinín ladharfhada**
Least Sandpiper **Gobadáinín bídeach**
White-rumped Sandpiper
   Gobadán bánphrompach
Baird's Sandpiper **Gobadán Baird**
Pectoral Sandpiper **Gobadán uchtach**

Sharp-tailed Sandpiper
  Gobadán earr-rinneach
Curlew Sandpiper **Gobadán crotaigh**
Purple Sandpiper **Gobadán cosbhuí**
Dunlin **Breacóg**
Broad-billed Sandpiper **Gobadán gobleathan**
Stilt Sandpiper **Gobadán scodalach**
Buff-breasted Sandpiper
  Gobadán broinn-donnbhuí
Ruff **Rufachán**
Jack Snipe **Naoscach bhídeach**
Snipe **Naoscach**
Great Snipe **Naoscach mhór**
Short-billed Dowitcher **Guilbnín gobghearr**
Long-billed Dowitcher **Guilbnín gobfhada**
Woodcock **Creabhar**
Black-tailed Godwit **Guilbneach earrdhubh**
Bar-tailed Godwit **Guilbneach stríocearrach**
Eskimo Curlew **Crotach Artach**
Whimbrel **Crotach eanaigh**
Curlew **Crotach**
Upland Sandpiper **Gobadán sléibhe**
Spotted Redshank **Cosdeargán breac**
Redshank **Cosdeargán**
Marsh Sandpiper **Gobadán corraigh**
Greenshank **Laidhrín glas**
Greater Yellowlegs **Ladhrán buí**
Lesser Yellowlegs **Mionladhrán buí**
Solitary Sandpiper **Gobadán aonarach**
Green Sandpiper **Gobadán glas**
Wood Sandpiper **Gobadán coille**
Terek Sandpiper **Gobadán Terek**
Common Sandpiper **Gobadán coiteann**
Spotted Sandpiper **Gobadán breac**
Turnstone **Piardálaí trá**
Wilson's Phalarope **Falaróp Wilson**
Red-necked Phalarope **Falaróp gobchaol**
Grey Phalarope **Falaróp gobmhór**
Pomarine Skua **Meirleach pomairíneach**
Arctic Skua **Meirleach Artach**
Long-tailed Skua **Meirleach earrfhada**
Great Skua **Meirleach mór**
Mediterranean Gull **Sléibhín Meánmhuirí**
Laughing Gull **Sléibhín an gháire**
Franklin's Gull **Sléibhín Franklin**
Little Gull **Sléibhín beag**
Sabine's Gull **Sléibhín Sabine**

Bonaparte's Gull **Sléibhín Bonaparte**
Black-headed Gull **Sléibhín**
Ring-billed Gull **Faoileán bandghobach**
Common Gull **Faoileán bán**
Lesser Black-backed Gull **Droimneach beag**
Herring Gull **Faoileán scadán**
American Herring Gull
  Faoileán scadán Mheiriceánach
Yellow-legged Gull **Faoileán buíchosach**
Caspian Gull **Faoileán Chaispeach**
Iceland Gull **Faoileán Íoslannach**
Glaucous Gull **Faoileán glas**
Great Black-backed Gull **Droimneach mór**
Ross's Gull **Faoileán Ross**
Kittiwake **Saidhbhéar**
Ivory Gull **Faoileán eabhartha**
Gull-billed Tern **Geabhróg ghobdhubh**
Caspian Tern **Geabhróg Chaispeach**
Lesser Crested Tern
  Miongheabhróg chíorach
Sandwich Tern **Geabhróg scothdhubh**
Elegant Tern **Gcabhróg ghalánta**
Roseate Tern **Geabhróg rósach**
Common Tern **Geabhróg**
Arctic Tern **Geabhróg Artach**
Forster's Tern **Geabhróg Forster**
Little Tern **Geabhróg bheag**
Whiskered Tern **Geabhróg bhroinndubh**
Black Tern **Geabhróg dhubh**
White-winged Black Tern
  Geabhróg bháneiteach
Guillemot **Foracha**
Brünnich's Guillemot **Foracha Brünnich**
Razorbill **Crosán**
Great Auk **Falcóg mhór**
Black Guillemot **Foracha dhubh**
Little Auk **Falcóg bheag**
Puffin **Puifín**
Pallas's Sandgrouse **Gaineamhchearc Pallas**
Rock Dove **Colm aille**
Stock Dove **Colm gorm**
Woodpigeon **Colm coille**
Collared Dove **Fearán baicdhubh**
Turtle Dove **Fearán**
Great Spotted Cuckoo **Mórchuach bhreac**
Cuckoo **Cuach**
Black-billed Cuckoo **Cuach ghobdhubh**

Yellow-billed Cuckoo **Cuach ghob-bhuí**
Barn Owl **Scréachóg reilige**
Scops Owl **Ulchabhán scopach**
Snowy Owl **Ulchabhán sneachtúil**
Little Owl **Ulchabhán beag**
Long-eared Owl **Ceann cait**
Short-eared Owl **Ulchabhán réisc**
Nightjar **Tuirne lín**
White-throated Needletail
    Gabhlán earrspíonach
Swift **Gabhlán gaoithe**
Pallid Swift **Gabhlán bánlíoch**
Alpine Swift **Gabhlán Alpach**
Little Swift **Gabhlán beag**
Kingfisher **Cruidín**
Belted Kingfisher **Cruidín creasa**
Bee-eater **Beachadóir Eorpach**
Roller **Rollóir**
Hoopoe **Húpú**
Wryneck **Cam-mhuin**
Green Woodpecker **Cnagaire glas**
Yellow-bellied Sapsucker **Súdhiúlaí tarrbhuí**
Great Spotted Woodpecker
    Mórchnagaire breac
Short-toed Lark **Fuiseog ladharghearr**
Woodlark **Fuiseog choille**
Skylark **Fuiseog**
Shore Lark **Fuiseog adharcach**
Sand Martin **Gabhlán gainimh**
Swallow **Fáinleog**
Red-rumped Swallow
    Fáinleog ruaphrompach
Cliff Swallow **Fáinleog aille**
House Martin **Gabhlán binne**
Richard's Pipit **Riabhóg Richard**
Tawny Pipit **Riabhóg dhonn**
Olive-backed Pipit **Riabhóg dhroimghlas**
Tree Pipit **Riabhóg choille**
Pechora Pipit **Riabhóg Pechora**
Meadow Pipit **Riabhóg mhóna**
Red-throated Pipit **Riabhóg phíbrua**
Rock Pipit **Riabhóg chladaigh**
Water Pipit **Riabhóg uisce**
Buff-bellied Pipit **Riabhóg tharr-dhonnbhuí**
Yellow Wagtail **Glasóg bhuí**
Citrine Wagtail **Glasóg chiotrónach**
Grey Wagtail **Glasóg liath**
Pied Wagtail **Glasóg shráide**

Waxwing **Síodeiteach**
Dipper **Gabha dubh**
Wren **Dreoilín**
Grey Catbird **Catéan liath**
Dunnock **Donnóg**
Rufous Bush Robin **Torspideog ruadhonn**
Robin **Spideog**
Thrush Nightingale **Filiméala smólaigh**
Nightingale **Filiméala**
Bluethroat **Gormphíb**
Black Redstart **Earrdheargán dubh**
Redstart **Earrdheargán**
Whinchat **Caislín aitinn**
Stonechat **Caislín cloch**
Isabelline Wheatear **Clochrán gainimh**
Wheatear **Clochrán**
Pied Wheatear **Clochrán alabhreac**
Black-eared Wheatear **Clochrán cluasdubh**
Desert Wheatear **Clochrán fásaigh**
Rock Thrush **Smólach aille**
White's Thrush **Smólach White**
Siberian Thrush **Smólach Sibéarach**
Swainson's Thrush **Smólach Swainson**
Hermit Thrush **Smólach díthreabhach**
Grey-cheeked Thrush **Smólach glasleicneach**
Ring Ouzel **Lon creige**
Blackbird **Lon dubh**
Fieldfare **Sacán**
Song Thrush **Smólach ceoil**
Redwing **Deargán sneachta**
Mistle Thrush **Liatráisc**
American Robin **Smólach imirce**
Cetti's Warbler **Ceolaire Cetti**
Fan-tailed Warbler **Ceolaire earrfheanach**
Pallas's Grasshopper Warbler
    Ceolaire casarnaí Pallas
Grasshopper Warbler **Ceolaire casarnaí**
Savi's Warbler **Ceolaire Savi**
Aquatic Warbler **Ceolaire uisce**
Sedge Warbler **Ceolaire cíbe**
Paddyfield Warbler **Ceolaire gort ríse**
Blyth's Reed Warbler **Ceolaire Blyth**
Marsh Warbler **Ceolaire corraigh**
Reed Warbler **Ceolaire giolcaí**
Great Reed Warbler **Mórcheolaire giolcaí**
Eastern Olivaceous Warbler **Ceolaire bánlíoch**
Icterine Warbler **Ceolaire ictireach**
Melodious Warbler **Ceolaire binn**

Dartford Warbler **Ceolaire fraoigh**
Subalpine Warbler **Ceolaire Fo-Alpach**
Sardinian Warbler **Ceolaire Sairdíneach**
Barred Warbler **Ceolaire barrach**
Lesser Whitethroat **Gilphíb bheag**
Whitethroat **Gilphíb**
Garden Warbler **Ceolaire garraí**
Blackcap **Caipín dubh**
Greenish Warbler **Ceolaire scothghlas**
Arctic Warbler **Ceolaire Artach**
Pallas's Warbler **Ceolaire Pallas**
Yellow-browed Warbler **Ceolaire buímhalach**
Hume's Warbler **Ceolaire Hume**
Radde's Warbler **Ceolaire Radde**
Dusky Warbler **Ceolaire breacdhorcha**
Western Bonelli's Warbler **Ceolaire Bonelli**
Wood Warbler **Ceolaire coille**
Chiffchaff **Tiuf-teaf**
Willow Warbler **Ceolaire sailí**
Goldcrest **Cíorbhuí**
Firecrest **Lasairchíor**
Spotted Flycatcher **Cuilire liath**
Red-breasted Flycatcher **Cuilire broinnrua**
Pied Flycatcher **Cuilire alabhreac**
Bearded Tit **Meantán croiméalach**
Long-tailed Tit **Meantán earrfhada**
Marsh Tit **Meantán lathaí**
Coal Tit **Meantán dubh**
Blue Tit **Meantán gorm**
Great Tit **Meantán mór**
Treecreeper **Snag**
Golden Oriole **Óiréal órga**
Red-backed Shrike **Scréachán droimrua**
Lesser Grey Shrike **Mionscréachán liath**
Great Grey Shrike **Mórscréachán liath**
Woodchat Shrike **Scréachán coille**
Jay **Scréachóg**
Magpie **Snag breac**
Chough **Cág cosdearg**
Jackdaw **Cág**
Rook **Rúcach**
Hooded Crow **Caróg liath**
Carrion Crow **Caróg dhubh**
Raven **Fiach dubh**
Starling **Druid**
Rose-coloured Starling **Druid rósach**
House Sparrow **Gealbhan binne**
Tree Sparrow **Gealbhan crainn**

Philadelphia Vireo **Glaséan Philadelphia**
Red-eyed Vireo **Glaséan súildearg**
Chaffinch **Rí rua**
Brambling **Breacán**
Serin **Seirín**
Greenfinch **Glasán darach**
Goldfinch **Lasair choille**
Siskin **Siscín**
Linnet **Gleoiseach**
Twite **Gleoiseach sléibhe**
Redpoll **Deargéadan**
Arctic Redpoll **Deargéadan Artach**
Two-barred Crossbill **Crosghob báneiteach**
Crossbill **Crosghob**
Common Rosefinch **Rósghlasán coiteann**
Bullfinch **Corcrán coille**
Hawfinch **Glasán gobmhór**
Black-and-white Warbler **Ceolaire dubh is bán**
Northern Parula **Parúl tuaisceartach**
Yellow Warbler **Ceolaire buí**
Yellow-rumped Warbler
    Ceolaire buíphrompach
Blackpoll Warbler **Ceolaire dubhéadanach**
American Redstart
    Earrdheargán Meiriceánach
Ovenbird **Éan oighinn**
Northern Waterthrush
    Smólach uisce tuaisceartach
Scarlet Tanager **Tanagair scarlóideach**
Fox Sparrow **Gealbhan sionnaigh**
White-throated Sparrow **Gealbhan píbgheal**
Dark-eyed Junco **Luachairín shúildubh**
Lapland Bunting **Gealóg Laplannach**
Snow Bunting **Gealóg shneachta**
Pine Bunting **Gealóg phéine**
Yellowhammer **Buíóg**
Ortolan Bunting **Gealóg gharraí**
Rustic Bunting **Gealóg thuathúil**
Little Bunting **Gealóg bheag**
Yellow-breasted Bunting **Gealóg bhroinnbhuí**
Reed Bunting **Gealóg ghiolcaí**
Black-headed Bunting **Gealóg cheanndubh**
Corn Bunting **Gealóg bhuachair**
Rose-breasted Grosbeak
    Gobach mór broinnrósach
Indigo Bunting **Gealóg phlúiríneach**
Bobolink **Bobóilinc**

Irish

References & Bibliography

Crowe, O. 2005. *Ireland's Wetlands and their Waterbirds: Status and Distribution*. BirdWatch Ireland.

Cummins, S. 2007. Red Grouse Survey. *Wings* 46, page 24. BirdWatch Ireland.

Curson, J., Quinn, D. & Beadle, D. 1994. *New World Warblers*. Christopher Helm.

D'Arcy, G. 1999. *Ireland's lost birds*. Four Courts Press.

Dempsey, E. & O'Clery, M. 2007. *Finding Birds in Ireland. The Complete Guide*. Gill & Macmillan.

Dempsey, E. & O'Clery, M. 2003 (second edition). *The Complete Guide to Ireland's Birds*. Gill & Macmillan.

Dempsey, E. 2008. *Birdwatching in Ireland with Eric Dempsey*. Gill & Macmillan.

Garner, M. 2008. *Frontiers in Birding*. BirdGuides Limited.

Gibbons, D.W., Reid, J.B. & Chapman, R.A. 1993. *The New Atlas of breeding birds in Britain and Ireland*. T & AD Poyser.

Gray, N., Thomas, G., Trewby, M. & Newton, S.F. 2000. The status and distribution of Choughs *Pyrrhocorax pyrrhocorax* in the Republic of Ireland 2002/03. *Irish Birds* 7: 2. BirdWatch Ireland.

Harris, A., Shirihai, H. & Christie, D. 1996. *The Macmillan Birder's Guide to European and Middle Eastern Birds*. Macmillan.

Harris, A., Tucker, L. & Vinicombe, K. 1989. *The Macmillan Field Guide to Bird Identification*. Macmillan.

Hutchinson, C. 1989. *Birds in Ireland*. T & AD Poyser.

Irish Rare Birds Committee. 1998. *Checklist of the Birds of Ireland*. BirdWatch Ireland.

Jonsson, L. 1992. *Birds of Europe with North Africa and the Middle East*. Christopher Helm.

Lack, P. 1986. *The Atlas of wintering birds in Britain and Ireland*. T & AD Poyser.

Lewington, I., Alstrom, P. & Colston, P. 1991. *A Field Guide to the Rare Birds of Britain and Europe*. Harper Collins.

Lovatt, J.K. 1984. *Birds of Hook Head, Co. Wexford 1883-1983*. Irish Wildbird Conservancy.

Lovatt, J.K. 2006. *Birds in Cavan*. BirdWatch Ireland.

Lynas, P., Newton, S.F. & Robinson, J.A. 2007. The status of birds in Ireland: an analysis of conservation concern 2008-2013. *Irish Birds* 8:149-167. BirdWatch Ireland.

Lysaght, L. 2002. *An Atlas of Breeding Birds of the Burren and the Aran Islands*. BirdWatch Ireland.

Malling, O. & Larsson, H. 1995. *Terns of Europe and North America*. Christopher Helm.

Malling, O. & Larsson, H. 2003. *Gulls of Europe, Asia and North America*. A. & C. Black, London.

McLoughlin, D. & Cotton, D. 2008. The status of Twite *Carduelis flavirostris* in Ireland, 2008. *Irish Birds* 8: 323. BirdWatch Ireland.

Mitchell, P.I., Newton, S., Ratcliffe, N. & Dunn, T.E. 2004. *Seabird populations of Britain and Ireland*. Christopher Helm.

Mullarney, K., Svensson, L. & Zetterstrom, D. 2010. *Collins Bird Guide, 2nd edition*. Harper Collins.

Murphy, J., Cooney, A., Rattigan, J. & Lynch, T. 2003. *The Shannon Airport Lagoon. A unique Irish Habitat*. Clare Branch, BirdWatch Ireland.

O'Clery, M. 2005. *The Dingle Peninsula Bird Report 2002-2004*. Corca Dhuibhne Branch, BirdWatch Ireland.

Robb, M., Mullarney, K. & The Sound Approach. 2008. *Petrels night and day*. Sound Approach.

Snow, D.W. & Perrins, C.M. 1998. *The Birds of the Western Palearctic, Concise Edition*. Oxford University Press.

Ruttledge, R.F. 1989. *Birds in Counties Galway & Mayo*. BirdWatch Ireland.

Sharrock, J.T.R. 1976. *The Atlas of breeding birds in Britain & Ireland*. T & AD Poyser.

Sibley, D. 2009 (second edition). *The North American Bird Guide*. Pica Press.

Annual or regular publications

Birding World. Monthly subscription-only journal.

British Birds. Monthly subscription-only journal.

Cork Bird Report.

Dingle Peninsula Bird Report.

Irish Bird Report. Published annually in *Irish Birds* by BirdWatch Ireland.

Irish East Coast Bird Report.

Northern Ireland Bird Report.

Useful websites

- www.birdsireland.com
Website of Eric Dempsey and Michael O'Clery. Identification workshops, bird art, bird tours, photography and consultancy.

- www.birdwatchireland.ie
Ireland's leading bird conservation organisation. Join online, conservation projects, online shop and links to branch networks and websites.

- www.irbc.ie
The Irish Rare Birds Committee website, with features on bird identification, the Irish List and the Irish Rare Bird Report.

- www.rspb.org.uk
Bird conservation in Northern Ireland.

- www.wwt.org.uk
Wildfowl and Wetlands Trust, with reserves in Northern Ireland.

- www.rte.ie/mooney
General wildlife information.

- www.ispca.ie
Local contacts for care of sick or injured birds in Ireland.

- www.countynaturetrust.tripod.com
Irish wildlife conservation projects in southern regions of Ireland.

- www.cr-birding.be
Database of bird colour-ringing schemes around the world.

- www.irishbirdimages.com
Bird photography by Paul and Andrea Kelly.

- www.irishbirding.com
Rare bird sightings and photographs.

- www.aaireland.ie
Route planning, road and traffic conditions.

- www.met.ie
Local, regional and national weather forecasts from Met Éireann, the Irish Meteorological Office.

Web

Index

265

Latin

Index

English

Albatross, Black-browed, 42–3
Auk, Great, 244
  Little, 132–3
Avocet, 78–9

Bee-eater, 146–7
Bittern, 52–3
  American, 233
  Little, 52–3
Blackbird, 170–71
Blackcap, 182–3
Bluetail, Red-flanked, 241
Bluethroat, 166–7
Bobolink, 228–9
Bonxie, 110–11
Brambling, 212–13
Bufflehead, 231
Bullfinch, 218–19
Bunting, Black-headed, 224–5
  Cirl, 243
  Corn, 224–5
  Indigo, 242
  Lapland, 220–21
  Little, 222–3
  Ortolan, 224–5
  Pine, 243
  Red-headed, 244
  Reed, 222–3
  Rustic, 222–3
  Snow, 220–21
  Yellow-breasted, 224–5
Bustard, Great, 235
  Little, 234–5
Buzzard, 64–5
  Honey, 233
  Rough-legged, 64–5

Capercaillie, 232
Catbird, Gray, 241
Chaffinch, 212–13
Chiffchaff, 186–7
Chough, 204–5
Coot, 76–7
  American, 234
Cormorant, 50–51
  Double-crested, 232–3
Corncrake, 74–5
Courser, Cream-coloured, 235
Crake, Baillon's, 234
  Little, 234
  Spotted, 74–5
Crane, 56–7
  Sandhill, 234
Crossbill, 218–19

Two-barred, 242
Crow, Carrion, 206–7
  Hooded, 206–7
  House, 244
Cuckoo, 138–9
  Black-billed, 138–9
  Great Spotted, 138–9
  Yellow-billed, 138–9
Curlew, 96–7
  Eskimo, 244
  Stone, 96–7

Dipper, 162–3
Diver, Black-throated, 36–7
  Great Northern, 36–7
  Pacific, 232
  Red-throated, 38–9
  White-billed, 36–7
Dotterel, 82–3
Dove, Collared, 136–7
  Mourning, 238
  Rock, 134–5
  Stock, 134–5
  Turtle, 136–7
Dowitcher, Long-billed, 98–9
  Short-billed, 98–9
Duck, American Black, 18–19
  Ferruginous, 24–5
  Long-tailed, 30–31
  Mandarin, 16–17
  Ring-necked, 26–7
  Ruddy, 28–9
  Tufted, 26–7
Dunlin, 92–3
Dunnock, 164–5

Eagle, Bald, 233
  Booted, 244
  Golden, 62–3
  Spotted, 234
  White-tailed, 62–3
Egret, Cattle, 54–5
  Great White, 54–5
  Little, 54–5
Eider, 30–31
  King, 30–31

Falcon, Gyr, 70–71
  Peregrine, 70–71
  Red-footed, 68–9
Fieldfare, 170–71
Firecrest, 192–3
Flamingo, Greater, 244
Flicker, Northern, 239
Flycatcher, Pied, 194–5
  Red-breasted, 194–5

Spotted, 194–5
Frigatebird, Magnificent, 233
Fulmar, 42–3

Gadwall, 18–19
Gannet, 42–3
Garganey, 22–3
Godwit, Bar-tailed, 98–9
  Black-tailed, 98–9
Goldcrest, 192–3
Goldeneye, 26–7
  Barrow's, 231–2
Goldfinch, 212–13
Goosander, 34–5
Goose, Barnacle, 10–11
  Bean, 12–13
  Brent, 10–11
  Cackling, 10–11
  Canada, 10–11
  Greylag, 14–15
  Lesser White-fronted, 231
  Pink-footed, 12–13
  Red-breasted, 244
  Snow, 14–15
  White-fronted, 12–13
Goshawk, 66–7
Grebe, Black-necked, 40–41
  Great Crested, 38–9
  Little, 40–41
  Pied-billed, 40–41
  Red-necked, 38–9
  Slavonian, 40–41
Greenfinch, 214–15
Greenshank, 100–101
Grosbeak, Rose-breasted, 228–9
Grouse, Red, 72–3
Guillemot, 130–31
  Black, 132–3
  Brünnich's, 238
Gull, American Herring, 120–21
  Black-headed, 114–15
  Bonaparte's, 114–15
  Caspian, 120–21
  Common, 116–17
  Franklin's, 116–17
  Glaucous, 122–3
  Great Black-backed, 118–19
  Herring, 120–21
  Iceland, 122–3
  Ivory, 122–3
  Laughing, 114–15
  Lesser Black-backed, 118–19
  Little, 114–15
  Mediterranean, 116–17
  Ring-billed, 116–17
  Ross's, 112–13